MODERN SCOTTISH LITERATURE

BOOKS BY ALAN BOLD

Poetry
Society Inebrious
The Voyage
To Find The New
A Perpetual Motion Machine
Penguin Modern Poets 15 (with Morgan and Brathwaite)
The State Of The Nation
The Auld Symie
He Will Be Greatly Missed
A Century of People
A Pint of Bitter
Scotland, Yes
This Fine Day

Stories
Hammer and Thistle (with Morrison)

Criticism
Thom Gunn & Ted Hughes
George Mackay Brown
The Ballad
The Sexual Dimension in Literature (ed)
Smollett: Author of the First Distinction (ed)
MacDiarmid: The Terrible Crystal

Anthologies
The Penguin Book of Socialist Verse
The Martial Muse: Seven Centuries of War Poetry
Cambridge Book of English Verse 1939–75
Making Love: The Picador Book of Erotic Verse
Mounts of Venus: The Picador Book of Erotic Prose
The Bawdy Beautiful: The Sphere Book of Improper Verse
Drink to Me Only: The Prose (and Cons) of Drinking

MODERN SCOTTISH LITERATURE

Alan Bold

LONGMAN
London and New York

LONGMAN GROUP LIMITED
Longman House, Burnt Mill, Harlow
Essex CM20 2JE, England
Associated companies throughout the world

*Published in the United States of America
by Longman Inc., New York*

First published 1983

BRITISH LIBRARY CATALOGUING IN PUBLICATION DATA
Bold, Alan
  Modern Scottish literature.
  1. Scottish literature – History and criticism
  2. English literature – Scottish authors – History
  and criticism   3. Gaelic literature – History
  and criticism
  I. Title
  820'.9'941   PR8511

  ISBN 0-582-49064-2

LIBRARY OF CONGRESS CATALOGING IN PUBLICATION DATA
Bold, Alan Norman, 1943-
  Modern Scottish literature.

  Bibliography: p. 321
  Includes index.
  1. Scottish literature – History and criticism.
  2. English literature – Scottish authors – History
  and criticism. I. Title.
  PR8512.B64   1983   820'.9'9411   82-8956
  ISBN 0-582-49064-2 (pbk.)   AACR2

Set in 10/11pt Linotron 202 Times Roman
Printed in Singapore by Four Strong Printing Co

For Christopher Murray Grieve (1892–1978)

CONTENTS

PREFACE

Many Scottish writers responded to questions of mine and I am glad to acknowledge their cooperation which is specified in the endnotes referring to letters and conversations. As there are, already, too many divisions in Scotland I have resisted the temptation to add to them in this work. Individual texts are discussed in broad formal contexts (poetry, fiction, drama) though the chapters are punctuated at significant thematic points. I have included no reference to my own poetry apart from this allusion to its existence.

I would like to thank David Morrison, Wick Branch Librarian, for supplying me with rare Scottish books from his extensive collection. Some passages of the text make use of material I contributed to *The Scotsman, The Sunday Times, TLS , Literary Review, Scotia* and *Akros*; and to my critical study of *George Mackay Brown* (1978). I gladly make acknowledgement to the editors involved. Finally, I must thank the various publishers of copyright material.

ACKNOWLEDGEMENTS

We are grateful to the following for permission to reproduce copyright material:

Martin Brian & O'Keeffe Ltd and Mrs Valda Grieve for extracts from the poems 'A Drunk Man Looks at the Thistle', 'The Watergaw', 'The Eemis Stone', 'Empty Vessel', 'Milk-Wort and Bog-Cotton' and 'In Memoriam of James Joyce' from *The Complete Poems of Hugh MacDiarmid 1920–1976*; the author, W. S. Graham, for extracts from his poems 'The Beast In the Space' and 'To My Mother' from *Collected Poems of W. S. Graham 1942–1977*; the author's agent, Curtis Brown Ltd, on behalf of the Estate of Lewis Grassic Gibbon for extracts from *Sunset Song*; Hutchinson Publishing Group Ltd for extracts from *The Dear Green Place* by Archie Hind; The Trustees of the National Library of Scotland for extracts from William Soutar's poems 'Autobiography', 'Cock-Crow' and 'Bawsy Broon'; Oliver and Boyd for extracts from *George MacKay Brown* by Alan Bold; Rhoda Spence for extracts from the poem 'The Prows o'Reekie' by Lewis Spence.

INTRODUCTION

Although Scotland is not officially an independent state, Scottishness is a recognised state of mind: sometimes an independent state of mind, occasionally a theocratic state of mind, frequently a confused state of mind. Still, it is a state of mind accepted by Scots and acknowledged by observers. Physiologically, the Scot may be no different from anyone else but has acquired a distinctive identity as a result of historical and cultural conditioning. A nation's history and culture are always interdependent; when that nation is denied its national status the history becomes the culture and vice versa. The Scot is sufficiently unsure of his independence to assert it aggressively. It is an argumentative issue, a crucial event that carries the burden of battles fought and lost. The extremism of the Scot, which ranges from lachrymose sentimentality to vicious brutality and from cosy domesticity to disorderly drunkenness, is evidence of uncertainty. Scottish literature seeks to make artistic sense of the confusion.

Writing to Mrs John F. Kennedy in 1964, John Steinbeck observed: 'You talked of Scotland as a lost cause and that is not true. Scotland is an *unwon* cause'.[1] The average Scot (so far as there is such a creature) would agree. Scotland is still fighting old battles, still obsessed by the past, still trying to convert defeat into victory. Scotland is a country uniquely haunted by history. With so many defeats to contend with the Scots have gradually come to regard themselves as born losers. The national penchant for pessimism relates to habitual defeatism. The traumatic impact of successive blows to the body politic has meant that the crucial moments of Scottish history are impressed on the national consciousness like dates cut deeply into tombstones. In 1513 the flowers of the forest were cut down at Flodden. In 1603 crown and court abandoned Scotland for the greater commercial glory of England. In 1699 an attempt to colonise Darien ended in disaster. In 1707 the Scottish parliament committed legislative suicide. In 1746 the defeat of the clans at Culloden represented a cultural catastrophe and initiated a quasi-genocidal policy against the Gael. The facts are easy to remember. They alliterate and impress. Scots recall them even while they wave Bannockburn banners at football matches (which also rehearse old grievances).

Scottish literature shows the various ways that the Scottish people live with the pressure and persistence of the past. When they want to rake over injustice they do so in terms of the Highland Clearances rather than referring to contemporary events. When they want to wound the auld enemy they dig over Culloden Moor. Any Scottish museum is a treasure house of old scores still to be settled. Any historical study is a handbook of injustice. This way of thinking is so strong it led an American scholar of folklore to an interesting conclusion:

> There operates . . . in Scotland . . . a most important sociological law . . . And that is *the petrifying but protective influence of great military defeats on those nations which have nevertheless managed to survive these defeats.* As the Scots themselves are the first to recognise, the whole cultural and political life of Scotland is still attuned, basically, to no later historical period than the mid- or late eighteenth century, except in the neo-Marxist atmosphere of Glasgow and the industrial area, which has entirely leapt the nineteenth century, into the present, owing to the challenge of the industrial blight. Cultured Scotsmen today still brood over their defeat by England – under the flattering pretense of 'Union' of the two kingdoms – in the early and mid-eighteenth century . . .[2]

Contrast and counterpoint, juxtaposition and antithesis, paradox and parallelism: these artistic techniques permeate Scottish literature because they correspond to a way of life.

Defeat is a divisive issue and division is responsible for the state of Scotland. Scotland is fragmented, cut to pieces by historical circumstances. Geographically there are differences between Highland and Lowland, east and west coast; linguistically there is a three-way split between English, Scots and Gaelic. Division is more than a physical presence, it is a mental condition. It can even be a pathological condition as in Stevenson's *The Strange Case of Dr Jekyll and Mr Hyde* (1886), which contains, or rather reveals, the classic artistic image of internal division. Stevenson did not, it should be noted, create the Jekyll and Hyde syndrome; he captured it in prose. Another Scot, Byron – who was 'half a Scot by birth, and bred/A whole one' as he says in *Don Juan* (X : 17) – noted the contradictory character of Scotland's national poet:

> [Dr John Allen] has lent me a quantity of Burns's unpublished and never-to-be published Letters. They are full of oaths and obscene songs. What an antithetical mind! – tenderness, roughness – delicacy, coarseness – sentiment, sensuality – soaring and grovelling, dirt and deity – all mixed up in that one compound of inspired clay![3]

Byron's definition of the 'antithetical mind' could be taken as a general description of Scottish literature. Burns was only being representative in his extremes.

Although Scottish writers would wish to piece together the fragments of defeatism in a healing image of artistic wholeness they, too, have been divided and therefore passionately involved in their material. Detachment is an unusual quality in Scottish writing. Scottish literature rarely strays from what G. Gregory Smith classified, in a classic phrase, as the Caledonian Antisyzygy:

> Perhaps in the very combination of opposites – what either of the two Sir Thomases, of Norwich and Cromarty, might have been willing to call 'the Caledonian antisyzygy' – we have a reflection of the contrasts which the Scot shows at every turn, in his political and ecclesiastical history, in his polemical restlessness, in his adaptability, which is another way of saying that he has made allowance for new conditions, in his practical judgement, which is the admission that two sides of the matter have been considered. If therefore Scottish history and life are, as an old northern writer said of something else, 'varied with a clean contrair spirit,' we need not be surprised to find that in his literature the Scot presents two aspects which appear contradictory. Oxymoron was ever the bravest figure, and we must not forget that disorderly order is order after all.[4]

That passage, from Smith's *Scottish Literature* (1919), became (as it were) the text for the secular sermon in which MacDiarmid announced the Scottish Renaissance.

In our own time the internal division has been investigated by the radical Scottish psychotherapist R. D. Laing, who began by defining the schizophrenic as an individual who 'does not experience himself as a complete person but rather as "split" in various ways'[5]; then later came to the conclusion that such a state of mind was a reasonable reaction to a disturbing environment:

> The normal state of affairs is that we know little of either [the inner and outer worlds] and are alienated from both, but that we know perhaps a little more of the outer than the inner. However, the very fact that it is necessary to speak of outer and inner at all implies that an historically-conditioned split has occurred, so that the inner is already as bereft of substance as the outer is bereft of meaning.
>
> We need not be unaware of the 'inner' world. We do not realize its existence most of the time . . . The process of entering into *the other* world from this world, and returning to *this* world from the other world, is as natural as death and giving birth or being born.[6]

Scottish writers would agree with Laing as they knowingly explore the inner world in their work. What Laing (who studied medicine in Glasgow) calls the Divided Self corresponds to what Gregory Smith called the Caledonian Antisyzygy and Byron called the Antithetical Mind. It is also a creative mind that requires a suitably expressive language.

In Scotland language is treated as a weapon in a national, and nationalistic, war. The Scottish writer makes a matter of decision – over the use of English, Scots, Gaelic – a matter of division. Again, though, it is ultimately a matter of history and prehistory. Prehistoric Scotland (north of the Forth anyway) was dominated by the broch-building Brythonic Celts we know as Picts; possibly they spoke a form of *p*-Celtic (Welsh). The Romans attempted to colonise Pictland as Caledonia then withdrew in 407. After the Roman withdrawal Alba (to use the Gaelic name) was fragmented into areas controlled by four groups, three of whom (Picts, Scots, Britons) were of Celtic origin with the fourth – the Angles of Lothian – being *Sasunnaich* to the Celts. The Scots, who gave their name to the land they came to (from Dalriada in *c*.500), spoke *q*-Celtic (Gaelic) which became the language of a united Celtic kingdom (Scotia) in 843 when Kenneth MacAlpin acquired Pictland more by kinship than conquest. Gaelic was thus once a national language which is why it has such emotive associations for Scots who know not a word of it. It is still regarded as the speech of a lost Celtic paradise. Scots are generally united in lamenting the way Gaelic was systematically destroyed as the national language of Scotland.

In Lothian the *Sasunnaich* spoke Anglo-Saxon and increasingly claimed to do so for the whole of Scotland. Lothian was the area favoured by the king and Malcolm III or Canmore (*Ceann mor* being Gaelic for 'great chief' rather than the schoolboy pejorative 'bighead') played an influential part in making Gaelic retreat to the relatively inaccessible Highlands and Islands. In 1069 Malcolm married Margaret, sister of the Anglo-Saxon heir to the recently conquered kingdom of England. According to the *Anglo-Saxon Chronicle* she transformed Scotland: 'she was destined to increase the glory of God in that land, to turn the king aside from the path of error, to incline him altogether with his people towards a better way of life, and to abolish the vices which that nation had indulged in in the past.' What Margaret actually did was persuade her illiterate husband to undermine Celtic tradition. He Romanised the Celtic church, he substituted Saxon for Gaelic as the court language, he replaced the clan system with a form of feudalism. Scotland was now polarised into a Highland area where the people adhered to the Celtic ways and Gaelic speech; and a Lowland area where they cultivated Anglo-Saxon attitudes.

The language of Anglo-Saxon Lothian was called *Inglis* and this was the medium used by John Barbour (1316–95) in his great historical narrative *Brus*; in other words, historical Inglis is what we call Scots. The confusion is typical. *Scottis* referred, originally, to Gaelic. It changed because observers needed to distinguish Lothian *Inglis* from English *Inglis* and called the former *Scottis*: by 1494 a Scotsman could call his Lowland speech *Scottis*.[7] But for an historical accident *Scottis* (as acceptable an Anglo-Saxon dialect as southern *Inglis*) would have become the national means of communication and hence used in prose as well as poetry. However, with the Knoxian revolution established in 1561, the triumphant Protestant reformers needed an extant translation of their sacred text. (A Scots translation of the New Testament did exist in manuscript but Murdoch Nisbet's version did not materialise in print until 1901.) In 1561 English refugees in Geneva had translated the Bible into English; Knox, an erstwhile resident of Calvin's Geneva, was naturally familiar with this. And Knox based the Reformation on the word of God. In 1561 the First Book of Discipline recommended that each parish should provide a minimum of four years schooling for every child; in 1579 the Scottish parliament decreed that every householder worth 300 merks had to possess 'a bible and psalme buke in vulgare language'.[8] The vulgar language was, fortuituously, English as the Reformers used the Geneva Bible which hence became the literary law of the land:

> Its language became familiar to the people as the language of solemnity and abstract thought, of theological and philosophical disputation, while Scots remained as the language of ordinary life, of the domestic, sentimental and comic, and from here we can trace the split mind that Scots have had about their native language ever since. A classic example is Burn's 'The Cottar's Saturday Night,' where the domestic scene is described in Scots, but as soon as the big ha' Bible is brought out the poem glides into English by the association of the Bible with the English language, which had gained spiritual prestige through the Reformation.[9]

Scotland's histrionic history continued to sabotage its indigenous culture. In 1603 James VI of Scotland achieved his ambition of moving his court to London as James I of a united kingdom. James anglicised himself and his writing: he revised his *Basilicon Doron* to make it intelligible to the English. Inexorably, the prestige of English increased immeasurably in Scotland. In 1707 English became the official language of the united kingdom; it was the speech of the London parliament and had the weight of the law behind it. Although Scots survived as an oral influence and in dialect verse it was not thought suitable for learned matters. In one of his letters Burns gives a rare glimpse of eighteenth century Scots prose:

> I hae dander'd owre a' the kintra frae Dunbar to Selcraig, and hae forgather'd wi' money a guid fallow, and mony a weelfar'd hizzie. I met wi' twa dink quines in particlar, ane o' them a sonsie, fine, fodgel lass, baith braw and bonnie; the tither was a clean-shankit, straught, tight, weel-far'd winch, as blithe's a lintwhite on a flowerie thorn, and as sweet and modest's a new blawn plumrose in a hazle shaw. They were baith bred to mainers by the beuk, and onie ane o' them had as muckle smeddum and rumblegumtion as the half o' some presbyteries that you and I baith ken.[10]

5

The intellectual giants who made Edinburgh the cultural capital of Europe during the eighteenth century would have recoiled in horror from such linguistic vulgarity. David Hume, who was (despite Dr Johnson's opinion to the contrary) a master of English prose, deliberately excised Scotticisms from his writing though he could not avoid the antithetical rhythm that gave his prose its Scottish character. In 1752 he attached a list of avoidable *Scotticisms* to some copies of his *Political Discourses*; by the time the list was reprinted in the *Scots Magazine* (in 1760) it was widely considered to be a solecism to employ Scotticisms. Hume and his friends corresponded with each other on the subject of offensive Scotticisms and Hume's literary club, originally called the Select Society (appropriately enough since the membership included Adam Smith, John Home the dramatist, and Allan Ramsay the painter), changed its name, in 1761, to the Society for Promoting the Reading and Speaking of the English Language. The situation in the eighteenth century was traumatic:

> The Scots were meeting a lot of English people, in Scotland or in London, and they found themselves being mocked at for their speech. This was the final demoralisation for a great many Scots. They really felt themselves to be uncouth . . . The Scottish Augustans seem to have bequeathed to us an inferiority complex and the Morningside accent.[11]

While Scots was gradually being eroded and reduced to the status of an embarrassing accent, Gaelic was being destroyed as a national language. The defeat of the clans at Culloden in 1746 was hammered home with a Disarming Act that took away distinctively Highland dress and music. Having deprived the Highlanders of their cultural identity the next step was to deprive them of their land so that sheep might take their place. The nostalgia for a glorious past, the lost Celtic paradise, has its historical basis in the tragedy of the Clearances. Writers have long been irresistibly drawn to the mythogenic possibilities of the fall of the Gael from his Eden. Two pseudonymous writers, Ossian and Fiona Macleod, reinforced the myth for different ages. James Macpherson's *Fingal* (1762) and *Temora* (1763), published in the name of the legendary warrior Ossian (son of Fingal), gave Europe a taste for spurious Celtism; Smollett's novel *Humphry Clinker* (1771) recorded the fact that 'The poems of Ossian are in every mouth'. In the Victorian period – when the 1872 Education (Scotland) Act suppressed Gaelic in Scottish schools – the taste lingered on and a Paisley man, William Sharp, imposed his eternally feminine soulmate Fiona Macleod on a responsive public. Fiona (who first appeared in *Pharais* in 1894) had an attractively melancholic appeal as will be evident in the following passage:

The last tragedy for broken nations is not the loss of power and distinction, nor even the loss of that independence which is so vital to the commonweal . . . The last tragedy, and the saddest, is when the treasured language dies slowly out, when winter falls upon the legendary remembrance of a people . . . It is a strange thing: that a nation can hold within itself an ancient race, standing for the lost, beautiful, mysterious ancient world, can see it fading through its dim twilight, without heed to preserve that which might yet be preserved, without interest even in that which once gone cannot come again. The old Gaelic race is in its twilight indeed; but now, alas! it is the hastening twilight after the feast of Samhain, when winter is come at last, out of the hills, down the glens, on the four winds of the world.[12]

Although Fiona, like Ossian, has been dismissed as a purely fanciful figure the sentiments expressed above would be endorsed by many Scottish writers and given popular currency by the formidable Marjory Kennedy-Fraser in her collections of Hebridean folksongs and her romantic autobiography *A Life of Song* (1929). It has long been assumed that it is possible to atone for Scotland's various defeats by learning Gaelic. Both Neil Gunn and Hugh MacDiarmid greatly regretted their ignorance of Gaelic and Fionn Mac Colla learned the language so that he could presume to speak (in English) for the Gael. Compton Mackenzie classified automatic genuflexion to Gaelic as the Lone Sheiling Complex.[13] The reference is to the Canadian Boat Song which had appeared anonymously in *Blackwood's Magazine* in 1829 and had been revived in 1885 when Joseph Chamberlain, in a speech delivered the year before a parliamentary Act guaranteed crofters fixed tenures, quoted the poem:

> From the lone shieling of the misty island
> Mountains divide us and the waste of seas;
> Yet still the blood is strong, the heart is Highland,
> And we in dreams behold the Hebrides . . .

> When the bold kindred, in the time long vanished,
> Conquered the soil and fortified the keep,
> No seer foretold the children would be banished
> That a degenerate lord might boast his sheep.

If the words still move it is because Gaelic civilisation is still seen as the innocent childhood that was denied to the Scottish nation.

The Lone Shieling Complex keeps alive the legend of Tir nan Og as did J. M. Barrie when he transformed the notion into the Neverland of *Peter Pan* and the enchanted island of *Mary Rose*. Not only celebrated sentimentalists like Barrie subscribed to the Lone Shieling Complex. Fionn Mac Colla constantly harped on the 'heartbreaking sense . . . that there had once been a Glory' and attributed Scottish drunkenness to a racial awareness of the lost Celtic paradise:

7

[Scottish drunkenness] is very largely due, and this applies to even the most seemingly coarse of Scots, to the fact that they retained in the benmost recesses of their consciousness, but insistent and demanding, a sense or awarness that there had been a Glory: and they lurched into drunkenness, excessive and senseless drunkenness it might well be, out of despair that they had lost contact with what might have given them dignity, and in the attempt to establish contact and connection. Their drunken 'gloriousness' was in compensation for a lost, authentic glory, unattainable now because of their society's and country's status of helplessness and dependence, and their own helpless inability to contribute positively to its destiny. I have all my life understood that beyond the drunkenness of the drunken Scot lay precisely such an ineradicable spiritual nostalgia.[14]

That spiritual nostalgia is the soft centre of Scottish culture.

Even among writers committed to the ideal of a regenerated Scotland there have been divisions. MacDiarmid fell out with Neil Gunn and he singled out Edwin Muir as a deadly enemy. In 1936 Muir had delivered himself of this statement: 'Scotsmen feel in one language and think in another . . . Scots poetry can only be revived . . . when Scotsmen begin to think *naturally* in Scots. The curse of Scottish literature is the lack of a whole language, which finally means the lack of a whole mind.'[15] That might seem an innocuous enough remark. In the context of Muir's general contention that the major work in Scotland would be cast in the English language it was cultural dynamite. MacDiarmid never forgave Muir the insult and henceforth treated him as a Judas. Thus was created another antithesis since the disciples of MacDiarmid felt they had to renounce the teachings of Muir. It was another battle to be joined to those of Knox versus Mary, Campbell versus Macdonald, Bonnie Prince Charlie versus Butcher Cumberland. The divided Scot needed heroes and villains. Knox is probably the best-known villain and has featured as such in a play by Bridie, a meditative book by Fionn Mac Colla, the poems of Edwin Muir and Iain Crichton Smith, the stories of George Mackay Brown. In 'Knox (2)' Alan Jackson put the matter succinctly:

O Knox he was a bad man
he split the Scottish mind.
The one half he made cruel
and the other half unkind.

Knox did nothing of the kind though the identification of one man with all the ills of a nation is symptomatic of national uncertainty. In fact Knox helped create the Scottish literacy without which none of the writers could castigate him. He has been portrayed as a sexual coward when he was a twice-married man and father of five; he is held to be synonymous with the narrowness of presbyterianism when Melville is meant; he is accused of Calvinistic sectarianism when two of his sons were Church of England clergymen; he is found guilty of cowardice when he was a remarkably courageous fighter willing to stand up to crowned heads.

Scotland seethes with moral indignation, though; it needs villains to blame and heroes to believe in. It needs a chamber of historical horrors and a current pantheon. Encouraged by the Calvinistic tendency to see the world in terms of absolute good versus absolute evil, the Scottish consciousness is full of archetypes and stereotypes. Scottish literature is peopled with such figures: the Domestic Tyrant, the Hardman, the Lachrymose Drunk, the Spiritual Celt, the Teetotalitarian Boor, the Gentle Highland Giant, the Canny Lowlander, the Kilted Clown. The Scottish public respond to these figures so emotionally that it is difficult to ascertain whether the stereotype is based on reality or whether the Scot conforms to given stereotypes. Sir Harry Lauder amassed a fortune making a public spectacle of himself as the Kilted Clown – one of the stereotypes. His special gift was in making the caricature available for export: 'I decided that if ever I got a footing in England I would not use words or idioms which would only befog my audience. I would sing my songs in English, I determined, *but with a Scottish accent*. The result was that I was more successful my first week in Newcastle than any other Scottish artiste who had appeared there.'[16] Lauderism was a powerful enough threat to Scotland's dignity for MacDiarmid to allude to it in many poems (including his masterpiece). Ironically enough, the first number of MacDiarmid's *The Scottish Chapbook* (the organ of the Scottish Literary Renaissance) carried, on the front page, a lion rampant and the motto 'Not Traditions – Precedents'; and, on the back page, a full-page advertisement for a pen, with the motto 'The inimitable Sir Harry Lauder uses the inimitable Waterman's Ideal – and he wouldn't like to be without it.' Alas, the advertisment was wrong and Lauder's image could be easily imitated and assimilated, especially with the mass production of stereotypes:

> The postcard boom of 1900–14 provided unlimited scope for an exploration and celebration of this Scotch caricature. Scotchness offered a rich vein of humour, sentiment and romance to the postcard artist. For the first time we discover what lies under the kilt . . . The Archetypal Scot. Mean, pawky, canny, fighting, sentimental and dressed to kilt in tartan and feathered bonnet. The wee yin leapt from a postcard onto the world's stage and back again. Captured forever on a picture postcard the iconography of Scotchness. The lost tribe roaming in the gloaming.[17]

That image was resisted by the best of the modern Scottish writers. They attempted to convey an alternative ideal. The Platonic supposition that the earthly world is an imperfect copy of an eternal ideal has been the philosophical force behind much twentieth century Scottish literature. It imagines a vision of Scottishness and was spread by selfconsciously visionary Scots. A man like R. B. Cunninghame Graham (1852–1936) emerged as the antidote to Lauder. Graham is the kind of Scot to whom MacDiarmid's Renaissance made sense. Graham was born in London, son of a Scottish laird and grandson of an eighteenth century Scottish songwriter. He took the world as his stage yet felt quintessentially Scottish. He was a Radical MP, a shaping spirit behind the Scottish Labour Party, and a founder member of the National Party of Scotland with Compton Mackenzie and MacDiarmid. MacDiarmid, never a man to give way to easy flattery, said of him: 'I valued Cunninghame Graham beyond rubies. We will never see his like again. He was unique and incomparable – a human equivalent of that pure white stag with great branching horns the appearance of which, tradition says, will betoken great good luck for Scotland at long last.'[18] As a writer Graham took his Scottishness seriously and wanted to liberate Scottish prose from the confines of the kailyard. As he wrote to Edward Garnett on 25 May 1898: 'In dealing with Scotland and things Scotch, one should avoid sentiment, it destroyed those awful McCroketts, and Larens, and is a snare to the pious chanting, hypocritical, hard, but at the same time sentimental, and whisky loving Scotchman. I am a Scotchman.'[19]

In a classic story, 'Beattock for Moffat', Graham described a man coming home to Scotland to die. The achievement of men like Graham, Mackenzie, Gunn and (above all) MacDiarmid encouraged a concept of Scotland as a place also capable of sustaining life. The best modern Scottish writers are individuals seeking to express the undivided self in an image of artistic wholeness. Whether they succeed or not they live up to the credo of individuality MacDiarmid integrated in *A Drunk Man Looks at the Thistle*:

> And let the lesson be – to be yersel's
> Ye needna fash gin it's to be ocht else.
> To be yersel's – and to mak' that worth bein'.
> Nae harder job to mortals has been gi'en.

That is an ideal clearly attainable in modern Scotland.

REFERENCES

1. Elaine Steinbeck and Robert Wallsten (eds), *Steinbeck: A Life in Letters*, Heinemann: London 1975; Pan edn p. 795
2. Gershon Legman, *The Horn Book*, University Books: New York 1964, p. 365

3. Alan Bold (ed.), *The Bawdy Beautiful*, Sphere: London 1979, p. xxvi
4. G. Gregory Smith, *Scottish Literature*, Macmillan: London 1919, pp. 4–5
5. R. D. Laing, *The Divided Self*, Tavistock: London 1960; Penguin edn p. 17
6. R. D. Laing, *The Politics of Experience & The Bird of Paradise*, Penguin: Harmondsworth 1967, p. 103
7. B.M. MS Harl. 6149, fol. 128b
8. *The Acts of Parliament of Scotland*, Vol. III, p. 139a
9. David Murison, *The Guid Scots Tongue*, Blackwood: Edinburgh 1978, p. 5
10. J. Logie Robertson (ed.), *The Letters of Robert Burns*, Walter Scott: London 1887, p. 59
11. Janet M. Templeton in A. J. Aitken (ed.) *Lowland Scots*, Association for Scottish Literary Studies: Edinburgh 1973, p. 7
12. Fiona MacLeod, *The Winged Destiny. Studies in the Spiritual History of the Gael*, Heinemann: London 1910, pp. 223–5
13. Compton Mackenzie, *The Monarch of the Glen*, Chatto and Windus: London 1941, Penguin edn p. 11
14. Fionn Mac Colla, *Too Long in This Condition* Caithness Books: Thurso 1975, pp. 20–1
15. Edwin Muir, *Scott and Scotland*, Routledge: London 1936, pp. 21–2
16. Sir Harry Lauder, *Roamin' in the Gloamin'*, Hutchinson: London 1928, p. 97
17. Brian Dunnigan in Murray Grigor (ed.), *Scotch Myths* exhibition catalogue, St Andrews 1981.
18. Duncan Glen (ed.), *Selected Essays of Hugh MacDiarmid.*, Jonathan Cape: London 1969, p. 127
19. Cedric Watts and Laurence Davies, *Cunninghame Graham: A Critical Biography*, Cambridge University Press: Cambridge 1979, p. 156

Part One

POETRY

1. THREE OPTIONS: DAVIDSON, McGONAGALL, *WHISTLE-BINKIE*

In a Victorian survey of *English Literature* (1879) the Rev. Stopford Brooke delivered himself of the following definition: 'Scottish Poetry is poetry written in the English tongue by men living in Scotland'.[1] The truth was rather more complicated. As the twentieth century dawned on Scotland, a Scottish poet could still think of himself as either a North Briton or as a Scotsman. If he inclined to the former he opted out of the national issue, treated his ethnic identity as a geographical accident of birth, and responded to Scottish topography in an English manner. This, basically, is the entirely honourable course pursued by Andrew Lang (1844–1912). On the other hand, it was possible for a Scottish poet to consider three indigenous options: the poetic radicalism of John Davidson, the broadside primitivism of William McGonagall, and the self-satisfied cult of pseudo-Burnsian verse. Despite the incongruity of this inheritance a new national style of Scots poetry did emerge as an alternative to the spectacle of 'poetry written in the English tongue by men living in Scotland'.

John Davidson (1857–1909) was brought up in Greenock, where he worked in a chemical laboratory before turning to schoolteaching which supported him (apart from a short spell of clerking in Glasgow) until he sought literary fame and fortune in London in 1889. In late Victorian London, Davidson's aggressively obvious Scottishness seemed out of place and a contemporary remembered him as 'rocky and stubborn and full of Scotch fight, with no little of Scotch pig-headedness'.[2] He quarrelled with his colleagues, Yeats included, and brooded on his neglect and poverty (relieved somewhat by the award of a Civil List Pension of £100 per annum in 1906). Davidson's self-destructive Scottishness alarmed George Bernard Shaw, who offered to help the poet:

> I urged Davidson to cast aside all commercial considerations and write the great poem I believed he had in him expressing to the full his Lucretian Materialism . . . I asked him how much he had to earn, and how long it would take him to write the poem. He said £500 a year, and six months. I sent him £250 and told him to go ahead with the poem, and give me half the profits until I was paid. The result was disastrous.[3]

Davidson wrote a feeble play instead of the poem Shaw hoped for. Nobody would produce the play and Davidson's sense of failure deepened. When he learned he had cancer he decided to take his own life by walking into the sea off Penzance in March 1909. The impact of this death was felt in Scotland by seventeen-year-old Christopher Murray Grieve who, as Hugh MacDiarmid, subsequently wrote a poem, 'Of John Davidson':

And something in me has always stood
Since then looking down the sandslope
On your small black shape by the edge of the sea
A bullet-hole through a great scene's beauty,
God through the wrong end of a telescope.

Davidson was a Scottish poet who eschewed an ostentatiously poetic diction and replaced it with a vigorous language, drawing its rhythmic life from everyday speech and its eloquent impact from scientifically informed sources. Davidson's *Ballads and songs* (1894) contained 'Thirty Bob a Week'[4] in which he presented as heroic the circumstances of a clerk with enough insight to realise the indignity of his particular human condition:

They say it daily up and down the land
  As easy as you take a drink, it's true;
But the difficultest go to understand,
  And the difficultest job a man can do,
Is to come it brave and meek with thirty bob a week,
  And feel that that's the proper thing for you.

It's a naked child against a hungry wolf;
  It's playing bowls upon a splitting wreck;
It's walking on a string across a gulf
  With millstones fore-and-aft about your neck;
But the thing is daily done by many and many a one;
  And we fall, face forward, fighting, on the deck.

These two final stanzas, with their internal rhymes, vivid images and alliteration, show Davidson's mastery of standard metrical forms. The colloquial tone, however, is radical and the poem greatly impressed T. S. Eliot:

for I also had a good many dingy urban images to reveal. Davidson had a great theme, and also found an idiom which elicited the greatness of the theme, which endowed this thirty-bob-a-week clerk with a dignity that would not have appeared if a more conventional poetic diction had been employed. The personage that Davidson created in this poem has haunted me all my life, and the poem is to me a great poem for ever.[5]

Davidson's other outstanding poems include 'A Runnable Stag' (who, like the poet, 'sank in the depths of the sea'), from *Holiday* (1906); and 'Snow' from *Fleet Street* (1909). In 'Snow' Davidson brings his poetic imagination to bear on a microscopic examination of a snowflake:

Every flake with all its prongs and dints
  Burns ecstatic as a new-lit star:
Men are not more diverse, finger-prints
  More dissimilar than snow-flakes are.

Worlds of men and snow endure, increase,
  Woven of power and passion to defy

> Time and travail: only races cease,
>   Individual men and crystals die.

Davidson's poem exhibits an intelligence entirely at odds with the solipsistic sentimentalism of Victorian poetry. He was acutely aware of social conditions, philosophically inclined to Nietzschean existentialism and also anxious to sustain a vision grand enough to admit microscopic matter to a Godless universe. For Davidson there was no absolute death ('Individual men and crystals die') but only a transition from earthly life to universal vitality. Davidson was a restless intellectual who nevertheless recalled his early environment with precision in his 'A Ballad in Blank Verse of the Making of a Poet' from *Ballads and Songs*. Here is Davidson's recollection of Greenock:

>   this grey town
> That pipes the morning up before the lark
> With shrieking steam, and from a hundred stalks
> Lacquers the sooty sky; where hammers clang
> On iron hulls, and cranes in harbours creak,
> Rattle and swing, whole cargoes on their necks;
> Where men sweat gold that others hoard or spend,
> And lurk like vermin in their narrow streets;
> This old grey town, this firth, the further strand
> Spangled with hamlets, and the wooded steeps,
> Whose rocky tops behind each other press,
> Fantastically carved like antique helms
> High-hung in heaven's cloudy armoury,
> Is world enough for me.

While Davidson was in London writing assertively about Greenock, a Dundee weaver was joining together crude rhymes in a way that laid him open to mockery and malice. Ironically, though, his work has survived, indeed flourished.

William McGonagall (1830–1902) suffered more than most from the calamities his hero Shakespeare summed up as 'outrageous fortune'. His vivid prose writings – like the 'Brief Autobiography' and 'Reminiscences' that preface his *Poetic Gems* – tell of his treatment at the hands of the various insensitive louts who tormented him. At school a teacher 'beat him unmercifully about the body and face, until his face was blackened in many places, with his hard Taws'[6]; as a performing artiste was a target for insults and *ad hoc* guided missiles; as a royalist he was mocked by one of Victoria's lackeys practising Balmorality; as a prominent Dundonian he was 'treated unkindly by a few ignorant boys and the Magistrates of the city'.[7] For all that, the posthumous treatment of McGonagall has been more malicious than anything that happened to him in his immensely productive and emotionally eventful life.

The orthodox opinion of McGonagall is that he was a sublimely bad poet: a posturing clown who got the hostility he deserved. His name is now a synonym for doggerel and many students seek to establish their intellectual superiority by declaiming his words with suitably knowing smirks. McGonagall has been parodied atrociously, has been used as the charismatic man in one-man theatrical shows, has inspired comics like Spike Milligan to attempt to improve on what they think of as blatant badness. McGonagall's achievement has been ridiculed by those who despise his lowly origins and humble verse. The joke, however, is on the anti-McGonallites for McGonagall himself was not really an unforgettably bad poet. He was an absolutely outstanding primitive poet.

McGonagall's poetic limitations are obvious enough and indicative of a primitive approach. He was totally indifferent to euphony, absolutely ignorant of imagery, quite unaware of the possibilities of verbal texture, unconcerned with the seductive power of rhythm. McGonagall was a narrative poet who constructed all his poems to a simple formula: all the lines had to be linked by obvious and emphatic rhymes (and his rhymes were no more eccentric than some of those used by a master like Gerald Manly Hopkins, e.g. *boon he on/ Communion*). This concept he shared with the first poets to avail themselves of rhyme, for the technique evolved as an aid to the memory of the reciter or ballad maker. McGonagall's poems may read like metrical tabloid journalism – full of hard facts, editorial comment and gossip – but they are recognisably the work of a man adhering to a metrical tradition and abiding by a rigid set of rules.

In his 'Brief Autobiography' McGonagall recalled the first visitation of his muse in 1877. He wrote,

> 'During the Dundee Holiday week' I sat thinking about the thousands of people who were away by rail and steamboat, perhaps to the land of Burns, or poor ill-treated Tannahill, or to gaze upon the Trossachs in Rob Roy's country . . . Well, while pondering so, I seemed to feel as it were a strange kind of feeling stealing over me, and remained so for about five minutes. A flame, as Lord Byron has said, seemed to kindle up my entire frame, along with a strong desire to write poetry.[8]

Obviously McGonagall is anxious to establish an impressive poetic pedigree so drops some celebrated literary names. However, there is little evidence in his poems to show the influence of poetic virtuosos like Burns and Byron (though doubtless he was responsive to the monotonous march of Scott's couplets). McGonagall's style is entirely based on the broadside ballad formula.

Francis James Child described broadside ballads as 'products of a low kind of art . . . from a literary point of view, thoroughly despicable and worthless.'[9] Because the broadside balladists were artisans, not literary elitists, they relied on hand-me-down rhymes and everyday subjects; like the makers of the traditional ballads they aimed at a popular style accessible to all and not at aesthetic originality. In the early nineteenth century most of the ballads emanated from London's seedy Seven Dials district and this quatrain comes from a typical broadside, 'Waterloo Fashions', printed by John Pitts:

> But a few months ago we were taught to rejoice
> And sing and give thanks with a loud cheerful voice
> For a victory great, if the tale be told true,
> That was won by a Duke, at or near Waterloo.

The do-it-yourself syntax (complete with inversions to force the sentences into the rhyming pattern), the metrical padding ('at or near') to drag out the linear movement, the matter-of-factual tone: all these elements reappear in McGonagall and explain what poetry-buffs regard as the mystery of his style. Here, in 'Beautiful Crieff', is the real McGonagall:

> Ye lovers of the picturesque, if ye wish to drown your grief,
> Take my advice, and visit the ancient town of Crieff;
> The climate is bracing, and the walks lovely to see,
> Besides, ye can ramble over the district, and view the beautiful
>   scenery.

We can imagine the young McGonagall, from garrulous Irish stock, positively rejoicing in the broadside ballads – the street litera-ture that shaped his imagination. With his lack of formal education ('all the education I received was before I was seven years of age'[10]) and his teetotalitarian attitudes he readily absorbed the broadside idiom and became a conscientious master of it. Self-styled men (and women) of letters appear in an unflattering light when we consider what they have made of McGonagall. In the history of painting Henri 'Douanier' Rousseau is treated as an admirable and earnest artist who made meaningful pictorial statements despite his primi-tive manner and lack of aesthetic sophistication. What Rousseau is to painting, McGonagall is to poetry.

McGonagall suffered, like many of his countrymen, from the illu-sion that a humbly born Scot could – with sufficient art and applica-tion – conquer the literary world. This, after all, was the precedent established by Burns in 1787. Burns constantly dismissed his unique gifts as commonplace, preferring to attribute his success to misplaced publicity: 'the novelty of a poet in my obscure situation, without any of those advantages which are reckoned necessary for that character, at least at this time of day, has raised a partial tide of public notice which has borne me to a height, where I am absolutely, feelingly certain, my abilities are inadequate to support me...'[11] After Burns came a deluge of imitation Burnses and Scot-tish poetry became a pastime for thousands of part-time poets. Hugh MacDiarmid was later to actually hold Burns personally re-sponsible for the ugly mixture of sentimentality and complacency discernible in Burnsian pastiche: 'Burns led directly to this sorry pass through his anti-intellectualism and his xenophobia. It is nonsense to say that he embodies all the great elements of the Scottish tradition when in these two main respects he in fact completely betrayed it.'[12] The problem was that Burns was, superficially, easy to imitate. In 'Tam O' Shanter' he used couplets magnificently and in his songs he did as the melody demanded. Usually, though, he relied on Robert Sempill's Standard Habbie measure so skilfully that it should be renamed the Standard Rabbie stanza in deference to his genius. Here is Burns speaking in defence of Lallans (or Lowland Scots) in the Postscript to his epistle 'To William Simpson':

> In days when mankind were but callans
> At grammar, logic, an' sic talents,
> They took nae pains their speech to balance,
>   Or rules to gie,
> But spak their thoughts in plain, braid Lallans,
>   Like you or me.

Burns was succeeded by poets as talented as Robert Tannahill (whose suicidal death by drowning anticipated Davidson's by a century) and Walter Scott (who cannily abandoned his narrative muse when Byron outdid him in commercial appeal). However, as Scottish fiction was reduced to the proportions of the kailyard so Scottish poetry got down to the level represented by the *Whistle-Binkie* collections. According to Jamieson's *Etymological Dictionary* a Whistle-binkie is 'One who attends a penny wedding, but without paying anything . . . a mere spectator, who is as it were, left to sit on a bench by himself, and who, if he pleases, may whistle for his own amusement.' In 1832, the year Scott died, the first series of *Whistle-Binkie* appeared. The impulse behind the publication was the desire to present a modern equivalent of Johnson's *Musical Museum*. The inspiration was, naturally, Burns. The preface to the two-volume edition of *Whistle-Binkie* (1853) claimed that the contents would 'express some feeling of sentiment which the heart delights to cherish', [13] a reference to Burns's claim (in the 'Epistle to John Lapraik') that

> My muse, though hamely in attire,
> May touch the heart.

Most of the poems in *Whistle-Binkie* try to touch the heart by celebrating cosy domesticity, the most famous being William Miller's 'Willie Winkie' whose first stanza achieved an oral reputation. More typically, though, there is the pseudo-Burnsian tone of James Ballantine's 'What Daur Meddle Wi' Me'' with its ridiculous fourth stanza about infant warriors:

> When Bruce at Bannockburn's red field
> Made Edward's doughty army yield,
> An' Southrons down in thousands reeled,

> Stark, still an' dour,
> The vera weans did thistles wield,
>   An' fought like stour.

According to the Scottish critic William Power the 'vernacular verses' of Robert Louis Stevenson were 'the real inspiration of the modern 'Scots vernacular revival'.[14] This dubious claim is based more on Stevenson's prestige as a Scottish writer of proven artistic integrity than on any examination of Stevenson's Scots poetry which is collected in Book 11 of his collection *Underwoods* (1887). In the first Scots poem, 'The Maker to Posterity', Stevenson imagines some 'auld professor or young heir' being perplexed by the poetic use of Scots.[15] Stevenson's answer is contained in the third and fourth stanzas:

> 'What tongue does your auld bookie speak?'
> *He'll speir; an' I, his mou to steik:*
> 'No bein' fit to write in Greek,
>   I wrote in Lallan,
> Dear to my heart as the peat reek,
>   Auld as Tantallon.

> 'Few spak it then, an' noo there's nane.
> My puir auld sangs lie a' their lane,
> Their sense, that aince was braw an' plain,
>   Tin a'thegether,
> Like runes upon a standin' stane
>   Amang the heather.'

Far from sounding a new note in Scots poetry, Stevenson shows himself a Burns imitator (right down to the mock contempt for learning). Like the Whistle-Binkies, Stevenson uses the Standard Rabbie stanza to wallow in a mood of self-congratulation.

2. DIALECT SCOTS

Stevenson's half-hearted usage of Scots was the metrical order of the day. There was nothing remotely radical about such verse; the lip-service paid to dialect was patronising, not patriotic. Dialect Scots, or regional Scots (since each poet added to the pseudo-Burnsian language phrases associated with a particular vicinity) reassured the reader that his intellectual expectations were not about to be tested. Scots was familiar from the poems of Burns and contemporary dialect Scots was conservative and fundamentally safety-first. It provided a cosy homely mood for enthusiastic versifiers; the serious poet, afraid of the domestication of the dialect, turned to English – as Davidson had done. To the Scottish reading public English verse acquired the associations of the schoolroom whereas dialect Scots verse sounded superficially like the songs still preserved in the oral tradition. Dialect Scots was popular and some of the poets attained considerable celebrity. They were well aware that the homely ring of the language had a commercial appeal.

James Logie Robertson (1846–1922), writing under the pseudonym Hugh Haliburton, concocted a volume, *Horace in Homespun* (1886), which presented the popular Hughie in Horatian roles. This was the poetry of a pedant seeking awkwardly to be at ease among the humble. When Hughie adopts a radical tone, in 'Hughie on Evictions: He Lectures a Greedy Landlord', [16]the sentiment is patently obvious and the Scots revealed as a mannerism to disguise the banality of the fundamentally English idiom:

> You spurn the cottar from his cot,
>   The cottage from the green;
> And where the poor man's home was not,
>   Your high ha' door is seen.
>
> But there's a Ha' wha's door is sma',
>   To which a' backs maun boo;
> And this great Ha' that waits us a',
>   Awaits baith them an' you.

Much more endurable was the verse composed by a poet Hugh MacDiarmid dismissed, for polemical reasons, as a man 'who has not only never written a line of poetry in his life, but [who] is constitutionally incapable of doing so.'[17].

Charles Murray is the closest Scotland has come this century to producing a genuinely popular poet, one revered by the ordinary people. His poems demonstrated the appeal of Scots so convincingly that when 'There's aye a something' appeared in the Aberdeen *Press and Journal* in 1933 the first edition sold out by 9 a.m. and two extra editions had to be printed. In a speech in Aberdeen on 2 December 1912 Murray said of his Scots poems: 'That these things should be written in the vernacular was neither accidental nor intentional. It was simply inevitable. If I had been forced to or tried to write in English I certainly could have done nothing'.[18] Murray's main strength was that he drew on the oral currency coined in his native Aberdeenshire, the centre of traditional balladry. He also responded to the precedent set by James Logie Robertson ('Hugh Haliburton'), whose forced literary Scots was brought down to earth by Murray's rural muse.

Murray was born in Alford in 1864 and emigrated to South Africa at the age of twenty-four. His break with his native land led him to dote on it and, in another speech in Aberdeen (25 October 1925), he described himself as 'having, during many years in a new country, kept warm my affection for the old, and retained my interest in its simple life, its old-fashioned characters and customs, and its couthy and expressive language'.[19] Murray's poetry was, then, initially an exercise in nostalgia as he acknowledged by calling his first collection *Hamewith* (1900).[20] 'Hamewith' means 'homewards' and Murray looked back to Scotland with the same kind of intense longing that made 'The Canadian Boat Song' such an obligatory part of the exile's emotional repertoire.

Still, he was no tear-jerking professional Scot; he was a formidable man who brought to poetry a natural gift for narrative and characterisation. In 'The Whistle', from *Hamewith*, he produced a poem that seemed to encapsulate the expectations of every Scottish child. There was the marvellous evocation of place and weather ('the winter brocht him dool'), the way youthful high spirits were dismissed by the ubiquitous Scottish bogeyman – the grim schoolteacher who 'lickit' the boy and 'brunt the whistle that the wee herd made'. The poignant cadence that closed the poem came after a glittering display of the Scots language at its most vivacious as in the passage that has the hero keeping the countryside alive with the traditional music of Scotland:

> He blew them rants sae lively, schottisches, reels, an' jigs,
> The foalie flang his muckle legs an' capered ower the rigs,
> The grey-tailed futt'rat bobbit oot to hear his ain strathspey,
> The bawd cam' loupin' through the corn to 'Clean Pease Strae';
> The feet o' ilka man an' beast gat youkie when he played –
> Hae ye ever heard o' whistle like the wee herd made?

That virtuosity had been lacking in Scottish poetry since the time of Burns. It is instructive to remember that Murray's poetry came as a cure for the hangover induced by the excesses of *Whistle-Binkie*.

Murray had begun the new century with a collection that, at its best, retouched the best features of the Scottish language. He wrote verse so memorable that it got the public response it deserved and, as Murray could create (in, for example, 'The Miller') a mood in a couple of lines ('Her teethless mou' was like a bell,/Her tongue the clangin' clapper') Scots was soon in a position to be treated with respect. The way was clear, in fact, for Lewis Spence to intellectualise Scots poetry and for MacDiarmid to invest the language with the dignity of individual genius.

The importance of Murray's contribution to Scottish letters was quickly appreciated by the likes of John Buchan, who said, at a presentation speech, 'let us see that the Scots we cultivate is a real speech – the broad Scots – not what I may be allowed to call a music-hall Scots . . . Let each of us cultivate the real language of his countryside with its racy words redolent of the soil, and its vigorous idioms which are a true reflex of local character'.[21] Murray certainly did that; he was no one-poem poet but a writer whose complete poetic works are worthy of examination. Murray was not content to reiterate the felicities of 'The Whistle' but was determined to go beyond it and write poetry relevant to the changing world he lived in.

Nowhere is his range more persuasively displayed than in his wartime volume *A Sough o' War* (1917). 'Dockens Afore His Peers' is a little masterpiece, a self-portrait of the Scot who is canny to the point of low cunning. Dockens is attempting to secure exemption for his youngest son and when he is unsuccessful at appealing to the conscience he unscrupulously appeals to the pocket. 'Harry Hears Fae Hame' comprises a series of epistles to a soldier and allows Murray to elaborate on a situation by presenting it from various points of view. Harry's father is selfconsciously casual in his apparent lack of concern; the "Gweed-Wife', however, puts the parental record straight:

> An' ilka day afore he tak's his denner,
>   He's doon the closs to see if Postie's come,
> An' brawly we can tell ye fae his menner
>   Foo things are gyaun atween the sea an' Somme.

Though sentimental it is acceptably so in language that effectively brings the war home to Aberdeen.

It became quite common to use dialect Scots for comic relief: Robert Service did this in, for example 'The Twa Jocks' in his *Ballads of a Bohemian* (1920). While expatriate Scots like Murray and Service fondly dwelt on the popular sentiments of the Doric, Scots at home began to confuse gravity with grandeur. The distinctive note of seriously intended Scots poetry was a long melancholy monotone. Violet Jacob (1863–1946) wrote assured verse that kept up the characteristic mood of resignation. It associated Scots poetry almost exculsively with dying falls, as in 'The Last o' the Tinkler'[22]:

> Ye'll rise tae meet the sun, lad,
>   And baith be trayv'lin west
> But me that's auld an' done, lad,
>   I'll bide an' tak my rest;
> For the grey heid is bendin'
> And the auld shune 's needin' mendin',
> But the trayv'lin 's near its endin',
>   An' the end 's aye the best.

The belief that 'the end 's aye the best' was shared by Jacob's colleagues who were therefore quite unprepared for the innovatory shock of MacDiarmid's lyrics. An admirer of Jacob, Marion Angus (1866–1946), made nostalgic raids on romantic Scottish history and came back with the usual antithetical images; in her 'alas! Poor Queen' it is the old battle of Knox versus Mary. However much MacDiarmid praised the likes of Jacob and Angus – and he did so with respect to their conscious artistry just as, later, he praised the homely muse of Helen B. Cruickshank – they offered no real direction for him to develop. In this respect the most remarkable of MacDiarmid's predecessors was Lewis Spence (1874–1955).

3. LEWIS SPENCE'S MIDDLE SCOTS

Spence was no shrinking Violet or home-made Marion but a man who put his patriotic ideals to a public political test. Spence was born in Broughty Ferry and worked as a journalist with *The Scotsman*, *Edinburgh Magazine* and the *British Weekly*. In 1926 he founded the Scottish National Movement, in 1928 he helped found the National Party of Scotland (as well as becoming its first vice-president), and in 1929 he became the first Scottish Nationalist to stand for parliament. Spence's nationalist energies were applied to the current state of Scots poetry and it seemed to him that the scope of the medium had to be extended by returning to the linguistic virtuosity of the great Makars:

> [in 1898] I had begun to make a serious study of Middle Scots literature, which appealed to me as the only trustworthy basis on which the rehabilitation of the Scots tongue could well be essayed. My main intention was to modernize that phase of Scots in such a manner as would make it serviceable for use at the present time in prose and verse by following the analogous process by which Chaucerian English had developed into modern English, this indeed being the simplest and most efficacious means to my hand.
>
> This process, indeed, occupied many years of labour in my spare time. By the late twenties I had completed perhaps half of my task when Mr MacDiarmid (who had applauded my endeavours and was fully knowledgeable concerning them) ventured upon his scheme for the formation of a generalized Scots drawn from all the known phrases and dialects of that tongue and which he described as 'Synthetic Scots'. Of course Mr MacDiarmid had a perfect right to formulate any such system as seemed good to him. This notwithstanding, I cannot believe that his efforts were founded on any tolerably scientific or rational basis.[23]

Spence, whose bitterness shows towards the end of that statement, was deliberately missing the point of MacDiarmid's achievement which was founded entirely on a creative basis and did not claim to be scientific or rational. Initially, though, MacDiarmid was enthusiastically aware of Spence's linguistic dexterity; in 1926 he saluted Spence as 'the first Scot for five hundred years to write "pure poetry" in the vernacular'.[24] William Power went even further:

> Lewis Spence stands out as the most marmoreal, the most completely artistic poet in modern Scotland . . .His exquisite sonnets in Middle Scots are an example . . .His poems on Edinburgh – apocalyptic, satirical, and majestically pictorial – are the finest things of the kind written in our time about any great city. Spence is a man of letters in the big, the French sense.[25]

The finale of one of Spencer's Edinburgh poems, 'The Prows o' Reekie'[26], demonstrates his gift of imagery and ability to see the sublime in the apparently ridiculous:

A hoose is but a puppet-box
To keep life's images frae knocks,
But mannikins scrieve oot their sauls
Upon its craw-steps and its walls:
Whaur hae they writ them mair sublime
Than on yon gable-ends o' time?

Spence later resented MacDiarmid's invasion of what he thought of as his exclusive poetic territory. He survived to regard himself as a forgotten man in his own lifetime. He deserves to be remembered as a minor Scots poet and major theoretical influence on MacDiarmid. Thanks to Spence the tradition that MacDiarmid inherited was alive to the possibilities of change. Spence had shown that Scots was not a dead-and-buried language but a literature that had been allowed to atrophy. It would obviously take a genius to shake Scots to its linguistic roots and make it bear the burden of great modern poetry. MacDiarmid was ready, willing and able to do just that.

4. HUGH MacDIARMID

During his lifetime MacDiarmid was such a massive presence in Scottish literary affairs that his work had an unsettling influence: his followers lavished praise on his poetry without considering it in a global context, and his enemies dismissed him as a virulent polemicist who used poetry for political ends. It is now possible to see what MacDiarmid actually achieved. He began writing after the First World War and wanted to help Scotland take her place in a radically new world in which independence would be granted to both individuals and nations. Although he was a nationalist he detested chauvinism and cultivated international contacts. He was convinced that Scotland needed saving from her own worst excesses and had the justifiable immodesty to assume that he could be a cultural saviour. As his work shows, he believed that poetry was an immensely more important force than politics so he began to revitalise Scotland by giving it a new poetic voice. He came to the conclusion that 'most of the important words were killed in the First World War' ('Talking with Five Thousand People in Edinburgh'), so set about liberating language from convention and complacency. He regarded the use of dialect Scots by poets such as Charles Murray as a manifestation of mindlessness; therefore he put in the place of dialect Scots an *ad hoc* idiom called Synthetic Scots, as it used the resources of the etymological dictionary and the expressive sound of the spoken language. MacDiarmid wanted Synthetic Scots to be as modernistic as Eliot's allusive English or Joyce's textured prose. In fact MacDiarmid's Synthetic Scots was the Scottish contribition to the literary experimentalism of the twentieth century.

Hugh MacDiarmid was born Christopher Murray Grieve in the little Border town of Langholm, Dumfriesshire, on 11 August 1892. His father was a rural postman and the family lived in the post office building underneath the local library, which gave young Grieve ready access to a collection of some 12,000 books. With characteristic immodesty he claimed to have read all these books by the age of fourteen and was fond, thereafter, of referring to his mind as one steeped in a 'strong solution of books'.[27] Grieve attended Langholm Academy (where Francis George Scott, the composer who set many MacDiarmid lyrics, taught English), then went to Edinburgh to train as a schoolteacher. When his father died in 1911, Grieve abandoned all idea of a steady career but decided to work at whatever would give him free time for writing: this meant journalism when he could get a job. During the First World War, Grieve served with the Royal Army Medical Corps and was invalided home from Salonika, suffering from cerebral malaria. In 1918 he married Margaret Skinner and the couple settled in Montrose where Grieve became chief reporter on the weekly *Montrose Review*, the father of two children, a Labour Member of the Town Council, a Justice of the Peace, a founder of the Scottish Centre of PEN, a co-founder of the National Party of Scotland, and founding editor of two periodicals. The first of these, *Northern Numbers*, was a fairly conventional poetry annual based on Edward Marsh's *Georgian Poetry* (1912–22). Grieve used it as a means to establish himself. The first issue appeared in 1920, the third and last in 1922. In those two years Grieve had used his editorial prerogative to oust the lesser lights and draw attention to his own brilliance:

> I began, when I issued my Northern Numbers anthology, by displaying the best of the work available by living Scottish poets; and side by side with it introduced work by younger and then quite unknown poets, including myself, who had very different ideas from those prevalent . . . The well-know poets represented alongside *les jeunes* in the earlier issues – Neil Munro, John Buchan, General Sir Ian Hamilton, Violet Jacob, Charles Murray, Lewis Spence, Donald A. Mackenzie – were speedily, and no doubt a trifle unceremoniously, 'dropped', and the field was left to the rising school.[28]

Grieve was writing in English and intially took a sceptical attitude to the attempts of the Vernacular Circle of the London Burns Club to preserve the Doric. His fertile mind, however, held two distinct possibilities: that the potential of Scotland could be expressed in poetry written in English with European terms of reference; or that Scotland could best realise her possibilities by exploring all the literary and patriotic possibilities of Scots. To do this the words in oral circulation would be extended by recourse to Middle Scots poetry (as Lewis Spence had done) and by consulting Jamieson's *Etymological Dictionary*. Never a man to limit himself, Grieve managed to get the best of both worlds by inventing an alter ego – Hugh MacDiarmid.

On 26 August 1922 Grieve's new magazine, *Scottish Chapbook*, was published in Montrose. In the first issue a 'Hugh M'Diarmid' made an appearance with a dramatic sketch, 'Nisbet, An Interlude in Post War Glasgow'. While he was launching *Scottish Chapbook*, Grieve was also contributing a series on 'Scottish Books and Bookmen' to the *Dunfermline Press*. On 30 September 1922 he referred to his ambivalent attitude to the Vernacular Circle of the London Burns Club but also indicated that his philological passion had been stimulated by the efforts of a friend who had been staying with him. This guest had studied Sir James Wilson's *Lowland Scotch as Spoken in the Lower Strathearn District of Perthshire* (1915) and had extracted from the dictionary enough unusual words to make two lyrics. The poems were 'The Water Gaw' and 'The Blaward and the Skelly', which thus appeared anonymously. In October 1922 the third issue of the *Scottish Chapbook* displayed, on its first page, 'The Watergaw'. Now it was attributed to 'Hugh M'Diarmid' and in defence of this poem editor Grieve wrote a forceful 'Causerie':

[Mr Hugh M'Diarmid] is, I think, the first Scottish writer who has addressed himself to the question of the extendability (without psychological violence) of the Vernacular to embrace the whole range of modern culture . . . the value of the Doric lies in the extent to which it contains lapsed or unrealised qualities which correspond to 'unconscious' elements of distinctively Scottish psychology. The recovery and application of these may make effectively communicable those unexpressed aspects of the Scottish character the absence of which makes, say, 'Kailyaird' characters shallow, sentimental, humiliating travesties . . . The whole trouble with the Doric as a literary language to-day is that the vast majority of its exponents are hopelessly limited culturally – and that the others (such as Mrs Violet Jacob, Mr Charles Murray and Miss Mary Symon) only use it for limited purposes . . . Stripping the unconscious form of the Vernacular of the grotesque clothes of the Canny-Sandy cum Kirriemuir Elder cum Harry Lauder cult, he has shown a well-knit muscular figure that has not been seen in Scottish literature for a long day.[29]

Although John Buchan felt that MacDiarmid's work was 'at once reactionary and revolutionary'[30] there is no doubt that MacDiarmid himself was primarily interested in the radically modernist effects of Scots. Perhaps the most significant historical fact about 'The Watergaw' is its appearance in 1922, the *annus mirabilis* of modernism: the year of Joyce's *Ulysses* and Eliot's *The Waste Land*. Grieve's English poetry, with its symbolist style, was modern in a derivative way; the poetry he composed for, and as, Hugh MacDiarmid was both novel and original.

From his Border childhood MacDiarmid had retained a reservoir of Scots words and to this vocabulary he added literary Scots. The oral rhythms and literary associations came together in a unique imaginative fusion:

> Ae weet forenicht i' the yow-trummle
> I saw you antrin thing,
> A watergaw wi' its chitterin' licht
> Ayont the on-ding;
> An' I thocht o' the last wild look ye gied
> Afore ye deed!
>
> There was nae reek i' the laverock's hoose
> That nicht – an' nane i' mine;
> But I hae thocht o' that foolish licht
> Ever sin' syne;
> An' I think that mebbe at last I ken
> What your look meant then.[31]

The poem expresses the poet's response to the death of his father (an event that is also alluded to in the later poem 'Kinsfolk'). By extending his imaginative sympathies the poet raises the memory of death to the level of a universal insight. 'The Watergaw' uses imagery for philosophical purposes, takes a symbol and invests it with an other-worldly importance. In the second stanza MacDiarmid refrains from interpreting the vital light that is both watergaw and life. Instead he lets the conclusion, like the symbol, hang in the air. The 'mebbe' in the penultimate line is not inserted in the interests of prosodic regularity; it is there to stress human vulnerability and the possibility that there just might be a transcendent answer to the question demanded by the existence of life. Stylistically, MacDiarmid had introduced a new note to Scots poetry. He had abandoned both the rigid quatrain and the Standard Rabbie stanza in favour of a more fluid format which closed on a clinching couplet. Above all MacDiarmid had intellectualised and modernised Scots poetry by isolating a particular image then seeking out its cosmic connotations. That was to be the method pursued in the Synthetic Scots lyrics in *Sangschaw* (1925) and *Penny Wheep* (1926) — and, indeed, in his later work. Two statements made by MacDiarmid go a long way to explaining his approach to poetry and the subsequent evolution of his verse. First, there is his theory of linguistic response:

> Because of a profound interest in the actual structure of language, like Mallarmé I have always believed in the possibility of 'une poesié qui fut comme deduit de l'ensemble des propriétés et des caractéres du language' – the act of poetry being the reverse of what it is usually thought to be; not an idea gradually shaping itself in words, but deriving entirely from words – and it was in fact (as only my friend F. G. Scott divined) in this way that I wrote all the best of my Scots poems . . .[32]

Secondly, there is his particular linguistic response to Jamieson's dictionary:

We have been enormously struck by the resemblance — the moral resemblance – between Jamieson's Etymological Dictionary of the Scottish Language and James Joyce's Ulysses. A *Vis comica* that has not yet been liberated lies bound by desuetude and misappreciation in the recesses of the Doric: and its potential uprising would be no less prodigious, uncontrollable, and utterly at variance with conventional morality than was Joyce's tremendous outpouring.[33]

MacDiarmid did not, therefore, regard the Scots language with anti-quarian affectations. He was determined to make Scots poetry an international force, to build a 'great Scottish Literary Renaissance'[34] for the rest of the world to marvel at the way they marvelled at Joyce's masterpiece. Having perfected an original lyric manner in 'The Watergaw' he produced two collections of lyrics that reached out into the vastness of space (as in 'The Eemis Stane'):

> I' the how-dumb-deid o' the cauld hairst nicht
> The warl' like an eemis stane
> Wags i' the lift;
> An' my eerie memories fa'
> Like a yowdendrift.

MacDiarmid's lyrics constantly jumped from the particular to the general and then came back, lovingly, to earth. In the lyrics in *Sang-schaw* and *Penny Wheep* MacDiarmid exhaustively pursued his method of opening up an image to cosmic consequences. He suggests a multi-dimensional view of reality by contrasting an earthly viewpoint with a God's-eye-view of the universe; this cosmic outlook simultaneously shrinks the world to socially manageable proportions and suggests the imaginative majesty of man who is capable of possessing the cosmos through creativity. MacDiarmid used God as an instantly accessible image of a meaningful universe and avoided the theological stereotype. In 'Crowdieknowe' God is not an omnipotent patriarch but an odious observer who has to contend with the truculent force of humanity in the shape of the unwillingly resurrected Langholm locals. MacDiarmid saw no point genuflecting before an abstract deity. In his poem 'Empty Vessel' he compared a girl crooning over a dead child to the intergalactic light that unfeelingly illuminates the universe:

> Wunds wi' warlds to swing
> Dinna sing sae sweet,
> The licht that bends owre a' thing
> Is less ta'en up wi't.

Paradoxically 'Empty Vessel' demonstrates how deeply MacDiarmid's modernity is rooted in tradition for the poem is a creative completion of a folk fragment.

In *Penny Wheep* MacDiarmid replied 'To One Who Urges More Ambitious Flights' by insisting 'We bit sangs are a' I need'. Five months after the publication of that statement he published *A Drunk Man Looks at the Thistle* (1926). Looking back on his masterpiece he said: 'The general (as beyond the particularly Scottish) theme of *A Drunk Man Looks at the Thistle* is to show "a beautiful soul in the making" – to trace, that is to say, its rise through all struggle and contradiction till it stands out a self-conscious, self-directing personality – a purified person'.[35] The poem amounts to much more than that, though; in *A Drunk Man* MacDiarmid virtually remade Scotland in his own image as symbolised by the thistle. He also made sure his poem functioned on various levels. Thematically the poem operates by taking the thistle through a startling series of metamorphoses. Stylistically it substitutes for the ineffable lyricism of *Sangschaw* an opinionated dramatic monologue. Structurally the poem is a Scottish odyssey with frequent interruptions and diversions. *A Drunk Man* can also be seen as an epic extension of Burns's 'Tam O' Shanter' since both poems describe an alcoholic odyssey homewards towards the arms of a nagging folk Penelope: Kate/Jean. In Burns's poem the Ulysses-figure returns on horseback and experiences a comic vision (corresponding to drunken hallucinations); in MacDiarmid's poem the Ulysses-figure staggers from the pub, collapses on a hillside, and experiences a regenerative vision of a new Scotland. MacDiarmid's Drunk Man is aware of all this and says

> I canna ride awa' like Tam,
> But e'en maun bide juist whaur I am.[36]

MacDiarmid is challenging Burns's image of Scotland (or the secondary image Burns clubbed into the national consciousness), and paying Burns the compliment of treating him as the only national poetic figure worth standing up to and for. And for that reason the Drunk Man quickly sets up an attack that separates Burns from his admirers:

> Rabbie, wad'st thou wert here – the warld hath need,
> And Scotland mair sae, o' the likes o' thee!
> The whisky that aince moved your lyre's become
> A laxative for a' loquacity.[37]

The Drunk Man is a real character as well as functioning symbolically. He is forever initiating quarrels and settling them to his own satisfaction. He is truculent rather than elegant, overwhelming rather than persuasive, adamant rather than agreeable. If at times he seems to be conducting an argument with himself that is because he believes in both dialect and dialectic (like his creator).

The Drunk Man begins in a state of exhaustion that corresponds to the national mood of Scotland. The poem opens memorably with a note of resignation – 'I amna' fou' sae muckle as tired – deid dune' – as the Drunk Man comes to. He has been drinking with Cruivie and Gilsanquhar and has left them to seek his bed. Instead he finds he is looking for his national identity for he is alone with himself:

> *Jean! Jean!* Gin *she*'s no' here it's no' *oor* bed,
> Or else I'm dreamin' deep and canna wauken,
> But it's a fell queer dream if this is no'
> A real hillside – and thae things thistles and bracken![38]

As his self, his individuality, is exposed under the searchlight beam of the full moon–'That's it! It isna me that's fou' at a',/But the fu' mune'[39] – he has to come to terms with what his self amounts to. He is a Drunk Man in a Scotocentric universe and is *au fait* (to use a favourite MacDiarmid phrase) with the international cultural context. He refers to T. S. Eliot, Dostoevsky, Mallarmé, Nietzsche, Freud, Schoenberg; he translates from the Russian of Blok and Hippius, from the French of Ramaekers and Rocher, from the German of Lasker-Schüller (at least MacDiarmid adapts extant translations to the Drunk Man's vernacular ends); he is aware of the strange artistic association of his own country with Sir Harry Lauder, Isadora Duncan, Mary Garden in Chicago, Duncan Grant in Paris. He sees Scotland as a mass of contradictions and feels archetypally Scottish in possessing a contradictory, contrary character:

> I'll ha'e nae hauf-way hoose, but aye be whaur
> Extremes meet – it's the only way I ken
> To dodge the curst conceit o' bein' richt
> That damns the vast majority o' men.[40]

The dialectical motion of MacDiarmid's poem – the to-and-fro movement of ideas, the counterpoint of images – makes it wide-ranging in reference and restless in movement. It emanates enough energy to fuel a nation. The Drunk Man gradually warms to his theme and attains a terrible clarity in his dawning sobriety: he sees through the superficially grim face of his nation and discovers a vision of unity-in-diversity. Through a series of evocative free-associations the Drunk Man celebrates the diversity. He jumps from the thought of a 'luvin' wumman'[41] to a majestic consideration of the eternal predicament of all women:

> O wha's the bride that cairries the bunch
> O'thistles blinterin' white?
> Her cuckold bridegroom little dreids
> What he sall ken this nicht.
>
> For closer than gudeman can come
> And closer to 'r than hersel',
> Wha didna need her maidenheid
> Has wrocht his purpose fell.[42]

This bride, at once virginal and vulnerable, is to be penetrated by the spirit of the new Scotland. She is to give birth to a poetic saviour who will be crucified on the thistle and then rise to resurrection. The Drunk Man is changing as this consciousness possesses him. In the process of metamorphosis he acquires the characteristics of his creator, Hugh MacDiarmid.

He looks at the thistle and is reminded 'o' the pipes' lood drone'[43] which takes him back to memories of Langholm (the Muckle Toon):

> Drums in the Walligate, pipes in the air,
> Come and hear the cryin 'o' the Fair.
>
> A' as it used to be, when I was a loon
> On Common-Ridin' Day in the Muckle Toon.[44]

He thinks of Scotland as 'THE barren fig'[45], then of the failure of the General Strike of 1926:

> Was it the ancient vicious sway
> Imposed itsel' again,
> Or nerve owre weak for new emprise
> That made the effort vain,
>
> A coward strain in that lorn growth
> That wrocht the sorry trick?
> — The thistle like a rocket soared
> And cam' doon like the stick.[46]

Holding together all the counterpointed images is the Drunk Man's increasingly steady vision of Scotland as a country with the potential to liberate itself from centuries of defeatism and develop a national ideal with universal implications for

> The thistle yet'll unite
> Man and the Infinite![47]

and

> The thistle rises and forever will,
> Getherin' the generations under't.
> This is the monument o' a' they were,
> And a' they hoped and wondered.[48]

The ideal Scot is a citizen of the universe, a man who offers the world the gift of his individuality. This is the philosophical point of the poem and MacDiarmid is quite explicit in his emphasis on the inviolability of each individual's individuality:

> And let the lesson be – to be yersel's,
> Ye needna fash gin it's to be ocht else.
> To be yersel's – and to mak' that worth bein',
> Nae harder job to mortals has been gi'en.[49]

There is nothing narrowly nationalist about this vision of unity-in-diversity for

> He's no a man ava',
> And lacks a proper pride,
> Gin less than a' the warld
> Can ser' him for a bride![50]

The conceptual basis of this great poem, then, is the possibility of national liberation through personal emancipation. The Drunk Man himself serves as an example by his metamorphosis from typically drunken Scot expatiating on Burns and booze to a sensitive and imaginative individual whose observations are worthy of a world's attention. By implication this path is open to every Scot who is willing to discard stereotypes, throw off the burden of historical defeat, and attain a dignified identity. Alone in his Scotocentric universe, the Drunk Man experiences a cosmic awareness of the circular movement of the galaxy. In terse and taut tercets the Drunk Man expresses his deepest conclusions:

> Whatever Scotland is to me,
> Be it aye pairt o' a' men see
> O' Earth and o' Eternity . . .
>
> He canna Scotland see wha yet
> Canna see the Infinite,
> And Scotland in true scale to it . . .
>
> The function, as it seems to me,
> O' Poetry is to bring to be
> At lang, lang last that unity . . .
>
> *A Scottish poet maun assume*
> *The burden o' his people's doom,*
> *And dee to brak' their livin' tomb.*[51]

MacDiarmid's own life was a record of dedicated artistic integrity; a decade after the publication of *A Drunk Man* he was living in penury in Shetland, heroically shouldering 'The burden o' his people's doom'. Having written *A Drunk Man* he had given Scotland cause to rejoice and a cause (a nation of developed individuals) to strive for. At the end of his poem the Drunk Man (now sober) reaches Penelope-Jean and offers her himself and his wordless eloquence. In MacDiarmid's own life artistic triumph was followed by personal trials.

In the thistle MacDiarmid had found an all-purpose symbol sufficiently familiar to provoke responses in all Scots and suggestive enough to sustain the poet's astonishingly inventive genius. For his next long poem *To Circumjack Cencrastus* (1930), he employed the Celtic symbol of eternity: the snake, or serpent, with its tail in its mouth. *Cencrastus* is inferior to *A Drunk Man*, but then so are most Scottish poems. It came as an anticlimax only because MacDiarmid had set himself such impossibly high standards in his masterpiece. It has generally been supposed that *Cencrastus* was weaker than its predecessor because the central symbol did not suit MacDiarmid's muse the way the thistle did. It is more basic than that. MacDiarmid never liked to repeat his successes. His whole career is a series of dramatic shifts in emphasis linked by the power of his personality; the dialectical motion of *A Drunk Man* corresponded to the contrary nature of MacDiarmid's own personality. In *A Drunk Man* MacDiarmid had sublimated his personality in the device of the dramatic monologue; in *Cencrastus* he decided to do without a poetic persona and, instead, expatiated on the state of the Scotocentric universe. *Cencrastus* is a series of autonomous poems and so regarded amounts to a splendid achievement. Poems like 'The Parrot Cry' and 'I'm the original/Plasm o' the ocean' search and satirise Scotland and the Scot. They are likely to be remembered without the benefit of the serpentine context. MacDiarmid's lyric gift was in evidence in the finest parts of the book although it had taken on a melancholy tone of uncharacteristic resignation:

> Nae wonder if I think I see
> A lichter shadow than the neist
> I'm fain to cry: 'The dawn, the dawn!
>   But ah
>   – It's juist mair snaw!*[52]*

Equally impressive is MacDiarmid's command of an elegiac English idiom in his translation of Rilke's 'Requiem für eine Freundin'. Yet the sequence is, overall, richer in opinion than in imagery and thereby demonstrates that MacDiarmid no longer took as his priority the revitalisation of Scots. He had personally fought that battle in his two collections of lyrics and *A Drunk Man*. During the next decade he was to be increasingly involved in personal survival and the embattled expression of his unpopular opinions.

The 1930s is remembered, in literary history, as a political decade; the era of the English pylon poets who took a fancy to Marxism and reinterpreted political comradeship in terms of public school chumminess. MacDiarmid bitterly dismissed them in a poem 'British Leftish Poetry, 1930–40':

> Auden, MacNeice, Day Lewis, I have read them all.
> Hoping against hope to hear the authentic call . . .
> And know the explanation I must pass is this
> – You cannot strike a match on a crumbling wall.

Yet Day Lewis acknowledged[53] that it was MacDiarmid who inspired the political poetry of the 1930s with his collection *First Hymm to Lenin* (1931). Although MacDiarmid did not join the Communist Party until 1934, the year after his expulsion from the Scottish National Party, this volume vividly revealed the colour of this politics. In the title poem the Synthetic Scots of the early 1920s is replaced by what is basically English with a Scottish accent. The poem, as the title makes abundantly clear, deifies Lenin (not individuality as in *A Drunk Man*) as the hope for the future of mankind. MacDiarmid, originally alive to the heroic individual, goes over to hero worship and the unMarxist assumption that Lenin personally orchestrated history by the force of his personality. In this poem MacDiarmid subscribes to the opportunist notion that the means justify the ends and that Lenin's policies, all of them, can be excused on pragmatic grounds:

> What maitters 't wha we kill
> To lessen that foulest murder that deprives
> Maist men o' real lives?

MacDiarmid's rhetorical question was answered by bitter hostility on the part of the readership who had seen him as the great white hope of Scotland. Now he was cast as the red terror, a man publicly committed to the overthrow of bourgeois society. That society took a terrible revenge on him.

Nevertheless, delighted by the impact of his secular first hymn to Lenin, MacDiarmid published his *Second Hymn to Lenin* in 1932. In the short satirical poems printed alongside the 'First Hymn' MacDiarmid had shown himself a master of succinctly expressed malice. The 'Second Hymn', again written in a Scottish-accented English, reduced politics to the first step in a long road to human emancipation which would ultimately depend on poetry:

> Sae here, twixt poetry and politics,
> There's nae doot in the en'.
> Poetry includes that and s'ud be
> The greatest poo'er amang men.
>
> —It's the greatest, *in posse* at least,
> That men ha'e discovered yet
> Tho' nae doot they're unconscious still
> O' ithers faur greater then it . . .
>
> Unremittin', relentless,
> Organized to the last degree,
> Ah, Lenin, politics is bairns' play
> To what this maun be!

MacDiarmid believed in the practical role poetry would play in the classless society that is the aim of theoretical Marxism. He was also painfully aware that, in the real world he lived in, poetry was the concern of a tiny minority. While he was making ringing statements on the state of the world his personal life was breaking down into various crises.

In 1929 MacDiarmid had been invited, by Compton Mackenzie, to go to London to edit the periodical *Vox*. The magazine, devoted to radio, collapsed after three months and the poet almost went down with it. He left his wife, Margaret, in London while he found a job as a Publicity Officer in Liverpool. After a catastrophic year he returned to London to be divorced in 1932. From that period dates his intense hatred of England and he was 'desperately anxious not to leave Scotland again'[54] Ironically the collection MacDiarmid published in that miserable year of 1932, *Scots Unbound*, contains some of his most delicate poems. 'Milk-Wort and Bog-Cotton' is a lyrical triumph. Its beautifully hushed majesty nevertheless contains a confessional reference to the poet's 'darkness':

> Wad that nae leaf upon anither wheeled
> A shadow either and nae root need dern
> In sacrifice to let sic beauty be!
> But deep surroundin' darkness I discern
> Is aye the price o' licht. Wad licht revealed
> Naething but you, and nicht nocht else concealed.

In complete contrast there is the onomatopoetic extravaganza 'Water Music' which, as the introductory stanza affirms, was inspired by the Anna Livia Plurabelle section Joyce worked into *Finnegans Wake*. MacDiarmid's delight in the sensuous possibilities of Scots was never more joyously expressed than in this poem:

> Archin' here and arrachin there,
>   Allevolie or allemand,
> Whiles appliable, whiles areird,
>   The polysemous poem's planned.
>
> Lively, louch, atweesh, atween,
>   Auchimuty or aspate,
> Threidin' through the averins
>   Or bightsom in the aftergait.

Such ecstatic moments were isolated, though, for MacDiarmid was taking up the challenge of a more bookish poetry, a verse entirely devoted to linguistic exploration. The result was poetry in which verbal grandeur alternated with passages reflecting the poet's lexical obsessions. MacDiarmid had evolved in his art and his life. After his divorce he married a Cornish girl, Valda Trevlyn, and the couple moved, with their baby, Michael, to an abandoned cottage on the Shetland island of Whalsay. MacDiarmid has described his condition bitterly:

> I could not have lived anywhere else . . . without recourse to the poorhouse. We were not only penniless when we arrived in Whalsay – I was in exceedingly bad state, psychologically and physically . . . I had no books. Indeed, we had practically no furniture . . . I have forgotten what that first winter was like; no doubt my wife remembers all too well – it must have been one long nightmare of cold and damp and darkness and discomfort.[55]

With island exile imposed on him by economic and psychological circumstances he began to investigate his environment and the poet-

37

ry he wrote then was neither Synthetic Scots nor everyday English. It was (as the opening of 'On a Raised Beach' shows) an erudite dictionary-based diction made poetic by the pressure of the poet's personality:

> All is lithogenesis–or lochia,
> Carpholite fruit of the forbidden tree,
> Stones blacker than any in the Caaba,
> Cream-coloured caen-stone, chatoyant pieces,
> Celadon and corbeau, bistre and beige,
> Glaucous, hoar, enfouldered, cyathiform,
> Making mere faculae of the sun and moon
> I study you glout and gloss, but have
> No cadrans to adjust you with, and turn again
> From optik to haptik and like a blind man run
> My fingers over you, arris by arris, burr by burr,
> Slickensides, truité, rugas, foveoles,
> Bringing my aesthesis in vain to bear,
> An angle-titch to all your corrugations and coigns,
> Hatched foraminous cavo-rilievo of the world,
> Deictic, fiducial stones.

MacDiarmid began to expand on even that idiom. He believed it was imperative that the poet should express the potentialities of the epic age he lived in and devoted his poetic efforts to the completion of a truly massive work that would include *In Memoriam James Joyce* (1955), *The Kind of Poetry I Want* (1961) and the projected *Impavidi Progrediamur*. Although he was Scotland's most distinguished living poet he refused to adopt any Grand Old Mannerisms but cherished his independence and idiosyncracy. He left Whalsay in 1942 and did warwork first as a fitter on Clydeside and then as a deckhand on a Norwegian ship. When the war ended he was technically unemployed. In 1951 he moved to a derelict, rent-free cottage in Biggar, Lanarkshire, and continued to plan the epic that was to be called *Mature Art*. Although critics despaired of the regurgitated bookish passages the poem is rich in personal moments perfectly expressed, as this extract from *In Memoriam James Joyce* shows:[56]

> In this realistic mood I recognise
> With a grim animal acceptance
> That it is indeed likely enough that the 'soul'
> Perishes everlastingly with the death of the body,
> But what this realistic mood, into which
> My mind falls like a plummet
> Through the neutral zone of its balanced doubt,
> Never for one single beat of time can shake or disturb
> Is my certain knowledge,
> Derived from the complex vision of everything in me,
> That the whole astronomical universe, however illimitable,

Is only one part and parcel of the mystery of Life;
Of this I am as certain as I am certain that I am I.
The astronomical universe in *not* all there is.

So this is what our lives have been given to find,
A language that can serve our purposes,
A marvellous lucidity, a quality of fiery aery light,
Flowing like clear water, flying like a bird,
Burning like a sunlit landscape.
Conveying with a positively Godlike assurance,
Swiftly, shiningly, exactly, what we want to convey.
This use of words, this peculiar aptness and handiness,
Adapts itself to our every mood, now pathetic, now ironic,
Now full of love, of indignation, of sensuality, of glamour, of glory,
With an inevitable richness of remembered detail
And a richness of imagery that is never cloying,
A curious and indescribable quality
Of sensual sensitiveness,
Of very light and very air itself,
– Pliant as a young hazel wand,
Certain as a gull's wings,
Lucid as a mountain stream,
Expressive as the eyes of a woman in the presence of love, –
Expressing the complex vision of everything in one,
Suffering all impressions, all experience, all doctrines
To pass through and taking what seems valuable from each.
No matter in however many directions
These essences seem to lead.

Although the idiom has altered the concerns are recognisably Mac-Diarmidian: language, individuality, unity-in-diversity. There is an artistic wholeness to his achievement in spite of, or because of since he was proud of his dialectical abilities, the contradictions. His poetry has the authority of a man who knows what it is to be possessed by imaginative powers, to be occasionally at the mercy of his material. Contrary to orthodox opinion, MacDiarmid did not take up Scots and then abandon it for English or vice versa. He used the two languages with a poet's indifference to dogmatic theory. He always hovered between Scots and English and in 1966, years after his supposed desertion of Lallans, could publish a poem like 'A Change of Weather' with its description of the sun 'strugglin' airgh and wan i' the lift'. The fact is that all MacDiarmid's work is cerebral: his Scots lyrics revealed an informed consciousness of the cosmos and his *Mature Art* project is a monumental exhibition of one man's erudition. Significantly enough, the first piece in Christopher Grieve's first book, *Annals of the Five Senses* (1923), is revealingly entitled 'Cerebral'. It is a prose composition delineating the thoughts that pass through the mind of a journalist as he writes a column on 'The Scottish Element in Ibsen'. It attempts to map the contours of a mind that free associates in a remarkably imaginative manner: 'His sense of actual cerebral disposition was acute and constantly employed.'[57] As MacDiarmid said in another context, 'That's me to a T.'[58] He was, after all, entitled to boast in 1972:

> I am accustomed to being accused of all sorts of contradictions, to which I have often merely answered, like Walt Whitman, 'I contradict myself. Very well! I contradict myself.' But . . .under the apparent inconsistencies and contradictions there is a basic unity . . .[In *Annals of the Five Senses*] I express the main ideas of all my subsequent work. I have demonstrably pursued these undeviatingly through my whole career . . .[59]

It was because of his determination to be utterly himself, albeit in a national context, that MacDiarmid spent so much time exposing as a cruel travesty the Lauderesque image of the Scot as a sentimental and silly fool. MacDiarmid rained down polemical words as hard as hail on the heads of his fellow Scots because he wanted Scotland to recognise itself so other nations would follow suit and recognise it as something worthwhile. He continually urged Scottish writers to show more responsibility, to be an exceptional part of the national community, to eschew the derivative and embrace the essential. In *Lucky Poet* he criticised his contemporaries for being 'hopelessly muddle-headed, anti-intellectual'[60] and the charge was repeated some twenty years later in *The Company I've Kept*: 'Most of our writers are backward-looking, consumed by a repetition complex, afraid to face up to and grapple with contemporary realities.'[61] In making his own subject-matter the total substance of Scotland he answered with a defiant negative his own rhetorical question in 'Direadh I': 'Scotland small? Our multiform, our infinite Scotland *small*?' Scotland is, MacDiarmid maintained, as large as the imagination can make it. MacDiarmid never claimed his was the only way; what he did was open up a world of possibilities and restore a sense of purpose to the national community. When he was buried in his native Langholm on 13 September 1978 there was no way his work would rest in peace. All his life he had welcomed criticism and combined celebration with cerebration. His hope was for a nation of individuals capable of thinking for themselves. If MacDiarmid's work was to have an influence then the process would recall the motto of *The Scottish Chapbook* – 'Not Traditions – Precedents'. If, for example, Synthetic Scots was to survive then it would support a Scottish national poetry. MacDiarmid, the self-styled saviour of *A Drunk Man Looks at the Thistle*, had little use for disciples, as his credo stressed individuality. To their credit the best of his followers attempted to adapt his idiom to their own needs.

5. SYNTHETIC SCOTS IN ACTION: SOUTAR, GARIOCH, GOODSIR SMITH

The first important poet on whom MacDiarmid exerted a powerful influence was William Soutar, whose appalling predicament as a bedfast invalid for the last thirteen years of his life (he died on 15 October 1943, aged forty-five) has been movingly recounted in Alexander Scott's biography *Still Life* (1958). Soutar was an active young man who passed out of Perth Academy into the navy in 1916 then contracted an illness which, after an unsuccessful operation in 1930, permanently confined him to bed in his room of the family home at Wilson Street, Perth. Soutar, who was never given to displays of self-pity, poignantly summed up the situation in his poem 'Autobiography'[62]

> Out of the darkness of the womb
> Into a bed, into a room:
> Out of a garden into a town,
> And to a country, and up and down
> The earth; the touch of women and men
> And back into a garden again:
> Into a garden; into a room;
> Into a bed and into a tomb;
> And the darkness of the world's womb.

Soutar began his poetic career as a writer of juvenilia in English and on 20 September 1923, prompted by MacDiarmid's Scots poems in *The Scottish Chapbook*, wrote three poems 'in the Doric'. He greeted the publication of MacDiarmid's *Sangschaw* (1925) with the comment 'Good work, Christopher, my lad – but the big things which Scotsmen have to do yet in literature must be done in English'[63]. Soutar was to change his mind radically on the subject. According to Alexander Scott, nine days after writing his rather dismissive words on *Sangschaw* Soutar wrote 'Cock-Crow', an announcement of the coming of a saviour:

> Fu heich upon the midden-bing
> It is His cronnie chaunticleer,
> Wha blaws the bugill o' oor King
> To lat the hale warld ken He's here,
> Liggan sae cumfie wi' the kye;
> An' a muckle, eerie licht ootby.

MacDiarmid's *Penny Wheep* did not seem to Soutar as good as *Sangschow* and he was so appalled at MacDiarmid's linguistically eclectic practices in *A Drunk Man Looks at the Thistle* (1926) that he wrote a humorous rejoinder 'The Thistle Looks at a Drunk Man':

> Wi' booze o' a' guffs he wud droon
> That honest Doric, as a loon,
> He throve on in a bonnie Toun
> Whaur fowk still speak
> Nae hash o' German, Slav, Walloon
> An' bastard Greek.

Before long Soutar felt a Wordsworthian 'Bliss was it in that dawn to be alive' euphoria about the renaissance initiated by Mac-Diarmid. He was too magnanimous a man to continue to protest in the presence of what was clearly genius and became convinced that MacDiarmid had solved the Scottish language problem by combining the rhythm of oral Scots with the richness of recorded Scots. In 1931 Soutar told MacDiarmid, in a letter, 'if the Doric is to come back alive, it will come on a cock-horse'[64]. His method of achieving a seminal impact on the Scottish people was to issue his *Seeds in the Wind* (1933), his first book of poems in Scots. By appealing primarily to children Soutar produced work that is as fine as any poetry can be when conceived for a deliberately limited audience. He triumphantly avoided the danger of patronising children by a rare mixture of mischief and melody, as in 'Bawsy Broon':

> Somebody nippit me,
> Somebody trippit me;
> Somebody grippit me roun' and aroun':
> I ken it was Bawsy Broon:
> I'm shair it was Bawsy Broon.

He went further than that in magical ballad-imitations like 'The Whale', which uses the unicorn as a symbol of fabulous Scottish vitality, something that Soutar must have devoutly wished for as he lay in his bed:

> I stude like ane that has nae pou'r
> An' yet, within a crack,
> My hauns were on the unicorn
> An' my bodie owre its back.
>
> Wi' ae loup it had skail'd the wud,
> An' wi' anither ane
> 'Twas skelpin' doun the gait I'd cam
> Thru vennel, wynd an' pen'.

In 1935 Soutar's *Poems in Scots*[65] appeared and it is on this volume that his reputation as a poet of real importance is based. The most substantial poem in the collection is 'The Auld Tree', which was composed between June 1929 and October 1931 and dedicated to MacDiarmid. It is a glowing verbal picture of a reborn Scotland whose prophets are a great patriot and two great poets: Wallace, Burns and MacDiarmid. Initially this dreamlike vision lifts

Soutar from his 'thowless banes' and brings him to 'a tree that lifts its hands/owre a' the worlds'. The dream is given poetic substance by the evocative use of descriptive couplets:

> But noo the nicht was comin' owre;
> The lither lift began to lour;
> As yont the hill the floichans flew
> Mair snell the yammerin' blufferts blew;
> Nae bleat was there o' beast or bird:
> I wud hae spak but had nae word.

The tree, of course, stands for Scotland and it has been weakened by living too long on past glories without rooting itself in the reality of the present and taking nourishment from the hopes of the future. Yet, like True Tammas (who is naturally mentioned in the poem because of his connection with the Eildon Tree), Soutar can foretell the future and imagines that

> a thistle stude
> Whaur aince had dwin'd the Eildon tree.

With guides like Burns, MacDiarmid and Wallace to show him the way, Soutar is elated by the prospect of the new Scotland and proud to be a part of it. If he allows himself at times to weigh the tree down with excessive symbolism then that is consistent with the conventions of the dream poem:

> And weel I kent, as it gaed by,
> That on a guidly hill was I;
> And that there breer'd, at ilka hand,
> The braid shires o' a promised land.
> Noo, as the day began to daw,
> The thistle wi' a warstlin' thraw
> Rax't out its airms – and was a tree
> Younglin' and green wi' fullyery.

'The Auld Tree' fully justifies its length and shows the direction Soutar might have taken if he had not been so cruelly cut down.

A comparison of Robert Garioch's poem 'The Percipient Swan'[66] with MacDiarmid's 'I'm the original/Plasm o' the ocean from *To Circumjack Cencrastus* shows what aspect of MacDiarmid Garioch found most useful to his own poetic personality. MacDiarmid's poem is a criticism of an interfering God:

> He ettles to use me
> Like a conjurer's hat
> And gar me evolve
> He disna ken what –

while Garioch's poem is an autobiographical credo complete with self-mockery:

> I hae ettled on land
> to hyst in the air,
> but I had to gie up,
> my feet were that sair.

Garioch's poem tells his readers that he's 'learning to sing' yet he has become associated not with song but satire and a rather guarded satire at that. Garioch (1909–81) was physically a small man (cf. 'the best of men are unco smaa', 'The Wire') and his most persistent stance is that of a wee fellae refusing to look up to his self-styled betters and verbally cutting them down to size.

His great master is Robert Fergusson, who is memorably brought back to life in the eulogy 'To Robert Fergusson' and claimed as a colleague:

> My ain toun's makar, monie an airt
> formed us in common, faur apairt
> in time, but fell alike in hert;
>   I whiles forget
> that ye ligg there ablow the clart
>   of Canongait.

Fergusson is also honoured in 'At Robert Fergusson's Grave' and, incidentally, in 'The Muir' ('And Fergusson, gyte, gyte in Darien'). Like Fergusson, Garioch was an Edinburgh poet who saw the whole divine comedy of life in his native city. Garioch was the son of an Edinburgh housepainter, went to school and university in Edinburgh and later taught at school and university (as Writer in Residence from 1971–73) in Edinburgh. Until the publication of his *Selected Poems* in 1966 (later expanded as the *Collected Poems* of 1977) his work was difficult to obtain: there were the privately published *Seventeen Poems for Sixpence* (1940), and *Chuckies on the Cairn* (1949); *The Masque of Edinburgh* (1954); and his Buchanan translations *Jephthah and The Baptist* (1959).

In the 1960s, however, Garioch found himself much in demand as a performer of his own poetry. He read with 'beat' and 'pop' poets whose greatest ambition was to achieve the instant poetic utterance which could be consumed, at one gulp, by the audience. Given the essentially superficial ambiance of such putative chamber recitals of verse, Garioch discovered that his humorous poems were warmly welcomed with gratifying enthusiasm while his serious pieces were tolerated in impatient silence. This public reaction encouraged Garioch to develop his humorous talent to the detriment of his serious gifts (he even became the Poet Laureate of the commercial station Radio Forth) and this direction was also favoured by Garioch's colleagues who have categorised him as the funny man and criticised his serious poetry. Sydney Goodsir Smith, a close friend of Garioch's, wrote: 'There is also a serious side to Garioch.

This comes out best, to my mind anyway, when expressed implicitly in the funny poems rather than explicitly in such thoughtful and considered works as 'The Wire'[67]; Maurice Lindsay insisted that 'Garioch's muse is high-spirited and fundamentally comic'[68]; and Alexander Scott confirmed the accepted view by opinionating: 'An early attempt at "achieving the imaginative sublime" in 'The Wire', an extended philosophical poem...founders in laboured movement and lack-lustre style, and 'The Muir'...which...is written in a mock-medieval manner disastrously at odds with its content'[69].

It is something more than a pity that Garioch was so ill advised to exclusively fire off his humorous sallies rather than sticking to his serious guns. He had the linguistic expertise and the poetic range to do great things in extended narratives. Without in any way detracting from his qualities as a comic writer, it seems reasonable to assume he could have spent more time courting his muse at length. For, on the evidence of his two most ambitious poems, he had the intelligence if not the inclination to take off where MacDiarmid left off in the 1930s (when he turned to an allusive epic poetry in English). That he did not do so is at once a criticism of the cautious cultural climate that has prevailed for so long in Scotland and the limited aims of the majority of Scottish poets and critics.

Garioch's long POW poem 'The Wire' is presented as a visionary ('This day I saw an endless muir') experience in which the human dream is reduced to a nightmare by the ghastly extremity of the situation. There are Dantean moments in the descriptive opening, the 'selva oscura' of the *Inferno* being transformed to the man-made hell of 'The Wire':

> And they are barbed wi twisted spikes
> wi scant a handsbreidth space atween,
> and reinforced wi airn rods
> and hung about wi bits of tin

The intensity of the introductory quatrains suggests a remarkably strong poetic imagination: the colourful flora ('Heather bell and blaeberry') contrast with the appallingly destructive tendencies of men. Garioch's glimpse of hell-on-earth is 'thrang wi folk' who simply endure their misfortunes fatalistically. There are no conspicuous heroes, only accidental acts of vulnerable individua'
Death, when it comes, is a casually brief matter and all the mo
horrific for that:

> A man trips up; the Wire gaes ding,
> tins clash, the guaird lifts up his heid;
> fu slaw he traverses his gun
> and blatters at him till he's deid.
>
> The dugs loup on him, reivan flesh,
> crunchin the bane as they were wud;

swith they come and swith are gane,
syne nocht is left but pools of bluid.

Bluid dreipan doun amang the roots
is soukit up the vampire stem
and suin the gaudy felloun flures
begowk the man that nourished them.

That is as deadly in impact as the best of modern war poems. Garioch has shrunk the human condition down to the proportions of the camp compound and allowed his creative mind to develop at full stretch. It is interesting to contrast that piece of writing with the Schweikian understatement of his prose account of captivity *Two Men and a Blanket* (1975).

By the auld alliance of experience and imagination Garioch is able to present the camp as a fully realised image of inhumanity so that the poem never becomes a purely personal fragment. Its form allows him to philosophise and he does so with a temperamental pessimism:

On this dour mechanistic muir
wi nae land's end, and endless day,
whaur nae thing thraws a shadow, here
the truth is clear, and it is wae.

(cf. 'here was truth, and it was wae', 'The Muir'). Still there is a recognition of the libertarian urge ('for aye they ettle to gang free') and the final impression made by the poem is of a world whose creative potential is continually threatened by its destructive tendencies.

In 'The Muir' Garioch gives his definition of heaven as 'Badenoch in simmer, wi nae clegs about'. It is a meditation on the implications of atomic theory as presented in J. Robert Oppenheimer's 1953 Reith Lectures on *Science and the Common Understanding*. Garioch ponders the paradox that while the external world feels substantial enough, if approached empirically, modern scientific theory has undermined commonsense by introducing rarefied notions like quanta and entropy.

The poem begins with an allusion to Dante's Hell and soon moves to Garioch's own attempts to comprehend a world that can conceive a mythical inferno and also make a real one at Hiroshima:

My heid is sair
wi thinkin o't; my hairt stouned wi despair;
my thocht is like a grain of gritty stuir
that blaws about the desert evermair.

This is no arid academic exercise but a poem that ingeniously links theology to physics. There are a few passages where Garioch merely regurgitates what he has gleaned from Oppenheimer but more often the scientific data are related to actual experience:

> it seems the bricht
> continuous rays vibratin frae the Sun
> come disparat, as we hae seen at nicht
> the tracer-bullets splairgin frae a gun,
> ae quantum at a time

In the end Garioch appeals for a global human embrace which will replace attempts to analyse the world into insignificance. The few flaws of the poem have nothing to do with the clever conception but with the execution in some parts:

> Glowran owre near at oniething, we kill
> the human meaning of this warld of stuir.

It is a questionable observation but 'The Muir' presents Garioch as a man with the intellectual equipment to undertake a long poem in his stride.

Deprived of the dimension of length, Garioch's talents display themselves in compact units textured with favourite nouns 'virr' and 'smeddum' and his favourite epithets 'fremmit' and 'gyte'. His most endurable monument in the abbreviated form is the sequence of Edinburgh Sonnets (of which there are eighteen in *Collected Poems*). In these sonnets Garioch stands and delivers ironical comments on the antics of the sort of folk who strut about the capital city like peacocks. Usually Garioch holds himself back to the last line before issuing his final judgement.

Garioch's great friend Sydney Goodsir Smith was born in New Zealand in 1915 and arrived in Edinburgh at the age of twelve. Henceforth he took the city to his heart and became, quite consciously, the boozy bard of Auld Reekie. His most characteristic theme was a dialogue between himself (usually with glass in hand) and a personified Edinburgh. In 'Lament in the Second Winter of War'[70] he wrote:

> Auld Embro's bluid is thin, the bars 're toom
> An cauld is her fierce iren hert, her black banes
> Rigid wi cauld, the bluid's fell thin aneth the snaw.

His affair with the personified city (cf. the image of Edinburgh, in *Under the Eildon Tree*, 'Flat on her back sevin nichts o' the week,/ Earnan her breid wi her hurdies' sweit') was conducted with good humour and grace. In *Skail Wind* (1941) the city is second only to the influence of MacDiarmid, whose presence is felt generally, and at detailed moments: 'the hail clanjamphrey' of the winter 'Lament' takes the last line of MacDiarmid's 'The Bonnie Broukit Bairn'; 'Lourd is my hert' (from 'Hornie wi the Green Ee') adapts a phrase ('Lourd on my hert') from *To Circumjack Cencrastus*.

Although Smith began as a doting disciple he had his own particular theme, which was the melancholy of the often solitary drinker, a very different thing from the ingenious insobriety of MacDiarmid's Drunk Man. In 'Song: The Steeple Bar, Perth', Smith begins

> O it's dowf tae be drinkin alane, my luve,
>> When I wud drink wi my dear,
> Nor Crabbie nor Bell's can fire me, luve,
>> As they wud an you were here.

That tone of resignation is sounded repeatedly through Smith's poetry. So there is an unholy trinity of influences in his work: the love of Edinburgh, the desire to emulate MacDiarmid, and the celebration of drink. Over and above all this there is the poet's sense of humour which always saved him from crying into his beer. It is gloriously present in his 'Epistle to John Guthrie' when, justifying the use of Scots by a poet, he asks rhetorically:

> Did Johnnie Keats whan he was drouth
> Ask 'A beaker full o the warm South'?
> Fegs no, he leaned acrost the bar
> An called for 'A point o bitter, Ma!'

Smith's volume *The Wanderer* (1943) contains his best-known lyric, 'Ma Moujik Lass'. Once more the theme is the solitary drinker lamenting his distant lover ('The lass I loo has turned away') and drowning his sorrows in drink:

> O fain I'd loo ma moujik lass,
>> O fain I'd haud her breist –
> I've nocht tae haud but a whusky glass,
>> A gey wanchancy feast.

The lyrical flow is exquisitely sustained and Smith is proof positive that a poet need not be born in Scotland to become a master practitioner of Scots poetry. Smith's next book, *The Deevil's Waltz* (1946), is very much a war effort: he makes all the right gestures, pays his tribute to John Maclean, and roundly condemns war. The publicly committed stance was not, however, a genuine poetic expression of Smith's personality; he was more at home with private emotions.

Smith is at his most enchanting in the long sequence of twenty-four elegies, *Under the Eildon Tree*, which was composed 'Embro toun, Dec. 1946–Feb. 1947', published in 1948 and revised in 1954. This poem has certainly received a torrent of adulation, much of it justified. The normally reticent Norman MacCaig called it 'the finest poetry to be published in Scotland since MacDiarmid's early work'[71] and that is saying something special; Alexander Scott was equally certain of its stature, calling it 'the greatest extended poem on passion in the whole Scots tradition'.[72] It is, without doubt, Smith's masterpiece and that in itself is a recommendation. Smith outfits the poem with some narrative apparatus taken from the ballad of 'Thomas Rymer' (Child No. 37) so that the poet is presented as an accurate prophet of his own fate in Elegy 23 ('The Time is Come'):

> True Tammas
> Neth the Eildons steers again

A more effective binding agent is the use – and abuse – Smith makes of the tradition of *amour courtois* where the poet is always a passive and unworthy worshipper at the shrine of the beautiful and unattainable lady. In Elegy 5 ('Slugabed') Smith is the, somewhat decadent, courtly lover:

> Smith the Slugabed
> Whas luve burns brichter nor them aa
> And whas dounfaain is nae less,
> > Deid for a ducat deid
> By the crueltie o' his ain maistress.

Later he parodies the courtly love conventions in his hilarious affair with the prostitute Sandra in Elegy 13 ('The Black Bull o Norroway').

Throughout the poem Smith is, as usual, bereft of the bodily comforts of his amorous companion, readily revealing in Elegy 17 ('The Faut Was Mine')

> The faut was mine, I admit.
> It was I abandoned ye; it's true . . .
> And see for lang I haena seen
> My lassie wi the midnicht een.

However, the object of his passion is not simply a lassie of flesh-and-blood but a Platonic ideal of female perfection beside whom earthly copies are inadequate. To convey this transcendental ideal Smith supplies his tale with a 'vast pantheon of passion' (Elegy 17), counterpointing his own misfortunes with those of couples like True Thomas and the Queen of Elfland, Aeneas and Dido, Abelard and Heloise, Tristram and Iseult, Cuchulain and Eimhir, Antony and Cleopatra, Burns and 'Highland Mary' Campbell, Orpheus and Eurydice, Aengus and Etain. The singing style is Orphic in its sense of remorse and the stylistic method is to produce a multilingual mixture whose main components are Latin and Lallans, as Smith concedes when he refers to himself as 'The Maker macironical' in Elegy 23. During the poem Smith portrays himself as an emotional extremist after the manner of MacDiarmid's Drunk Man who would 'aye be whaur/Extremes meet'. Elegy 6 ('What Wey Should I') spells it out:

> For I was born excessive, Scorpio,
> In aathing and in luve;
> Eneuch's no near as guid's a feast til me,
> The middle airt, the Gowden Mean,

> Has little recommandan it
> As far as I can see,
> And in the hert's affectioun
> I find nae exceptioun.

The state of defeatist nostalgia is rudely interrupted in the bawdy Elegy 13 when squalid urban reality contradicts the lofty abstract ideals of love the poet has so far presented. His partner in this elegy is no classical or Celtic heroine but a real woman with a commercial attitude to the flesh and, with reservations, the embodiment of desire:

> A bien and dernit fleeman's-firth
> And bodie's easement
> And saft encomforting!
> O, Manon! Marguerite! Camille!
> Any maybe, tae, the pox –
>   Ach, weill!

Smith was never again to manage so superb a coalescence of the earthly and eternal, the squalid and sublime, the passionate and Platonic; nor was he to attempt such an artistically complex poem again. He returned to short poems and when his muse needed room to stretch in he adopted a gossipy conversational mode. In his collection *Figs and Thistles* (1959) Smith included 'The Grace of God and the Meth-Drinker' which, with 'Ma Moujik Lass', was to become a standard anthology piece. Robert Garioch considered the meth-drinker poem 'a major poem in the presence of all the poems in the World' [73], an assessment hardly supported by the actual performance, stylish though it is. The poem is constructed parenthetically around the rather platitudinous sentiment that there-but-for-the-Grace-of-God-go-I. It depicts the meth-drinker clearly enough ('The stink/O' jake ahint him') and fairly crackles with vernacular panache, but the use of an unfortunate creature to summon up *schadenfreude* is not necessarily the stuff of which major poems are made. 'Ach, weill!', as Smith would have said.

Much more acceptable are the three conversational longish poems. *The Vision of the Prodigal Son* (1960) finds the poet celebrating the 200th birthday of Burns and in reflective and painfully honest mood before the poem develops into a pubscape, a territory so familiar to Smith that he is probably the greatest exponent of its glories (and otherwise). *Kynd Kittock's Land* (1965), a television poem, is Smith's guided tour of the city he so lovingly adopted:

> This rortie city
> Built on history
> Built of history
> Born of feud and enmity

The third of the conversational poems, *Gowdspink in Reekie* (1974), is an irreverent meditation of Goldsmith's 'Where wealth accumulates and men decay'. Again the noisy centre of Smith's world is the pub and in this artificial environment he is visited by his muse who turns out to be Graves's White Moon Goddess. In a passage (which virtually repeats a similar section in *The Vision of the Prodigal Son*) he describes the moment of creative truth:

> But we were standing at the bar . . .
>   When, there she was!
> The door bust open wi a thrang
> O' orra buddies, students and conspiratoories
> All on the bash to celebrate I dae ken what –
> And there she was, a lassie frae the mune direct,
> That smiled at me.

Fortunately for Scottish poetry the muse smiled often on Smith, especially during the composition of *Under the Eildon Tree*. He was able to shape out his sybaritic life-style into poems that are often warm and lovable and occasionally rather sentimental. He is the poet of ends, of lost causes, of the world remembered through a hangover. His favourite season is winter, his favourite time night. When the rest of the city retired to bed Smith was ready for poetic action and his nocturnal habits are described with admirable honesty in his poems.

6.   LALLANS AFTER THE SECOND WORLD WAR

Soutar, Garioch and Smith were three poets who responded creatively to the linguistic gospel according to MacDiarmid and who each produced individual verse. To the poets who emerged after the Second World War, Lallans (which was the term most of them preferred to Synthetic Scots) was not only a cultural cause; it was a poetic banner to be waved in the face of English verse which was held to be effete and irrelevant to the needs of modern Scotland. MacDiarmid was virtually deified as the 'greater Christ . . . greater Burns' whose birth was announced in *A Drunk Man*. There were many mini-MacDiarmids who believed that by imitating the master they were flattering Scotland. The Scottish Renaissance had taken place in the 1920s; by the 1940s the Renaissance had established itself as the Lallans movement equipped with its own publisher, William Maclellan, and (as edited by Maurice Lindsay) its own organ – the annual anthology *Poetry Scotland*. In the changed circumstances Lallans proved attractive to assorted romantic patriots as well as to genuine poets.

Douglas Young (1913–73) was more of a political powerhouse

and cultural propagandist than a poet though his witty 'Last Lauch' is endlessly anthologised and has even been cast in concrete and integrated into the pavement design of a shopping centre in Glenrothes New Town. Young had style, panache and the courage to go to prison for his convictions; he was sentenced to twelve months' imprisonment for refusing to be conscripted into the British army. He alludes to his incarceration in his preface to *Auntran Blads* which the Glasgow publisher William McLellan issued in 1943: 'I am greatly obliged to Mr David Murison, my umquihile colleague in the Greek Department at King's College, Aberdeen, for correcting the proofs, a task which I was not permitted to perform as a guest of His Britannic Majesty.' Young was a Greek scholar, an accomplished linguist who used Scots (in poems and his Lallans versions of two comedies by Aristophanes) because he believed, in principle, that there should be a modern Scots literature to inspire modern Scots. He was anxious to join forces with MacDiarmid and, when Young was elected chairman of the Scottish National Party in 1942, MacDiarmid did begin to feel that things were beginning to go his way. Young's original poetry was, with few exceptions, entirely derived from the MacDiarmid grand manner and his translations (like the following 'Wald Ye Be Atween a Lassie's' from the Gaelic of Sorley Maclean) often read like parodies of MacDiarmid:

> Wald ye be atween a lassie's houghs
> wi your mou on her breists sae fair and sauchin,
> and the Red Army warsslan to daith,
> jurmummlit and forfochen?

Young persevered with his Scots in his translations: in *Auntran Blads* there are thirteen translations from the Gaelic of Sorley Maclean, one from the Gaelic of George Campbell Hay; also translations from the Erse, the Greek, the German, the Chinese and the Russian. He even translated Burns into Greek ("Ae Fond Kiss' i' the Doric').

Unlike Young, Tom Scott has had no university seat[74]. He is something of a loner who speaks in his own voice or, more poetically, the Scots voice he rediscovered in 1950 while travelling Italy and Sicily on the proceeds of an Atlantic Award. Scott's distinctively abrasive poetic approach is a product of his early environment. In 1931 Scott's boiler-maker father had to leave Glasgow, during the economic slump, and begin a new life as a builder in St Andrews. In these two communities – radical-industrial Glasgow and conservative-academic St Andrews – he came across contrasts that sharpenned his class consciousness. Consequently his work is informed by a MacDiarmidian dialectic: a fellow feeling for builders, creators, producers and a corresponding dislike of careerists, destroyers, exploiters. When *The Ship* (1963) appeared Scott was forty-five, a mature man, no acorn newly planted on Parnassus. He was technically confident, able to move from the iambic pentameters of the title-poem to more intricate stanzaic patterns as in, for example, 'Fergus' with its schematic view of Scottish history and feminist sympathies:

> They kaaed doun Woman frae the throne and skies,
>   And even frae the chair,
> Hapt her bewtie in a dow disguise
>   And sat her on the fluir.
> Degradan her, they undermined theirsels
>   Wi casuistic laws,
> And brutalised their future in the schuils
>   Wi never-idle taws.

Scott's most impressive achievement in Scots is 'The Ship', his 763-line allegory based on the tragedy of the *Titanic* (the self-styled unsinkable White Star Liner that sank, in 1912, drowning 1,500 people). Scott sees the event symbolising the collapse of European civilisation, a collapse that led inevitably to two World Wars and a Cold War:

> We follaed up the Ship wi ae gret war,
> Refused to change, sae anither follaed that,
> And refusan to change, a cauld war follaed that.

The Ship has ten God-given commandments and, in addition to this religious ethic, the formal perfection of art plus technology. However, in making the Ship (or building European civilisation) the division of labour has alienated man from his fellow-men and so Scott's idealised original community of mankind has been destroyed:

> Union wes broken, and unionism born.
> In sicna warld the Ship cam til completion:
> Aa real values tint in ostentation.

Thus we have, on board, the 'dividit bodie o mankind'; humanity is split into classes, then conditioned to conform to class orthodoxy. The class war is apparent everywhere. The 'first-class sauls' (aristocracy) disdain the vulgarity of the *nouveau riche* 'middle fowk' (bourgeoisie) who in turn despise the propertyless state of the 'laichest fowk' (working class). Together they sail into tragedy which comes in an epic simile:

> The slain bull, wi' steel deep throu his hert,
> May stand fair stotious for whit seems an age
> Afore he slawlie sinks doun on his knees,
> And slawlier still, keels owre – sae the Ship,
> Slain by an ayebydan matador,
> Stopped in its trecks afore it settled doun.

Since then Scott has had his most conspicuously successful moments in long, or longish, poems. *At the Shrine o the Unkent Sodger* (1968) is an earnest anti-war poem; *Brand the Builder* (1975) is a powerful study of the poet's father and the life he led. In the course of the poem Scott contrasts the powerful personality of his father with lesser contemporaries like the butcher Broun or the emasculated academic Polyphemus Goast. In the finest section of the poem, 'Auld Sant-Aundreans: Brand the Builder', there is a vivid portrait of a man struggling towards a consciousness of the larger life beyond his immediate environment:

> The supper owre, Brand redds up for the nicht.
> Aiblins there's a schedule for to price
> Or somethin nice
> On at the picters – secont hoose –
> Or some poleetical meetin wants his licht,
> Or aiblins, wi him t-total aa his life
> And no able to seek a pub for relief frae the wife,
> Daunders oot the West Sands 'on the loose'.
> Whitever tis,
> The waater slorps frae his elbuck as he synds his phiz.
> And this is aa the life he kens there is?

After *Brand* Scott turned to extended poems in recondite English: *The Tree* (1978), a meditation on evolution stressing the creative qualities of the abstract heroine Woman; and *The City*, a work in progress.

Alexander Scott (b.1920) has been a pedagogic force in Scotland, working enthusiastically on behalf of the aims of MacDiarmid's Scottish Renaissance. He was appointed head of the Department of Scottish Literature in Glasgow University in 1971 and has made his presence felt on various academic boards, editorial committees and anthologies. Surprisingly enough (or perhaps not, given the circumstances), he has been reluctant to investigate in depth the most crucial period in his life – his participation in the Second World War.

Instead there are isolated references to the war in which he was awarded the Military Cross for leading a company attack on a German regimental headquarters at the battle of the Reichswald in 1945. His poem 'Coronach'[75] begins with what is, in an emotional context, a remarkable frankness that is characteristic of the resolutely unsentimental Scott:

> Waement the deid
> I never did,
> Owre gled I was ane o the lave
> That somewey baid alive
> To trauchle my thowless hert
> Wi ithers' hurt.

The use of pararhymes is both astute and appropriate. Scott is always at a considerable distance from his material, never a man to be at the mercy of his feelings. Perhaps he is too conscious of the sentimental connotations of post-Burnsian Scots to indulge in emotional confession. In his snappy sequence 'Scotched' he defined 'Scotch Passion' ironically:

> Forgot
> Mysel.

Scott has preferred, at any rate, to forget the war he fought in to concentrate, instead, on issues that affect him as a citizen of postwar Scotland.

Scott has functioned effectively enough as an occasional poet (remembering Goethe's use of that term for poems composed for special occasions). His method is to respond cautiously to an impersonal experience. Thus the death of film star Jayne Mansfield suggests a poem, the memory of Marilyn Monroe another poem, the film *King Kong* demands two poems ('Beast Fable' and 'Kong was King'), television programmes on Miss World ('Ballade of Beauties'), Isadora Duncan ('Dear Deid Dancer'), and bestselling records ('Top of the Pops') are all covered in occasional poems. It is as if Scott was searching for a theme that is implicit in a war poem such as 'Front Line' which begins with a biblical allusion then reaches a crescendo of pain

> While my all-too-obedient servants,
> the soldiers at my command,
> my brothers, my sons,
> they too,
> with bullets bashing their brains,
> they fell

Scott's poetic persona is that of the worldweary cynic who has seen so much he can put everyday incidents into an historical perspective. He stands guard over his own emotions like a sentry on duty. Only when he relaxes do we discern the poetry (as opposed to the always well-made verse). In 'Continent o Venus' he shows how successful he can be when avoiding merely vicarious experience; in this much anthologised poem he substitutes for the conventions of courtly love a personal response to a particular woman. In his long poem on Aberdeen, 'Heart of Stone', he devotes several lively descriptive passages celebrating, albeit ironically, his predicament in being made in the stony image of his native city:

> Our sins in stane,
> The graveyairds sprauchle gantan, their granite teeth
> Asclent wi a deid skinkle, a gless girn
> At nichtgouned angels far owre lourd to flie,
> And nappied cherubs far owre cauld to flichter,

> And whim-wham scrolls, and whigmaleerie urns,
> The haill jing-bang bumbazed in a sacred scutter
> To fleg the deid wi a fate that's waur nor daith.

Particular poets such as the two Scotts, and the talented William Jeffrey (1894–1946), have been able to use Scots as an adequate idiom for a life's work and generally the quality of post-MacDiarmid Scots poetry has been agreeably high. The tendency has been away from the intellectuality of MacDiarmid's Synthetic Scots to a diction based on conversational street (or strath) Scots. J.K. Annand, who followed Soutar's example in writing bairnsangs, attempted to stabilise the spelling of the language in his energetic promotion of the Scots Style Sheet adopted by the Makars' Club in Edinburgh in 1947. However, Scots poets have preserved their phonetic idiosyncracies in deference to regional rhythms. This celebration of regionalism is not (or not usually) a neo-Whistlebinkian parochialism as we can see in the poems of the most outstanding post-MacDiarmid makars. George Campbell Hay (b.1915) was brought up in Argyll. As the son of the author of *Gillespie* (see pp. 117–23) he had an outstanding literary inheritance and brought to poetry a rich marine imagery. His work is of a very high order. The enigmatic quality of longing in many of his lines is successfully married to sudden stark images like those contained in the close of his 'The Land of Promise'

> Ye wull druft wi the tides as they shuft an' swing by the side o the
> [land,
> an' quate the fush wull glim at ye oot o cauld eyes,
> an' there ye wull rock in the tangle an' turn, till the deid rise,
> an' the hunners that socht a shore that seeker nevar fand.[76]

Scots shows no signs of dying out as a linguistic means of communicating a strong sense of Scottishness. William Tait (b.1918) alternates between Shetland dialect and Scots verse, William Neil (b.1922) between Gaelic and Scots.[77] The Aberdeen poet Alastair Mackie (b.1925) has the intellectual ability to use Scots for disturbing psychological subjects and has a useful line in aphorism (as in 'Weet Kin'):

> Ach, Scotland, a back close i the mind,
> the doup o the seck, let doun country.[78]

Duncan Glen (b.1933), editor of the pro-Scots magazine *Akros*, uses a conversational Scots for casual domestic subjects and David Morrison (b. 1941) has responded to his life in Wick. Donald Campbell, who was born in Wick in 1940, uses the speech-rhythms of the area in his Scots poems (and even more memorably in his play *The Widows of Clyth*).

In some ways Scots had come full circle. MacDiarmid's Synthetic Scots was planned as an antidote to the conservatism of dialect Scots as used by Charles Murray and others. This fact was gradually obscured as the Scottish Renaissance lost its original experimental urgency and became the Lallans movement of the period following the Second World War. By the 1960s poets were using dialect Scots while proclaiming allegiance to the poetry and politics of Hugh Mac-Diarmid. Dialect Scots – regional Scots – was being used, often awkwardly, to deal with contemporary subjects. The irony of this was appreciated by the few poets who saw the experimental possibilities of regionalism. Stephen Mulrine (b.1938) wrote 'The Coming of the Wee Malkies' in honour of the speech of Glasgow:

> Whit'll ye dae when the wee Malkies come,
> if they dreep doon affy the wash-hoose dyke
> an' pit the hems oan the sterrheid light,
> an' play wee headies oan the clean close-wa',
> an' blooter yir windae in wi' the ba',
> missis, whit'll ye dae.[79]

Tom Leonard (b. 1944) has taken this to its logical conclusion by selectively transcribing the Glasgow patois. Presented in print this reveals the surprisingly deep linguistic ambiguity of street talk, as in 'The Good Thief':

> heh jimmy
> ma right insane yirra pape
> ma right insane yirwanny uz jimmy[80]

The comic possibilities of this found-poetry are considerable.

Although Scots enjoyed the prestige of its association with Hugh MacDiarmid it has never been above criticism; Scotland is too combative a place for that. A literary scholar, David Craig, has spoken for many in denouncing the diction of some MacDiarmid disciples (Goodsir Smith, Maurice Lindsay, Tom Scott):

> it is easy to compose in a language so akin to Scots as English is and then
> simply to put in some 'Scotsness' in the form of Scots synonyms for
> nouns, adjectives, etc . . . The curious limping flatness of such verse – the
> lack of vital movement, or of real vividness for all the display of
> adjectives – feels as though it were due to piecing together sentences
> from words which are not second nature to the writers.[81]

Dr Craig is simplifying matters, for if it were 'easy' to translate English thoughts into Scots verse it would be correspondingly 'easy' enough to translate Scots poems back into the putative English original. This is not the case. However, the criticism is worth recording as is its appearance in Alan Jackson's witty 'A Scotch poet speaks':[82]

> Och, I wish you hadn't come right now;
> You've put me off my balance.
>
> I was just translating my last wee poem
> Into the dear auld Lallans.

A much heavier blow against Lallans was delivered by one of its ablest practitioners. Maurice Lindsay had been one of MacDiarmid's most fervent disciples, had edited *Poetry Scotland* and had written MacDiarmidian poems in Scots. However, by 1962 he had come to the conclusion that Scots was no longer adequate for the challenge of a new era and explained away his personal apostasy with a generalised assault:

> Lallans was a brave last-ditch effort to restore to Lowland Scotland its ancient language. It failed to arouse any measure of popular support. During the 'Fifties, the Scots tongue receded more rapidly than ever before under the impact of television, and has now been reduced to a mere matter of local accent. It is utterly unthinkable that this poor wasted and abandoned speech, however rich in theory its poetic potential, can possibly express what there is to be expressed of the Scottish *ethos* in the age of the beatnik and the hydrogen bomb. The fact is that Lallans has not been used with contemporary significance by any writer during the greater part of the last decade.[83]

Ironically enough, Lindsay's words have dated as drastically as the language he was anxious to eliminate. Phrases like 'the impact of television' and 'the age of the beatnik' are journalist platitudes and poor arguments in favour of Lindsay's Pauline conversion to English. Still, the fact that he felt it necessary to dispute the supremacy of Lallans showed the Scottish Renaissance had become an establishment strong enough to create an enemy within. In the 1920s MacDiarmid had worked for a national movement and, by the 1960s, it had a respectable literature – too respectable for some (including MacDiarmid no doubt). Poetically inclined Scots were drawn to Lallans which was almost obligatory on those with nationalist sympathies. By the 1960s Lallans had won a propagandist victory; this triumph even detracted from the achievement of poets who continued to write in English because it was the language that came most naturally to them.

7. EDWIN MUIR

It is an astonishing fact that a small country like Scotland has produced, from its two geographical and temperamental extremes, two of the greatest poets of the twentieth century: the Borderer MacDiarmid and the Orcadian Muir – men who were first great friends and then great enemies. MacDiarmid began his poetic career in a blaze of lyrical glory; Muir's first poetic steps were painfully slow yet he stuck to his craft so tenaciously that he was eventually revealed as a writer of sublime gifts whose vision of eternity complemented

MacDiarmid's concept of the uniqueness of the individual. Edwin Muir was born in the Folly, his father's rented farm in Deerness parish, Orkney, in 1887. He was the youngest of six children. When Muir was two the family moved to the small Orkney island of Wyre and the six idyllic years spent there provided the basis for Muir's experience of Eden. The expulsion from Eden was traumatic. The Muirs were driven out of Wyre by the landlord who features in the poem 'The Little General'. In 1901 the family came to Glasgow. Muir looked back on this period as the Fall into a nightmarish labyrinth from which there was no easy escape. He had to work in an office, a beer-bottling factory, a bone factory and a shipbuilding office. Psychologically he was broken by a series of personal tragedies: during the Glasgow years his father died of a heart-attack, his brother Willie of consumption, his brother Johnnie of a brain tumour, and his mother from an internal disease.

In 1918 Muir married Willa Anderson, a classics graduate of St Andrews, then lecturing in a women's college in London. Muir was thirty-two, in a wretched state psychologically and with poor financial prospects. Supported by Willa, however, Muir was able to recover his mental stability and repossess, imaginatively, his childhood Eden. He later said: 'My marriage was the most fortunate event in my life.'[84]. Muir found London a difficult place to adjust to. He did part-time work with Orage's *The New Age* but still suffered from mental anguish associated with his urban experiences. The size of London intimidated him as 'the vast solidity of my surroundings and my own craving emptiness threw me into a slightly feverish state, drove fear up into my throat, and made my lips dry'.[85] He agreed to undergo a course of psychoanalysis to alleviate his troubles and as part of the treatment was encouraged to record his dreams. Many of his poems – for example, 'The Combat' – are based on dream experiences.

By 1921 the Muirs were ready to leave London to spend some time abroad: in Czechoslovakia, Germany, Italy, Austria. In Prague Muir felt psychologically settled for the first time in years. Then, in 1922 (the year of *The Waste Land* and *Ulysses* and C.M. Grieve's creation of Hugh MacDiarmid), he began to write poetry in Dresden and Hellerau. He was thirty-five:

> I had no training; I was too old to submit myself to contemporary influences; and I had acquired in Scotland a deference towards ideas which made my entrance into poetry difficult. Though my imagination had begun to work I had no technique by which I could give expression to it. There were the rhythms of English poetry on the one hand, the images in my mind on the other. All I could do at the start was to force the one, creaking and complaining, into the mould of the other . . . I began to write poetry simply because what I wanted to say could not have gone properly into prose. I wanted so much to say it that I had no thought left to study the form in which alone it could be said.[86]

Although he had taken to poetry he knew it would not support him; after he and Willa returned to London in 1925 they worked at German translations, including the definitive versions of Kafka's novels which contained situations Muir could readily identify with.

On the outbreak of war (which deprived the Muirs of income from their German translations) Edwin had to take a job in the Food Office in Dundee while Willa returned to teaching. After the war, Muir went to Prague as the Director of the British Council Institute there until the Communist coup of 1948. He was horrified at the change in Prague, 'The Good Town'[87]:

> Look at it well. This was the good town once,
> Known everywhere, with streets of friendly neighbours,
> Street friend to street and house to house. In summer
> All day the doors stood open . . .
>   If you see a man
> Who smiles good-day or waves a lordly greeting
> Be sure he's a policeman or a spy.
> We know them by their free and candid air.

Horrified, Muir left Prague and went as Director of the British Council Institute to Rome where he experienced a conversion to the ideals of Christianity. Although he could never join the Roman Catholic Church he remained subsequently sympathetic to Catholicism.

Since the publication of *Scott and Scotland* in 1936 Muir had been under sustained attack from MacDiarmid for daring to suggest that 'Scotland can only create a national literature by writing in English.'[88] Nevertheless he felt he could find some peace in Scotland if, through imaginative effort, he could regain his childhood Paradise with an informed innocence due to experience. Life, he felt, was not an everyday story, but an eternal fable – the first version of his autobiography was called *The Story and the Fable* (1940) – and he was sure that 'the life of every man is an endlessly repeated performance of the life of man.'[89] The publication of *The Labyrinth* in 1949 confirmed his status as an internationally important writer and he returned to Scotland in 1950 to spend five years as Warden of Newbattle Abbey adult education college outside Edinburgh. There he encouraged George Mackay Brown, Tom Scott and Archie Hind.

Muir enjoyed his work with staff and students but, irritated by the pettiness of committees, was glad to deliver the 1955–56 Charles Eliot Norton lectures at Harvard (published as *The Estate of Poetry* in 1962). He returned from Newbattle and, with the money earned in America, bought a cottage in Swaffham Pior outside Cambridge. He died in 1959 and had attained the reputation of being, like Neil Gunn, something of a secular saint. Scotland needed a complete contrast to MacDiarmid and Muir seemed to conform to that image.

Perhaps the strongest influence on Muir's poetry was the symbolic discursiveness of Wordsworth, though Muir felt that Wordsworth
was not a poet to be imitated. He shared with Wordsworth an ability to elevate, by imaginative pressure, an otherwise prosaic occurr-
ence. There was also a crucial indigenous influence. In his childhood
Muir had heard his mother reciting ballads, and their simple narrative logic informed his own strophic narrative poems such as 'The
Little General' and 'The Combat'. From the ballads too he learned
the strength of conventional rhymes. Thus the mechanics of a Muir
poem are relatively simple: he frequently opens with a descriptive
passage, moves to a piece of action, then provides a philosophical
commentary on the poetic events. Muir used language for functional
clarity rather than sensuous impact and always pointed to a meaning
independent of euphony. He is a philosophical poet and his thought
is, to a large extent, his poetry. In his last poem, 'I Have Been
Taught', he composed a credo:

> And now that time grows shorter, I perceive
> That Plato's is the truest poetry,
> And that these shadows
> Are cast by the true.

Muir was a Platonist who believed that earthly events were imperfect
copies of eternal ideals. He felt his poetry could reveal to the reader
the eternal fable behind the time-tied story.

Three poems from *The Labyrinth* illustrate Muir's visionary
approach. The title-poem is a meditation on the trauma of being
trapped by circumstances. It uses the Greek myth of Theseus in a
strongly autobiographical fashion. In Muir's treatment of the myth
the labyrinth Theseus has to escape from stands for the restrictive,
soul-destroying aspects of the man-made environment. It is probable he was thinking particularly of the infernal period he spent in
Glasgow when he composed the labyrinthine opening sentence of
the poem:

> Since I emerged that day from the labyrinth,
> Dazed with the tall and echoing passages,
> The swift recoils, so many I almost feared
> I'd meet myself returning at some smooth corner,
> Myself or my ghosts, for all there was unreal
> After the straw ceased rustling and the bull
> Lay dead upon the straw and I remained,
> Blood-splashed, if dead or alive, I could not tell
> In the twilight nothingness . . .

The poem evokes the negative fears that haunted Muir and suggests
a transfigured imaginative alternative. 'The Transfiguration' shows
the world transformed by religious ecstasy. Muir learns from Christ
the affirmative way out of the labyrinth:

> For he had said, 'To the pure all things are pure.'
> And when we went into the town, he with us,
> The lurkers under doorways, murderers,
> With rags tied round their feet for silence, came
> Out of themselves to us and were with us,
> And those who hide within the labyrinth
> Of their own loneliness and greatness came,
> And those entangled in their own devices,
> The silent and the garrulous liars, all
> Stepped out of their dungeons and were free.
> Reality or vision, this we have seen.
> If it had lasted but another moment
> It might have held for ever! . . .
> But he will come again, it's said . . .
> Then he will come, Christ the uncrucified,
> Christ the discrucified, his death undone,
> His agony unmade, his cross dismantled –
> Glad to be so – and the tormented wood
> Will cure its hurt and grow into a tree
> In a green springing corner of young Eden . . .

The poem holds all Muir's interests: there is the biblical inspiration (Matthew 17: 1, 2), the use of dream images (for Muir had dreamed of the man with rags round his feet), the contrast between 'Reality or vision' leading to a visionary insistence on humanity going back to Eden as a prelude to the poet's own return to his Edenic childhood.

'The Combat' is Muir's most disturbing, dreamlike poem. He felt 'that sleep, in which we pass a third of our existence, is a mode of experience, and our dreams a part of reality'.[90] One of his dreams, of which there is a prose account in *An Autobiography*, confronted him with the imagery of 'The Combat'. It tells of two unevenly matched animal antagonists fighting a perpetual battle. The animals act out their destructive impulses in an allegory of aggression which depends on a heroic resistance to the monstrous desire to dominate:

> A while the place lay blank, forlorn,
> Drowsing as in relief from pain.
> The cricket chirped, the grating thorn
> Stirred, and a little sound was born.
> The champions took their posts again.
>
> And all began. The stealthy paw
> Slashed out and in. Could nothing save
> These rags and tatters from the claw?
> Nothing. And yet I never saw
> A beast so helpless and so brave.
>
> And now, while the trees stand watching, still
> The unequal battle rages there.
> The killing beast that cannot kill

Swells and swells in his fury till
You'd almost think it was despair.

Muir's most famous poem, 'The Horses', from *One Foot in Eden* (1956), shows him at the height of his creative powers bringing creative imagery and intense experience to bear on his vision of Eden. There has been some confusion over whether Muir intended the horses to be real or symbolic.

For Muir they were both: they were real horses displaying the characteristics of their ideal counterparts. Reality and vision had merged in an artistic wholeness. In *An Autobiography* Muir said, of his early work, 'when I wrote about horses they were my father's plough-horses as I saw them when I was four or five'.[91] That is the period of Muir's Eden, his agricultural idyll on Wyre. Muir reaches back for this image as a contrast to the destructive impulses of the nuclear age. In 'The Horses' the human fascination with technology has destroyed man-made civilisation. In the time it took the biblical God to create the heavens and the earth, technological man has 'put the world to sleep'. Technology is reduced to rubble and is quite useless:

On the second day
The radios failed; we turned the knobs; no answer.
On the third day a warship passed us, heading north,
Dead bodies piled on the deck. On the sixth day
A plane plunged over us into the sea. Thereafter
Nothing.

Like a healing vision the 'strange horses' arrive. They beat out a new rhythm ('a distant tapping... A deepening drumming'), different from the biblical pastiche of the opening of the poem. Muir has gone beyond description into the fabulous dimension of his Platonic vision. If there is to be a future for mankind, he suggests, it will depend on a recovery of 'that long-lost archaic companionship' between all living things:

Among them were some half-a-dozen colts
Dropped in some wilderness of the broken world,
Yet new as if they had come from their own Eden.
Since then they have pulled our ploughs and borne our loads,
But that free servitude still can pierce our hearts.
Our life is changed; their coming our beginning.

In the aftermath of nuclear destruction Muir imagines man regaining Eden by going back to his roots in nature.

Unlike MacDiarmid, Muir brought no movement into being: there are no doting disciples reiterating texts in the tones of the master. His influence has been most obviously felt by Kathleen Raine, who has shared Muir's Platonic approach, and George

Mackay Brown, who has constantly sought out the fable behind the story. Kathleen Raine (b.1908) has also been an egregiously enthusiastic advocate of the informed mysticism of Blake; her *William Blake and Traditional Mythology* (1968) combines scholarship with a personal statement of belief in a transcendent world. Raine studied natural science at Cambridge and was able to make her mysticism accessible by allowing it to develop from empirical foundations, as in the 'Celtic Cross' section of her sequence 'Eileann Chanaidh':

> Against grain of granite
> Hardness of crystalline rock-form mineral
> Form spiritual form is countergrained, against nature traced
> Man's memories of Paradise and hope of Heaven.
> More complex than Patrick's emblem green trifoliate
> Patterning the tree soul's windings interlace
> Intricate without ends its labyrinth.[92]

Her elegantly precise diction, cutting across the lines with enjambement, is evidence of an intelligence all too often lacking in modern poetry.

8. PHYSICAL AND METAPHYSICAL: BRUCE AND MacCAIG

Muir's emphasis on the metaphysical resonance of English was a revelation to Scots who realised that this ancient speech need not be the language of cultural betrayal. In the 1930s, writing the long poems conceived in his Shetland exile, MacDiarmid himself had turned from Synthetic Scots to Synthetic English. For certain perceptive poets maturing during the Second World War the use of Scots, Synthetic or otherwise, was a way of using a voice from the past. English poetry was apparently capable of endless renewal, since the 1940s saw English poets hovering between realism and surrealism. Similarly Scottish poetry in English could be sharply physical or delicately metaphysical as the work of, respectively, George Bruce and Norman MacCaig showed.

George Bruce believes in 'a spare language trusting that it gathers to itself, more than the statement it evidently makes'.[93] Bruce's first book, *Sea Talk* (1944), made his reputation as the poet of Buchan and one of the finest writers of English verse to emerge in Scotland since Muir. Bruce was born in 1909 in Fraserburgh where his father ran 'the oldest curing firm in the North of Scotland'.[94] His poems are taut with the tension of the sea town. His lines are short, terse and always tapping out the persistence of the past (as in 'Inheritance'):

This which I write now
Was written years ago
Before my birth
In the features of my father.[95]

Bruce rejected the Aberdeenshire dialect as used by Charles Murray and turned instead to a precision influenced by the Pound of *Hugh Selwyn Mauberley*. In an autobiographical essay Bruce explained his method:

The distinguishing feature of an upbringing in the town where the sea thundered its blessing and curses was the presence of an absolute. Whereas each piece of landscape draws attention by its difference from any other to locality, the sea proclaims its universality . . . Perhaps that world of stone, air, light and dark could only have become known and its experience available at the point I heard the special merit in the phrase: 'A boat has gone.' That phrase had already been purified, not by the poet, but by the community which required a spare, athletic language for survival's sake, and in this case words which could convey terrible news quickly and with a minimum of emotion.[96]

Bruce's desire to let the words do the work without any extravagant poeticising is evident in, for instance, 'My House', which begins

My house
Is granite
It fronts
North

Obviously there is a danger of going so far towards simplicity as to achieve only an arid absence of adornment. It is evident that Bruce was writing with a programmatic purpose and felt his poetry should correspond to a social bleakness. Though the poems in *Sea Talk* recall Bruce's childhood they were written in the 1930s when, as the poet said, 'I saw the approaching cataclysm of war as the nadir preordained by the disappearance of a personal society before the rapid advance of a mechanistic society which equated progress with financial profit'.[97] So he was both preserving, in direct language, that personal society and making an artistic stand against the rhetoric that now seemed irrelevant. He especially liked Pound's application of formal modes to contemporary subjects and admired Pound's bitter irony. 'The Curtain' describes the return of his father from an attempt to rescue the crew of a sunk ship:

My father came home,
His clothes sea-wet,
His breath cold.
He said a boat had gone.

After the brief allusion to tragedy ('a boat had gone') Bruce introduces an Imagist counterpoint:

I remembered
The blue glint
Of the herring scales
Fixed in the mat,

And also a foolish crab
That held his own pincers fast.
We called him
Old Iron-clad.

Stylistically Bruce is (or was when he published *Sea Talk*) fonder of alliteration than rhyme. He was also happiest when recalling the obligatory childhood idyll. When he moves on to philosophical territory he is unsure; 'Kinnaird Head', a much anthologised poem, undermines reality with an unconvincing symbolism ('Fit monument for our time') and the poem ends by pitting the personified rock against impersonal history.

In subsequent years Bruce became a BBC producer and promoted the work of other poets. He never again managed the urgent intensity of *Sea Talk*. Other collections showed him a man of warmth and good intention who could turn out a polished performance. He could write 'Three Love Poems for My Wife' with a measured passion, he could drop into Lallans, he could respond emotionally to a television war report and compose his own report on 'Laotian Peasant Shot' with a hint of the old tautness:

When he fell the dust
hung in the air
like an empty container
of him.

Like so many other Scottish poets, he did not demonstrate decisively a power to stay the course after the promise of an outstanding debut. To use a sporting analogy, Scottish poets tend to be sprinters who do well over a short distance for a short time. Reputations are, however, made by the man who keeps going and it is appropriate that, in 'Sketch of a Poet', Bruce admiringly describes

MacCaig angular in a wind-rainy day,
long, lithe striding to a shop

MacCaig is Norman MacCaig, who is generally regarded as the finest English-writing Scottish poet since Muir.

Like Edwin Muir, Norman MacCaig has produced a voluminous body of verse in English and has won a position as one of the greatest Scottish poets to choose English as his first language. Although he was one of Hugh MacDiarmid's closest friends (in which capacity he delivered a moving funeral oration at Langholm in 1978) he has never been tempted to use Scots in any creative capacity. In fact MacDiarmid's work exerted no apparent stylistic influence on MacCaig, whose closest contemporary model is the American poet Wallace Stevens. MacCaig dislikes the romantic connotations of the bardic role and has avoided public pronouncements. He has cultivated a persona as the poet who simply gets on with the job of making a good poem. It all sounds ridiculously simple: 'I've got no powers of invention . . . All my poems are about actual things that happened, mostly to me or to people I know well. I sometimes slightly decorate the truth but they are all things that happened.'[98] In private MacCaig is a dignified, highly articulate man with a great capacity for kindness. His poems exhibit the qualities associated with the man. They are concerned with human kindness, visually obsessed with the landscape of Assynt (where MacCaig has a summer-holiday cottage), and stylistically unbreakable. MacCaig gives the impression that if a poem doesn't come complete he simply junks it rather than worrying over it.[99] However, the evidence suggests otherwise: the finished product has a polish, a craftsmanship, that is beyond most of his comtemporaries.

MacCaig was born in Edinburgh in 1910 and has been content to stay in his native city during the year: his holidays are spent around Lochinver where he is, as the title of a poem has it, 'A Man in Assynt'. His background stretched back to Gaeldom:

> My mother came from Scalpay, Harris, at the age of sixteen, with no word of English in her mouth.
> My father came from Dumfriesshire, near Castle Douglas (went to school at the Haugh of Ur – there's a name for you), but his father, who was a carter, came from Argyll and married a pukka Borderer. Three of my grandparents, therefore, were pure Gaels.
> My father worked in and came to own a chemist shop in Dundas Street, Edinburgh.
> Neither of them influenced me on [what you call] 'the high road to literature', though they lived damned skimpily to put me through school (Royal High) and University.
> I discovered N.W. Sutherland before the war, fell for it (it's rather like Harris) and have spent all summer holidays there ever since and it's there I found my closest friends – as close as Sydney [Goodsir Smith] and Chris [Grieve] were.[100]

MacCaig read Classics at Edinburgh University and the discipline shows in his work which stands, supremely, for verbal clarity and the intelligent exposition of accessible subject-matter. He spent most of his life teaching in primary schools in Edinburgh, a career MacDiarmid characteristically commented on: 'Norman is a schoolteacher and one with a real vocation. He is now [1966] a deputy headmaster, but he ought to have been a headmaster long ago – and would have been if it had not been for the fact that he was, a conscientious objector and served a term of imprisonment on that account.'[101] MacCaig did eventually become a headmaster and thereafter Reader in Poetry at the University of Stirling. Yet there is nothing ostentatiously academic about him and he has not done any sustained scholarly work in prose. It is as a poet that he has operated and deserves attention.

As MacCaig began his poetic life as a member of the Apocalypse it is worth recalling, briefly, what that ephemeral movement stood for. Led by the triumvirate of Henry Treece, J.F. Hendry and G.S. Fraser, the negative rationale of the group was hostility to the political pylon poetry of the 1930s. The Apocalypse rejected the solutions offered by technology and offered an apolitical romanticism tinged with surrealistic technique. After dabbling with Apocalyptic mannerisms in his early collections, *Far Cry* (1943) and *The Inward Eye* (1946), MacCaig cultivated a Metaphysical manner: the exposure of a stream-of-consciousness became less important to him than the exhibition of formal control over his material. MacCaig's special gift is to make Metaphysical sense of the external world, to impose poetic order on a mass of sensations. The tension in his poetry is created by the poet's selfconscious references to the act of creation. There is an awareness of the distance between the thing observed and the poetic possession of it.

This Metaphysical approach is well illustrated in the poem 'Climbing Suilven'[102]:

> Parishes dwindle. But my parish is
> This stone, that tuft, this stone
> And the cramped quarters of my flesh and bone.
> I claw that tall horizon down to this;
> And suddenly
> My shadow jumps huge miles away from me.

The poet surprises himself by taking subjective liberties with the objective world. Texturally MacCaig's work is distinguished by his ingenious Metaphysical imagery and intellectual agility. Thematically he has three favourite subjects: landscape, animals, people. Stylistically he has moved from a very tight strophic poetry to a more open verse, fluid rather than free. The poem 'Fiat' encapsulates his early addiction to strict form for the stanzas rhyme *ababcc* and the basic rhythm is the old faithful iambic pentameter:

> I cannot stammer thunder in your sky
> Or flash white phrases there. I have no terse
> Exploding passion, and cannot vilify
> My dulcet world through flute-holes of a verse,
> But gently speak and, gently speaking, prove
> The everlastingness in which you move.

A later poem, 'Brooklyn Cop', written after a poetry-reading trip to the USA, shows how far he had opened up in his own verse to achieve a relaxed wit:

Built like a gorilla but less timid,
thick-fleshed, steak-coloured, with two
hieroglyphs in his face that mean
trouble, he walks the sidewalk and the
thin tissue over violence.

MacCaig's poems are first personal. Whereas MacDiarmid addressed the world, MacCaig assumes an audience of one (and a loved one at that). With this other he conducts a public private argument, usually about the inadequacy of words to convey emotional experience. He claims that poetry is insufficient to his needs then refutes his own argument by making a poem out of this internal conflict. In 'Gifts' he invokes the gorgeous symbolic world of Yeats then refuses to enter it:

I need no fancy to mark you as beautiful,
If you are beautiful. All I know is what
Darkens and brightens the sad waste of my thought
Is what makes me your wild, truth-telling fool
Who will not spoil your power by adding one
Vainglorious image to all we've said and done.

After this he does exactly what he promised not to and adds a 'Vainglorious image' about 'A cloak of the finest silk in Scotland'. A much later poem, 'Return to Scalpay', used the same arcane approach and sums up the technique of the mature MacCaig. As we have seen, MacCaig's mother came from Scalpay, so the poet is going home. The poem rhymes elaborately and uses both iambic pentameter and syllabic lines. The first stanza establishes, with deft poetic shorthand, the sense of place, the novelty of a motorcar on Scalpay, the strangeness of the Gaelic language, the precise location of the poetic landscape ('by Craig Lexie over to Bay Head'). In the second stanza MacCaig emphasises the transformation of the place: there is a house 'where no house should be', there is the absence of 'Aunt Julia's house', there is the destruction of the Red Well. In the third stanza MacCaig recalls happy times on the island which leads him (in the fifth stanza) to the emotional heart of the poem:

Scalpay revisited? – more than Scalpay. I
Have no defence,
For half my thought and half my blood is Scalpay,
Against that pure, hardheaded innocence
That shows love without shame, weeps without shame,
Whose every thought is hospitality –
Edinburgh, Edinburgh, you're dark years away.

Two more stanzas follow, describing MacCaig's emotional encounter with Johann who 'laughs and cries and laughs, as she always did' and the poem moves towards an image of the poet 'filled with love and praise and shame'. Whereas the early poems took some trouble to conceal emotions, the mature poems reveal them.

MacCaig has written splendid poems about animals. Whereas Ted Hughes, say, empathises with animals – anthropomorphises them – MacCaig relishes the otherness of animals. In 'Goat' he refers to this apartness:

> The nothing like him goat, goat-in-itself,
> Idea of goatishness made flesh, pure essence
> In idle masquerade on a rocky shelf

and contrasts this with the selfconsciousness of the human observer. It was MacDiarmid's contention that his friend was apolitical by nature[103] and a reading of MacCaig's animal and landscape poems might give the impression that this marvellously gifted poet is more at home with flora and fauna than with human issues. That would be an erroneous impression. MacCaig is no party-liner but warms to isolated individuals. And because he is stimulated by art rather than ideology he is no aesthetic escapist. He has spent a creative lifetime, in fact, refusing to have critical labels pinned to him. His work speaks volumes for his human sympathies: in the poem 'Assisi' he distinguishes between human pretension and human indignity. When he sees a misshapen dwarf outside 'three tiers of churches built/in honour of St Francis' he feels the misery more deeply because of its ironic contrast with an ecclesiastical monument to saintly humility. MacCaig is a poet who loves paradox, who is doubly enchanted by the world he sees so paradoxically. His range is really as wide as his human sympathies, which appear to increase with age.

In MacCaig's book *The Equal Skies* (1980) there is a remarkable sequence of 'Poems for Angus' in which MacCaig – master of the short poem – sustains his grief over twelve interconnected poems. It is arguably his finest achievement. In this piece the tragedy of a friend's death is evoked but the poet preserves his linguistic dignity. He does so by externalising mood and making sadness elemental. The sequence opens with 'Notes on a winter journey, and a footnote': the journey to the frozen north of Scotland seems appropriate and yet, ominously, 'a death waited for me'. The death is described in the second, and most immediate, poem, 'A.K. MacLeod'. Having gone to his favourite landscape MacCaig is met at Ullapool by his dear friend:

> Next morning the man who had greeted me
> with the pleasure of pleasure
> vomited blood
> and died.

This dissolves into 'Highland funeral' in which MacCaig contrasts the pagan landscape with the sanctimonious voice of the minister. MacCaig's fastiduous attitude to the integrity of language makes him shy away from the ritualistic platitudes of institutional religion which has a verbal crumb of comfort for every occasion. MacCaig's own feelings on death are expressed (after the passage of time in 'A month after his death') in 'Triple burden':

> I know I had my death in me
> from the moment I yelled upside-down
> in the world.

Now he is burdened by another death and feels the weight of it pressing down on him. He thinks (in a rare use of abstraction) of 'the sea of unknowing' and his own final voyage to go 'beyond knowledge, beyond memory'.

After a little poem ('Comforter') we are at last given a portrait of the man whose death moved the poet so profoundly:

> He went through a company like a lamplighter –
> see the dull minds, one after another,
> begin to glow, to shed
> a beneficent light.

In 'From his house door' MacCaig reflects on how this man 'enriched his life'; finally, in 'Defeat' (which follows 'Angus's dog', 'Dead friend', 'In memoriam'), MacCaig come back to his instinctive conviction that words can never be adequate to the ineffable quality of human friendship

> For all I can say of him
> is no more
> than a scribble in the margin
> of a lost manuscript.

MacCaig's poetry is a creative answer to his own doubts about the limitations of language.

9.   SCOTS IN EXILE: FRASER AND GRAHAM

By remaining in Scotland as one of MacDiarmid's closest friends MacCaig provided a semblance of cultural coexistence. He was a Scot who expressed himself in an elegantly literary English and, what is more, enjoyed the approval of MacDiarmid himself. Otherwise the period following the Second World War found Scotland, as ever, in a state of cultural civil war as two opposing factions fought a linguistic battle over the status of Scots and English. It is not surprising that a few Scottish poets put a distance between themselves and the issues raging in their native land. Among the most interesting of the poetic exiles were G.S. Fraser and W.S. Graham.

Towards the end of 1979 the present writer received an undated letter from G.S. Fraser, who surprised me with his valedictory tone:

'I have always tried to write simply and lucidly but in too formal a way, I think, and sometimes with too wide a range of reference. I have always avoided since that disastrous early business of the New Apocalypse being committed to any group, including groups of mavericks. But I am grateful to poetry ... I hope at my age, if you reach it, you also may say "Well, if the shadows must fairly soon close in on me, at least I have enjoyed life, and given some enjoyment to others." It may seem a modest ambition, but it is one rarely achieved.' At that time he was only sixty-four but with a chronic heart weakness that made him face up courageously to the closeness of death. He died on 3 January 1980.

Fraser was an acute critic who conveyed a passion for poetry in his studies of Pound and Yeats and in books like *The Modern Writer and his World* (1953) and *Vision and Rhetoric* (1959). One imagines him, at the end of his life, acting like a line from his poem 'Memories of Swansea' – 'A dying man, still crazy about poetry.'[104]

Fraser was an admirably frank man who openly acknowledged his poetic limitations. He knew he was temperamentally library-bound and apt to draw his inspiration from poetry rather than non-literary experience. Although he later regretted his association with the New Apocalypse (which also attracted Scots like J.F. Hendry and Norman MacCaig) his poetry remained full of apocalyptic resignation to such an extent that he always seemed to contemplate life in the past tense as in 'Elegy for Certain Resolutions':

> I used to ride upon a horse, with reins
> Curved in the fingers of a feeble hand,
> Would play at single-stick on Saturdays,
> Had Algebra and Euclid to understand

Fraser was earnest and intense in the 1940s; in the 1950s and 1960s he expended a great deal of energetic enthusiasm in encouraging young poets to bring their work to him for criticism. What he valued was a contented marriage of manner and matter, a coming-together of inspiration and craftsmanship. His own favourite poets are obvious from his own poems: Yeats, Eliot and Auden. MacDiarmid he admired but could not empathise with.

Born in Glasgow in 1915, Fraser was educated at Aberdeen Grammar School and St Andrews University. After the Second World War, Fraser did not want to go back to Scotland and, instead, had the critical (if not creative) time of his life in London then Leicester. He probably left Scotland because of his aesthetic distaste for the hard-bitten anti-poetic lifestyle endured by the natives. This reason is tentatively put forward in his poem 'Meditation of a Patriot':

> He sings alone who in this province sings.
> I kick a lamp-post, and in drink I rave:

> With Byron and with Lermontov
> Romantic Scotland's in the grave.

Fraser seemed to enjoy literary gossip and the company of poets and his own verse reflects this exclusively bookish world. In a revealing poem, 'Problems of a Poet', he broods on his defects and his 'handful of talents' and admits to a terrible paucity of theme:

> 'What will you write about? Trees, politics, women . . .'
> I shall write about nothing at all.
> They shall say, his basket was emptied early,
> He bowed, but did not come for the curtain call.

In a fundamental sense, then, Fraser's poems are vicarious: they are not about first-hand experience but are poems about poems. His voice is not direct but a literary affectation based on the hesitant tones of Eliot's Prufrock. He sounds selfconscious and apologetic.

There is no doubting Fraser's sincerity, his critical intelligence, his concern to uphold literary values. In a creative context, though, he was probably too diffident – too aware of his shortcomings – to even attempt to write really endurable poetry.

W.S. Graham is a poet whose principal theme is the making of poetry. This makes his imagery elusive and his manner frequently obscure. He creates a private world of symbol and sometimes writes as if he resents the reader's intrusion in his creative privacy. 'The Beast in Space'[105] begins:

> Shut up. Shut up. There's nobody here.
> If you think you hear somebody knocking
> On the other side of the words, pay
> No attention. It will be only
> The great creature that thumps its tail
> On silence on the other side.
> If you do not even hear that
> I'll give the beast a quick skelp
> And through Art you'll hear it yelp.

The use of the word 'skelp' is part of Graham's Scottish heritage; similarly his sequence 'Malcolm Mooney's Land' refers to 'bonny friendly beasts' and 'Early hunters/Skittering across the ice'.

Graham was born in Greenock (the home of John Davidson, Alan Sharp, Bill Bryden) in 1918, educated at Greenock High School and worked as a structural engineer before resuming his more formal education at Newbattle Abbey College. From his background we might expect an aggressively proletarian verse; yet Graham rejected the pylon poetry of the 1930s and warmed instead to the influence of Dylan Thomas. Greenock still featured in his work as a familiar and vigorous presence, as in a poem 'To My Mother':

> In words I change them further
> Away from the parent fire.

> Look. Into life or out?
> What son did you inherit?

> The flowing strongheld Clyde
> Rests me my earliest word
> That has ever matchlessly
> Changed me towards the sea.

> That deep investment speaks
> Over ship-cradles and derricks
> And ebbs to a perfection's
> Deadly still anatomies.

Graham outgrew the affectations of the Apocalypse movement but escaped from Greenock: he has spent most of his adult life in Cornwall. Several collections show him heavily under the influence of Dylan Thomas, whose metaphorical density he admired. *The Nightfishing* (1955) comprises the title poem, ballads and letters. In 'Letter 1' we see Graham cultivating morbid thematical material in the manner of Thomas. Watching the water (as he has done so compulsively since his Greenock days) Graham envisages his own end, overlaid with an epithet ('second-sighted') worthy of Dylan Thomas:

> And I saw my death flash
> For an instant white like a fish
> In the second-sighted sea.

Graham's love of rich verbal textures also leads to obsessive punning:

> . . . but over
> Flowing all ways I make
> My ways. Always I make
> My ways.

His essentially private poetry has led him to conduct, over the years, an exploration of the imaginative territory presided over by Malcolm Mooney:

> As Mooney's calls Time this moment . . .
> Mooney's called Closing . . .
> ('Letter 111')
> And hears old Mooney call Time
> Bogtongued like doomsday over
> The bar and hears Mooney's
> Hanging lamp lapping
> The sweet oil from its bowl.
> ('Letter 1V')
> In Malcolm Mooney's Land
> I have heard many
> Approachers in the distance
> Shouting . . .
> Elizabeth, my furry

> Pelted queen of Malcolm
> Mooney's Land . . .
>> ('Malcolm Mooney's Land')
> What is the language using us for?
> Said Malcolm Mooney . . .
> Slowly over the white language
> Comes Malcolm Mooney the saviour
>> ('What is the Language Using Us For?')

When Graham was asked to expand on the presence of Malcolm Mooney in his poetry he replied as follows:

> Forgive me taking so long to reply to your letter. You have caught me in the blizzard season. I know my writing is a bit off. It is because I am writing with my left hand. What was it you wanted to know?
>
> Yes, I have seen myself in some of Sydney's writings with me not knowing whether I was being used for good or ill. I am a simple man. What was it you wanted from me? I am Malcolm Mooney. That has always been my name. I would like to be known as having crossed the great glacier with dogs. Good beasts, good friends. I still have the best three. Ludwik, Tralee, Marchy. She is a born leader and keeps us all in order. But you want to know about Mister Graham.
>
> I help him when I can. Why doesn't he speak easier and let himself be? I remember him young. And me younger than I am now with my hand on the tiller.
>
> I hope I have been of some help. I leave you now. I have to feed my dogs.
>> Malcolm Mooney

Further comment is rather superfluous.

10. CONVERSING IN ENGLISH: LINDSAY TO MORGAN

Graham is unfairly neglected in Scotland, where readers tend to respond most readily to the poets in their midst. The English-writing Scottish poets who have attracted attention have had in common no compelling theme, no poetical party-line. Instead they have aimed at a conversational ease, a casual approach that simulates the familiarity of the speaking voice. Narrative formality is generally contained in formal stanzaic units; the result is a low-pressure poetry that has something in common with the English Movement poetry of the 1950s. At another level conversational English verse can be regarded as the equivalent in English of dialect Scots poetry, for in both cases the oral origins confine individuality to an area. As this conversational English poetry aims at urbanity much of it is delivered in the tones of the professional middle-class Glaswegian as is the case with Maurice Lindsay or Edwin Morgan. It can also make a virtue of its geographical location as in the war poetry of Hamish Henderson. Perhaps the most recognisable voice belongs to Maurice Lindsay, whose literary career has been linked to his visibility as a television performer.

Lindsay was born in 1918, the son of an insurance manager who was every inch a selfmade man. Lindsay was drawn to the arts, first as a musician then as a prolific writer, but always followed his father's footsteps by making sure of his financial security. His parentally acquired confidence helped him become a weel-kent voice and face on radio and television; his concern for the environment eventually led to his becoming a Director of the Scottish Civic Trust. We have come to expect poets to be rough and ready, impolite and poor; Lindsay's incongruous position as a middle-class Glaswegian member of the Scottish establishment may have done wonders for his bank balance but has prevented a real assessment of his poetry, which is, of course, unfair. Wallace Stevens, the great American poet, was an executive of an insurance company; T. S. Eliot worked in a bank and as a director of a publishing firm. The supposition that poets must be relentlessly bohemian is a romantic fallacy for there is no automatic connection between great poetry and grinding poverty. What Lindsay has lacked, in choosing to be a part-time poet, is the time and inclination to essay the long poem and thereby strike the major note. His poems are short and to the point, statements rather than suggestive meditations: he has written minor poetry of unusual interest. The lasting impression is of much intelligence and self-discipline; the selfless passion we expect from great poetry is absent but Lindsay claims only be 'an enjoyable poet' and not a great one.

There are two main types of Lindsay poem: poems of affirmation and poems of irritation.[106] 'Love's Anniversaries' is a touching evocation of the decay of erotic intensity into 'the unutterable language of content'; 'These Two Lovers' reworks the theme in a more lively prosody and also ends on an image of resignation with the poet

> like you, content
> should this togetherness we're lent
> prove to be all that living meant.

Again, in 'Two Weddings', Lindsay returns to a celebration of his own good fortune, how he and his wife

> learnt love's best accomplishment
> let daily touching presence stray
> us gently into shared content.

There are few poets who return so lovingly to the word 'content'. It is perhaps an indication of Lindsay's security.

Whatever interferes with Lindsay's contented life, however, is treated not with compassion but annoyance. His family (the folks who live on the hill) constitute the positive aspect of the poet's life. Those who unwittingly intrude on the idyll shoulder the brunt of Lindsay's resentment. Sometimes the voice is exactly that of an infuriated motorist fulminating at those who hinder his progress – and there are many allusions to Lindsay's status as a car-owner. 'Subjective Projective' depicts a driver being brought to a halt by the traffic lights. He opens the window and sees a man spitting down a drain, which moves him to the eccentrically unreasonable conclusion that the man is

> hairy enough to be a poet
> too damn many of them
> any bugger can be a poet
> now that you can't nail thoughts with rhyme

Lindsay is able to convey exactly the driver's inability to empathise with those less fortunate than himself. It is a feeling he seems to share. That poem, and others of a similarly irascible ilk, do not use satire so much as succumb to indignation.

When Lindsay does display sympathy it is very much a family affair. 'Glasgow Orange Walk' lampoons the

> Spread women, ugly men and little children
> dressed in the Sunday best of bigotry

because they impinged on his daughter's wedding. The deeply felt 'An Elegy' is concerned with the poet's father and his heroic refusal to accept various medical verdicts on his life expectancy. It is a remarkably revealing poem, full of the middle-class virtues that Lindsay has built into a credo. He believes, above all, in decency and this shines through the poem and justifies the intensely personal terminal image of a man tumbling from grace. At such moments Lindsay makes the reader query his preconceptions.

Lindsay's thematic complacency is shared by several English-writing poets who avoid the epic aspiration. Hamish Henderson (b. 1920), however, embraced a universal theme in his war poems but has largely renounced the practice of poetry since then. Whereas Lindsay is an example of a sophisticated Scottish man of letters, Henderson has made his lasting reputation as a man of the people. He is internationally known as a collector of folk poetry and has established, in the School of Scottish Studies in Edinburgh, an archive containing many variants on the traditional Child ballads. During the Second World War, Henderson served as an Intelligence

Officer in North Africa and Sicily; from that period came *Elegies for the Dead in Cyrenaica* (1948). These poems are grave with a quiet grandeur and remain among the most moving human statements on the subject of war and its eternal victims:

> There were our own, there were the others.
> Therefore, minding the great word of Glencoe's
> son, that we should not disfigure ourselves
> with villainy of hatred; and seeing that all have gone down like curs
> into anonymous silence,
> I will bear witness for I knew the others.
> Seeing that littoral and interior are alike indifferent
> and the birds are drawn again to our welcoming north
> why should I not sing *them*, the dead, the innocent ?[107]

Henderson has published isolated poems since then but nothing to equal the sustained power of his martial sequence.

The theme of death, so appropriate to Henderson's elegies, is never far from the surface of Scottish verse, whether in Scots or in English. Alasdair Maclean (b. 1926) has turned to it positively: '[My mother's death] confirmed me... in my belief that death was the noblest and most profound of the great themes of poetry, or what the love poets turn to when they put away childish things.'[108] Maclean's response to this great theme is indicative of the seemingly casual tone of much Anglo-Scots poetry. The form is tight, the rhythm smooth, and the attitude matter-of-factually casual (in 'At Home'):

> From a city slum you were transported north,
> a Lowland bride who was not yet my mother.
> You went in one day's journeying from class
> to race; one ghetto, that is, to another.
> No voice came through these narrow entrances
> to shout a welcome to the dark inside
> where herring folk cooked supper over peat
> and made smoked salmon out of Highland pride.

The conversational tone of the poem owes something to the casual diction of the English 'Movement' poets of the 1950s. Yet the dourness of the theme is recognisably Scottish because it takes life so seriously.

Edwin Morgan has attempted to avoid monotony by being an eclectic writer open to countless influences. He was born in 1920 in Glasgow where his father worked in a firm of iron and steel scrap-merchants. Morgan's home was not a bookish one but he acquired a passion for literature, went on to study English at Glasgow University, and eventually became a Professor of English at the same university. He has gloried in Glasgow and writes about the streets and people of the city from the viewpoint of the concerned observer. In 'Glasgow 5 March 1971' he describes a violent incident:

With a ragged diamond
of shattered plate-glass
a young man and his girl
are falling backwards into a shop-window.
The young man's face
is bristling with fragments of glass
and the girl's leg has caught
the broken window
and spurts arterial blood
over her wet-look white coat.[109]

Superficially the poem has the impersonality of photographic naturalism and the deadpan indifference of tabloid journalism. What distinguishes the writing is the control the poet imposes on his material. He dwells on telling details so that, for example, the theme of
facial expression runs through the poem: the faces of the victims are
shocked, the faces of the two attackers are blank, the faces of two
witnesses are averted.

In his 'Glasgow Sonnets' Morgan shows another aspect of his versatility. 'Glasgow 5 March 1971' uses rhythmic rapidity to create a
scene; the fifth Glasgow sonnet uses rhyme to weld together the bits
and pieces of a political argument:

'Let them eat cake' made no bones about it.
But we say let them eat the hope deferred
and that will sicken them. We have preferred
silent slipways to the riveters' wit.

In Morgan's poetry there is very little tender human contact between people. The poet stands back to admire or observe but does
not willingly participate directly. Since Glasgow is synonymous with
poverty and violence Morgan focuses much of his attention on the
stereotypical viciousness of the city. The citizens do not have meet-
ings but confrontations. 'The Suspect', a dramatic monologue, presents one such confrontation:

Asked me for a match suddenly/with his hand up
I thought he was after my wallet
gave him a shove/he fell down
dead on the pavement at my feet
he was forty-two, a respectable man they said
anyone can have a bad heart I told the police
but they've held me five hours and don't
tell me the innocent don't feel
guilty in the glaring chair

The nervous halting rhythms of the poem simulate the speaker's
mental state. Morgan is, technically, a clever writer whose poems en-
gage the reader's intellect rather than his emotion. He has great
facility for word play but lacks a central vision or an obsessive
theme. Many of his poems are based on reading or viewing ('The

Suspect' leans on television thrillers, not actual experience) and, like Alexander Scott, he approaches subjects vicariously. 'The Death of Marilyn Monroe' manufactures a poem by playing on the emotive power invested in a great sex-symbol. He is more successful when the vicariously known subject is technological.

Morgan is one of the few poets to make science fiction and scientific fact an integral part of his work. He has responded enthusiastically to the space age and written poems that penetrate deep space imaginatively. The theme seems to encourage the free exercise of his imagination. 'Spacepoem 3: Off Course' conveys the plight of the distressed astronaut by the disintegration of the language. The adjectives and nouns seem to float above syntax:

> the crackling somersault   the smuggled orbit
> the rough moon   the visionary rendezvous
> the weightless headphone   the cabin debris
> the floating lifeline   the pitch sleep
> the crawling camera   the turning silence
> the space crumb   the crackling beard
> the orbit mouth-organ   the floating song

There are no sentences in that poem; only a catalogue of items. In a much lighter poem, 'The First Men on Mercury', Morgan invents a language for the people of Mercury. English begins to merge with Mercurese in an alarming manner:

> – Men come in peace from the third planet
> which we call 'earth'. We are earthmen.
> Take us earthmen to your leader.
>
> – Thmen? Thmen? Bawr. Bawrhossop.
> Yuleeda tan hanna. Harrabost yuleeda.
>
> – I am the yuleeda. You see my hands,
> we carry no benner, we come in peace.
> The spaceways are all stretterhawn.
>
> – Glawn peacemen all horrabhanna tantko!
> Tan come at'mstrossop. Glawp yuleeda!
>
> – Atoms are peacegawl in our harraban.
> Menbat worrabost from tan hannahanna.
>
> – You men we know bawrhossoptant. Bawr.
> We know yuleeda. Go strawg backspetter quick.
>
> – We cantantabawr, tantingko backspetter now!
>
> – Banghapper now! Yes, third planet back.
> Yuleeda will go back blue, white, brown
> nowhanna! There is no more talk.

11. CULTIVATING THE GARDEN: IAN HAMILTON FINLAY

Morgan's linguistic and typographical experiments, and those of Alan Riddell (1927–77)[110], are inspired by the example of Ian Hamilton Finlay, whose internationally celebrated work has made him probably better known outside than inside Scotland. He is unique and does not really fit into any literary school or pattern; what is certain, though, is that he has exhibited more sheer artistic ingenuity than perhaps any other resident of twentieth-century Scotland. Finlay was born in 1925 in Nassau, Bahamas, and returned to Scotland in his early youth. He rapidly made a reputation as a writer of short stories and a witty poet using traditional measures. In the 1960s he began to combine verbal statements with visual images and the result was classified as Concrete Poetry. Finlay does not, however, regard his work as revolutionary but as traditional. His is a conceptual art in which the initial intellectual concept is carried through to a precisely logical conclusion. He transforms images into three-dimensional forms and gives the pun an artistic life of its own: a pink stone, for example, is engraved with the motto 'Sea Pink'. Most of his images are perfectly natural. Autumn becomes, in a stone inscription, *One (Orange) Arm Of The World's Oldest Windmill* and a swallow is *The Cloud's Anchor*. His typographically arranged poems really have to be seen to be believed.[111] Finlay looks for classical perfection in his work and in life; those who do not conform to his ideas of artistic integrity are cast as enemies. He is combative but, above all, creative. And his greatest creative work is incorporated in his garden. No survey of poetry in Scotland can afford to ignore this garden.

In his *Lives of the Poets* (1779–81) Dr Johnson commented on the work of Shenstone, the poetic gardener, and his ability.

> to point his prospects, to diversify his surface, to entangle his walks . . . to plant a walk in undulating curves . . . to place a bench at every turn where there is an object to catch the view; to make water run where it will be heard, and to stagnate where it will be seen; to leave intervals where the eye will be pleased, and to thicken to plantation where there is something to be hidden.*

Finlay has adapted Shenstone's ambitions to the Scottish landscape which means that Shenstone has entered into Scottish literature at two critical phases as Burns too was greatly impressed by the English poet. At home at Stonypath in Dunsyre, Lanark, Finlay creates his own cultural environment.

---

* There are no page references for classics available in a number of editions.

Some twenty-five miles south-west of Edinburgh, on a hillside in the Pentlands, Finlay presides over his recently established 'republic of Little Sparta'. The existence of this miniature state (of about three acres) is recognised on the Ordnance Survey map of Scotland; it is an even more important feature on the cultural map. Since moving there in 1967, Finlay and his wife have transformed it from a neglected farmhouse and farm on the estate of Sue Finlay's father into a literary-philosophical garden complex of considerable profundity.

Finlay was never satisfied with the two-dimensional presentation of his early work. He required a spatial element and Stonypath gave him the opportunity to translate his ideas into action. Finlay's work is based on collaboration with calligraphers, sculptors, carvers, photographers, pictorial artists, typographers and other craftsmen. In creating the garden he achieved a new collaboration, a working relationship with nature. Whereas Cézanne wanted to do Poussin again after nature, Finlay wants to do 'nature over again after Poussin' (to cite the title of a Finlay exhibition). He began with neither money nor gardening expertise; he was, however, motivated by a vision of making an English neoclassical garden, albeit on a cottage scale. The realisation of this vision was to involve both a rediscovery of the classical tradition and contain a revolutionary proposition.

Much of Finlay's neoclassical work is informed by the principle of the three-dimensional pun and the spirit of the paradox. He compels us, through his verbal wit and visual imagery, to confront nature with culture and vice versa. For example, an inscription on a stone reproduces the rowan's leaf-shape and tells us that *The Rowan/Is Learning/To Write* and we see the point illustrated graphically and botanically before our eyes. He also likes to play on our preconceptions and tease meanings out of our perceptions. A bridge, carved with a massive facsimile of Claude's signature, alters our outlook on the spectacle before us. We see it, simultaneously, as a real landscape and as a scene from a seventeenth century landscape painting (as if nature copied art). Whereas some artists have been anxious to achieve synthesis, Finlay's awareness of the organic life of his environment has resulted in an imaginative symbiosis.

The extraordinary range of cultural references throughout the garden is a guide to Finlay's pugnacious philosophy. He is concerned with the contemporary indifference to culture and the atrophy of the great neoclassical garden tradition; consequently Finlay's heroes generally have some revolutionary significance. In the Front Garden are two juxtapositions which metaphorically transform trees into columns by placing stone column-bases against them: on the left (looking from the Sunken Garden) is a tribute to Fabre d'Eglantine, who composed the French Revolutionary calendar; on the right is a similar salute to Saint-Just. Near the Top Pond in Little

Sparta the notion is expanded into a hillside Pantheon celebrating Jules Michelet (whose *History of the Revolution* is a favourite of Finlay's), Robespierre, Jean Jacques Rousseau, Corot and the fantastic landscape painter Caspar David Friedrich. This Pantheon is installed, on a larger scale, in the Kroller-Muller Museum at Otterlo in The Netherlands.

As a practical visionary who works with a talented team of craftsmen and welcomes visitors, Finlay is no isolationist. Nor is his garden a retreat. As he writes in his *Unconnected Sentences on Gardening* (modelled on Shenstone's aphoristic observations) 'certain gardens are described as retreats when they are really attacks'.[112] Finlay's garden is certainly an attack: artistically it is an assault on complacency and philosophically it is a positive demonstration of the proposition that modern life could be restructured according to classical proportions. In his courtyard, Finlay had a gallery where he could exhibit and sell his work; subsequently he redesignated this as a temple with rusticated pilasters and a dedication reading *To Apollo/His Music/His Muses/His Missiles*.

12. THE PARISH AND THE ISLAND: GEORGE MACKAY BROWN AND IAIN CRICHTON SMITH

Finlay's work flourishes in Little Sparta, so by cultivating his own garden he has commanded the attention of the informed world. The spirit of Voltaire is consciously present; the locality expands imaginatively into another world. What makes the difference between flat regionalism and an artistically precise universality is the imaginative dimension. It is conspicuously there in the work of Finlay; it is also there in the writing of George Mackay Brown and Iain Crichton Smith. Two epithets of abuse often thrown at writers are parochial and insular; George Mackay Brown and Ian Crichton Smith are, literally, parochial and insular as their work relates to (respectively) a singular parish and a particular island. However, they have transformed their origins imaginatively to such an extent that dismissive epithets of abuse become inoperative and we enter worlds of invention.

George Mackay Brown (b.1927) lives in Stromness, which is the centre of his artistic universe. He is probably best known as an outstandingly gifted prose stylist. It was, however, as a poet that Brown first established his literary reputation and his poetic work remains an important part of his total output. He is a versatile poet whose most obvious virtues are formal clarity and an impressive command of verbal music. He has been influenced by the inscape and sprung rhythms of Hopkins, by the ecclesiastical tone of the later Eliot, by the metaphorical density of Dylan Thomas, by the melancholy resignation (complete with refrain) and iconography (complete with tinkers) of Yeats. He has three distinct styles in his repertoire: a simple direct style, usually rhymed, which is employed for contemporary themes; a measured style of great dignity, normally in free verse, which simulates the saga voice; and a highly-wrought intricately patterned ornamental style which deals with ceremonial subjects.

Brown's fascination with literary forms has resulted in a wide variety of stylistic effects. He can be sensuous in a thoroughly contemporary manner; he can be stark and austere; he can expertly imitate archaic forms. His immersion in the past has left him with a fondness for runes and kennings. Runes, like the Norse examples in Maes Howe, were statements cut in stone: doubtless the effort involved accounts for their brevity. Brown has written a large number of runic verses distinguished by sheer verbal compression. Kennings were euphemistic metaphors employed by, among others, the Icelandic skalds. Brown has revived rune and kenning in his poems so that the Viking past is omnipresent in many of them. From Scotland itself he has drawn heavily on the formal majesty and dramatic intensity of the great traditional ballads.

What Brown excels at in his poems is the rhythm of speech, particularly the rhythm of Orkney speech. Orcadians speak in an inquisitive manner with a reversed cadence that begins on a low note and rises to a high one. It is full of pondered silences and Brown includes these in his poems; the pause between stanzas is an integral part of the total artistic execution. In *Greenvoe* Brown describes Orkney speech as 'slow and wondering, like water lapping among stones'[113], and this quality is apparent in his poetry. When he wants to present a voice from the past he adopts another voice, shot through with archaism, abstraction, and syntactical inversion, as in 'The Blind Helmsman' in *Fishermen with Ploughs*.[114]:

> Man goes, man voyages, into the blackest sun.
> Nor doth hero long keep
> Lithe limb or lissomness or laughter.
> Honey is bitter at last in the mouth.
> Fareth a shadow to the ghostly feast-halls.

Apart from the use of alliteration – where the liquidity of the 'l' sounds onomatopoetically suggest the surge of the sea – that opening is absolutely typical of Brown in that it announces the voyage theme that is basic to his approach. In this sense most of his poems have a strong narrative element – even his lyrics are going somewhere, taken up on a voyage from exile to home. He is not a first-personal poet – when an 'I' speaks it is usually in the context of a dramatic monologue.

One of the finest poems Brown has published is 'Hamnavoe'. This is a moving tribute to his father, who was born and died in Stromness; a posthumous gift of images to a father whose 'gay poverty... kept/My seapink innocence/From the worm and black wind'. The poem is a portrait of one day in the life of Hamnavoe (Stromness) and comprises a steady accumulation of marvellously vivid images so that the people of the town come to life:

> A tinker keened like a tartan gull
> At cuithe-hung doors. A crofter lass
> Trudged through the lavish dung
> In a dream of cornstalks and milk.

More than that, the town itself seems alive with incident, glorying in its 'pipe-spitting pier-head', its 'ignorant closes', its 'kirk, in a gale of psalms', its 'tumult of roofs'. The universe, too, becomes a familiar part and parcel of the little seaport, for the moon hangs like a 'buttered bannock'. Through this world Brown's postman father voyages with stops to deliver his 'penny letters'. The felicitous details and rhythmic fluency enable Brown to wrap up the town in a cosy parcel of images so he can deliver them to his father.

Like Brown, Iain Crichton Smith has a reverence for the English language and an abiding interest in a limited number of themes. Smith was born in 1928 on the Outer Hebridean Island of Lewis. It is axiomatic that environmental factors play some part in shaping the creative development of any writer; Smith has created his best poems entirely through a sustained exploration of the insular world he inhabited until the age of seventeen when, for the first time in October 1945, he left Lewis to study English at Aberdeen University. He later taught English at Oban High School and wrote poetry and prose in both Gaelic and English.[115]

Smith's early life with his widowed mother (his father died of TB which produced in Smith's mother a morbid fear of illness) reinforced his tendency to accept life as a gift which, once unwrapped, presented the inevitability of death. The first poem in *Thistles and Roses* (1961) – the book that did most to consolidate Smith's early reputation as an important poet – was 'Old Woman'. It is a portrait of a life that has crumbled before the encroachment of age (as cliffs crumble when assaulted by the sea). It is an image of indignity:

> And she, being old, fed from a mashed plate
> as an old mare might droop across a fence
> to the dull pastures of its ignorance.

This reduction of the human being to a specimen of decay is treated by Smith as the supreme tragedy of life; it is the principal theme that has haunted his poetry as well as the novel *Consider the Lilies* (1968) which views the Highland Clearances through the consciousness of 'an old woman'.

The Old Woman theme is, then, a starting point for any examination of Smith's work. It is absolutely crucial to it. When I asked Smith about the importance of this theme to him he answered:

> I think this came from my mother, whom I used as a paradigm of many Highland traits. For some reason I think of the old woman as being stronger than the old man. There is a strong will and determination there that attracts me. There is also a pathos which I find very moving for most of the old women I knew had received very little from life, though that did not diminish their grip on it. Many of them too were religious, as my mother was. Not all of the old woman are based on my mother directly but the impetus came from her life.[116]

In Smith's published works there are several poems about old women and each of them draws from Smith his deepest emotions and/or his profoundest sympathy. The poem 'For my mother' is, naturally, full of admiration for a woman who has weathered the storms of seventy years:

> as if her voyage were
> to truthful Lewis rising
> most loved though most bare
> at the end of a rich season.

A second poem bearing the title 'Old Woman' (and beginning 'Your thorned back') presents a less sympathetic character (probably the darker side of his mother), a woman moulded by the narrow religious principles of the Free Church:

> Your set mouth
> forgives no-one, not even God's justice
> perpetually drowning law with grace.

'Old Woman with Flowers' and 'If You Are About to Die Now' delicately invoke the poet's thoughts on the final moments of his mother whose death is recorded, and life celebrated, in the first part of the collection *Love Poems and Elegies* (1972).

This sequence of poems shows Smith at his most alert so that every sound and sight around him assumes a significance which he attributes to the death of his mother. In the fine first poem of the sequence, 'You lived in Glasgow', the poet combines sharp observation with visionary meditation as he sits in Glasgow and thinks about her:

> Now I sit here in George Square
> where the War Memorial's yellow sword glows bright
> and the white stone lions mouth at bus and car.
> A maxi-skirted girl strolls slowly by.

I turn and look. I might be you. But no.
Around me there's a 1970 sky.

Here the solemnity of the mood is emphasised by the deliberately formal pattern of the verse: the emphatic reliance on rhyme and the frequent use of iambic pentameter ('A maxi-skirted girl strolls slowly by'). In 'This island formed you' Smith thinks of Lewis with 'its black hatted men/and stony bibles' then he follows that with 'The space-ship'. Here there is an unexpected metamorphosis whereby his mother, dying of lack of oxygen, becomes 'an astronaut lacking air,/dying of lack of it in the depths of space'. The final poem in the sequence, 'The earth eats everything', suggests the unforgettable impact of this particular death on the poet:

I have forgotten it over and over.
Life is explainable only by life.
I have read that on paper leaves.

In the Old Woman poems we see Smith's technical practices as well as one major part of his thematic repertoire. His is a poetry of statement heightened by poetic intensity; the statements are supported not by argument but by imagery. In a recent essay on his childhood Smith remembered what he had taken, as an artist, from Lewis: 'It gave me images of the sea and the bare mind... It has made me, I think, unhealthily concerned with religion... There is a certain pessimism which may perhaps have to do with growing up among an ageing population so that I seem to know more about the old than I do about the young.'[117] As well as the Old Woman theme, three further subjects are referred to here: the sea, religion, and an historical pessimism. These subjects sometimes appear on their own, sometimes as part of the Old Woman theme. The sea, for an islander like Smith, is an uncertain and treacherous element so there is nothing remotely romantic about his poems on that theme. 'For the Unknown Seamen of the 1939–45 War Buried in Iona Churchyard' is an elegiac tribute to the dead. Smith is not concerned with great cosmic meanings but in conveying the commonplace quality of the collective, and theologically pointless, death:

What happened was simply this, bad luck for those
who have lain here twelve years in a changing pose.

Smith is not a poet of passion so much as a poet obsessed by the denial of passion (an emotional feature that can be traced back to his childhood in Lewis). There is a characteristic reticence about the poem, a prosaic ('One simply doesn't/know enough') inability to fully embrace the subject, that indicates how uneasy Smith is with abstractions. For him there is no clear concept of Death; there is only the particular death. And yet the poem is saved from bathos by Smith's sheer poetic expertise which is best displayed in the final stanza (unobtrusively rhyming *ababb*) with its terminal pararhyme (a device borrowed, appropriately enough in the circumstances, from Wilfred Owen):

> Best not to make much of it and leave these seamen
> in the equally altering acre they now have
> inherited from strangers though yet human.
> They fell from sea to earth, from grave to grave,
> and, griefness now, taught others how to grieve.

Another sea-poem, 'By Ferry to the Island', contrasts the immense surge of the water by juxtaposing it with the esentially trivial pursuits of the visitors: 'Someone made coffee, someone played the fool'. In the fourteen-poem sequence 'By the Sea' the sea is also used as a symbol of permanence beside which human activities are squalid.

Smith's concern with religion is a product of his desire to move clear away from the negativity of the Free Church religion so it is a particularised issue, not an abstract consideration of religion as a philosophical discipline. (The Free Church of Scotland was formed when, in the Disruption of 1843, a body of Scottish presbyterians seceded from the Established Church of Scotland.) As a sect the Free Church has become, in Scotland, associated with the things it is proverbially against: drink, merriment on Sunday, permissive morals. As such it has been frequently caricatured as a naysaying conspiracy of hypocrites dedicated to a rigid kirkianity rather than to the teachings of Christ. Smith has said (16 May 1979) 'I was brought up in the Free Church and I have felt since that as a religion it is too constricting, dictatorial and lacking in joy.'[118] In 'Sunday Morning Walk' Smith depicts the island of Lewis in the cold grip of a Free Church Sabbath, a bizarre situation involving the islanders' calculated indifference to the glorious summer that surrounds them:

> Sunday of wrangling bells – and salt in the air –
> I passed the tall black men and their women walking
> over the tight-locked streets which were all on fire
> with summer ascendant. The seas were talking and talking . . .

Obviously this bleak denial of life, in the name of religion, has disturbed Smith; in the title poem of his collection *The Law and the Grace* (1965) he adopts an argumentative attitude to those he imagines might condemn his lack of Free Church religion:

> It's law they ask of me and not grace.
> 'Conform,' they say, 'your works are not enough.
> Be what we say you should be,' even if
> graceful hypocrisy obscures my face.

This guilty struggle, with the religion he was conditioned to as a child, could have resulted in an obsessive poetry disfigured by the same sort of religious prejudice Smith was so anxious to avoid. However, he wrote his way out of that predicament by proclaiming his own artistic credo in 'I Build an Orange Church'. In this poem Smith still has something to believe in but he has replaced conventional religion with a colourful commitment to the insights of art:

> I make a ceiling of intensest blue.
> The seats are heliotrope, the bibles pink,
> hymn books are apple green.

13. SINGER AND NEWER VOICES

Smith's contemporary, James Burns Singer, was born in New York in 1928 but brought up and educated in Scotland where he worked as a marine biologist before moving to London in 1955. In 1956 he married a black American psychologist, Marie, and the success of this relationship helped compensate for the tragic element in his life, for his father had gone insane and his mother had committed suicide. He achieved some success in 1957 with two books: a collection of poems, *Still and All*; and a novel, *Living Silver*. He was immensely promising and Hugh MacDiarmid has said he has seldom 'met a more extensively read man'[119] than Singer. However, the promise was not to be fulfilled for Singer died in Plymouth, in 1964, at the age of thirty-six.

What we are left with is the work of a poet whose ambition, as Anne Cluysenaar recalls, was 'to write a poem which does not contain a line of poetry – that would be the great accomplishment'.[120] In pursuit of this ambition Singer stripped his poetry of obvious emotional connotation and created a cerebral style that is more analytical than poetic. It is a poetry of propositions and argument. 'An Apology', for example, begins:

> It is the unforgivable
> Essence of individual acts
> Which uncontrollably attracts
> Words through the incommunicable.

Singer sought a kind of perfection, a poetry that would insinuate itself rather than force itself on the reader. His ideal was the wordless eloquence of shared silence, and he wanted to utilise – as he says in 'Verses from a Distance' – 'a vocabulary made of silence'.

This contradiction provides a mood in Singer's work: on the one hand he is using words to communicate, on the other hand he is reluctant to communicate anything specific. The result is a consistent reticence with occasional jarring justifications of his method: 'I come down here to gather/Recollection' ('The Present'). The trouble with abstract concepts in poetry is that the verse becomes a clinical exercise precluding any sensuous language. Obviously Singer realised this and there are glimpses of a more memorable style, as when he talks of his wife's 'dark body deepening gradually' ('Wife').

It is as if Singer were afraid of his feelings or, at least, afraid of making an exhibition of them. In guarding over his own poetic impulses he erred on the side of timidity. Still, Singer was determined to make his own style and to use his keen intellect and scientific training to rescue poetry from romantic excess. He is an unfinished poet in that he did not live long enough to triumph creatively over his own initial theory, but he completed enough work to show a clear direction.

No poet younger than Smith or Singer can be considered to have a securely established reputation though there are several reputations in the making. During the 1960s a new generation of poets emerged in Scotland; they affected a transatlantic accent, cultivated a cosmopolitan tone, confused restlessness with rootlessness and claimed to have outgrown the petty moral conventions of presbyterian Scotland. However, the incessant obsessive references to Scotland suggested they were protesting so much because they were painfully aware of the inescapable pressure of their Scottishness. Tom Buchan (b.1931) wrote poems that energetically expressed his sense of fun but his most telling lines contained serious comments on the state of Scotland. His 'Scotland the wee' conveys, in the shorthand of readymade images, what the poets of the 1960s felt was so disastrously wrong with Scotland[121]:

> Scotland the wee, crèche of the soul,
> of thee I sing
>
> land of the millionaire draper, whisky vomit
> and the Hillman Imp
>
> staked out with church halls, gaelic sangs
> and the pan loaf

A similar disenchantment pervades the work of Alan Jackson (b.1938). Jackson adapted to his own satirical ends the mocking anarchical manner of the American Beats and scorned what he took to be Scotland's outmoded and hypocritical moral preoccupations. With genuinely witty irreverence Jackson ridiculed establishment institutions and tried to replace presbyterian timidity with permissive liberalism. He was an active campaigner on behalf of unilateral nuclear disarmament and tried to bring a feeling of festivity to Scotland. He initiated a series of poetry readings at Edinburgh's Traverse Theatre and, for a while, made poetry as much a part of the cultural calendar as music and drama. Jackson was, briefly, Scotland's unofficial spokesman for the alternative culture of the

1960s and his best poems are aphoristic celebrations of the euphoria of the daft existential moment (in 'Nothing'):

> Nothing in my woman's head
> didn't worry about that
> Took her into C and A's
> and bought her a great big purple woolly hat.[122]

Iconoclasm was an important feature of two Scottish surrealists: George Macbeth (b.1932) and David Black (b.1941). Macbeth displayed a devil-may-care black comedy, surprised the reader with macabre imagery, and generated a genre of sick (and slick) verse. His usual technique was to take a subject and flog it to death, pursuing the theme to the point of exhaustion. It is polished, manufactured poetry; occasional verse that sometimes falls bathetically to the occasion. In a poem on his own death, 'And I bequeath'[123], he offers a typically morbid image:

> And I bequeath my empty head,
> My hollow flesh, and leaking bones,
> To those well nourished upon groans
> Who operate upon the dead.

Very occasionally Macbeth's sardonic humour gives way to confessional poems about his Scottish upbringing. In 'St Andrews' he writes:

> My child's Belief
> (I now believe) was a Scots exile's: gone
> With loosened roots. When the sick wish returns
> For the lost country, the dream-Scotland grief
> Was noble in, I clutch at *things* . . .

David Black's work is astonishingly inventive, a fluent catalogue of Gothic and surrealistic images. He was one of the most individual voices of the 1960s in Scotland with his freeflowing fluent verse that turned dreamlike and nightmarish incidents into incisive narratives. His stylish dramatic monologues brought disturbing figures to Scotland: the Red Judge, the Black Judge, the Hangman ('From the Privy Council'). Black invariably set his strange scenarios in an utterly mundane Edinburgh context so that the expressionistic content of the poems would stand out stark against a bleak background. 'Leith Docks', an unlikely subject, was even treated with Black's eerie atmosphere and nervous energy:

> Kandahay, O kandahay. I
> run spinning in the
> wet lights, past
> morose burghers. An
> amazing length, Leith Walk. On
> down Constitution Street – O

io! the
Corn Exchange – and into
an immense dockland. Dim
lights on glimmering water, dark
bulk of piers.[124]

A more solemn poetry was attempted by Stewart Conn (b.1936), who derived some of his solidity from the muscular influence of Ted Hughes; and Robin Fulton (b.1937), whose terse understatements avoid rhetoric at the risk of predictably anticlimactic endings.[125] Giles Gordon (b.1940) did some delicate work and Douglas Dunn (b.1942) made an impact, with *Terry Street* (1969), as the second poet of his adopted Hull, a lesser Larkin. The classification was unfair for Dunn is an impressively intelligent poet who has published fine individual poems. 'Drowning', from *Barbarians* (1979), is situated round the river Gryfe in Dunn's native Renfrewshire. The poem recalls the death of a boy whose name has been forgotten as being of no public consequence. Dunn remembers how he and his friends swam in the same river and how, previously, he had glimpsed the little death:

Too young for swimming then, I was in goal,
When, from our pitch, I saw the dead boys come.[126]

The intention is to give a sense of dignity to the occasion and to rebuke those who forget their working class childhood because conditioned to equate poverty with nonentity.

Dunn brings to his poetry a pictorially precise gift of observation and he is a skilful craftsman: his use of rhyme controls the conversational ease of his poetry and the rich alliteration is integral rather than ornamental. His collection *St Kilda's Parliament* (1981) contains some of his best poems and shows him an artist capable of development. In the title poem he meditates on the difference between the real Scotland and the tourist image:

Traveller, tourist with your mind set on
Romantic Staffas and materials for
Winter conversations, if you should go there,
Landing at sunrise on its difficult shores,
On St Kilda you will surely hear Gaelic
Spoken softly like a poetry of ghosts
By those who never were contorted by
Hierarchies of cuisine and literacy.

Almost every line of Dunn's verse shown an empirical intelligence; he is not fanciful or lyrical but a poet who allows observation to dissolve into speculation. He is a thoughtful writer who broods over everyday subjects.

Liz Lochhead (b.1948) is a feminist poet who nevertheless admits sexually provocative images to her verse, as in 'Bawd'[127]:

I'll be a torment, haunt men's dreams,
I'll wear my stockings black with seams.
I'll rouge my cleavage, flaunt myself, my heels
will be perilously high, oh
but I won't sway.

Lochhead has managed to combine the shrill, terminal tone of Sylvia Plath with the snappy knowall manner of the glossy woman's magazine. The texture of her verse is spikey (like those high heels she always writes about) and her tone is confidential rather than strictly confessional. Her contemporary, Walter Perrie (b.1949), takes a more didactic line. His long poem *A Lamentation for the Children* (1977) used both Scots and English in a search for the poet's own roots. *By Moon and Sun* (1981) is the account of an amorous and political odyssey through a flawed world made whole by passion.[128]

   Although the present writer knows no Gaelic it would be presumptuous to close this account of modern Scottish poetry without some reference to Sorley Maclean, the great Gaelic poet. Maclean was born in 1911 in Osgaig on the island of Raasay and evolved, in the opinion of a reliable bilingual judge like Iain Crichton Smith, into 'a major poet . . . the most original poet we have had in Gaelic this century'.[129] As a Gael, Maclean felt drawn to the traumas of modern history and his work is directly related to political struggles of his time: the Spanish Civil War, which provided the tragic backdrop for the intense love affair recounted in *Dain do Eimhir* (1943); the Second World War in which Maclean was seriously wounded; the Class War, which provided Maclean with his personal pantheon of revolutionary heroes like James Connolly and John Maclean; and the Cold War whose changing landscape features in his later work (for example, 'The Lost Mountain' with its reference to Vietnam). Maclean's poems have been translated into Scots by Douglas Young and English by Crichton Smith. Maclean himself, however, feels

> No poetry is translatable, and the more verse approximates to poetry the more untranslatable it is. Gaelic poetry is especially difficult for many reasons: Gaelic is so much outside the Western European traditions; it has so little Latin/Greek/Romance vocabulary (although it has some), unlike English, French, etc.; by far the primary sensuousness of Gaelic poetry has always been sound; Gaelic is a mid-European language and therefore Scots is too Teutonic or Nordic for it and English is too much affected by its huge accretions of Romance vocabulary, the ratio of quantity of long and short vowels is much greater in Gaelic than in English or Scots.[130]

Maclean's range is international, his passions are both sensual and political, and his greatest poems are both heroic and elegiac. As his own translations apparently come closest to the music and meaning of the Gaelic original I close with a stanza from his translation of his 'The Woods of Raasay'[131] showing his response of the old Scottish ideal of wholeness:

> To believe with flesh,
>   with brain and heart,
>   that one thing was complete,
>   beautiful, accessible:
>   a thing that would avoid the travail
>   of the flesh and hardship,
>   that would not be spoiled by the bedragglement
>   of time and temptation.

REFERENCES

1   John Richard Green (ed.), *English Literature by the Rev Stopford Brooke*, American Book Company: New York 1900, p. 62

2   Maurice Lindsay (ed.), *John Davidson: A Selection of his Poems*, Hutchinson: London 1961, p. 12

3   Ibid. pp. 22–3

4   Ibid. All Davidson texts are quoted from Lindsay's edn

5   Ibid. p. xii

6   William McGonagall, *Last Poetic Gems*, David Winter: Dundee 1978, p. 6

7   William McGonagall, *Poetic Gems*, David Winter: Dundee 1890, p 12

8   Ibid. pp. 6–7

9   Francis James Child, *The English and Scottish Popular Ballads* (5 vols), Houghton, Mifflin: Boston 1882–98; reprinted New York (1965) Appendix p. 757

10   William McGonagall, *Poetic Gems*, p. 5

11   J. Logie Robertson, *The Letters of Robert Burns*, Walter Scott: London 1887, p. 48

12   Hugh MacDiarmid, *Burns Today and Tomorrow*, Castle Wynd Printers: Edinburgh 1959, p. 23

13   *Whistle-Binkie or The Piper Of the Party*, (2 vols) Glasgow 1878, Preface p. vi

14   William Power, *Literature and Oatmeal*, Routledge: London 1935, p. 155

15   Stevenson text from *Underwoods*, Chatto and Windus: London 1887

16   Hugh Haliburton, *Horace in Homespun*, Blackwood: Edinburgh 1886

17   Hugh MacDiarmid, *Contemporary Scottish Studies*, London (Leonard Parsons) 1926; Scottish Educational Journal reprint (1976), p. 6

18   *Proceedings at Dinner in Honour of Charles Murray*, Aberdeen, 1912, p. 21

19   *Proceedings at Presentation of Portrait and Bust to Mr Charles Murray*, Aberdeen, 1925

20   Murray texts from *Hamewith: The Complete Poems of Charles Murray*, Charles Murray Memorial Trust: Aberdeen 1979

21   *Proceedings at Presentation of Portrait and Bust*, p. 21

22   John MacQueen and Tom Scott (eds), *The Oxford Book of Scottish Verse*, Clarendon Press: Oxford 1966

23   *Scotland's Magazine*, vol 50, no 8, August 1954, p. 34

24   Hugh MacDiarmid, *Contemporary Scottish Studies*, p. 62

25   William Power op. cit. pp. 180–1

26   *The Oxford Book of Scottish Verse*

27   C. M. Grieve, *Annals of the Five Senses*, Porpoise Press: Edinburgh 1930, p. 20 and preliminary 'In Acknowledgement'

28   Hugh MacDiarmid, *Lucky Poet*, Methuen: London 1943; Cape reprint (1972), pp. 178–9

29   *The Scottish Chapbook*, vol. 1, no. 3, Oct. 1922, pp. 62–3

30   Hugh MacDiarmid, *Sangschaw*, Blackwood: Edinburgh 1925, p. x

31   Texts of all MacDiarmid poems from Michael Grieve and W. R. Aitken (eds), *Hugh MacDiarmid: Complete Poems 1920–1976*, 2 vols., Martin Brian and O'Keeffe: London 1978

32   Hugh MacDiarmid, *Lucky Poet*, p. xxiii

33   *The Scottish Chapbook*, vol. 1, no. 7, Feb. 1923, p. 183

34   Ibid. p. 182

35   *The Voice of Scotland*, vol. 9, no. 1, 1959, p. 5

36   Hugh MacDiarmid, *Complete Poems*, p. 109. Because of the length of *A Drunk Man Looks at the Thistle* page references to *Complete Poems* are provided, whereas short poems are identified by title.

37   Ibid. p. 85

38   Ibid. p. 86

39   Ibid. p. 86

40   Ibid. p. 87

41   Ibid. p. 102

42   Ibid. p. 102

43   Ibid. p. 96

44   Ibid. p. 97

45   Ibid. p. 105

46   Ibid. p. 121

47   Ibid. p. 98

48   Ibid. p. 152

49   Ibid. p. 107

50   Ibid. p. 114

51   Ibid. pp. 161–5

52   Ibid. p. 205

53   Hugh MacDiarmid, *Lucky Poet*, p. 158

54   Ibid. p. 41

55   Ibid. p. 45

56   Hugh MacDiarmid, *Complete Poems*, pp. 822–3

57   C. M. Grieve, *Annals of the Five Senses*, Porpoise Press: Edinburgh 1930, p. 18

58   Hugh MacDiarmid, *Lucky Poet*, p. 58

59   Ibid. p. xi

60   Ibid. p. 44

61   Hugh MacDiarmid, *The Company I've Kept*, Hutchinson: London 1966, p. 20

62   The Soutar texts are from *Seeds in the Wind*, Andrew Dakers: London 1943 and *Poems in Scots*, Moray Press: Edinburgh: 1935. Soutar's

papers are in the National Library of Scotland. MacDiarmid's edition of Soutar's *Collected Poems*, Andrew Dakars: London 1948 is misleadingly incomplete, containing nothing from *Seeds in the Wind* and *Poems in Scots*. A selection of Soutar's *Poems in Scots and English*, Scottish Academic Press: Edinburgh 1975, is available

63   Alexander Scott, *Still Life*, Chambers: Edinburgh 1958, p. 57

64   Ibid. p. 116

65   'The Auld Tree' is included in neither the 1948 *Collected Poems* nor the 1975 *Poems in Scots and English* but the text (as printed in the *Poems in Scots* of 1935) can be consulted in the National Library of Scotland

66   The Garioch texts are from *Collected Poems*, Macdonald: Edinburgh 1977

67   Introduction to Robert Garioch, *Selected Poems*, Macdonald: Edinburgh 1966, p. 8

68   Maurice Lindsay, *History of Scottish Literature*, Robert Hale: London 1977, p. 392

69   Alexander Scott (ed), *Modern Scots Verse 1922–1977*, Akros: Preston 1978, p. 17

70   The Smith texts are from *Collected Poems*, John Calder: London 1975: that volume, however, mispells Eildon (in *Under the Eildon Tree*) as Eldon throughout

71   *Saltire Review*, vol. 1, no. 1, April 1954, p. 16

72   Norman MacCaig (ed), *For Sydney Goodsir Smith*, Macdonald: Edinburgh 1975, p. 11

73   Ibid. p. 53

74   Tom Scott's poems appear in *The Ship*, Oxford University Press: Oxford 1963 and *Brand the Builder*, Ember Press: London 1975

75   Alexander Scott, *Selected Poems 1943–74*, Akros: Preston 1975

76   A selection of George Campbell Hay's poems appear in Gordon Wright (ed.), *Four Points of a Saltire: The Poetry of Sorley Maclean, George Campbell Hay, William Neill, Stuart MacGregor*, Reprographia: Edinburgh 1970

77   William Tait, *A Day Between Weathers: Collected Poems 1938–1978*, Paul Harris: Edinburgh 1980 and Neil's selection in *Four Points of a Saltire*

78   Alastair Mackie, *Clytach*, Akros: Preston 1972

79   Maurice Lindsay (ed.), *Modern Scottish Poetry*, Carcanet: Manchester 1976

80   Tom Leonard's poems appear in *Poems*, O'Brien: Dublin 1973 and *Bunnit Husslin*, Third Eye: Glasgow 1975

81   David Craig, *Scottish Literature and the Scottish People 1680–1830*, Chatto and Windus: London 1961, pp. 242–3

82   Alan Jackson, *All Fall Down*, Kevin Press:Edinburgh 1965

83   Maurice Lindsay, *Snow Warning*, Linden Press: Arundel 1962, p. 7

84   Edwin Muir, *An Autobiography*, Hogarth Press: London 1954, p. 154

85   Ibid. pp. 155–6

86   Ibid. p. 205

87   The Muir poems are from *Collected Poems 1921–1958*, Faber: London 1960

88   Edwin Muir, *Scott and Scotland*, Routledge: London 1936, p. 178

89   Edwin Muir, *An Autobiography*, p. 49
90   Ibid. p. 49
91   Ibid. p. 207
92   *Penguin Modern Poets 17: David Gascoyne, W. S. Graham, Kathleen Raine*, Penguin: Harmondsworth 1970
93   Letter, 23 June 1979
94   George Bruce, *Collected Poems*, Edinburgh University Press: Edinburgh 1970, p. 119
95   Bruce's poems are taken from the above volume
96   Maurice Lindsay (ed.), *As I Remember*, Robert Hale: London 1979, p. 29
97   Ibid. p. 26
98   Interview with George Bruce, Radio Scotland, 14 January 1979
99   In conversation he rejects the romantic notion of inspiration and claims to throw away unsatisfactory poems rather than rework them.
100 Letter, 18 Feb. 1979
101 Hugh MacDiarmid, *The Company I've Kept*, p. 235
102 The MacCaig poems are from *Old Maps and New*, Hogarth Press: London 1978 and *The Equal Skies*, Chatto and Windus: London 1980
103 Hugh MacDiarmid, *The Company I've Kept*, p. 235
104 Fraser's poems were posthumously collected in *Poems*, Leicester University Press: Leicester 1981
105 Graham's poems appear in *Penguin Modern Poets 17* (see note 92), and *Malcolm Mooney's Land*, Faber: London 1970
106 Lindsay's poems appear in *Collected Poems*, Paul Harris: Edinburgh 1979
107 Hamish Henderson, *Elegies for the Dead in Cyrenaica*, Lehmann: London 1948
108 Alasdair Maclean, *Waking the Dead*, Gollancz: London 1976
109 Morgan's poems appear in *The Second Life*, Edinburgh University Press: Edinburgh 1968; and in the selections included in *Penguin Modern Poets 15* (1969) and Geoffrey Summerfield (ed.), *Worlds* Penguin: Harmondsworth 1974
110 Alan Riddell, *Eclipse*, Calder and Boyars: London 1972
111 Ian Hamilton Finlay, *Poems to Hear and Sea*, Macmillan: New York 1971
112 Ian Hamilton Finlay, *Nature Over Again After Poussin*, University of Strathclyde: Glasgow n.d., p. 22
113 George Mackay Brown, *Greenvoe*, Hogarth Press: London 1972, Penguin edn, p. 15
114 George Mackay Brown, *Fishermen With Ploughs*, The Hogarth Press: London 1971 and *Poems, New and Selected*, The Hogarth Press: London 1971
115 Iain Crichton Smith, *Selected Poems*, Gollancz: London 1970
116 Letter, 6 May 1979
117 Maurice Lindsay (ed.), *As I Remember*, p. 118–19
118 Letter, 6 May 1979
119 Hugh MacDiarmid, *The Company I've Kept*, p. 217
120 Anne Cluysenaar (ed.), *Burns Singer: Selected Poems*, Carcanet: Manchester 1977, p xxi and text
121 Tom Buchan, *Dolphins at Cochin*, Barrie and Jenkins: London 1969

122 Alan Jackson, *The Grim Wayfarer*, Fulcrum: London 1969
123 George Macbeth, *Collected Poems 1958–1970*, Macmillan: London 1971 and *Poems of Love and Death*, Secker and Warburg: London 1981
124 The selection of David Black's poems in *Penguin Modern Poets 11: D. M. Black, Peter Redgrove, D. M. Thomas* Penguin: Harmondsworth 1968
125 Robin Fulton, *Selected Poems 1963–1978*, Macdonald: Edinburgh 1981
126 Douglas Dunn, *Barbarians*, Faber: London 1979 and *St Kilda's Parliament*, Faber: London 1981
127 Liz Lochhead, *The Grimm Sisters*, Next Editions: London 1981
128 Walter Perrie, *A Lamentation for the Children*, Canongate: Edinburgh 1977 and *By Moon And Sun*, Canongate: Edinburgh 1971
129 Sorley Maclean, *Poems to Eimhir*, (trans. Iain Crichton Smith) Northern House: Newcastle 1971, p. 11
130 Letter, 19 June 1979
131 Sorley Maclean, *Spring Tide and Neap Tide: Selected Poems 1932–72*, Canongate: Edinburgh 1977

Part Two

FICTION

14. THE PERSISTENCE OF THE PAST

Scottish fiction in the twentieth century has been stylistically conservative and thematically consistent. It has limits rather than limitations and has observed various literary rules; there has been no Scottish *Ulysses* and no general dissatisfaction with the traditional pattern of the novel as a story fleshed out with characters who struggle heroically towards a clearly defined conclusion. Some of the rules were laid down by Sir Walter Scott. Although his posthumous deification by the Victorians harmed his reputation as a serious writer, it was the Laird of Abbotsford who first realised the possibilities of fiction firmly set in a Scottish context. The publication of *Waverley* in 1814 was the beginning of a new career for Scott who had previously built up a considerable market for his narrative poetry before Byron came on the scene. Scott first invented, then perfected, the historical novel. He evoked the past so vividly that readers felt they were actually participating in historical events. To Scott (and lesser Scots) the past was a meaningful experience, not an escapist fantasy or a Gothic extravaganza. Scottish history – with its broken men, crushed ideals, and lovingly remembered defeats – was the stuff which Scottish dreams and nightmares dotes on. The Scots loved to dwell on the past and fiction gave a form to the habit of searching yesterday for the meaning of today. Since Scott, the Scottish novel has tended to expand within an historical matrix.

Scott's main theme was the persistence of the past; his style hovered between literary and oral modes. There was always a distinction between refined English writing and rough-and-ready Scots speech. David Hume worked hard to eradicate from his prose the presence of Scottish mannerisms; Scott used the linguistic conflict to sustain creative tension and to vary the texture of his texts. In 1824 Scott published *Redgauntlet*, probably his most subtle and deeply felt novel. The characterisation is rich, the narrative methods ranging from the epistolary to the third-personal. In Letter XI from Darsie Latimer to Alan Fairford, Scott includes the vernacular *tour de force* 'Wandering Willie's Tale'. This chilling episode is drawn from Scott's immense knowledge of the oral tradition and represents a living tradition of spoken Scots:

> Men thought [Sir Robert Redgauntlet] had a direct compact with Satan – that he was proof against steel – and that bullets happed aff his buff-coat like hailstanes from a hearth – that he had a mear that would turn a hare on the side of Carrifra-gawns – and muckle to the same purpose, of whilk mair anon. The best blessing they wared on him was, 'Deil scowp wi' Redgauntlet!'*

*There are no page references for classics available in a number of editions.

That is conspicuously Scottish: the language turns on a knowledge of the supernatural and a familiarity with the devil. Scott's world-wide success as a novelist demonstrated what Burns's poetry had already shown, namely that a Scottish writer could appeal to an international audience by using Scots albeit, in Scott's case, in moderation. Since then Scottish writers have been able to follow Scott's example by using literary English for their narrative and simulating oral Scots for dialogue. Stylistically this encourages contrast and counterpoint; a paradoxical prose, an antithetical imagery. Fiction haunted by history and constantly aware of linguistic division becomes distinctively Scottish when it admits an element of unsettled psychology. Then Scottish character is convincingly portrayed as a being agonisingly aware of extreme options. The search for the unity behind the split personality is a familiar fictional odyssey in Scotland. Out of this obsession with internal division Robert Louis Stevenson created a masterpiece, a book that projected the Divided Self (see p. 3) on to the consciousness of the world.

15. STEVENSON AND SCHISM

In publishing his novel *The Strange Case of Dr Jekyll and Mr Hyde* in January 1886, Robert Louis Stevenson unleashed on the world the classic image of the divided personality, a being torn between extremes. Stevenson apparently conceived the novel in a dream and transcribed it rapidly because he needed money. Financial pressure must have concentrated his mind wonderfully for the finished product (the result of revisions suggested by his wife, Fanny Osbourne) is both psychologically penetrating and aesthetically satisfying. Scottish people had long been internally divided before Stevenson classified the Jekyll and Hyde syndrome; after 1886 they had a clear artistic image of a national pathological condition. Although Stevenson's novel is ostensibly set in London there can be little doubt that it recreates Victorian Edinburgh. A consummate artist, Stevenson shifted capitals in order to gain some objectivity. The novel remains an expert diagnosis of the Scottish character by a writer who had experienced two aspects of life in his native Edinburgh. G. K. Chesterton, writing in 1927, understood how Scottish *Jekyll* was:

> it seems to me that the story of Jekyll and Hyde, which is presumably presented as happening in London, is all the time very unmistakably happening in Edinburgh . . . Mr Hyde indeed possesses the cosmopolitan charm that unites all nations; but there is something decidedly Caledonian

about Dr Jekyll; and especially something that calls up that quality in
Edinburgh that led an unkind observer (probably from Glasgow) to
describe it as 'an easy-windy, west-endy place'.[1]

To Scott's history-drenched themes, Stevenson added some
perennially relevant Scottish topics: the divided personality, the
concept of childhood as an idyll, the constant conflict between
father as domestic tyrant and son (or, in abstract terms, between authority and imagination). Life was never equal to Stevenson's imagination and he remained essentially a product of an infirm childhood enlivened by the vicarious delights of Skelt's model theatre
and the strange stories told him by his nurse Cummy (Alison Cun-
ningham). In Edinburgh he lived two lives: in his father's house he
subscribed, reluctantly, to the Victorian notion of filial duty; in the
streets of Edinburgh he cultivated the company of prostitutes and
relished the bohemian life. The proximity of good and evil fascinated him and in 1878 he began to collaborate with W. E. Henley on
a play about Deacon Brodie, the Edinburgh cabinet-maker whose
nocturnal activities scandalised Edinburgh. Muriel Spark's Jean
Brodie gives a good account of the Deacon:

> I am a descendent, do not forget, of Willie Brodie, a man of substance, a
> cabinet maker and designer of gibbets, a member of the Town Council of
> Edinburgh and a keeper of two mistresses who bore him five children
> between them. Blood tells. He played much dice and fighting cocks.
> Eventually he was a wanted man for having robbed the Excise Office –
> not that he needed the money, he was a night burglar only for the sake
> of the danger in it. Of course, he was arrested abroad and was brought
> back to the Tolbooth prison, but that was mere chance. He died cheer-
> fully on a gibbet of his own devising in seventeen-eighty-eight. However
> all this may be, it is the stuff I am made of . . .[2]

Every Scot has day and night in his makeup, the result of a history
soaked in bloody divisions. Stevenson wanted to give this theme
artistic embodiment. The Stevenson/Henley play about Deacon
Brodie flopped in Britain and America but Stevenson surely remembered the character when he dreamed up Dr Jekyll and Mr Hyde.

What is so Scottish about the novel is the familiarity with hypoc-
risy, the pretence that there is no moral middle ground but a world
populated by men who are either absolutely good or absolutely evil.
Another ingeniously indigenous touch is the means by which Dr
Jekyll achieves his monstrous metamorphosis. The doctor is given to
strong drink and this is the conventional means of releasing the dark
side of the Scottish character: his potion makes him 'conscious of a
heady recklessness'. The most brilliant part of the novel is contained
in the final section, purporting to be 'Henry Jekyll's Full Statement
of the Case'. Here, in Jekyll's own words, is the moral predicament
of the Scotsman:

I concealed my pleasures . . . I stood already committed to a profound duplicity of life. Many a man would have even blazoned such irregularities as I was guilty of; but from the high views that I had set before me, I regarded and hid them with an almost morbid sense of shame . . . Though so profound a double-dealer, I was in no sense a hypocrite; both sides of me were in dead earnest . . . man is not truly one, but truly two . . . It was on the moral side, and in my own person, that I learned to recognize the thorough and primitive duality of man; I saw that, of the two natures that contended in the field of my consciousness, even if I could rightly be said to be either, it was only because I was radically both.

As a novelist Stevenson was especially adept at delineating personality; at getting inside his characters. He shows us Scottish characters stricken by conscience, vitiated by guilt, agonising over morality. His characters are much more introverted than Scott's; they were aware of the subjective nature of man-made ethical codes. Scott could recreate period detail brilliantly and his novels judge men by their actions. Stevenson introduced an element of ambiguity. His readers are encouraged to speculate, to doubt. In Stevenson's world there is no clear distinction between haloed heroes and diabolical villains. Human nature is as complex as it is cunning and the reader is confronted by this reality. Stevenson is a student of morality; this is true of all the important Scottish novelists who have followed him.

In *Weir of Hermiston* (1896), his unfinished novel, Stevenson's prose is at his most polished. Aesthetically, the performance is assured. In this fiery father-versus-son novel Stevenson sounded yet another leitmotif in Scottish fiction: the assault on established authority. The tense relationship between the rigidly dogmatic Hermiston and his more imaginative son is, on an allegorical level, the story of Scotland with patriarchal arrogance in opposition to the idealism of youth. 'Hanging' Hermiston's fallibility, his grim determination to appear more ruthless than he actually is, his domestic tyranny – these factors make him a symbol of prejudice. His wife (whose 'philosophy of life was summed up in one expression – tenderness') represents the feminine principle of tenderness. Archie – impressionable Archie – is far from heroic but stands for a Scotland struggling to be free of unthinking obedience to a viciously retributive morality. Stevenson was seeking to define a principle of natural justice, to substitute emotional flexibility for dogmatic morality. Consider Archie's outburst to Glenalmond:

I do not love my father; I wonder sometimes if I do hate him.
There's my shame; perhaps my sin; at least, and in the sight of God, not my fault. How was I to love him? He has never spoken to me, never smiled upon me; I do not think he ever touched me.

The sons of John Gourlay (*The House With the Green Shutters*) and

Gillespie Strang (*Gillespie*) might have reiterated the sentiment for they are of the same lineage as Archie. The Victorian reliance on God-the-Father was a barrier Stevenson always wanted to break down. He questioned authority for authority's sake and thus remains a fascinating novelist who suggested a clearly valid direction for Scottish novelists. At the end of the nineteenth century, however, his influence was overshadowed by a triumvirate who reduced Scotland to the size of a kailyard or cabbage patch. They were not so much an alternative tradition as a collective aberration; at least that is how serious Scottish novelists came to regard them. In order to establish worthwhile creative credentials the Scottish novelist felt obliged to denounce the kailyarders. To the serious writer the novel was an edifying art form; to the kailyarder it was a convenient package that could be stuffed with entertaining bits and pieces.

16. THE CONFINES OF THE KAILYARD: BARRIE AND COMPANY

Stevenson died on 3 December 1894 and with his death Scottish fiction went into a temporary decline. Kailyardism had come in Stevenson's lifetime: Barrie's *Auld Licht Idylls* appeared shortly after *Jekyll* and the most influential works of the kailyard genre pre-dated the publication of *Weir of Hermiston*. Stevenson actively encouraged Barrie and Crockett; indeed, he considered Barrie to be a genius (which arguably he was, though more of the commercial than the artistic variety.) Kailyardism had a ready market and went from success to success. Barrie's tales of Thrums caught on with the public and Crockett was able to give up the ministry thanks to the income from his writing. Maclaren's *Beside the Bonnie Brier Bush* (1894) was a bestseller that quickly went through a quarter of a million copies in the UK and half a million in the USA. So we should be wary of categorising the kailyarders as sentimental fools; they were men who had a shrewd judgement of the public taste and the public responded by adoring the intellectually undemanding entertainment the kailyarders produced.

Unlike Stevenson, the kailyarders were sure of their morals, mindful of their artistic manners, and certain they had God on their side. They were presbyterians who smiled benevolently on the parish. They operated within a theological ambiance and had a platform once. The Rev. Will Robertson Nicoll founded and published (on 5 November 1886) the first number of the *British Weekly*. Nicoll, a Free Church man, encouraged Barrie and discovered Ian Maclaren. Little wonder he encouraged the kailyarders for this was a literary movement that adhered to the theological doctrines of the Free Church. Barrie was brought up in the Free Church; S. R. Crockett and Ian Maclaren (the pseudonym of John Watson) were both Free Church ministers. A consequence of the Disruption of 1843, the Free Church stood for presbyterian fundamentalism and a rejection of state interference; the kailyard novelists put their faith in God and pinned their fortune on God's chosen. Kailyardism was not only a sentimental outpouring that travestied Scottish life; it was a type of writing guaranteed to bring monetary rewards to those who stuck to the rules. Kailyard fiction portrayed 'life as seen through the windows of the Free Kirk manse'[3]; from this viewpoint Scottish characters were always quaint, the way Scots spoke was comical, the situations Scots found themselves in were coy.

The use of the word kailyard to denote a whimsical style of writing was initially the work of J. H. Millar in an article in W. E. Henley's *New Review* of 1895. Millar wrote that Barrie 'is fairly entitled to look upon himself as *pars magna* if not *pars maxima* of the kailyard movement'.[4] Henley, with editorial expertise, gave the article the title 'Literature of Kailyard'. Of course, by 1895 the genre cried out for a name to identify it. It had been launched by Barrie with his two volumes of Thrums stories – *Auld Licht Idylls* and *A Window in Thrums* (1889) – and his first novel, *The Little Minister* (1819). Barrie's clerical novel had been imitated in S. R. Crockett's *The Stickit Minister* (1893) and 1894 deserves to be remembered as the supreme moment of kailyardism with the publication of Crockett's *The Lilac Sunbonnet* and Ian Maclaren's *Beside the Bonnie Brier Bush*. Maclaren prefaced his collection of prose sketches with lines from a traditional song reworked by Burns for James Johnson's *Musical Museum*:

> There grows a bonnie brier bush in our kail-yard,
> And white are the blossoms on't in our kail-yard.

It is interesting to speculate what different connotations would have been attached to the word 'kailyard' had Maclaren chosen the bawdy variant that was in oral circulation in his time:

> There is a thorn bush in oor kail-yard,
> There is a thorn in oor kail-yard,
> At the back of thorn bush there stands a lad and lass
> But they're busy, busy hairin' at the cuckoo's nest.

Ironically, too, the location of the best-known Scottish bawdy song is Kirriemuir where Barrie was born and which he fictionalised as Thrums.

What Barrie, Crockett and Maclaren had in common was a theological attitude to life and a facility for writing light prose. They did not dictate the course of Scottish fiction but they amounted to an example that subsequent Scottish writers deplored. George Blake, author of *The Shipbuilders* (1935), looked back in considerable anger to the kailyarders:

> a small group of sentimental, if gifted, Scots gratified Victorian sentimentality by representing the real life of their country in terms that were quite hopelessly out of date for all practical purposes . . . They were perhaps victims of the chronic Scots disease of nostalgia, of the urge to escape back into the comprehensible conditions of their original, independent state and away from the new, incomprehensible turmoils of the industrial age. It is above all significant that the successful practitioners were mostly ordained ministers of one of the numerous Scottish churches – the Free Church – and that the one who was not, James Matthew Barrie, adhered to the Free Church and dealt largely in scenes from clerical life.[5]

Barrie was certainly the biggest cabbage in the kailyard. His ability to assess and exploit the public taste is as celebrated as his emotional immaturity; yet his sentimentality was sincere, and while he was occasionally an acutely embarrassing example of a Scotsman on the make he was also capable of great kindness. The hero of Barrie's *Sentimental Tommy* (1896) not only justifies the titular epithet but is confirmed in his longings by no less an authority than Sir Walter Scott:

> *Waverley* revealed to him that he was born neither for the ministry nor the herding, but to restore to his country its rightful king. The first to whom he confided this was Corp, who immediately exclaimed: 'Michty me! But what will the police say?'
> 'I ken a wy,' answered Tommy, sternly.[6]

The boyish sense of adventure and the comic Scots are typical of Barrie in his kailyard period. The style reminds us that kailyardism did not entirely die out: it continued to assert its principles in the comic-strips ('Oor Wullie' and 'The Broons') contributed by Dudley D. Watkins to the presbyterian newspaper *The Sunday Post*.

Barrie had a narrative gift that was quite exceptional and what he lacked in artistic integrity he compensated for in sheer fluency. He is the man who might have carried on the tradition created by Scott and confirmed by Stevenson and doubtless he imagined he was doing just that. Barrie's greatest fictional triumph came, in fact, towards the end of his life. It was a short story, not a novel. Still, the Scottish short story is the Scottish novel writ small; the Scottish short story reflects the Scottish love of gossip and is often cast in an oral mould. Because of this the Scots language features strongly and there is a stylistic link between three of the finest Scottish short stories: Scott's 'Wandering Willie's Tale', Stevenson's 'Thrawn Janet' (1882) and Barrie's 'Farewell, Miss Julie Logan'. After the drowning of Barrie's adopted son Michael Llewellyn Davies in 1921 Barrie preserved a literary silence. This was broken in 1931 when 'Farewell, Miss Julie Logan' was offered as the only fiction supplement ever issued by *The Times*. The story brings back the Jacobites beloved by Scott and Sentimental Tommy and disliked by the Rev. Adam Yestreen who narrates this tale. The glen is locked and haunted by Strangers (ghostly rebels from the 1745 uprising) and a Spectrum. Adam Yestreen meets the Spectrum and falls in love with Miss Logan (both developments amounting to the same thing); and drops Miss Logan when she admits to being a Papist. Twenty-five years later Yestreen returns to the scene of his folly and broods on the significance of it all. The mood is superbly sustained and the use of Scots conveys the sardonic nature of Yestreen:

> there is a hantle of small farms in the glen, forbye shepherds' sheilings and bothies, and an occasional roadside bigging of clay and divot in which may be man or beast; truly, when I chap I am sometimes doubtful which will come to the door.[7]

Barrie could write with subtlety and linguistic sensitivity when he wanted to; usually he simply trusted in his own spontaneous outpourings. 'Farewell, Miss Julie Logan' is a finely crafted story, the work of a delicate artist. It suggests that Barrie could have researched the Scottish psyche instead of profitably trivialising it. It was this tendency to opt out of artistic responsibilities that made the kailyarders an object of scorn.

17. *GREEN SHUTTERS*: THE NEW HOUSE OF SCOTTISH FICTION

Millar's attack of 1895 did not destroy the credibility of the kailyarders for the public continued to consume their books. What Millar did so effectively was to identify the enemy for a new generation of Scottish novelists. Young men who regarded literature as a vocation held the names of Maclaren, Crockett and Barrie in contempt and were determined to oppose their methods. Where the kailyarders portrayed sweetness and light the new novelists painted a picture, complete with dramatic (and sometimes melodramatic) chiaroscuro, of malice and gloom. First, and supreme, among the new novelists was George Douglas Brown (1869–1902). Chronologically and thematically twentieth century Scottish fiction begins with Brown's *The House with the Green Shutters*. (1901). It is not revolutionary in manner but rather a return to the exploratory style used by Stevenson in *Weir of Hermiston*; it is seemingly revolutionary in matter only when considered in a Scottish context where the ambitions of the novelist had been reduced to the confines of the kailyard. In retrospect James Bridie saw the movement away from kailyardism as an inevitable swing of the pendulum:

The Kailyard School appears. Another school reacts from it and, if I
call it the Midden School, I hope you will misunderstand me. A Midden
is necessary if we are to have growth. These writers enriched our soil. Its
gentle origin is seen here in George Douglas Brown's *House with the
Green Shutters*, and it has grown to formidable proportions . . .[8]

George Douglas Brown was born in Ochiltree, Ayrshire, the illegitimate son of a farmer and an illiterate dairy worker, Sarah Gemmell.
Brown was named after his father, who was known around Ochiltree as 'Smudden' (after his farm Drumsmudden) and as a child
young George had to endure unbearably malicious gossip:

He heard rough-tongued men refer to him as 'Smudden's bastard', and
there was no doubt what the hateful term implied. Because his mother
was unmarried, he was not the same as other children. And when he saw
Smudden driving through Coylton [where Brown went to school]', his
face clouded. In his deep, secretive manner, he hated the small, dark
man, hated him for being his father and yet for not being his father.[9]

Brown left Coylton parish school to work as a pithead boy at Tar-
bolton. However, his old teacher from Coylton, impressed by the
brilliance of the boy, got him a place at Ayr Academy where he was
taken under the wing of the rector, William Maybin, an enthusiastic
classicist. At Glasgow University, Brown took a First in Classics,
won the Eglinton Fellowship of £100 per year, then won in 1891 the
Snell Exhibition Scholarship which – at £130 for three years – took
him to Balliol College, Oxford. At Oxford he fretted about the
health of his mother (she died in 1895 from heart failure) and his
loss of interest in academic studies was reflected in the Third he received at Oxford. In London he struggled to make a living from
literary hackwork; eventually he went to a cottage in Haslemere, Surrey, to write the novel that had obsessed him since he first conceived
of it as a long short story.

Before approaching Brown's novel direct it is instructive to imagine its impact on a country conditioned by kailyardism to accept a
caricature of itself. We can do this by comparing Brown's realistic
classic with a kailyard classic. In the opening sketch of *Beside the
Bonnie Brier Bush*, 'Domsie', we are introduced to the precocious
prizewinning scholar George Howe who goes to university, sweeps
the scholastic board, and returns home to meet his maker philosophically:

When George came home for the last time, Marget went back and
forward all afternoon from his bedroom to the window, and hid herself
beneath the laburnum to see his face as the cart stood before the stile. It
told her plain what she had feared, and Marget passed through her
Gethsemane with the gold blossoms falling on her face. When their eyes
met, and before she helped him down, mother and son understood.

'Ye mind what I told ye, o' the Greek mothers, the day I left. Weel, I
wud hae liked to have carried my shield, but it wasna to be, so I've come

home on it.' As they went slowly up the garden walk, 'I've got my degree, a double first, mathematics and classics.'

'Ye've been a gude soldier, George, and faithfu'.'

'Unto death, a'm dootin, mother.'

'Na,' said Marget, 'unto life.'

Drumtochty was not a heartening place in sickness, and Marget, who did not think our thoughts, endured much consolation at her neighbours' hands . . . When I found George wrapped in his plaid beside the brier bush whose roses were no whiter than his cheeks, Kirsty [Stewart] was already installed as comforter in the parlour, and her drone came through the open window.[10]

In *The House with the Green Shutters* we meet a very different type of scholar; not a saint but a very Scottish sinner. Brown's insight into human nature, especially human nature of a Scottish kind, is authentic and impressive:

With his second year [Young Gourlay] began the study of philosophy, and that added to his woes. He had nerves to feel the Big Conundrum, but not the brains to solve it – small blame to him for that since philosophers have cursed each other black in the face over it for the last five thousand years. But it worried him. The strange and sinister detail of the world, that had always been a horror to his mind, became more horrible, beneath the stimulus of futile thought. But whiskey was the nightly cure . . . with whiskey humming in his blood, he paced onward in a happy dream. The wretched puddles by the way, the frowning rookeries where misery squalled, the melancholy noises of the street, were passed unheeded by. His distracted powers rallied home; he was concentrate, his own man again, the hero of his musing mind. For, like all weak men of a vivid fancy, he was constantly framing dramas of which he was the towering lord . . . As he walked in a tipsy dream, he was 'standing up' to somebody, hurling his father's phrases at him, making short work of *him*! If imagination paled, the nearest tavern supplied a remedy, and flushed it to a radiant glow. Whereupon he had become the master of his world, and not its slave.[11]

Brown's concept of literary style was formed by his study of Classics; his enthusiasm for European literature convinced him that the function of the novelist was to present to the public the results of a deep research into life. No details, however unpleasant, were to be hidden. In the first instance Brown was undoubtedly activated by a desire to erase kailyardism from Scotland. On 24 October 1901 he wrote to his friend Ernest Barker:

Well, I suppose you have read the *Green Shutters* by this time. 'Tis a brutal and bloody work; too sinister, I should think, for a man of your kindlier disposition. There is too much black for the white in it. Even so it is more complimentary to Scotland, I think, than the sentimental slop of Barrie, and Crockett, and Maclaren. It was antagonism to their method that made me embitter the blackness; like Old Gourlay I was going to 'show the dogs what I thought of them.' Which was a gross blunder, of course. A novelist should never have an axe of his own to grind. If he allows a personal animus to obtrude ever so slightly it knocks his work out of balance. He should be an aloof individual, if possible, stating all sides and taking none.[12]

Brown does himself an injustice here for if the anti-kailyard impetus provided the anger that sustained him, his own talent supplied enough formal strength to contain that anger. In a positive way Brown wanted to give a classical perfection of form to the Scottish novel. He succeeded in doing so in *The House with the Green Shutters* but his death, the year after its publication, deprived Scotland of a great novelist. (It is worth noting that Scottish fiction has had its unfair share of – to borrow Wordsworth's phrase for Chatterton – marvellous boys that perished in their pride, for Stevenson died at the age of forty-four and both George Douglas Brown and Lewis Grassic Gibbon died at the age of thirty-three.) Brown may have gone on to produce a whole series of great novels. When he died he was contemplating a new novel, apparently a Cromwellian romance. He may have felt the need to move outside of Scotland for his next theme; we simply do not know.

The House with the Green Shutters is the work of a careful, self-conscious stylist. There had been nothing quite as structurally shapely as it in previous Scottish fiction. The whole book is contained within a parabola described by the rise and fall of the House of Gourlay. Brown makes sure this shaping principle will not be lost on the reader. He begins the novel with the description of a liquid arch:

> The frowsy chamber-maid of the 'Red Lion' had just finished washing the front door steps. She rose from her stooping posture, and, being of slovenly habit, flung the water from her pail, straight out, without moving from where she stood. The smooth round arch of the falling water glistened for a moment in mid-air. John Gourlay, standing in front of his new house at the head of the brae, could hear the swash of it when it fell. The morning was of perfect stillness.[13]

Ezra Pound thought that great literature was 'simply language charged with meaning to the utmost possible degree'.[14] Brown's opening paragraph therefore qualifies as great literature. It contains the seed of the whole story that is about to unfold – the rise and fall of the arch symbolising the rise and fall of the House of Gourlay, the unlovely nature of Barbie's inhabitants ('frowsy . . . stooping . . .') as represented by the chamber-maid, the image of Gourlay standing in front of his imposing new house, the bustling reality behind the rural idyll.

The arch image is crucial so, at the end of the novel, when the psychological and physical House of Gourlay has collapsed, Brown returns to it:

Their loins were loosed beneath them. The scrape of their feet on the road, as they turned to stare, sounded monstrous in the silence. No man dared to speak. They gazed with blanched faces at the House with the Green Shutters, sitting dark there and terrible, beneath the radiant arch of the dawn.[15]

Pride comes before a fall, or as Brown paraphrases it in his novel 'Pride *will* have a downcome'[16]: that gloating piece of folkwisdom is at the heart of *Green Shutters*. Brown had suffered from malicious gossip in his own life and had formed a bitter impression of Scottish smalltown life. Scots, according to Brown's experience, were motivated by malice: they resented any man who surpassed the situation he inherited. Such a man would, thanks to the workings of a Calvinist God, get his just desserts. A humble man was a Godfearing man; an overbearing man was diabolical. John Gourlay was proud and unbearably overbearing so, to the locals of Barbie (Brown's fictional recreation of Ochiltree), was simply tempting fate. The Greeks had a word for it – *hubris* – and it was to the Greek model that Brown went for his bleak study of a Scottish tragedy. Gourlay's *hubris* invites disaster but he is also destroyed by the bodies; the malicious gossips who comment on his character, proleptically gloat over his downfall, and contribute to the inevitable catastrophe. In elevating a group of Scottish gossips to the status of a Greek chorus, Brown made use of his classical training. In his 'Rules for Writing', collected at the end of 1901 and intended to form the basis of a theoretical treatise, he discussed

The value of The Chorus. (1) It gives the moral environment. (2) In its composite character it is an actor contributing to the final results. The gossips in *The House with the Green Shutters* act directly on the two Gourlays. (3) It adds a convincing reality to the central characters . . . (4) To shew the mind of an essential character through the mind of a secondary character.[17]

Brown thought deeply, then, about the structural possibilities of the novel; the finished product demonstrates more architectonic power than any Scottish novel of comparable length. Brown did not see himself in the restricted role of storyteller but as a man with a visionary grasp of the nature of the novel. He set out, quite deliberataly, to write a masterpiece and succeeded in doing just that. When reduced to a paragraph-length paraphrase *Green Shutters* sounds like a melodrama; Brown's style, however, informs the story with significance and brings out all its subtleties. It is the story of a divided community and, as such, a microcosm of the story of Scotland itself. As we read it on one level the secondary allegorical level attracts our attention.

John Gourlay is the top man in Barbie. The biggest fish in a little pond, for Barbie is only 'a dull little country town'.[18] He revels in his position of power as the only carrier in Barbie and, to emphasise his monopolistic power-base, builds the grandest house in the town. All Gourlay's pride is contained in the house and just as the house looks down on the town so Gourlay looks down on the people:

> At the beginning of a new day to look down on the petty burgh in which he was the greatest man, filled all his being with a consciousness of importance. His sense of prosperity was soothing and pervasive; he felt it all round him like the pleasant air, as real as that and as subtle; bathing him, caressing. It was the most secret and intimate joy of his life to go out and smoke on summer mornings by his big gate, musing over Barbie ere he possessed it with his merchandise.[19]

Gourlay has married into money and has nothing but contempt for his wife; she has fulfilled her monetary function and is of no more use to Gourlay. He is incapable of appreciating human nature as an intrinsically loveable quality but prefers to quantify everything from goods to family. Appalled at Gourlay's hostility, his wife has succumbed to squalor, and this provokes the violence in him. After being bested in a business deal Gourlay returns to witness his wife:

> The sight of the she-tatterdemalion there before him, whom he had endured so long and must endure forever, was the crowning burden of his night. Damn her, why didn't she get out of the way, why did she stand there in her dirt and ask silly questions? He struck her on the bosom with his great fist, and sent her spinning on the dirty table.[20]

Gourlay is not only vindictive he is brutal: the archetypal Scottish hardman who strikes first and asks questions later. There are few in Barbie with the character to confront Gourlay face-to-face for he is physically formidable and temperamentally aggressive. Their vindictive grudge against Gourlay is expressed behind his imposing back. Seeking strength in numbers the malicious gossips of Barbie (the bodies) gather together at the Bend o' the Brae to plan their little strategies. Brown's description of the bodies is deservedly famous because it is so devastatingly accurate:

> In every little Scotch community there is a distinct type known as 'the bodie'. 'What does he do, that man?' you may ask, and the answer will be, 'Really, I could hardly tell ye what he does – he's juist a bodie!' The 'bodie' may be a gentleman of independent means . . . fussing about in spats and light check breeches; or he may be a jobbing gardener; but he is equally a 'bodie'. The chief occupation of his idle hours (and his hours are chiefly idle) is the discussion of his neighbour's affairs. He is generally an 'auld residenter'; great, therefore, at the redding up of pedigrees . . . The genus 'bodie' is divided into two species: the 'harmless bodies' and the 'nesty bodies'. The bodies of Barbie mostly belonged to the second variety . . . Gourlay spoke of them as a 'wheen damned auld wives'. But Gourlay, to be sure, was not an impartial witness.[21]

Green Shutters is a book fired by conflict just as Barbie is pola-rised between the forces represented by, respectively, Gourlay and James Wilson – the molecatcher's son whose business acumen breaks Gourlay's monopolistic control of the carrying trade, and initiates his financial ruin. The eponymous House is at once a realistic edifice and a symbol with biblical overtones for 'if a house be divided against itself, that house cannot stand'.[22] Moreover, in Gothic man-ner, there is a curse on the House of Gourlay:

> And so, gradually, his dwelling had come to be a passion of Gourlay's life. It was a by-word in the place that if ever his ghost was seen, it would be haunting the House with the Green Shutters. Deacon Allardye, trying to make a phrase with him, once quoted the saying in his presence. 'Likely enough!' said Gourlay. 'It's only reasonable I should prefer my own house to you rabble in the graveyard!'[23]

Gourlay, as Brown makes perfectly clear, is a man who lusts after possessions for the power they convey on the possessor. Having attained the heights of personal success, Gourlay falls because of his inherently petty nature (which links him with the bodies he de-spises) and his soul-destroying environment. His ambition stops at the frontiers of Barbie. For all that he is a more impressive man than the bodies and his tragedy is the tragedy of the Scotsman brought down by a history of acquired inferiority:

> Even if Gourlay had been a placable and inoffensive man, then, the malignants of the petty burgh (it was scarce bigger than a village) would have fastened on his character, simply because he was above them. No man has a keener eye for behaviour than the Scot (especially when spite wings his intuition), and Gourlay's thickness of wit, and pride of place, would in any case have drawn their sneers . . . his repressiveness added a hundred-fold to their hate of him. That was the particular cause, which acting on their general tendency to belittle a too-successful rival, made their spite almost monstrous against him.[24]

Gourlay, always obsessive about his possessions, begins to act hysterically from a desire to get the better of Wilson: 'Wilson and Gourlay were a pair of gladiators for whom the people of Barbie made a ring'[25]. Events, like the coming of the railway to Barbie, overtake Gourlay and he has to compensate by vicarious triumphs. Because Wilson sends his son to the High School of Skeighan, Gourlay does likewise; because Wilson's son goes to university Young John Gourlay is sent to study for the ministry. Surprisingly enough, Young Gourlay begins auspiciously by winning the Raeburn essay-prize, much thought of in Barbie. Unfortunately Young Gourlay has inherited all his father's arrogance without any of his father's strength of character; he begins to indulge his alco-holic impulses and act accordingly. Eventually he is expelled from university for insulting a lecturer and this is not only an insult to the

Gourlay name but an injury to the House of Gourlay. Gourlay himself, owing interest on a mortgage and unable to get a loan, takes his wrath out on his son:

> He had a triple wrath to his son. He had not only ruined his own life, he had destroyed his father's hope that by entering the ministry he might restore the Gourlay reputation. Above all he had disgraced the House with the Green Shutters. That was the crown of his offending. Gourlay felt for the house of his pride even more than for himself – rather the house was himself; there was no division between them. He had built it bluff to represent him to the world. It was his character in stone and lime. He clung to it, as the dull, fierce mind, unable to live in thought, clings to a material source of pride. And John had disgraced it. Even if fortune took a turn for the better, Green Shutters would be laughed at the country over, as the home of a prodigal.[26]

That passage demonstrates the limitations of Gourlay's life; the bodies are the mirror he looks to for approval.

When Gourlay comes to deal with his son his attitude is diabolical and he stands as the absolute and hideous image of the authoritarian Scottish patriarch, the Calvinist God of vengeance on earth. Brown describes this with acute psychological penetration in one of the most powerful passages in a powerful book:

> [Gourlay] meant to sweat punishment out of [Young John Gourlay] drop by drop, with slow and vicious enjoyment . . . To bring a beaten and degraded look into a man's face, rend manhood out of him in fear, is a sight that makes decent men wince in pain; for it is an outrage on the decency of life, an offence to natural religion, a violation of the human sanctities. Yet Gourlay had done it once and again. I saw him 'down' a man at the Cross once, a big man with a viking beard . . . Gourlay, with stabbing eyes, threatened, and birred, and 'downed' him, till he crept away with a face like chalk, and a hunted, furtive eye . . . To break a man's spirit so, take that from him which he will never recover while he lives, send him slinking away *animo castrato* – for that is what it comes to – is a sinister outrage of the world. It is as bad as the rape of a woman, and ranks with the sin against the Holy Ghost – derives from it, indeed. Yet it was this outrage that Gourlay meant to work upon his son. He would work him down and down, this son of his, till he was less than a man, a frightened, furtive animal. Then, perhaps, he would give a loose to his other rage, unbuckle his belt, and thrash the grown man like a wriggling urchin on the floor.[27]

Gourlay, we see plainly, is a tyrant; a vicious domestic tyrant at that. Brown, who normally keeps a respectful distance from his material, invades that passage with personal opinions and its fervency suggests it harks back to his own experience as a figure of fun in Ochiltree.

Eventually the worm turns and, in front of his mother and sister, Young John Gourlay murders his father. This climactic act is conveyed with rare artistic precision and symbolic resonance: the murder weapon has, in previous pages, insinuated its ominous way into the narrative and Gourlay's last gesture is typical of the man as it shows him looking down from the top of a ladder. Brown mixes realistic with melodramatic modes, classical catastrophe with Gothic effect:

> 'By God, I'll kill ye,' screamed John, springing to his feet, with the poker in his hand . . . Mrs Gourlay screamed and tried to rise from her chair, her eyes goggling in terror. As Gourlay leapt, John brought the huge poker with a crash on the descending brow. The fiercest joy of his life was the dirl that went up his arm, as the steel thrilled to its own hard impact on the bone. Gourlay thudded on the fender, his brow crashing on the rim.
>
> As the blow fell there had been a cry as of animals, from the two women. There followed an eternity of silence, it seemed, and a haze about the place, yet not a haze, for everything was intensely clear, only it belonged to another world. One terrible fact had changed the Universe. The air was different now; it was full of murder. Everything in the room had a new significance, a sinister meaning. The effect was that of an unholy spell.[28]

The three remaining Gourlays – mother, son and daughter – attempt to disguise the patricidal catastrophe as an accident but the curse on the House of Gourlay brings its insubstantial presence to bear. Young Gourlay is haunted by the fearsome image of his father and dying of drink; his sister Janet is dying from a lung complaint; and his mother is, as a result of the blow inflicted on her by Gourlay, dying of an abscess of the breast. The three of them have nothing to live for now that Gourlay has gone in dreadful circumstances. Therefore the three of them take their own lives: first Gourlay's son, then his wife, then his daughter take poison. The book ends as the postman spreads the news of the final fall of the House of Gourlay. We can imagine that the bodies will dwell on the events for the rest of their lives.

Thematically Brown's book gathered together all the strands of Scottish realism: it has a domestic tyrant, a downtrodden woman, a drink problem, a group of malicious gossips, an explosive situation, supernatural overtones, and a classical catastrophe. Stylistically it is a model of literary excellence. All the elements are so beautifully integrated into the texture of the book that each new reading reveals different levels. *Green Shutters* was a self-conscious work of art, something Scottish writers could emulate. It was not only an important literary event; it was a precedent acknowledged by succeeding Scottish novelists. *The House with the Green Shutters* is the most seminal novel in modern Scottish literature and its offspring are still appearing.

18.   J. MacDOUGALL HAY: GOURLAY INTO *GILLESPIE*

In a structural sense *Gillespie* is an epic expansion of *The House with the Green Shutters*; J. MacDougall Hay, with his intimate knowledge of the sea, wove wave after wave of variation on a theme announced by George Douglas Brown. J. MacDougall Hay was born on 23 October 1881 in Tarbert, Loch Fyne, Argyllshire; an important biographical detail since Tarbert is featured, under the pseudonym Brieston, as the setting of *Gillespie*. Hay, the son of a steamship agent, was a Scottish lad-o-pairts of the type so beloved by the kailyard novelists. He became a prizewinning scholar (at Glasgow University), worked as a freelance journalist, then became a schoolteacher in Stornoway and Ullapool where he contracted rheumatic fever. He gave up schoolteaching and returned to Glasgow University to study divinity, supporting himself with freelance journalism. After serving time as a probationer in Morven, Argyll, he became as assistant minister in Glasgow, then (in 1909) minister of Elderslie (birthplace of Sir William Wallace). The new minister of Elderslie married Catherine Campbell, a daughter of the manse, and used his evenings for literary work: *Gillespie* was written and re-written three times before it was published in March 1914.

Like Brown, Hay had only a brief literary career. In 1916 he published a second novel, *Barnacles*, and planned a third, *The Martyr*, with a theological background. Towards the end of the First World War he published a volume of free verse poems, *Their Dead Sons*, and in 1919 his sermon of commemoration for the fallen, as preached in Elderslie church, was published at the request of the congregation. On 10 December 1919 Hay died of tuberculosis. He was thirty-eight years old.

Hay was a great admirer of Dostoevsky and there is ample internal evidence to suggest that *Gillespie* was planned as a sprawling psychological fiction on the Russian scale. However, Hay's first debt was to Brown. Hay's son, the poet George Campbell Hay, acquired his father's library and regarded his range of reading as orthodox: 'Burns, Scott, Galt, Stevenson, Brown's *The House with the Green Shutters*'.[29] The emphasis should be on the last name in that list for the tragic, elemental fictional house of *Green Shutters* was revisited – or, rather, re-haunted – in J. MacDougall Hay's novel. It is no disservice to Hay's book to say it derived from Brown's precedent; nor is it an insult to either book to point out that both were motivated by an anti-Kailyard impetus. The motivation of a work of art is of secondary importance to its achievement, yet it is necessary to acknowledge the intellectual matrix in which the work was conceived. An introduction to the latest edition of *Gillespie* dismisses the sug-

gestion that it is 'a sort of adjunct to or variation on George Douglas Brown's *The House with the Green Shutters*'.[30] Adjunct no;
variation yes.

It is crucial to consider this connection as one that does all credit
to Hay. As an ordained minister, like Maclaren and Crockett, he
had the theological qualifications to revitalise the Kailyard movement. In choosing to receive the Scottish realist gospel authorised
by Brown he made sure that *Green Shutters* would not be an isolated
phenomenon but a creative home frequented by Scottish writers.
One book cannot force a tradition; two books can certainly suggest
one. With the publication of *Gillespie* Scotland could see the contours of an exploratory tradition that has accounted for most of the
major successes of modern Scottish fiction.

Any reader of *Gillespie* will be able to see how brilliantly Hay
varied the themes he adapted from Brown: the indignity of the cash-
register creed, the iniquity of patriarchal tyranny, the inequality of
parochial society. As if to acknowledge his debt, Hay made a direct
allusion to *Green Shutters*, which, as we have seen, opens as 'The
smooth round arch of the falling water glistened for a moment in
mid-air'. Hay cherished that moment when he included in his own
book a parallel passage:

> Not a few of the bowed windows in the Back Street give upon the
> Pump, so that Lucky can lean out for a chat with Nan at Jock, the same
> who is Jock Sinclair's wife, while she draws water. Sometimes the
> windows do not serve; great occasions woo them to a closer intimacy at
> the Pump. After this fashion. In the still afternoon there is a curve of
> water in the air. Slap! it takes the quiescent street along its drowsy
> length. This humid scavenging marks one bell. Towsy heads pop out of
> doors and rummage at the windows.[31]

These towsy heads were first attached to the bodies of *Green Shutters*.

As well as the novel influence of Brown, and relating to it, Hay
draws on an earlier mode of Scottish writing. In his critical survey of
The Scottish Novel, Francis Russell Hart sees the beginnings of indigenous Scottish fiction in 'what we might cautiously call the
Gothic tendency'[32]; Hay's novel is full of Gothic surprises. It is
quickly established that there is a curse on the House of Strang for
over the door of the Ghost Inn (and that name alone is full of supernatural significance) hangs a sign full of macabre import:

> Attention, however, was attracted, not to the gables, but to a sign which
> hung over the door. Dimly traced on this heart-shaped sign was the
> half-defaced head of a man, and a hand grasping a dagger. The hand
> stabbed down with sleuth-like malignity. The place had once been an inn
> and of considerable repute; but horror came to nest there in the
> inscrutable way in which it attaches to certain places.[33]

The inn has witnessed a murder and the man who finds the corpse takes to drink and dies insane. No native of the West Highlands would be associated with such a sinister property and it is acquired by an incomer from Ayrshire. This is Gillespie's father, Richard Strang. At the moment of Gillespie Strang's birth the sign reappears like a curse:

> Stunned, [Richard Strang] could answer nothing; and when he was again at the foot of the stair he was listening to a wail which, borne down upon the wind of Time out of an inimical midnight past, and passing beneath the heavens like an arrow of God, struck unerringly into his heart, as he stood listening to the scurry of the wind rasping the rusty dagger overhead. With every swing of the drunken sign the dagger was plunged downwards with a snarl.[34]

Moreover the sign prefigures the ghastly finale of the book. As Gillespie comes back to the Ghost to die (in torment from lockjaw contracted by stepping on his wife's broken whisky bottle) he is confronted by

> A house of no resort; a house of silence, save for the jangling of the sign over the door. A faint smile came over Gillespie's face as he recognised the sign. The smile redeemed his face, for, like the house, his aspect was wizened and gaunt. The old familiar creak over the door wakened the past out of its sleep . . . [35]

At the end of the book, with the house of Strang about to vanish with the imminent death of old Richard Strang, the sign reacts:

> At the sound [of gulls squawking] which, perhaps, stirred some memory of the sea, the glazed eyes of old Mr Strang turned from the ceiling to the window. His wife was dead; dead was his son in the kitchen; dead were his grandchildren; and he, as borne on a tide of sleep, was slipping into the shadows. The sign above the door was at peace in the windless air. Passion and greed, love and dreams, lust and madness, were all vanquished, were all vanished; grief and shame, yearning and hope, were all at rest; faces had faded away; things dissolved; nothing was left but the earth, about to renew life at the hands of another transitory ploughman. With a long, deep sigh old Mr Strang closed his eyes in the House of Ghosts, to meet the everlasting silence, and look into the things of eternal rest. The sunset flamed along the sea and hung out banners in the heavens. It flooded the 'Ghost' with golden light. It shone upon the features of Gillespie, exposed in a ghastly grin. It irradiated the still, white face of old Mr Strang.
> 'Earth to earth, dust to dust,' murmured Mrs Galbraith, as she shook the tears from her eyes. The ploughman on Muirhead Farm went on ploughing the lea, ministering to the faith that is imperishable in the breast of man.[36]

Hay sustains his symbolic curse throughout the book, then, and it is a reminder that Gillespie Strang is not a simple black-hearted villain but a man ruined as much by circumstances as by his insatiable greed. In a better society than Brieston (or, by implication, Tarbert)

Gillespie's immense energies might have been diverted to more humanitarian ends.

Whereas John Gourlay, in *Green Shutters*, suffers from *hubris* another classical concept is introduced to account for Gillespie: 'The profile of nemesis now was turned full face upon him'.[37] Whereas Gourlay's arrogance infuriates the bodies of Barbie, Gillespie is hated for two reasons: first he is ruthless; second, he is an outsider, 'of a Lowland breed. It was not only hardship but shame and dishonour that such an incomer should hold the reins of the town'.[38] Gillespie is not alone in his relentless quest for self-advancement, and we feel the difference between him and the villagers he dominates is one of degree. Had they his formidable drive they might well have done as he did. He hounds the farmer Galbraith to his death by insisting on payment of a debt and he has designs on Mrs Galbraith. When she leaves Muirhead Farm he takes it and marries Morag Gillespie; his wife is sexually demanding and he obliges her with two sons but that is the sum total of his concern for her. Sexually abandoned by Gillespie, Mrs Strang degenerates into alcoholism.

Gillespie's rise to financial supremacy is dramatic. He takes over the fishing business and incurs the wrath of the fishermen by buying their catch and selling at a profit. The mystery of the sea is an omnipresent part of the novel. There is a great climactic scene when three fishermen find a headless body in the sea and spitefully dump it at Gillespie's curing-shed. Gillespie is more than equal to the insult for he sees an eel inside the corpse so that, when the body moves, he, the depised Lowlander, can remain in control of his faculties while the superstitious and supernatural fisherman panic. One of them is drowned and Gillespie is held to be responsible which makes him causally involved in the deaths of three men: Galbraith (the farmer Gillespie hounded to death), Andy (the fisherman Gillespie frightened to death), and, later, Iain (the son Gillespie sent to his death by letting him sail in an inadequate boat). Gillespie survives the headless corpse crisis, though:

> Within a fortnight [of the headless corpse affair] Gillespie was back in Brieston with a steamer. The idea of the steamer was monstrously simple. At the opening of the spring herring season, he meant to buy in her and 'kill the smacks' . . . Gillespie now fawned on every one with a sort of angelic devilry . . . His touch was a cat's with sheathed claw . . . He imagined that in the genial sun of this duplicity Brieston was again warming towards him. He reckoned on the gullibility of the public, and was about to prove his reckoning correct.[39]

In such ways Brieston builds Gillespie up, places him on a pinnacle he is bound to fall from. From the onset of his career his massive greed is fuelled by the little greed of the Brieston folk. Gillespie might disgust his wife (who retaliates by disgracing him) but the locals reluctantly give him his dues and in this light he appears as a more cunning kinsman of Gourlay:

> Few in Brieston fathomed Gillespie. He had had the best of luck. Times were good . . . The substantial beginnings of a fortune in his hands, and the possibilities of its ultimate attainment had sharpened his business faculty to a monstrous degree. There was something hawk-like in the man, as he hovered over the town spying out chances and occasions. He had always been crafty, and had veiled his actions so adroitly in hypocrisy, and was so cordial, even to his enemies, that he was held as a first-rate man.[40]

In making Brieston his world and this tiny world his oyster (literally, for he goes into oyster-catching) Gillespie courts retribution. When things go disastrously wrong he is made to suffer.

Brieston is visited by a plague and the vindictive locals blame this on Gillespie and attack his house and shop. With the enthusiastic support of Mrs Galbraith (widow of the farmer hounded to death by Gillespie) the fishermen burn Gillespie's boats though he recovers from this triumphantly by renting new boats to the men. However, the catastrophe edges closer with every page and it transpires that Gillespie has cheated on a relative, Barbara Strang, who is in love with Gillespie's son, Eoghan. Eoghan, driven to distraction by the deviousness of his father and the decadence of his mother, dies in the bloody set-piece that comprises the catastrophe of the book. Hay was determined to go even further than Brown in presenting a realistic account of violence and the mother-and-son confrontation deserves to be quoted at length:

> 'Oh, Jesus Christ, lead her sorrow and her woe into my breast', he cried. The chimney suddenly belched smoke. Her gloomy face lightened with a fierce expression of joy, and with incredible swiftness she half arose, seized him by the hair, jerked his head back savagely, and drew the glittering blade of the razor across his throat. A tiny artery spurted upon her hand. The hot blood drove her crazy. She tightened her knees upon him as with a vice, and deepened her clutch in his hair. Profound astonishment paralysed him. His head was viciously wrung back again, and in a horrible silence she, with the savage strength of a demoniac, slashed his throat open through the muscles, till the razor scraped on the surface of the bones of the neck. A huge gout of arterial blood spouted on her face, blinding her, and pumped far across the room, splashing on the wall. He glimpsed the stained blade in her hand as, with a superhuman effort, he heaved himself up. The chair toppled; she crashed backwards; the thud of her head on the back of the fender mingled with the brittle sound of the broken whisky bottle. She rolled over on her side, her face smeared with his blood, and in her right hand the dripping razor. Neither had spoken a word.
> Astonishment, incredulity, anger swept rapidly over him, and gave way to deep-seated fear, to horror unspeakable. A dark steady stream poured and poured down his neck and shirt. This is death, he thought: my life is pouring out of me. His body burned and became cold. He

121

clapped his hands to his throat and staggered up on his feet. From the cut windpipe a mound of bloody froth hissed and crackled. He strove to cry out for help. There were bands of light appearing and disappearing before his eyes. He swayed upon his feet, fainting into an enormous region of darkness; crashed down on the floor and lay like dead in a pool of blood. He was aware of a vast terrible silence, which isolated him from humanity. Panic-stricken, he got up again and lurched to the sink, turned on the tap, and attempted to wash his neck. Again he fell on the floor in a pool of red and dark blood . . . Nailed on the sky above were the heads of malefactors, whose blood fell on the earth like rain. It ran on his face and throat; God Almightly, it was his own blood . . . Again he got to his feet, stumbled to the kitchen door, his face like dough, reeled through the passage into his own room, where again he crashed on the floor, face downwards, and lay still in a sea of blood, his pupils wide and staring into a damnable abyss of horror.[41]

What Hay gives us, in this novel, is an account of a society mis-shapen by the conditions prevailing in a shabby pocket of Victorian Scotland. He shows humanity in the raw, unredeemed by finer aspirations. In his creation of so many sordid characters, and in his running commentary on them, Hay implies that Gillespie Strang is not unique but a figure fairly typical of an era when the accumulation of wealth was pursued as an end in itself. To measure up to the materialistic expectations of a Calvinist community, Gillespie has to become a ruthless capitalist; so ruthless, indeed, that the novel occasionally assumes the brooding tonality of a Victorian melodrama. As a human being Gillespie is born with his future fixed for him within the boundaries of Brieston; he inherits a supernatural curse and a natural greed. Gillespie's tragedy is the tragedy of the ambitious Scot who succumbs to the values inherent in a deadly environment. Hay was a Church of Scotland minister; in this context his treatment of squalid reality seemed blasphemous. When *Gillespie* was first published it apparently cost Hay an appointment to the parish church at Grantown-on-Spey, as Lady Seton of Grant Castle had recoiled from the book's brutality. When *Gillespie* was re-printed in 1979 the Church of Scotland bookshop in Edinburgh refused to display copies because of the offensive content of the novel. Too much, though, can be made of the sensational aspects of *Gillespie*. Hay was a superlative literary stylist, a man whose prose is charged with vitality and close observation. This description of the industry of sea would not be surpassed in Scottish fiction until Neil M. Gunn came to write *The Silver Darlings* (1941):

There is nothing which gives to one ashore such a profound impression of the riches of the sea as a herring-gutting scene. The wings of angels hover upon the silvery mass as one looks abroad over a field of fish in many boats. Those beautiful fish, silk-shot with a greenish-blue through the scales, are the strongest hostages against penury. From the cold deep they have come to brighten the hearth; fashioned in silver in the dark, as diamonds in the bowels of the earth. The burnishing of knives was a labour of love in the Back Street. What a sight it was to see again the big fishing-boats laced with scales and the shining pile in the Square. The women sat on empty herring boxes by the pile, their arms bared and dappled with blood . . . When the dusk came the work was continued within the store, whose interior, lit with torches, presented a weird spectacle. Beneath the glare of the torches mingled with smoke, the gutters with blood-stained hands sat around, their faces starting out of the reek in the murky light and falling again into shadow. The pile of herring smouldered in pools of dull gold.[42]

Stylistically *Gillespie* is a monumentally solid novel, demonstrating Hay's command of sensuous descriptive narrative and symbol-tinted realism. Thematically it is limited to the narrow range of a protagonist who can never escape from the standards of his neighbours.

19. JAMES LESLIE MITCHELL AND THE ENGLISH

Both Brown and Hay cast their narratives in English prose while reporting the demotic speech of the natives as colourfully as they could. In other words, they respected the historic division between literary English and oral Scots. Lewis Grassic Gibbon's dream was to resuscitate a fully functional Scots prose that would convey the rich texture of a revitalised Scottish consciousness. Like Brown and Hay, Gibbon died in his thirties and left behind a Scottish masterpiece; like Brown and Hay, too, he fulfilled many of his ambitions and left behind much more than promise. Lewis Grassic Gibbon was born James Leslie Mitchell in 1901, at the Hill of Seggat farm, near Auchterless, central Aberdeenshire; thus the year 1901 represents the *annus mirabilis* of Scottish fiction as the year when *The House with the Green Shutters* was published and the author of *A Scots Quair* born. When Mitchell was eight his family moved and settled in Bloomfield, a farm-croft on a hill above Arbuthnott village in the Mearns (another name for Kincardineshire). This landscape featured as the enduring reality in the imaginative world created by Lewis Grassic Gibbon. At Arbuthnott school, Mitchell impressed the village schoolmaster, Alexander Gray, with his expertise as an essayist and Gray preserved the 'Essay Book kept by James Leslie Mitchell, Arbuthnott School, 1914'. These schoolboy essays are remarkably accomplished for a boy of thirteen as the following extract demonstrates:

Everything around seemed to acclaim harvest. The wide fields of waving corn, gleaming yellow in the morning sunshine, the sharp click! click! of the binder, the voice of the driver calling his horses, who seem greatly to relish a few mouthfulls of ripe grain and the busy workmen rapidly 'stooking' (I think that's the way you spell it) the sheaves – all of them acclaim the same thing.[43]

Mitchell went on to Mackie Academy in Stonehaven, the county town of Kincardineshire; he left after a year to work as a reporter on, first, the *Aberdeen Journal*, then the Glasgow *Scottish Farmer*. His experience of Glasgow was unfortunate for he was sacked for tampering with his expense account and, in a fit of depression, seriously considered suicide. Of Glasgow he later wrote, 'It may be a corpse, but the maggot-swarm upon it is very fiercely alive.'[44] In 1919 Mitchell became a clerk in the Royal Army Service Corps; later he did the same work for the RAF. By using the army as a passport to other places he gained something substantial from his military service though his artistic temperament made him the odd-man-out in barrack-room banter. Thanks to his military service he gained first-hand knowledge of life in the Middle East and made a contact that led to his subsequent trip to Central America where he speculated on the Maya civilisation (the subject of his 1934 volume *The Conquest of the Maya*). In 1928 he published his first book, *Hanno*, and began his career as a full-time writer. From then, until his death in 1935 at the tragically early age of thirty-four, he published seventeen books and various essays. He was a compulsive writer who divided his day into three portions, planning to complete 1,500 words in each portion: *Sunset Song*, acknowledged as his masterpiece, was written in six weeks.

Adopting as his pseudonym Lewis Grassic Gibbon (a name derived from his mother's maiden name) Mitchell alternated between English and Scots prose. He was impressed by MacDiarmid's Synthetic Scots and polemical manner and collaborated with the poet in a book called *Scottish Scene* (1934). In this he expressed concern at the linguistic diffidence of Scottish writers:

> The prose – or verse – [of Scottish writers using English] is impeccably correct, the vocabulary is rich and adequate, the English is severe, serene . . . But unfortunately it is not English. The English reader is haunted by a sense of something foreign stumbling and hesitating behind this smooth facade of adequate technique: it is as though the writer did not *write* himself, but *translated* himself . . . Nearly every Scots writer of the past writing in orthodox English has been not only incurably second-rate, but incurably behind the times.[45]

Now this point has been made by almost every Scottish Nationalist who can point to the obvious evidence: that Burns's source of inspiration dried up drastically when he turned to Augustan English instead of Scots; that Scott's most memorable prose occurs in the vernacular *tour de force* 'Wandering Willie's Tale' from *Redgauntlet*.

Mitchell's disciples have tended to take him at his word and prefer to ignore his English prose while worshipping the Scots of *A Scots Quair*. However, Mitchell was a very fine exponent of English prose (and even settled in England, in Welwyn Garden City). It is salutary to examine his finest English writing. Thus Mitchell's second novel, *The Thirteenth Disciple* (1931), is an impressive work suggesting that the work of its author should be treated as a whole and not split schizophrenically into two.

Although it is not his greatest single achievement this novel is a powerful enough fiction to take a distinguished place in the twentieth century. It is an autobiographical novel: like Mitchell, the hero, Malcom Maudslay, is brought up in Aberdeenshire (the real Arbuthnott becomes the fictional Leekan), becomes a journalist in Glasgow where he is sacked for altering his expense account, joins the army, becomes a Diffusionist, and makes a journey to Central America to speculate on the culture of the Maya. Maudslay, whose invented memoirs form the textual basis of the novel, is no mere colourful character. He is supposed to embody a vision and his odyssey is symbolic as well as consistently believable. Malcom, son of a tenant-farmer, begins his selfconscious life by contemplating suicide but spares himself after experiencing the spectacle of the horizon. Thus his intellectual journey opens on Stane Muir where the nineteenth century ends, optimistically, with a bonfire above the summit's neolithic stone circle. The nineteenth century, with all its Victorian connotations, is at an end forever – or so the scene suggests.

Mitchell's fervent Diffusionist belief that the Golden Age of the primitive hunter had been destroyed by the curse of civilisation pervades the novel. It is haunted by the tragic impact of civilisation, inspired by the hope of rediscovering the ancient culture. Malcom regards himself as of Azilian descent (through his Argyllshire mother) and his despair at the squalor of modern life is transformed into hope when he encounters, in the army, John Metaxa and becomes devoted to the man. Metaxa, an architect turned explorer, expounds Diffusionism for Malcom's benefit. He dismisses the idea that civilisation is civilising and contrasts the kindness of the Old Stone Age with the cruelty of contemporary Europe. To illustrate the accuracy of Metaxa's analysis Mitchell has him martyred in the First World War. Malcom is overwhelmed by the traumatic shock of it all and hides himself away in Chelsea in the 1920s.

Just as Metaxa is the ideal (uncivilised) man, so Domina Riddoch is the ideal (uncivilised) woman. She endorses Metaxa's condemnation of civilisation and enthuses Malcom with a desire to find the lost City of the Sun apparently built by the Maya somewhere in America. Malcom, whose awareness erupted on the Scottish hills, takes to the hills again renaming a Central American range after

125

Domina – thus giving the symbolism a sexual dimension. As the book ends he has a glowing vision of the City of the Sun. In this novel Mitchell combined a provocative theory with convincing human details so the reader feels sympathy for Malcom and his ideals.

Mitchell was to go from strength to strength as a novelist in English. *Spartacus* was published in autumn 1933 immediately after *Cloud Howe* and one year before *Grey Granite*. The story of Spartacus was well known: the Thracian gladiator led a revolt of gladiators and slaves at Capua in 73 BC, decisively defeated several Roman armies, gathered a great army around him, and was eventually defeated and killed by Crassus in 71 BC. The name had another significance for Mitchell: Liebknecht's Spartacus League of 1916 eventually became the German Communist Party in 1919. As early as 1919 Mitchell thought of himself as a communist though, as we shall see, it was a very individual and eccentric kind of communism.

As *Spartacus* is, formally, an historical novel it takes some cues from Scott. It seeks to make the period relevant, vibrantly alive, so that the reader is drawn into the action and gets the feel of the period. Mitchell does this quite brilliantly and the comparison with Scott is especially valid in the early part of the book as Mitchell creates an atmosphere. In Scott's *Waverley* (1814), the hero travels northwards after hearing of the catastrophe at Culloden:

> As he advanced northward, the traces of war became visible. Broken carriages, dead horses, unroofed cottages, trees felled for palisades, and bridges destroyed, or only partially repaired, – all indicated the movement of hostile armies.

Here is a comparable passage from *Spartacus* when Publius Varinus is sent by the Senate to crush the rebellious army:

> Presently he was in a land that another army seemed to have devastated. Houses stood looted and roofless, with the smoke still curling from the charred beams and starving dogs snuffling amid the ruins; farms were deserted, the storehouses sacked, gates open and herds straying untended.[46]

As the novel progresses, however, Mitchell's prose becomes increasingly drenched in blood as he seeks, successfully, to capture verbally the sight and sound of man-to-man combat. War has provided some of the greatest moments in literature, from Homer onwards, and Mitchell's contribution to this martial genre was extreme. His novel drips blood and is not designed for the squeamish. Spartacus himself is gentle in repose but possessed by blood-lust when battle has to be done. Mitchell spares nothing, but recreates in fast-moving narrative the 'wrenching of tearing flesh and . . . crackle of breaking bones.'[47]

Because the history of Spartacus is so well known, Mitchell had to sustain the reader's interest by creating compelling characters.

Kleon, a focal figure in the story, is an intellectual eunuch who immediately joins the revolt after slitting the throat of his master – and, as a gesture against his own mutilation, castrating him. He is inspired by the vision of his favourite author, Plato, and sees the gladiator revolt as an opportunity to test the ideals of *The Republic*. Spartacus comes over as a slow, stolid character with an instinct for guerilla warfare and military leadership; his Roman adversaries admire his cunning but despise him for his clemency and refusal to torture prisoners. Kleon gradually works his way up to become Spartacus's right-hand man, his adviser. Safe in this position of privilege, Kleon works on his plan of moulding Spartacus into a living image of Plato's concept of the Leader of a New Republic. There are fascinating secondary characters like Gershom ben Sanballat, a Jewish aristocrat enslaved for his political beliefs; and Gannicus, who resents Spartacus's assumption of leadership. The Romans, too, are presented in some depth. Still, Mitchell's finest artistic effect is to give a collective voice to the slaves themselves. Here, confronted by a menacing Roman army, the slaves realise exactly what they have in common:

> With that realisation there came on the slaves hate with remembrance – hate built on memories dreadful and unforgivable, memories of long treks in the slave-gangs from their native lands, memories of the naked sale, with painted feet, from the steps of windy ergastula, memories of cruelties cold-hearted and bloody, of women raped or fed to fish to amuse the Masters from their lethargy, of children sold as they came from the womb, of the breeding-kens of the north, where the slaves were mated like cattle, with the Masters standing by.[48]

Mitchell not only wrote at white-heat; he seethed with moral indignation as he did so. There is no pretence at historical impartiality in *Spartacus*; it is always clear that Mitchell is on the side of the slaves. For all that *Spartacus* is a triumphant historical novel; a novel that reposseses time past and gives it contemporary meaning. Mitchell applied his narrative skill to a familiar genre (one made in Scotland by Scott) and showed a total command of it. He also brought to the historical novel a sense of urgency, an intense mood that makes the reader care passionately about the events described and take sides. *Spartacus* the novel is a tract for the times (the hungry thirties); Spartacus the man, as recreated by Mitchell, is an example to others. This is established at the close of the book. Spartacus has been killed, his army defeated. Crassus, the Roman victor, has more than six thousand prisoners and all are to be crucified – 'one by one nailed on the new-made crosses'.[49] The description of the final agony of the insurrectionists is extremely moving, an example of Scottish realism moving into a mythical dimension. Kleon is still alive on his fourth morning on the cross. Nearing death, he has a vision in which Spartacus is seen as a sacrificial victim who will come again to save the lowliest people on earth. Paradoxically, Scottish realism often tends to acquire mythical connotations as if to affirm the universal truth of particular verities. Mitchell is a master of this tendency as the magnificent conclusion to *Spartacus* shows:

> And the day passed, the sun swung its arc of brightness across the sky so slowly that [Kleon] thought of it as many days, long stretches of darkness and long stretches of light; and his tongue swelled out between his teeth; and death would not come; and the spiked wheel in his brain grew and grew till it filled the sky, till it burst from his head and he saw the earth in torment. And about him, in little spaces between his own agony, he heard the last cry of men who died, and saw their bodies bulge and shudder and pass to ease at last . . . And then again pains seized and tore at his heart and passed again; and wildly, a last wild moment, he raised his eyes.
>
> And he saw before him, gigantic, filling the sky, a great Cross with a figure that was crowned with thorns; and behind it, sky-towering as well, gladius in hand, his hand on the edge of the morning behind that Cross, the figure of a Gladiator . . . And he saw that these Two were One, and the world yet theirs: and he went into unending night and left them that shining earth.[50]

Mitchell the novelist in English may yet attain the prestige of Gibbon the novelist in Scots when the published work is seen as the product of a singular imagination. Before moving on to *A Scots Quair*, however, it is instructive to look at Mitchell's philosophy in so far as it played a significant part in the trilogy. Mitchell was a Diffusionist. In other words, he believed that primitive man lived in a Golden Age until warped by the curse of civilisation. The primitive hunters, according to Diffusionist doctrine, were nomadic. They gathered their food and lived the good life without recourse to rigid institutions or punitive laws. They were not savages; their Golden Age predated civilisation. Now (the Diffusionists argue) this destructive phenomenon known as civilisation was no inevitable part of human evolution. It was something that happened by chance on the banks of the Nile. Let Mitchell explain in his own words:

> All human civilisations originated in Ancient Egypt. Through the accident of time and chance and the cultivation of wild barley in the Valley of the Nile, there arose in a single spot on the earth's surface the urge in men to upbuild for their economic salvation the great fabric of civilization. Before the planning of that architecture enslaved the minds of men, man was a free and happy and undiseased animal wandering the world in the Golden Age of the poets (and reality) from the Shetlands to Tierra del Fuego. And from that central point in Ancient Egypt the first civilizers spread abroad the globe the beliefs and practices, the diggings and plantings and indignations and shadowy revilements of the Archaic Civilization.[51]

Apparently the men of the Archaic Civilisation reached Scotland in search of copper and gold and pearls and, according to Mitchell, found a green and pleasant land and 'Golden Age hunters – men perhaps of Maglemosian stock . . . men naked, cultureless, without religion or social organization, shy hunters, courageous, happy, kindly.'[52] The civilisers buried Scotland under their rites and religions; the priestly overlords 'built the rings of the Devil Stones on the high places from Lewis to Aberdeenshire.'[53] Then, even worse, Scotland was invaded by the savage Celts who knew nothing but viciousness, who came to conquer the Picts. Mitchell could become passionate about the false idea scholars had about the Celts:

> They were, and remain, one of the greatest curses of the Scottish scene, quick, avaricious, unintelligent, quarrelsome, cultureless, and uncivilizable. It is one of the strangest jests of history that they should have given their name to so much that is fine and noble, the singing of poets and the fighting of great fights, in which their own actual part has been that of gaping, unintelligent audition or mere carrion-bird raiding.[54]

After being softened up by the Celts, Scotland endured a succession of traumatic shocks and could only manage a handful of great leaders like Wallace and Knox (of whom Mitchell says, 'Knox himself was of truly heroic mould; had his followers, far less his allies, been of like mettle, the history of Scotland might have been strangely and splendidly different').[55] For all that, the 'ancient Pictish spirit'[56] still permeated Scotland and accounted for the country's finest aspects. Such was Mitchell's outlook; it did not rigidly determine the fiction of Lewis Grassic Gibbon but forever hovered in the background.

20. LEWIS GRASSIC GIBBON AND THE SPEAK

A Scots Quair comprises a trilogy of novels of which the first, *Sunset Song*, was published in 1923. The title is meaningful, for Gibbon recalled a way of life that vanished as the First World War darkened the world. Mitchell's favourite lines of poetry – which appeared as the epigraph to his first book, *Hanno*, and his last, *Nine Against the Unknown* (1934) and hung above his fireplace in Welwyn Garden City – came from Tennyson's 'Ulysses':

> The lights begin to twinkle from the rocks;
> The long day wanes; the slow moon climbs; the deep
> Moans round with many voices. Come, my friends,
> 'Tis not too late to seek a newer world.
> Push off, and sitting well in order smite
> The sounding furrows; for my purpose holds
> To sail beyond the sunset, and the baths
> Of all the western stars, until I die.
> It may be that the gulfs will wash us down:
> It may be we shall touch the Happy Isles.

The first novel in Gibbon's great trilogy represents the sunset the author wanted to sail beyond. Set in the parish of Kinraddie – so it is, literally, parochial life under scrutiny – *Sunset Song* portrays a harsh, cruel world. The song of the title is the age-old song of Scotland, haunted by memories of defeat:

> . . . it came on Chris how strange was the sadness of Scotland's singing, made for the sadness of the land and sky in dark autumn evenings, the crying of men and women of the land who had seen their lives and loves sink away in the years, things wept for beside the sheep-ouchts, remembered at night and in twilight. The gladness and kindness had passed, lived and forgotten, it was Scotland of the mist and rain and the crying sea that made the songs . . .[57]

Like J. MacDougall Hay, Gibbon was writing with a conscious contempt for kailyard fiction and an enormous admiration for Brown's *The House with the Green Shutters*. At the end of the Prelude to *Sunset Song* we learn that the new minister described the parish of Kinraddie as

> the Scots countryside itself, fathered between a kailyard and a bonny brier bush in the lee of a house with green shutters. And what he meant by that you could guess at yourself if you'd a mind for puzzles and dirt, there wasn't a house with green shutters in the whole of Kinraddie.[58]

As we have seen, J. MacDougall Hay echoed, in *Gillespie*, the 'arch' passage in *Green Shutters*. In the same way, Gibbon introduces a parallel to the *animo castrato* passage (see above, p. 115) in *Green Shutters*. In *Sunset Song* John Guthrie's son Will innocently gives the name Jehovah to a horse. Guthrie, immediately assuming the habits of the tyrannical Calvinist patriarch, smells blasphemy and knocks his son down:

> And mind, my mannie, if I ever hear you again take your Maker's name in vain, if I ever hear you use that word again, I'll libb you. Mind that. Libb you like a lamb.
> So Will hated father, he was sixteen years of age and near a man, but father could still make him cry like a bairn.[59]

And again, after Will has used Guthrie's gun without permission:

> And up to the barn [Guthrie] went with Will and took down his breeks, nearly seventeen though he was, and leathered him till the weals stood blue across his haunches; and that night Will could hardly sleep for the pain of it, sobbing into his pillow, till Chris slipped into his bed and took him into her arms and held him and cuddled him . . .[60]

Such familiarity with domestic (and/or educational) ritualised violence is a permanent feature of Scottish fiction.

Technically, Gibbon's prose is the most ambitious experiment to be undertaken by a modern Scottish novelist (Sydney Goodsir

Smith's *Carotid Cornucopius* being more in the nature of broad farce than controlled fiction). Gibbon's stylistic innovation was to convey, in literary prose, the rhythm of oral Scots. *A Scots Quair* is constructed to a tight pattern yet it unfolds like a story told by word of mouth, a collective tale of the folk. Thus the narrative constantly invokes the impersonal 'You' which is at once the reader, the writer and the character referred to. The continuity of the narrative is expressed in conversational expressions like 'Folk said...' and 'So that was...'. Gibbon felt that the emotive power of Scots was essential to a story telling of the inner development of a quintessential Scot, a story that related people to the land they came from. Of his own prose, Gibbon said: 'The technique of Lewis Grassic Gibbon in his trilogy *A Scots Quair*... is to mould the English language into the rhythms and cadences of Scots spoken speech, and to inject into the English vocabulary such minimum number of words from Braid Scots as that remodelling requires'.[61] Gibbon begins *Sunset Song* by tracing the history of Kinraddie parish back to the reign of William the Lion (1165–1214) when a Norman, Cospatric de Gondeshil, was knighted for slaying a gryphon. This instantly takes us into the world of folklore where gossip is as sacred as holy writ and rumours become legends by virtue of their longevity. Kinraddie is a cluster of croft-farms though by 1911, when the action of *Sunset Song* begins, there are only nine left. Blawearie farm – consisting of 'coarse, coarse, land, wet, raw, and red clay'[62] – is leased by John Guthrie, who is an archetypal agricultural Scot. He is bigoted, brutal, insensitive and ignorant. His daughter, Chris, is the central figure in the trilogy and she and her brothers live in fear of Guthrie's outbursts. His whole attitude to life is one of negativity. Chris loves the Standing Stones of Blawearie but Guthrie says they are 'coarse, foul things.[63] Life itself, to Guthrie and his like, is coarse. 'Coarse', in fact, is the essential epithet of abuse throughout the book (just as to be compared to a 'tink' is a deadly insult): 'Next door the kirk was an olden tower, built in the time of the Roman Catholics, the coarse creatures'[64]; there is the 'coarse moorland behind the Mill'[65]; and 'Most said it was a coarse thing, learning, just teaching your children a lot of damned nonsense'.[66] A key passage, that introduces the inevitable presence of split personality, distinguishes between oral and literary modes thus:

> So that was Chris and her reading and schooling, two Chrisses there were that fought for her heart and tormented her. You hated the land and the coarse speak of the folk and learning was brave and fine one day and the next you'd waken with the peewits crying across the hills, deep and deep, crying in the heart of you and the smell of the earth in your face, almost you'd cry for that, the beauty of it and the sweetness of the Scottish land and skies. You saw their faces in firelight, father's and mother's and the neighbours', before the lamps lit up, tired and kind,

faces dear and close to you, you wanted the words they'd known and used, forgotten in the far-off youngness of their lives, Scots words to tell to your heart, how they wrung it and held it, the toil of their days and unendingly their fight. And the next minute that passed from you, you were English, back to the English words so sharp and clean and true – for a while, for a while, till they slid so smooth from your throat you knew they could never say anything that was worth the saying at all.[67]

Chris is a thinker and therefore a rare, rather than a coarse, creature. She goes to college in Duncairn to acquire some experience of life outside Kinraddie parish. However, she is attached to the people of Kinraddie: to Chae Strachan, socialist and farmer of Peesie's Knapp; to Long Rob of the Mill, who denies religion and whistles his way through life; and, eventually, to Ewan Tavendale, the foreman at Upperhill. Ewan represents vitality to Chris – who is worn out by the relentlessly grim paternalism of John Guthrie.

Chris's life is dramatically altered by three events (and, as befitting a trilogist, Gibbon arranges everything in triplicate). First, her mother poisons herself and her twins rather than face another pregnancy and the concomitant heartache; then Guthrie dies a broken man (and Chris weeps for him at his funeral, remembering that his spirit had been crushed by the unequal challenge of making a living from the land); then Chris marries Ewan Tavendale – who is Highland and coarse according to Will Guthrie – and makes him the master of Blawearie. Chris has come to realise that the land conditions and contains the crofters:

And then a queer thought came to her there in the drooked fields, that nothing endured at all, nothing but the land she passed across, tossed and turned and perpetually changed below the hands of the crofter folk since the oldest of them had set the Standing Stones by the loch of Blawearie and climbed there on their holy days and saw their terraced crops ride brave in the wind and sun. Sea and sky and the folk who wrote and fought and were learned, teaching and saying and praying, they lasted but as a breath, a mist of fog in the hills, but the land was forever, it moved and changed below you, but was forever, you were close to it and it to you, not at a bleak remove it held you and hurted you.[68]

That is not the pathetic fallacy taken to extremes; it is at once an expression of belief in determinism and a habitual tendency to empathise with nature.

Chris is emotionally dependent on her peasant origins yet occasionally ashamed of them. So far her life has been a mixture of pantheistic euphoria and circumstantial tragedy. As the novel approaches its end (which is the beginning of the second part of the trilogy) the mood becomes increasingly bleak. War breaks out and destroys what was left of Kinraddie's communal identity. The World War is reflected in microcosm in the bitter infighting that overwhelms Kinraddie. Chae Strachan enlists but Long Rob of the Mill, unwilling to distinguish between bad Germans and bad Scots, wants nothing to do with a war he regards as a blunder. The parish is divided; and the Conscription Act simply makes the divisions more emphatic. Ewan is initially excused military service on account of his status as a farmer; Long Rob of the Mill refuses to fight and pays for this display of conscience by being tormented in jail (an act of brutality that anticipates the torture of young Ewan in *Grey Granite*). Ewan, unable to live with the aura of cowardice that seems to cling to every non-combatant, decides to enlist and leaves Chris with their child Ewan.

When Ewan comes back on leave before going to France he is transformed. Whereas once he had been caring and tender, now he is indifferent and crude. The expectation of war and the preparations for it have moulded him into an efficient uniformed unit; a fighting machine with no time for niceties. War is more than a specific conflict; it is a general condition sweeping the world and breaking up traditional bonds between communities (like Kinraddie) and families (like the Tavendales). Chris and Ewan part as bitter enemies in a domestic war. Later Chris learns from Chae Strachan that Ewan has been shot as a coward and deserter. The story, as relayed by Chae is that Ewan, sickened by the European situation, recalled the marital security he shared with Chris. He had attempted to get back to Blawearie. Chris understands this romantic gesture; cherishes the memory of Ewan and the promise of young Ewan. As the novel ends she is somewhat wiser than she was, less of an ideal and more of a woman. She prepares for a new kind of life as the wife of Robert Colquohoun, the new minister of Kinraddie.

Just as *A Scots Quair* was planned in three books, so each book is made to operate on three distinct levels. There is the narrative level (the story of Chris), the poetic level (the singing Scots prose), and the mythical level (the persistence of the past, the symbolic meaning of Chris's life). At the end of *Sunset Song* Robert Colquohoun has the Standing Stones of Blawearie made into a war memorial for the Kinraddie dead (Ewan, Chae and Long Rob – who eventually succumbed to pressure and enlisted). This has a certain irony for, in the Diffusionist scheme of things, the Stones represent the coming of civilisation and organised religion which, together, destroyed the life led by the Golden Age primitives. The Stones represent a marker for a way of life that vanished yet could, given a recrudescence of the old Pictish spirit, come again. Chris is not a New Woman (in the Ibsenite or Shavian sense); she is a phenomenon, a survival of the primitive type.

Gibbon chose his titles carefully. The sunset in the first book of *A Scots Quair* is the fading of the peasant age. *Cloud Howe* (1933) constantly refers to the passing of the clouds over Seggett and Gibbon means us to take the clouds as a symbol of nebulous ideals that pass and leave the land as it was. Chris, married to Robert Colquohoun, broods on this in a key passage:

> She minded then as she worked at that tree, an apple tree, and set smooth the earth, and reached her hands in the cling of the mould, that saying of Robert's, long, long ago, the day he unveiled the new-hallowed Stones up by the loch on Blawearie brae – that we'd seen the sunset come on the land and this was the end of the peasant's age. But she thought, as often, we saw more than that – the end forever of creeds and of faiths, hopes and beliefs men followed and loved: religion and God, socialism, nationalism – Clouds that sailed darkling into the night. Others might arise but these went by, folk saw them but clouds and knew them at last, and turned to the Howe from the splendid hills – folk were doing so all over the world, she thought, back to the sheltered places and ease, to sloth or toil or the lees of lust, from the shining splendour of the cloudy hills and those hopes that had followed and believed, everlasting. She herself did neither, watching, unsure: was there nothing between the Clouds and the Howe?[69]

Gibbon had a tight formal plan for his trilogy and, having employed it triumphantly in *Sunset Song*, stuck rigidly to it. This enabled him to compose quickly by pouring his prose into a familiar mould. Each book was to have a specific social environment (parish, borough, city); each book was to have a different type of husband for Chris (Ewan Tavendale, Robert Colquohoun, Ake Ogilvie); each book was to relate to a great social event (the First World War, General Strike, Class War). Chris was the common factor, the constant and eternal feminine principle of creativity and endurance. In *Cloud Howe* Chris has left Kinraddie, 'a countryside that was dying or dead'.[70] Married to Colquohoun, she is delighted when he becomes minister of the borough of Segget. She can keep her distance from Kinraddie but retain her regard for her heritage. Just as Kinraddie has its Standing Stones, so Segget has its Kaimes, 'a long line of battlements under the hills, midway a tower that was older still, a broch from the days of the Pictish men'.[71] Chris is irresistibly attracted to the Kaimes, so they become a surrogate monument for her; another reminder of the Pictish spirit of Scotland. The novel explores Chris's romantic nature, the idealistic Christian Socialism of Colquohoun, and the steady development of young Ewan Tavendale who shapes up as a stronger personality than his father. Again the symbolism is striking: on the outbreak of the First World War Chris had given birth to Ewan; while the General Strike is collapsing she miscarries Colquohoun's son. Chris is vibrantly aware of the vagaries of history.

Having made Chris such a memorable character and *Sunset Song* such a deep artistic experience, Gibbon had the problem, in *Cloud Howe*, of sustaining interest in a sequel in which each image moves increasingly towards abstraction. He does this by frequent flash-backs to Chris's early life and these incidents are often richer than the main narrative of *Cloud Howe*. Instead of the extension of a central personality *Cloud Howe* tends to dissipate its energies on a host of quaint characters: like the garrulous Ag Moultrie, possessed of 'a tongue for news that was awful'[72] and known as the Roarer and Greeter; Sim Leslie, known as Feet, the plodding policeman of Seg-get; Hairy Hogg, the pompous provost of the borough; Ake Ogilvie, the joiner, who 'wrote his ill bits of poetry and stite – he thought himself maybe a second Robert Burns'[73]; Stephen Mowat, the young laird, whose English accent amuses the locals; station-porter Jock Cronin, who, as the son of a spinner, claims to speak for the poor folk of the Old Toun (as distinct from the bourgeoisie of the New Toun of Segget).

For much of *Cloud Howe*, in fact, we are back with the bodies of *Green Shutters*. The Scottish penchant for malicious gossip simul-taneously amuses and distresses Gibbon for it is the expression of a broken and spiteful people. Gibbon took this as seriously as Brown did:

> [Colquohoun] laughed . . . and then laughed again, a second laugh that was dreary, Chris thought. My God, were there ever folk like the Scots! Not only THEM – you and I are as bad. Murderous gossip passed on as sheer gospel, though liars and listeners both know it is a lie. Lairds, ladies, or plain Jock Muck at the Mains – they'd gossip the heart from Christ if He came, and impute a dodge for popularising timber when He was crucified again on His cross![74]

and, as an example of this murderous gossip, an event after the Seg-get Show:

> Near Skite a farmer went out to his barn, early next morning, and what did he see? Two childes and two lasses asleep in his hay. And he was sore shocked and went back for his wife, and she came and looked and was shocked as well, and if they'd had a camera they'd have taken photographs, they were so delighted and shocked to see two queans that they knew in such a like way, they'd be able to tell the story about them all the years that they lived on earth; and make it a tit-bit in hell forbye.[75]

Cloud Howe is less integrated than *Sunset Song*. Basically it com-es down to a stream of anecdotes and character sketches held together by the presence of Chris and the duplication of the struc-ture of *Sunset Song*. Thus there is a feeling of *dèja-lu* in the reading of it. The locals gossip about each other, fight each other, and cor-dially hate each other. It is a portrait of a community in a state of disintegration, a people without a shared point of view. Gibbon, of course, wanted to expose the fragmentary nature of a society dis-figured by commerce and he underlines the element of distrust and the habit of thinking the worst of people. The locals dislike Chris and Robert – Chris because of her apparent snobbery and Robert because of his theologically misplaced radical notions. When Chris is observed, by Ag Moultrie, coming down from the Kaimes her air of innocence is interpreted as shameful indifference. Ag thinks up a story that brings out the twisted nature of the Scottish gossip:

> Ag was real shocked, for the Kaimes was the place where spinners and tinks of that kind would go, of a Sabbath evening, and lie on the grass and giggle and smoke and do worse than that – Ay, things that would leave them smoking in hell, as the old minister said that they would. So no decent folk went up there at night, this creature of a woman was surely a tink.[76]

Ag, true to her nature, puts it around that Chris has been up the Kaimes with an amorous spinner. Robert Colquohoun, despite his ministerial status, fares no better at the hands of the people. His pulpit insistence on Christian Socialism is misinterpreted by the locals as a frontal attack on their faults. They conclude that Colquohoun is dangerous and immoral.

As Gibbon examines the internal divisions in Segget he puts matters in perspective by introducing a deeper dimension. The General Strike is supported by the Segget spinners and Colquohoun; but the credibility of the radicals collapses with the return to work. Defeatism seems to be the order of the day and despondency deepens when the forces of reaction form a National Government under Ramsay MacDonald (who was the subject of a vituperative essay by Gibbon in *Scottish Scene*). Chris miscarries her child. Robert thinks he has seen the risen Christ and succumbs to a pious and passive religiosity before dying in church on his bible when his lungs, damaged by gassing in the First World War, finally give out. Segget is a sorry spectacle and even young Mowat, the laird, 'was ruined and hadn't a penny, the whole of Segget mortgaged to the hilt'.[77]

So much pessimism might have detracted from the positive impact of the book but Gibbon skilfully combines the thematic saga with incidental humour, though the humour is often cruel (as when a slaughtered pig is put into a man's bed). *Cloud Howe* is a much more didactic book than its predecessor and Gibbon's authorial viewpoint is stated throughout the book which contains as many opinions as observations. For example, the young laird tells Peter Peat his opinion about the Scottish Literary Renaissance and these views are the polar opposite of Gibbon's own:

> Yes, [Mowat the laird] believed in Devolution for Scotland, but not this mad nationalism now rampant, only the Unionist Party would see that Scotland got her dues in the end. And he told Peter more of the coarse new Nationalists, not the flower of the country's gentry, as once, Scotland had lost her chance once again, the new leaders a pack of

socialists and catholics, long-haired poets, a fellow called Grieve, and Mackenzie and Gunn, hysterical Highlandmen.[78]

Moreover there are the obligatory references to the golden hunters of the Golden Age; and the early deification of young Ewan who had 'something within him hard and shining and unbreakable as rock, something like a sliver of granite within him'[79], who was 'hard and cool as – grey granite'.[80]

Grey Granite is the final part of the trilogy and here Gibbon is concerned with finding a political solution to the story of Scotland: for he certainly meant his heroine to be, symbolically at least, the spirit of Scotland. Robert Colquohoun, in *Cloud Howe*, had exclaimed 'Oh Chris Caledonia, I've married a nation'[81] and this identity is suggested throughout the trilogy. In *Sunset Song* Chris was the fertile wife; in *Cloud Howe* she was the loyal companion; in *Grey Granite* she is the protective mother. She has left Segget and come to the industrial city of Duncairn to be Ma Cleghorn's partner in running a boarding house. She is adored by the boarders though, as a minister's widow, has the reputation of being a toff (which is the urban equivalent, in terms of abuse, of the rural tink). Ewan, too, is regarded as a toff and is initially the object of scorn when he takes a job stoking a furnace at a steel foundry. Ewan may be grey granite down to the core but his aloof appearance disguises the fact. His mates torment him. Ewan, however, is no soft touch and takes on tough Alick Watson in the kind of pugilistic set-piece we expect in Scottish fiction:

> Ewan dripped blood like a half-killed pig, but he didn't know that, infighting, they were both thick-streaked with blood and snot, holding and fighting, Alick tried to kick, Ewan felt a stab of pain like a knife, and loosened his hold and Alick broke away – looked, swung, and struck, it caught Ewan's neck, he gave a queer grunt and twist, the fight finished, queer that silence to Alick and the way the sheds shook.[82]

When he returns to the foundry Ewan is welcomed by Alick and the others. From being scorned as a toff he becomes adored as a tough leader.

Ewan regards Scots as 'that blunted and foolish and out-dated tool'[83] and speaks an educated English; the other characters speak in tones appropriate to the city. Thus there is a noticeable change of style from the first two novels to the last. *Grey Granite* is only partly written in the fluent oral rhythms of *Sunset Song* and *Cloud Howe* and the mixture is awkward. The descriptive passages in English are mannered (as if Gibbon was forcing the political content against the grain of his prose) and the English dialogue forced. Ewan is given to saying things like 'There's nothing new under the sun'[84] and Ellen Johns – an English schoolteacher who becomes his lover – retorts with platitudes like 'Ewan, oh my dear!'".[85] Ellen is the most important of the secondary characters; the others are Sim 'Feet' Leslie, the policeman from *Cloud Howe*, now a sergeant in Duncairn; Big Jim Trease, Duncairn's leading communist; and Ake Ogilvie, from *Cloud Howe*, who get a job as foreman-joiner at Provost Speight's sawmills.

The main point of the novel is to show Ewan's transformation from an idealistic socialist into a hard-bitten communist willing to twist the means to justify the revolutionary end. When the novel opens we are plunged into the depressed 1930s with the dramatic increase in unemployment and the growing threat of world war. Ewan, appalled at the foundry's willingness to manufacture weapons of destruction, organises a strike. Despite his attempts to control the strike democratically violence erupts; a blackleg is drowned and the police have pepper thrown in their eyes. At this stage Gibbon abandons his commonsense sequence of events to introduce a melodramatic touch. Alick Watson's sister is pregnant and Alick suspects Ewan of being the father; therefore he tells 'Feet' Leslie that Ewan was the brains behind the drowning and the attack on the police. When Alick discovers his mistake it is too late. Ewan has been arrested by the police.

Once in the hands of the police Ewan is brutalised and tortured. And he is, in his moment of martyrdom, the symbol of the oppressed through the ages as Gibbon makes clear in probably the most powerful passage in the book:

> And still he'd said nothing, setting his teeth, though the pain behind his teeth had clamoured to him to let go, to confess to anything, anything they wanted . . . But that real self that transcended himself had sheathed its being in ice and watched with a kind of icy indifference as they did shameful things to his body, threatened even more shameful, twisted that body till his self cowered in behind the ice and fainted again . . . And now, as he thought, the morning was near.
>
> He moved a little the arm he'd thought broken, it wasn't, only clotted with bruises, the dryness had left his throat, he lay still with a strange mist boiling, blinding his eyes, not Ewan Tavendale at all any more but lost and be-bloodied in a hundred broken and tortured bodies all over the world, in Scotland, in England, in the torture-dens of the Nazis in Germany, in the torment-pits of the Polish Ukraine, a livid, twisted thing in the prisons where they tortured the Nanking Communists, a Negro boy in an Alabama cell while they thrust the razors into his flesh, castrating with a lingering cruelty and care. He was one with them all, a long wail of sobbing mouths and wrung flesh, tortured and tormented by the world's Masters while those Masters lied about Progress through Peace, Democracy, Justice, the Heritage of Culture – even as they'd lied in the days of Spartacus, lying now through their hacks in pulpit and press, in the slobberings of middle-class pacifists, the tawdry promisings of Labourites, Douglasites . . . [86]

The experience hardens Ewan, takes all the sentimentality out of him, and he dedicates himself to becoming a fulltime Communist agitator, an organiser in London. Chris is a spectator in this novel: she watches as Ewan grows away from her; she understands when Ewan breaks from Ellen; she makes a marriage of convenience with Ake Ogilvie and sympathises when he leaves her to seek a new life in Canada. At the end of the trilogy she leaves Duncairn and goes back to live on her father's croft in Cairndhu. She has come full circle, gone back to her genesis. In a sense, she has gone to ground. *Grey Granite* is an episodic book; the trilogy loses its emotional impetus the further it gets from Chris and her outlook. Whatever its incidental flaws, though, *A Scots Quair* was a monumental advance in Scottish literature. Gibbon had magnificently renewed the central tradition of Scottish fiction. As with Brown and Hay we can only speculate as to what sort of work would have followed. Among the papers found after Gibbon's death was the manuscript of a new novel and the style shows him returning to the anecdotal fluency of *Sunset Song*:

> The last Stratoun there had been the laird John who drank like a fish, nothing queer in that, a man with a bit of silver would drink, what else was there for the creature to do if he was a harmless kind of man? But his downcome had been that he swam like some kind of damned fish as well, he was always in and out of the sea, and the combination had been overmuch . . . he'd filled himself up with a gill of Glenlivet and gone for a swim, and been taken with cramp.[87]

21. NEIL M. GUNN: IN SEARCH OF THE SYMBOL

So far we have considered novelists who died full of promise: George Douglas Brown, J. MacDougall Hay and Lewis Grassic Gibbon had only started to sing a song. Neil Miller Gunn, however, is one Scottish novelist who enjoyed a long career and even outlived the publication of his last novel by almost two decades. More than that, he always knew where he was going from first (*The Grey Coast* in 1926) to last (*The Other Landscape* in 1954); Gunn's is a consistent vision that gradually unfolds during an active literary career stretching over thirty years. He is revealed as a craftsman carefully shaping his dreams into the reality of the traditional novel and yet though plot, character and structure impress by their solidity there is another level invoked by theme, archetype and texture. Gunn saw everyday reality as a surface riddled with symbolic significance; he used the symbols as points of entry into a magical world beyond. Because of the persistence of the folk memory and the recurrence of elemental human situations this magical world is always attainable. It is also recognisable as the earthly paradise associated, in Gunn's imagination, with the Gaelic world that obtained before Culloden.

Gunn constantly recalls the pre-Culloden paradise lost (or almost lost) by the exercise of inhumanity. It is the dramatic scene on which his vision focuses. The clan system, despite all its human imperfections, represented a social system Gunn admired and partly inherited through his links with his father and his father's father and so on. Gunn liked to imagine that Gaeldom was not entirely destroyed but subtly persisted. As a young man Gunn was greatly attracted to the Celtic Twilightry of Fiona Macleod (William Sharp) and though he later found fault with Fiona's highly-coloured prose he never entirely shook off the influence. Clearly he saw the Celtic light shining through the darkness of the contemporary world. Whereas the big sprawling industrial-urban ideologies celebrated rootlessness, Gunn's Celtic credo affirmed a sense of community in a closely observed locality. Idealism meant more to Gunn than ideology and clan meant more than class. In his informative treatise on *Whisky and Scotland* (1935) he tentatively explores the issue:

> Almost from the beginnings of recorded history, there has been a world drive against the Celts . . . And the process is still going on, none the less deadly or ruthless because in these days it may be less bloody – the process of driving them off the ultimate rocks into the sea . . . In all sorts of ways, by all sorts of peoples, then, that which is Celtic or Gaelic has been driven back to the mountains, driven into the sea. Until at last, among many of the Gaels themselves, a shame of their heritage comes over them, and they have been known to deny it with a curious and introverted hate.[88]

As a positive answer to such negativity Gunn celebrated the atom of delight that activated the modern Gael and gave him a unique place in the contemporary world. Gunn presented characters who were both substantial and symbolic enough to embody his belief in an affirmative fiction. Gunn's pellucid writing is restorative rather than wildly inventive for it reveals a world the reader perceives to be there. To do so it ranges philosophically from Platonic eternals to Jungian archetypes and uses plots that have the illustrative impact of parables. Lewis Grassic Gibbon regarded civilisation as a curse; Gunn saw it as something with flaws man had occasionally to escape from. This escapism was not irresponsible but obligatory, for man was biologically determined to search. Whether the quest was for intellectual solutions or for food it remained a quintessentially human instinct:

> If man has been on this earth for about a million years, only the last six thousand or so have been what we call civilized. For a stretch of time inconceivable to the mind he was a hunter. That this has conditioned the

cells in his body and most of them in his head may be taken as
biologically reasonable . . . From the beginnings of their human history
the Highlands have been a hunting ground.[89]

The Highland environment recognises the hunting instinct whereas
the urban ambiance represses it. Gunn is always most at home in his
native Highlands.

In several of Gunn's novels we see the tension between
elemental, instinctual man as hunter and civilised man as domesti-
cated provider. A man is torn between the two extremes. He might
be happy enough with his family and subscribe to Burns's comfy notion (expressed in the epistle 'To Dr Blacklock') that

> To make a happy fire-side clime
> To weans and wife,
> That's the true pathos and sublime
> Of human life.

However, there will be moments when he craves the elemental challenge. Some activities satisfy this need and, for Gunn, fishing (with
its Christian connotations) is supreme among them. Archetypal man
is, thus, divided between the urge to hunt and the urge to settle.
Archetypal woman is a more consistent creature; she uses her hom-
ing instinct, feels her destiny to be domestic (though this might seem
a heresy to feminist writers) and employs her gifts to bring man
down to earth (which is her own element). Gunn's image of the
home has nothing to do with the bourgeois household, incidentally.
It is a subtle evocation of the ancient concept of settlement. Woman
(in Gunn's novels) wants to settle, man is always aware of a need to
expand, to 'get rid of the burden, drop the shackles and run'.[90]

As we read Gunn's novels we are aware of an eternal story being
retold in an exactly described setting. Like Edwin Muir, Gunn was a
Platonic visionary who saw the everyday object as an imperfect copy
of an eternal ideal which could be approached by the power of creative writing. Like Muir, he combined the Platonic vision with a use
of the bible as a source-book of instantly accessible images. Hence a
heroic fisherman, to cite an obvious example, is inevitably made in
the image of Christ. As a child Gunn would have been well aware of
the relevance of such images to his own life. He was born in 1891 in
a village on the Caithness coast: Dunbeath, the setting of *Morning
Tide*, *Highland River* and *The Silver Darlings*. His father was a
fishing captain (the heroic figure to whose memory *The Silver Darlings* is dedicated). Gunn's horizon was usually set on the changing
aspects of the sea. It seemed to be infinite. On the other hand the
physically finite (though imaginatively limitless) world was contained in the local environment. Gunn often shrunk experience to
the proportions of a child's daydream which began with an exploration and extended outwards into an allegory:

In the Highlands of Scotland a strath is a small glen. For a small boy – a boy up to ten or twelve year of age – a strath is ideal in size, because its physical features are not so vast or extensive but they can be encompassed on foot yet are extensive or 'far off' enough never to be exhausted in interest or wonder or the unexpected. A glen can be too big, its mountainous sides too high, its cataracts or river too fierce or deep to cross, its distances too bare and forbidding for a small boy to know with any intimacy more than his own home part of it. Our Strath we knew throughout its length – or very nearly. To walk its full length to the river source – always called the Waterhead – was the ultimate adventure and the thought of it inhabited the mind with a peculiar strangeness.[91]

That attitude is basic to Gunn's novels. Man escapes from the familiarity of the strath into the expansive mystery of the sea. It is significant that Gunn's greatest descriptive passages seek to capture the appearance and appeal of the sea.

In his teens Neil Gunn entered the Civil Service and from 1923 to 1937 was excise officer attached to an Inverness whisky distillery. In 1937 Gunn scored a great popular success with *Highland River*. Buoyant with this triumph the novelist resigned from the Civil Service and went, as the title of his next book explained, *Off in a Boat* (1938) with his wife, Daisy, sailing from Skye to Inverness. He published his mystical autobiography in 1956; lived comfortably enough with his wife until her death in 1963; then gradually declined until his own death in 1973 at the age of eighty-two. Even the briefest outline of his life suggests he had pratical knowledge to go with his vision. This vision was both physical and metaphysical. Although Gunn participated in Scottish Nationalist politics he eschewed doctrinaire solutions and preferred more philosophical answers. He felt that modern Scotland was to be remade in the image of the spiritually superior Gael: this creative myth sustained him through his writing career of thirty years during which he produced his twenty novels; novels which could be structurally schematic and stylistically repetitive.

Gunn establishes his Platonic mood carefully then populates it with archetypes. A selfconsciously Celtic Innocent searches in the River of Life for the hazelnuts of Knowledge and the salmon of Wisdom and finds the Vision in the Source. It all sounds too abstract to be true, but Gunn – for all his personifications, symbolically representative figures and bible-based stereotypes (prodigal sons, sacrificial victims, redeemers) – nevertheless brought a new quality to the Scottish novel. His first novel, *The Grey Coast* (1926), was received as the most powerful Scottish fiction since *Green Shutters* but Gunn intended to depart from the realist norm.

Gunn was a moralist, a man fascinated by the human capacity for good and evil. He retells the old story of innocence and experience as it takes place in a Scottish landscape with Edenic associations. In Gunn's ideal world the individual realises that he is apart from na-

ture rather than a part of it and at that moment he has lost his innocence and become aware that life is a challenge with various options. The instant of awareness is crucial as it is both a fall from
grace and a profound insight into the fate of humanity. In Gunn this
conscious struggle torments the individual as he moves towards
maturity. In his autobiographical summing-up *The Atom of Delight*
(1956) he recalled how the moment happened to him, how he saw
his second self. Just as the innocent Adam had his apple, so Gunn
as archetypal innocent ate the hazelnuts of knowledge (real nuts
with allegorical overtones):

> The shallow river flowed around and past with its variety of lulling
> monotonous sounds; a soft wind, warmed by the sun, came upstream
> and murmured in my ears as it continuously slipped from my face. As I
> say, how I got there I do not remember. I do not even remember
> whether anyone had been with me on that expedition, much less what
> anxieties might have to be resolved with 'excuses' when I got home. I
> was just there.
>
> Then the next thing happened, and happened, so far as I can
> remember, for the first time. I have tried hard but can find no simpler
> way of expressing what happened than by saying: *I came upon myself
> sitting there.*
>
> Within the mood of content, as I have tried to recreate it, was this self
> and the self was me . . . Perhaps this second self is what others have
> described as the essence or the soul. I am not too sure . . . It apprehends
> a whole greater than itself, but of which itself is part, and in this
> apprehension is delight's essence.[92]

A delightful sensation, however, that brings problems to occupy the
individual for the rest of his life.

In *Bloodhunt*, Gunn remarks, 'Of all the stories man had made
only two were immortal: the story of Cain and the story of Christ.'[93]
The child can grow into a Cain or into a Christ or can be a bit of
both. It is yet another variant on the Jekyll and Hyde syndrome.
Gunn's unique quality comes from his sureness of touch and his un-
forced allegorising. The vision comes naturally to him. When we
read Gunn we respond to the symbols and the allusion because they
are woven into the texture of his novels. The characters may be
symbolic yet are also recognisably real (most of the time); it is the
same with the dramatic situations. Through the suggestive beauty of
his writing Gunn implies that each simple incident has a larger
meaning. For example, if he describes a family we are made to feel
that the family is a unit corresponding to the Celtic *clann* which, in
turn, is the heart of the Gaelic community which is a model for
mankind to consider. All this is expressed so memorably that it comes as a shock to note the technical means Gunn has at his disposal.
On a purely figurative level Gunn's books are virtuoso exercises in
synecdoche since every item carries its symbolic burden. Gunn
brought the Celt out of the twilight and into the contemporary

world – a world that had its hideous reality as well as its magical possibilities. His novels therefore add up to an account of the twentieth century by a Celtic visionary with few illusions about man's capacity for both destruction and creation.

Gunn's first novel, *The Grey Coast* (1926), is a suitable prelude to the work that follows it for it sounds, quietly, the major themes that Gunn builds on in subsequent novels. These themes concern the perpetual struggle of good and evil, the Celtic consciousness, the persistence of history, the racial memory of the Highland Clearances, the economic situation prevailing in the Highlands and the place of the Gael in the contemporary world. Ivor Cormack, the penurious fisherman, is made in the image of Christ and apparently ready for his local martyrdom. Donald Tait of Tullach is a landowner, which is to say he is the epitome of evil. Like other Highlanders, Gunn learned of the Highland Clearances through the bitter facts preserved in the oral tradition. He knew of the hideous metamorphosis of clan chief into cynical landlord: in his view any man who presumed to possess the land for solely exploitative purposes committed a crime against nature. The novel develops as both men desire the same woman: Maggie, who looks after the croft of her cunning old uncle Jeems. Jeems is the Gael as survivor; eventually his will to endure overcomes the avarice of Tullach. Primitive good, aided and abetted by experience, triumphs over evil. Gunn's fictional debut is didactic in tone yet noteworthy for its subtle descriptive power and structural clarity.

Morning Tide (1930) represents a stylistic advance on the basic theme of making the right choice. In Gunn's visionary world men make major choices: they confront a challenge directly or they shrink from it by clinging to familiar features. Metaphorically their choice hovers between danger and security, physically it homes in on the proximity of a mate. Part of every Gunn novel is the eternal female as physically seductive reality and elemental force. The earth and the sea, as elements, are both female but in a drastically different way: whereas the earth is like a mother the sea is like a mistress. The woman is able to compromise with the earth but remains suspicious of the sea and the rivalry it represents. It threatens her, makes emotional claims on her man. Gunn's second novel reveals the psychosexual nature of this conflict by detailing the temperamental growth of heroic fisherman's son Hugh Macbeth. Hugh's life is related to the predicament of his family who develop like a community in microcosm. Hugh's brothers either drown at sea (like Duncan) or escape to exotic shores (like Alan, who emigrates to Australia) and his sisters are gradually revealed to him as sexual strangers with a magic of their own. Hugh's own relationship with the environment is what finally matters in the novel. What makes the book important, though, is not so much the development of the plot as the way the elements are integrated into the affairs of men. By the sensuous impact of his prose Gunn claims the mysterious and seductive sea as his special concern. Here is young Hugh becoming aware of the scale of the sea that surrounds him:

> The loneliness of the bouldered beach suddenly caught him in an odd way. A small shiver went over his back. The dark undulating water rose from him to a horizon so far away that it was vague and lost. What a size it was! It could heave up and drown the whole world. Its waters would go rushing and drowning. He glimpsed the rushing waters as a turbulent whiteness released out of thunderous sluices. 'But you can't,' he half-smiled, a little fearfully, glancing about him. A short distance away, right on the sea's edge, he saw one of the boulders move. His heart came into his throat. Yet half his mind knew that it could only be some other lonely human in the ebb.[94]

The Lost Glen (1932) shows Gunn using some of the conventions of Scottish realism for his own carefully formulated artistic ends. It is a novel that shows how seriously Gunn took his countrymen (even the most pretentious of them). Gunn knows that intellectual Scots deliberately play a part in the tragic destiny of their nation so he supplies a suitably histrionic plot. We meet, once again, the disgraced student: Ewan is another version of the Prodigal Son, a figure Brown used with such skill in *The House with the Green Shutters*. Gunn's most sympathetic critic has found *The Lost Glen* a relative failure because in 'shifting his dramatic centre from the simple croft girl Maggie [of *The Grey Coast*] to the young Highlander returning disgraced from his university, Gunn loses the naturalistic intensity of the first novel . . . This is tragedy marred by melodrama'.[95] However, Gunn had every reason to avoid melodrama and the plot is not really outrageously far-fetched. Gunn had a point to prove, too, in his third novel. He wanted to show that he was no tame traditionalist, no regional writer reposing in the Celtic Twilight. He wanted to make the Gael a powerful figure; *The Lost Glen* is a novel Gunn felt Scotland needed. It is a strong social drama with a doomed Gael and a hauntingly actual landscape.

In *Morning Tide* we watched the innocent coming to terms with the challenge of the world. Hugh was content to discover Eden. Ewan MacLeod is depicted in a bleaker quest. Gunn seems eager to demonstrate his grasp of narrative essentials: he shows off his ability to vary the pace and to construct a strong story. Instead of dwelling, with leisurely detail, on the exposition he makes the first paragraph carry a punch so the sinner is named and the censors (Brown's bodies in a Highland guise) grouped into the background:

> Ewan MacLeod was aware that his disgrace was known before the bus drew up by the small post office a hundred yards short of the hotel. The usual waiting group all looked at the outcast student, the older ones secretively, but the youngsters with a stare . . . Eyes, when they could,

peered at him with inhuman penetration, for he personated so much in the way of monstrous behaviour . . . And so every house would live under the shadow of Ewan's return.[96]

Obviously Ewan has long since passed the innocent Adam stage (celebrated in *Morning Tide*). He remains, though, a potentially tragic hero who sometimes spoils his chances by ostentatiously carrying on Christ-like shoulders the burden of his people. He acts out a role, gives in to self-pity and survives by cultivating a stoicism that degenerates into cynicism. Gunn's belief in the Gaelic ideal is put to the test in this novel. It is a test he is anxious to pass with the demonstrative quality of his fiction. All Gunn's books consider, directly or by implication, the possibility of restoring Gaeldom to its former glory. In this novel Gunn incorporates a suggestion of the healing power of the Celtic instinct (which seems synonymous with the creative instinct). It is not, to Gunn, a reactionary point of view:

Not a revival of the old, but the old carried forward, evolved, into the new, and the creative instinct at work once more, and all the more powerfully for being free of the increasing nightmare of city civilizations.
The ghost might put on flesh and blood. And humanity be given a new vision.[97]

Linguistically Gunn is at a theoretical disadvantage and he recognises the paraodox involved in writing about the beauty of Gaelic (as the apocryphal language of the Garden of Eden) in English – as MacDiarmid did in his 'Lament for the Great Music'. Occasionally Gunn bends his English into an unusual syntax so his prose either shines with a strange brilliance or – when the experiment fails – reads like a translation rather than a native language. This can, admittedly, be disastrously gauche as when Ewan lusts after the incomer Clare Marlowe in feelings expressed thus:

In this lust was an underswirl of triumph, so that his wide-open look did not waver but stared steadily, letting realisation seep about the inner retina, letting the full possibility rise up and flood hotly the mind . . . And she had come to life beside him, her flesh flushing warm, and looked at him – or not looked at him. He had caught the hidden pause in her thought.[98]

As expected, Ewan does turn out to be one of Gunn's archetypes – the innocent Adam forced, by circumstances, to assume the role of Prodigal Son. We learn that he has been studying for the ministry at Edinburgh University, learning divinity at the expense of his Uncle Will who happens to be a hypocritical publican. A flashback establishes what happened on 'that last fatal night in his Edinburgh lodging'[99] when he gave his uncle the flimsiest of excuses for disowning him. An undergraduate argument, fired by drink, had developed to the point where Ewan felt obliged to defend the tragic melancholy of the Gael against the Lowland opportunism of the aptly named Lothian. Ewan thus accepted the role of the defeated and paid the ultimate price. It is the latest in a long line of defeats so he heads home carrying his shame like a tattered banner. Ewan is a thinker who sees everything in a cosmic context. Standing with his forgiving father, for example,

> A moment of piercing divination came to Ewan wherein he saw their twin bodies caught up against a fateful eternity, not dark, but faintly silvered, like the far and utter loneliness of the sea.[100]

He also speculates on the motives that makes martyrs as he puts himself in exalted company:

> Christ and Gautama and Tolstoi – the leaders of humanity had all searched back for the lost glen of their vision, breaking, as a first step, the shackles of personal ambition and material success. That was the *fact*. The vision of what they searched for was greater than any vision they had ever had.[101]

The titular lost glen is the source of the vision and its music is contained in the pibroch composed by Ewan's great piper friend, Colin McKinnon, who lives in a croft on the lip of a corrie with his daughter Mary. She is the eternal female principle; something that Ewan is not yet equipped to fully conmprehend. Ewan is distracted by Clare Marlowe and tells her what Colin's pibroch signifies, namely 'a glen where never a human foot had been before'.[102] A musical approximation of innocence.

Against this speculative background the story rapidly develops. Ewan is dangerously apt to involve others in his actions and is instrumental in his father's drowning. He alters those he comes into contact with. He appeals to Mary and he toys with Clare. He strikes up hostile attitudes to the villain, Colonel Hicks – who represents Commercial Man as ruthless exploiter of the Gael. To underscore his base instincts the Colonel is also anxious to spoil women, especially pure young women, for we learn that the 'Colonel has a pleasant weakness for young women'[103] and that he 'was always brightened by a good-looking young woman'.[104] Obviously the Colonel will complete the picture of exploitation by attempting to despoil Mary, the eternal female; sure enough he tries to ruin her by rape. In this episode Gunn drops his usual poise and resorts to a frenetic shorthand that merely confirms that his gifts are more suited to portraying mood than to empathetically rendering abrupt action:

> He had her now. At that moment it was not so much perhaps the satisfying of the instinct of lust as the gratifying of the instinct of dominance; male dominance, a man's final pride. He stood against the door, watching her through the faint gloom; saw her panting breasts, the feverish hands that clutched the torn revealing jumper . . . He had her –

cornered in the cow's stall. His body surged in a harmony of power. The concentration of his advance fascinated her. The dreadful intention that sat in his face weakened her. His mouth moved and the lower jaw set. His shoulders hunched a trifle. Her body fluttered to weak acts of mimetic rejection.[105]

Ewan's response to all this is indecisive. He speculates on the proper course of action, treating the incident like a text for a sermon. Eventually, though, his intellect is submerged in his instinct and he kills the Colonel and surrenders to the sea in a final ethically apposite act.

As his confidence grew in the exercise of his art so Gunn's ambition swelled and he next tried to make a book that was more of a visionary statement than an entertaining tale. To achieve the necessary distance he plunged into the past and set *Sun Circle* (1933) in ninth century Caithness. The difficulty of avoiding period quaintness prevents Gunn from painting a totally convincing picture; yet the book coheres thematically. It opens atmospherically as Gunn, making good use of the pathetic fallacy, describes the feminine contours of the coast and draws proleptic conclusions:

> All down the West the islands lie to the sea under this hot summer sky inviting and unprotected, and the long gaze narrows with foreknowledge of their certain rape.
> Narrows and lingers a moment on one last island of all, where men, robed and cowled like women, their backs to the pagan West, are meditating the triumph of the light of Christ. And that island, too, shall be raped.[106]

We are made acutely aware that a change is coming, that an external threat is about to materialise, that local history has reached a critical period. What man holds sacred, Gunn contends, is a projection of the best human qualities. Man makes his faith in his own imagery; the book examines the imagery.

It is a tale full of capital-lettered importance, so that the mysterious Master – the mentor of Aniel – comes from a Grove. And he acts symbolically by drinking from the well of fear and eating from the tree of good and evil. Aniel himself watches over his world as it progresses from cradle to credo. Life (so the book implies) is a perpetual test of human endurance. Therefore the secret of life is the ability to survive various assaults or, to switch to a more Gunnian metaphor, to weather the storms. An individual becomes whole by combining innocence and experience; he reposseses the inner vision of childhood and adds to it the knowledge that comes with the possession of the second self. A community requires a faith to sustain it, to complete a sun circle of mythical strength. For Haakon and the Vikings faith is combative, for Aniel and the Celts it is reflective. Stronger than both of these beliefs is Christianity with its central doctrine of sacrifice. Haakon's faith drives him to wanton acts of

destruction so that inevitably he brings destruction on himself and
Nessa. Aniel rejects the legendary Nessa and chooses Breeta for her
affinity to mother earth. Through Aniel's cogitations we are treated
to an exposition of Gunn's conclusions about life and vital belief:

> Aniel would bring back the young chief with his Christian religion. But
> he need not be hopeless about that. At the end of all religions that which
> is offered is always the same thing. That might be difficult, more difficult
> than all else to feel and to believe, and impossible for the old. But if
> Aniel had to satisfy his own people in the old ways, then he would do so,
> even if he had to do it secretly. For there was only one law in the end:
> the spirit has to be satisfied. In the fullness of time the Christian religion
> might satisfy it, for it, too, was based on blood and sacrifice. There were
> many religions in the world and the gods had many names. The rest was
> loyalty. Only of one thing were we sure, that there are dark beings,
> malignant and cruel; that pain and terror and disease and disaster and
> death over-take us. Each man was a lonely being in that battle. He had
> to hold the gods and demons at bay by propitiation, by sacrifice, but
> even more by the strength within himself. Let him be as one in his circle.
> Then the gods will respect him and the demons fear him, and he will
> know that joy which gives the only vision. Our past was in the earth, and
> our roots are in our past. We live for a little on the surface, drawing
> from our roots and sending new shoots to the Sun. The earth beneath,
> the sun above, and we the children of their union. That is all we know,
> and perhaps all we need to know to find the power that has serenity at its
> heart.[107]

In *Butcher's Broom* (1934) Gunn presents his most deeply felt, if
not always perfectly realised, consideration of the Gaelic past. It is a
novel he, as author, intrudes into with various asides. Gunn broods
on the Clearances that came after the catastrophe of Culloden and
he does so in a novel that has the scale of Scott's historical work and
the symbolic charge of his own, by now characteristic, fiction. In
this book Gunn fairly seethes with moral indignation at the genocidal cruelty unleashed on the Celt. It is something he simply cannot be
objective about. Nevertheless he achieves perspective, if not emotional distance, by going back in time. A new century, the
nineteenth, has commenced. While Napoleon nurses his territorial
ambitions the Celts ponder the remnants of the shattered clan system. Gunn relates the two situations in a passage that describes a vicious circle of suffering:

> It could hardly be within God's irony that a world which had forgotten
> [the Highlanders'] very tongue should be concentrating all its forces of
> destruction upon them. What could the pride and power of emperors
> have to do with this little pocket of self-sufficing earth lost in the hills,
> this retreat, this end of an age, this death of a culture which a
> millennium before had been no more offensive to the nations of the
> West than to set Christianity and learning amongst them? When tragedy
> thus completes itself has it not earned in a people the dignity of saying 'It
> is finished'?[108]

Anxious to impose the meaning of the Gaelic tragedy on the modern reader's consciousness Gunn develops a persuasive argument and illustrates it with incident and symbolic image. In the Highlands, he contends, there was a system that worked; that produced art and culture and cared for the people as a whole community. It was patriarchal and protective and it persisted until the ideal asserted itself in the romantically doomed cause of the adventurer Bonnie Prince Charlie. Then an inferior system based on commerce had gone in for the kill and the clansmen had been scattered. Commerce scored a victory over culture. The clan chief, the head of the communal family, had betrayed his people with Judas-like duplicity and the folk had been swept away in the interest of a financial proposition. Men had been shunted off so that sheep might take their place:

> Accordingly, by virtue of his sole ownership of the land, the chief came to hold territorial power over his clansmen that was absolute, and their value to him shifted from that of fighting men to rent-paying men. The chief had turned from a great leader into a great landlord, and with the law in all its power behind him, his concern became the acquisition of the greatest possible amount of annual tribute in cash.[109]

In almost every instance Gunn's titles are carefully chosen so that they reverberate with significance. *Butcher's Broom* is no exception. It involves a pun and a principle. Butcher's broom is a shrub featured on the Sutherland clan badge; ironically enough the Countess of Sutherland functioned as the clearing instrument (or broom) doing the dirty work of the victor of Culloden – the Butcher Cumberland. Against the treachery of the Sutherland chief there is the voice of the people, eloquent and wise in the ways of the oral tradition. Dark Mairi, the Gaelic eternal female, endures like the sea so long as she is allowed to. She is quintessential, a perpetually mothering presence. She is spiritual yet substantial, elusive yet omnipresent:

> She was a small woman, roundly built, deep chested and straight, yet she did not give an impression of bodily strength so much as of something delicate and hardy that persists evenly . . . But perhaps the suggestion of persistence, of abidingness, that was the silent note struck by her person, was sustained most distinctly by the cheek-bones . . . Her head was raised in a watchfulness that was sometimes direct and glimmering and sometimes staring-blind.[110]

The people she seeks to preserve are reduced to a broken family who have a culture in common and a language equal to it:

> In truth, it is an immensely old tongue, and a thousand years before Mairi it was richer in its knowledge, wider in its range, and was given to metaphysics and affairs of state. The thousand years have slowly pushed it back, have shut it up in the glens, where it has developed its instinct

for human value, and may flash out of the mouth of a tempestuous fighter or grow silent in him who with fixed eyes stares through the material world and sees what takes place outside our notions of time and space.[111]

In this novel Gunn preaches to the converted since modern readers deplore the Clearances and recognise the Sutherland Clearance especially as a symbol of inhumanity. Gunn's book thus fitted in well with the literary mood of the 1930s when writers were politically conscious and were determined to question the dark forces in nature. Gunn saw this as a problem as ancient as it was urgent:

> There would seem to be a power in nature that once set on harrying is not content to defeat and break, but must with malignant intensity pursue its quarry into a physical death of revolting and bloody cruelty. And to bring this about it uses forces that appear oddly disconnected, set blindly in motion by divergent causes, over great areas of the earth.[112]

Dark Mairi alone is no match for this power, especially as it has become an organised destruction. The men have gone and she has to draw on her own, admittedly considerable, resources. She mothers Elie (and her fatherless child), she carries with her an affirmative attitude. Still, the destructive power is at large; the dogs are having their day. At the end of the novel Mairi is torn to pieces by the dogs of the shepherd who watches the animals that have replaced men:

> The human mother carrying on her ancient solitary business with the earth, talking good and familiar sense with boulder and flower and rock, and now and then following a root below the surface . . . The two dogs started . . . They were hunting the human quarry out of this place. It was their only sport. They leapt among the lambs, and one, madly eager to be in before his fellow, sprang at the woman. She screeched as she went down and the brute ripped and tore. The white wave swirled away from her. The second dog pounced, and the two snarled and slashed, but not the woman now so much as each other, for they were mad with excitement . . . [113]

Given Gunn's allegorical approach such an ending was inevitable, even predictable. Dark Mairi had to die dramatically so we could feel a bit of Gaelic culture being murdered anew on the printed page. *Butcher's Broom* is meant to be a disturbing book, a story that reminds us of the crimes committed in the name of commercial progress. After *Butcher's Broom* Gunn returned to the subject he was most at ease with: the childhood dream that suddenly wakens to the nightmarish possibilities of the external world yet transcends all difficulties in an affirmative vision of the inviolability of individuality. *Highland River* (1937) is Gunn's best-known novel. Its financial and artistic success made a full-time writer of him, for he was suddenly able to give up his excise work in Inverness, go *Off in a Boat* (1938) with his wife, Daisy, sailing from Skye to Inverness, and settle down to life in Braefarm House. The novel raises some stylistic questions we have to answer in making a case for Gunn as a major Scottish novelist. Principally there is the nature of allegory as a form with definite limitations. To rely entirely on allegorical implications means that the writer is more concerned with ethical abstractions than with human relationships. We have to feel some sympathy for fictional characters and regard them as something more than Jonsonian humours or purely representative figures. They have to be persons before they are personifications. Gunn's use of names often suggests that they are labels: Kenn, in *Highland River*, represents knowledge (since 'ken' is idiomatic Scots for 'know') just as Young Art and Old Hector represent, respectively, creativity and experience in *Young Art and Old Hector* and *The Green Isle of the Great Deep*. Kenn's appeal as a character demonstrates that he is more than a personification of knowledge.

In fact Kenn does come alive in the pages of the novel, principally because he is a self-portrait of the artist as a boy. We know this to be so since so much of *Highland River* corresponds to the odyssey outlined in the autobiographical memoir *The Atom of Delight*. For this novel Gunn turned inwards then projected that second self he discovered as a child. The analysis of this process frequently dissolves into a description of Dunbeath; the novel contains some of Gunn's most stunningly beautiful stretches of writing. Kenn has to learn a lesson from nature, namely that the individual is a being born of a source that has psychological as well as local colour. Just as the baby is carried in the amniotic fluid the boy is almost umbilically attached to the river. Individuals are, metaphorically, rivers that run into the oceanic mass of humanity. Yet they retain their uniqueness if they are aware of origins. This is the secret Kenn discovers on tracing his Highland river back to its source. In the beginning Kenn fights with a thirty pound salmon in the Well Pool; single-handed he captures it. This is the greatest event in his life, more important even than his immersion in the First World War when he is gassed and hospitalised until he recovers his sight (or vision):

> From that day the river became the river of life for Kenn . . . For Kenn, then, the river was primarily not a concern of the folk who lived near its banks. Its communal importance had little interest for him. In all his outings, by himself or with his companions, the river was an adventure often intense and always secretive . . . Going from the mouth to the source may well seem to be reversing the natural order, to be going from the death of the sea, where individuality is lost, back to the source of the stream, where individuality is born. Yet that is the way Kenn learned his river and, when he came to think of it, that is the way he learned life.[114]

In his own life in Dunbeath – the strath, the river, the rush to the sea – Gunn-Kenn is aware of a model of perfection. Such a realisation is something Gunn is profoundly grateful for and he incorporates in the novel some vivid insights into village life. To convey the nature of the mature Kenn the novel switches to the present tense. Kenn has done well at school, survived a world war, qualified as a scientist. His empirical temperament is often at odds with his racial memories of his Caithness past. He has to bring the two together and does so by an imaginative return to the Highland river. Caithness endures with its archeological markers to a way of life both primitive and profound:

> This bare, grim, austere Caithness, treeless, windswept, rock-bound, hammered by the sea, hammered, too, by successive races of men, broch-builders and sea-rovers, Pict and Viking . . .[115]

Kenn realises that innocence is the way the world was before touched by human hand and he senses his own part in an eternal story:

> . . . the grown Kenn knows quite exactly one quality in the scent of the primrose for which he has an adjective. The adjective is innocent. The innocency of dawn on a strath on a far back morning of creation. The freshness of dawn wind down a green glen where no human foot has trod . . . For the heirs of brutal savages, the inheritors of brutish instincts, whence this troubling vision of primrose dawns and wood fires, of fleet running and laughter, whence the mounting effect of it all to a flame-bright ecstasy?
> There is no denying that however it comes about, whatever the cause, such a state of happiness is produced. Kenn has experienced it over and over again. He has deliberately gone back to his Highland river to experience it afresh.[116]

Highland River is beautifully written in a spare language studded with images and overlaid with symbolism. It is a story made fabulous by the power of art. It is basic Gunn – the writer using the traditional art of storytelling to suggest magical possibilities. Kenn has to live with the pain of his brother's death and to accept his own end as inevitable. This does not prevent him from responding fully to life. He has learned his lesson, has come to understand and value his uniqueness. After all, the book is a prolonged meditation on Gunn's perception of the oneness of life. Kenn recalls the Celtic people with their imaginatively expansive ways, their natural faith derived from the hazelnuts of knowledge and the salmon of wisdom. It is an ecstatic novel. After *Highland River* Gunn attempted two different genres in an effort to play the literary market in his own way.

Wild Geese Overhead (1939) and *Second Sight* (1940) have to be regarded as occasional novels inspired by Gunn's desire to diversify before returning to an obsessive research into the meaning of life. In *Wild Geese Overhead* Gunn moves out of the rural environment and asks the reader to empathise with Will Montgomery, a journalist conditioned by the harsh ambiance of Glasgow. Still, even a city dweller has a second self for Will's epiphanies (symbolised by the sight of wild geese overhead) suggest that there is more to life than meets the urban eye. Another glimpse of the hidden depths is given in *Second Sight*, a supernatural thriller in a Highland setting. Gunn cleverly deploys all the trappings of the genre: an idyllic setting (a lodge in the wilderness), a contest between man and beast (the stag King Brude), a sinister apparition involving a corpse (of a character very much alive and out for King Brude's blood). Gunn includes frequent asides to air his opinions (on clairvoyance, on the theories of J. W. Dunne, on the Brahan Seer) so the novel is informative as well as suspenseful. Both books are slight in comparison with his next, *The Silver Darlings* (1941).

The Silver Darlings is Gunn's most highly rated novel: it is also his most accessible since the symbolism does not hold back the splendidly spectacular action of the book. It is at once an adventure and an odyssey. Like *Butcher's Broom* it is set in the first part of the nineteenth century; the main difference between the two books is that the later novel is more engaging. Gunn immerses his imagery in an everyday industry as full of hope and the promise of economic progress as it is rich in symbolism. The silver darlings are 'the herrings, the lithe silver fish, the swift flashing ones, hundreds and thousands of them, the silver darlings'.[117] They are a perfect physical base for Gunn's images.

The novel opens in 1816. Catrine, a teenage bride, is intent on a lifetime of happiness with her husband, Tormad. She carries his child and cleaves to his strength. Tormad loves her; he is also in love with the sea and this affection destroys him. In a scene full of furious action he is taken by the press-gang. Catrine is left to cope with her life as the custodian of a child. For she knows, through intuition more than experience, that her maternal duty is her priority. In a poignant passage Catrine dwells on Tormad's death for he comes to her as a revenant (with the force of a figure from a ballad):

> It was the fifth night after his capture that she saw Tormad again . . . He did not speak, he could not speak, but stood there mute, asking her forgiveness. And she knew why he asked her forgiveness: not for anything that had happened between them, not for anything in the past, but because he was dead.[118]

Catrine has to seek a new life so she moves from Dale to Dunster (which is actually Dunbeath). She carries the future within her, but it is problematic for the child has no father, yet is named after Gaeldom's great organisational hero Finn MacCoul.

Throughout the novel we watch Finn's consciousness evolve. He has to come to terms with a triple challenge: first, the persistence of the past; second, the coexistence of good and evil; third, the rivalry of other men for a beloved woman. The past of Dunster is symbolised by the House of Peace, a knoll marking the site of an old monastery. Finn is naturally, or preternaturally, drawn to it. As a child Finn chases and kills a butterfly which means that 'the terrible knowledge of good and evil was in him'.[119] His rival, and model, is Roddie Sinclair, the most dynamic captain in Dunster. Roddie is a competitor for the love of Catrine; he is captivated by her and wants to wed her. He is also, potentially, a surrogate father who lives with the knowledge of Tormad's ghostly claims on Catrine. For some considerable time. Tormad is conspicuous by his absence for his death is not officially acknowledged. So Catrine waits, like the sea. Her embrace is elusive.

Gunn's heroes are manly men who accept responsibilities; his women are sturdy but comely wenches who know how to keep a house in good order so they might make man the adventurer accept his role as a domestic creature. Gunn does not always rise above the stereotypical man and woman but he usually does so in *The Silver Darlings* by dealing with Catrine, Roddie and Finn in revealing episodes. Roddie has his 'six feet of sure manhood'[120] and Finn is aware of 'the growth towards responsible manhood'.[121] At the same time both Roddie and Finn require a mate, a figure combining sexual allure with maternal comfort. Because of this elemental approach to amorous relationships Gunn makes the coming together of manly man and comely wench sound more like a contest than a congress. Men and women tend to lock like wrestlers in a physically formidable embrace. Catrine remembers Tormad as a wrestling partner, 'her fingers going through his hair, sometimes gripping it and hanging on until he yelled and threatened her and they rolled and fought in an ecstasy of living'.[122] Finn is drawn to Una in similarly aggressive terms:

> . . . though she was a well-built girl, Finn pinned her arms and broke her strength . . . She gripped him more strongly as if she felt what was coming. He pushed her head back relentlessly. She struggled against showing what he would find in her face. But he found it and the world went blind against her mouth.[123]

That encounter in the Birch Wood shows Gunn's peculiarly primitive reading of romance. It is always a test, an all-embracing ordeal.

As competitors Finn and Roddie are linked. At first the contest is an unequal one between a boy and a man. Thus Finn the child is taken to the market where he stands in awe of Roddie. Finn, determined to establish some personality of his own, wants to blow his own trumpet both literally and symbolically (which is a typical Gunn touch). Roddie shows him how. Later Finn watches Roddie assert his muscular masculinity by effortlessly ringing the bell in a strongman contest. Finn subsequently discusses the day with his mother.

He clearly envies Roddie his strength and mastery of the sea. He too wants to be a skipper. Catrine is alarmed; having lost one man to the waves she is not about to lose another. Not if she can prevent it. She asks Finn to promise her he will never go near the sea. He avoids the issue. Catrine is no longer the single influence in his life. Still, Catrine despises the sea. The sea is a bitch, a womanly rival. Finn respects her but sails his toy boat in imitation of his elders. He dreams of being like Roddie, of being 'the greatest man in the world'.[124] Strangely, the world is not much larger than Finn's day-dream – as he is about to prove.

Climactically Finn and Roddie go on a voyage together. It is built up as an epic voyage, the first time a Dunster boat has attempted to go beyond the Moray Firth. What follows is full of incident and narrative power. The boat rounds Cape Wrath, the men land in Stornoway where Roddie displays his manliness yet again by proving himself the toughest man in town. Most memorable of all, though, is the test Finn passes: the climbing of the ultimate obstacle, the sheer rock Eilean Mor. The crew have lost their way and will surely perish without water. The only possibility of survival depends on a heroic ascent of the rock. The person who does it will be a man among men, both friend and saviour – a Caithness hero to be compared with Finn MacCoul and even Christ. Finn surpasses himself and in his moment of glory understands his relationship with Roddie:

> He could see that for a long time he had been afraid of Roddie, of a strange terrible power that was in him. Now he was no longer afraid. He could hold his own against Roddie.[125]

When Roddie and Finn return they do so as men ready to meet their mates. Catrine and Una, respectively, are destined to become skippers' wives. Finn has become a man after all, an extraordinary man able to cope with life and carry it forward. He is the ideal fisherman, legendary and lifelike at the same time. As the novel comes to a majestic close he contemplates his second self born of the awareness that he is both himself and part of something seemingly larger than life:

> There had been one moment of revelation that would outlast all others. It occurred in the Birch Wood. Una and himself had been sitting talking, and from them all self-consciousness, all stress, had fallen away. She was talking quietly of something they would do together, when suddenly he did not hear so much what she was saying as the tone of her voice, and its intimacy put about them a ring of silence. They were within this ring alone, in league for ever, the two of them, cut off from all others in the world . . . Time became a stilled heart-beat. Stealthy, climbing sounds. Finn's body drew taut, heaved up on to supporting palms. Whisperings, the movement of the top of a small birch-tree here and there whose

trunk invisible hands gripped. The hunters in their primordial humour
were closing in. Life had come for him.[126]

In *The Serpent* (1943) we run through Gunn's entire repertoire so
smoothly that the author seems ironically aware of the familiarity of
it all and exclaims: 'High heaven save us from the symbolists, from
the abstracters! Give us back the earth and the flesh and the lovely
currents that flow in and between them!'[127] The Gunn vision is experienced by Tom Mathieson who is successively nicknamed Tom
the Atheist, Tom the Serpent and then (definitively) the Philosopher. It is the Philosopher in whose image the book is made; he
reflects on the life he has lived in flashbacks that reveal the disastrous consequences of daring to deviate too radically from the
naysaying norm of his Highland village. As a child Tom had been
mischievous enough to play cruel practical jokes capable of back-
firing; as a young man his blasphemy had hastened his father's death
(in a set piece where father suffers a heart attack in attempting to
strike his rebellious son); as an adult he has contemplated murder in
the name of love.

All the Gunn quintessentials are present. There is the
monumental link with the past (the knoll of the Stones, the contrast
between Highland rural idyll and Lowland industrial inferno as Tom
goes to Glasgow to learn about life and politics), the sexual rivalry
(since both Tom the Atheist and Donald the minister's son are after
the same girl) and the obligatory discovery of the hazelnuts of
knowledge in a Highland river in childhood:

> When he was a small boy, perhaps about ten, he had gone nutting in the
> wooded burn which wanders down the steep slope of the Glen just
> beyond Taruv. Johnny Munro, the blacksmith's son, a boy of about
> thirteen, had been with him. Johnny said that the best trees were near
> the top of the wooded stretch. There the nuts came out of the clusters a
> deep dark brown and had a rich flavour – a 'whisky taste', Johnny called
> it. They wandered, and filled their pockets, and cracked the nuts with
> their teeth, and ate them during long hours on a Saturday in October.[128]

Then there is the symbolism: the serpent as biblical Satan versus the
serpent as Celtic emblem of eternity. At the end of the book the
Philosopher's musings are interrupted when he is touched by an
earthly serpent (an adder) which subsequently emerges from his
left arm to the horror of his great friend, the shepherd. As Tom is
given Gunn's thoughts on life it is in *The Serpent* that we get the
simplest statement of his own philosophy which is an ardent indi-
vidualism:

> So he came back to the individual, and as the only individual he would
> ever have a chance of knowing was himself, he drifted from his
> preoccupations with socialism and freethought into a tentative reading of
> philosophy. For manifestly each individual was born by himself, lived by

himself, and died by himself. There was no getting past that. That was central. All the rest was added to it, was superstructure . . . Perhaps amid the intellectual and spiritual efforts of man, literature in its detachment from any specific field of effort, as an observer in all fields, had the job of synthesising for and in the individual all the theses and anti-theses, and bringing the result with some coherence to walk on its own two feet amid the tall grasses! The ultimate of what is felt and thought and experienced by all, expressed in terms of life. The living essence of the communal whole. The living individual.[129]

In *Young Art and Old Hector* (1942) Gunn had introduced the two titular characters as rather obviously named personifications of imagination and experience. The book cast Art Macrae in the role of listener, Hector Macdonald as the storyteller recalling the legendary Gaelic past. Having created such useful characters Gunn brought them back together in the dystopia *The Green Isle of the Great Deep* (1944). Understandably, given his quiet humanity, Gunn had been appalled at the horrific reports of the atrocious cruelty practised in Nazi Germany. His imaginative answer to it was a novel that used his own iconography to make some inroads into an apparently inhuman political situation. In the event the ancient Gaelic wisdom proves more than a match for the contemporary totalitarian mentality. The individual (armed with imagination and knowledge, or Young Art and Old Hector) acquires the wisdom to overcome the institution. The community proves more endurable than the collective. Thus the novel is an extended piece of wishful thinking on Gunn's part.

The book opens up with a discussion of contemporary affairs involving brainwashing and concentration camps. Old Hector is disturbed by this and takes Young Art to the river of life, the 'fabled River'[130] where they will find the hazelnuts of knowledge and the salmon of wisdom. Unfortunately the river has been contaminated by contemporary events (symbolised by a newspaper containing reports of concentration camps). Art and Hector have lost their sense of direction so are plunged into the river to emerge in a dream that rapidly become a nightmare. They have descended to the Green Isle of the Great Deep.

In the Green Isle they see the Tree of Knowledge and eat the forbidden fruit. The biblical relevance is reinforced when they find room at the Inn and befriend Robert and Mary. Old Hector realises that Robert and Mary are of the earth, for Mary 'was different from the other inhabitants of the Green Isle. She thought below the surface of her face. She was almost human, in the way that he himself had always known human beings. Last night, in a fancy of his mind, the others on the Green Isle had seemed to him like clean empty shells on a strange seashore.'[131] The Green Isle, with its institutional rigidity, threatens to engulf the two visitors though Young Art keeps escaping. Old Hector wonders, in his confusion, why the citizens tolerate an autocratic order imposed from above and Robert answers ' "Did you rise against the lairds and the factors and the clergy when they told you that you had to be cleared off your own ancient lands and your homes burnt down?" ' ' "No," said Old Hector sadly.'[132] Still, Old Hector has his belief in the power of art, 'the vision of the immortal boy'.[133] Art is elusive, difficult to pin down. Even when he is captured he manages to break free, for by then he has met God (in the guise of the Starter from Clachdrum, a rather simplistic play on the meaning of the starter of a – human – race). The reader wise in the ways of Gunn will anticipate the end of the book. A totalitarian society will always be opposed by the 'immortal three – knowledge, wisdom and magic'.[134] With this lesson learned Young Art and Old Hector return to their earthly home which is re-freshingly imperfect in comparison to the inhuman abstraction they have left behind in their collective nightmare. Gunn's attempt to come to creative terms with urgent current affairs is admirable rather than achieved; he was still open to a thematic challenge but too set in his literary ways to be capable of novelty. Gunn takes his own vision too much for granted and, as he parades all the usual symbolic paraphernalia, the unconverted reader will find it difficult to see how Celtic innocence could possibly undermine Barbaric cruelty.

In his postwar fiction Gunn tended to operate to a rather rigid formula; each novel exhaustively explores the narrative and thema-tic possibilities implicit in a symbolically significant title. Thus *The Key to the Chest* (1945) is a psychological thriller with a difference: the victim (a seaman found drowned clutching the eponymous chest) is more of a curse than a corpse and the villain is not a graceless in-dividual but the destructive force that divides a community against itself (a schism that keeps Charlie MacIan, the token Prodigal Son, from his unpleasant brother Douglas the shepherd). *The Drinking Well* (1947) shows Gunn reaching for new symbolic depths (switch-ing from the River of Life to the Well of Life) as he sends Iain Cat-tanach away from the Highlands and into Edinburgh in a maternal-ly-approved attempt to improve, commercially at least, on his crof-ter-father's humble station in life. In the city, learning law in an office, Iain is (metaphorically and actually) like a fish out of water although he comes to value his patience for the 'one thing the coun-try had taught him was how to endure'.[135] In Edinburgh he finds a Lowland girl to compensate for his Highland Mary and finally loses his legendary patience with an arrogant colleague who duly suffers some traditional Highland ferocity. Iain returns to the Highlands to reunite with Mary, to drink from the Well of Life, and to take up the challenge of an economically rejuvenated Highland plan for Mary believes he should translate his dreams into practical schemes:

'Oh Iain, wouldn't it be lovely if you got things going, and all the young fellows, and the girls, too, were in it, happiness and work, and your fiddle going, and dancing! And one day – it would be the people's glen.'

'Dreams!'

'Wherever we go, what have we at the end of the day but our dreams – and our hands? What has any people, whether in Australia or Russia, but just that? Haven't I heard you say it? The Highlands will never be anything – but what we make them.'

'I did not know – you thought like that.'[136]

Thus the novel ends on an upward surge of hope. Iain is aware of the Gaelic past but determined to avoid further defeat if he can; with the Well of Life and the folk wisdom of Mairag the local witch and the love of Mary, he is at least entitled to think of himself as a man with a future.

The Shadow (1948) is a psychological thriller like *The Key to the Chest*. Nan Gordon is living under the shadow of a nervous collapse caused by the London blitz. The healing Highland idyll she hoped for turns out to be illusory since she is in the wrong frame of mind. She hears of the murder of a local, she befriends the artist Adam who betrays her trust by assaulting her, and in attempting to shake off Adam she discovers the drowned body of another local. Nan's Aunt Phemie brings Nan's Communist friend Ronald Surrey to the scene of the crimes and he goes for revenge. The novel shows Gunn's habit of looking apprehensively at the sinister way contemporary negativity casts a shadow over everything worth while.

Gunn's novels increasingly appeared to function as endlessly extended metaphors (*The Drinking Well* runs to more than four hundred pages of print) with the only variable factor being the genre chosen for a particular purpose. *The Silver Bough* (1948) is a character study of a man tormented by modernity and therapeutically drawn towards the primitive myth-making prehistoric past as marked by the archeological site investigated by Simon Grant in the novel. Grant's search leads him into conflict with Andie Mackenzie, his *ad hoc* assistant and local idiot; and with Donald Martin, landowner, on whose property the all-important chambered cairn lies. There is also an infant innocent, Sheena, and a silver bough; more precisely, two silver boughs, one being the legendary apple-bearing bough of musical miracles, the other being an earthly replica made for Simon by a friend in Edinburgh. Gold is discovered, a coffin is unearthed, Andie vanishes and apparent opposites like Simon and Donald find human qualities in common. The common touch likewise links the characters in *The Lost Chart* (1949). Dermot Cameron, spy, is given a strategically crucial chart of a Hebridean island. In rescuing a damsel in distress, an island acquaintance Christina McNeil, the chart is lost. All is not lost with it, however, as Dermot suspects that Cold War Communists are using the lovely Christina to further their nefarious ends. There is much discussion on political matters, the essential point being the immorality of institutional authority.

Neither of these novels occupies the place in Gunn's output accorded to *The Well at the World's End* (1951), a beautiful little book – little, that is, by Gunn's standards – providing probably the most perfect example of Gunn's artistry. It begins with an anecdotal trifle and expands into a profoundly philosophical conclusion. In some novels Gunn's symbols are pressed embarrassingly on the reader whereas in this book they arise naturally from the text as the author achieves his own ideal of using the skills of a lifetime to reveal an insight so perfectly innocent that a child could understand it. The book pursues the way of the mystic seeking the mystery of life: it follows the Zen Buddhist path towards the ineffability of the absolute and Jung's mythical road on which modern man searches for his soul.

Everything in the novel shines with a symbolic glow, from the filling of a kettle from a well or the eating of a salmon sandwich to the appreciation of a glass of whisky (not surprisingly since the Gaelic word for whisky, *uisge-beatha*, means water of life, the implications of which are thoroughly discussed in Gunn's *Whisky and Scotland*). Gunn relates global conflicts to a particular flaw in humanity, a hunger that is too often unsatisfied, a lust for solutions. He finds the so-called maturity of modern civilisation spurious and rejects it in favour of an awareness of innocence. The earthly paradise might be an imperfect impression of the eternal one but it is accessible to the individual willing to take an imaginative leap into the unknown. Gunn is optimistically looking for Tir nan-Og, 'the living essence that philosophers, lost in meditation, called the divine Ground and ordinary men, lost in dream, called eternal youth'.[137]

Peter Munro, Professor of Ancient History, is on a Highland holiday with his wife, Fand. He has asked an old woman for water and been directed to a well so clear it looks empty. Peter learns that it only gives up its elemental contents to those who make the effort to look deep, beyond the surface, into the bottom of things. Suddenly he decides to seek out the mystery of life. The transition from well-watching to spiritual odyssey is not so abrupt as apposite for Gunn has created a mood of enchantment so compelling that the reader is immersed in the subsequent events. The delicate relationship between Peter and Fand is absolutely convincing and the dialogue is both natural and knowing, representing 'the kind of talk that . . . might start in the personal but . . . went beyond the horizon. Its heart-beat was light, its speculation had wings'[138] Here is an example of what Gunn has in mind in a section that reveals that author's mastery of the majesty of the novel:

A moon must have risen behind the hill they had climbed, for its radiance was spilling everywhere. The silence was now absolute, and, when she listened to it, it went from her, ballooning up and away into a remoteness that was like the remoteness of another land, of a place beyond.

'That was odd – about the water in the well,' he said.

'Yes.'

'What's that legend again about the well at the world's end?'

'An old Gaelic legend – with a tragic end.'

'Tragic?'

'Yes. It's about a goddess that went off to find the well in the land beyond ours, the Land of Youth. When she found it, she couldn't have done the right thing – though what she should have done we don't know. The water in the well got angry and rose up and drowned her, for her body was found on a bank of the river that now flowed from the well.'

He was silent for a little while. 'What did she expect to find in the well?'

'Knowledge and poetry. There are hazels above the well, and they burst into blossom when you find it, and inspirations and wisdom fall into the well, and the well surges. You'll often find mention of this well in the old legends.'

'You've got to hand it to them,' he said. 'My God,' he said, reaching for his glass, 'if ever there was a time when we could be doing with that well, it's now.'

She was silent.

'You see what I mean? This gloom that hangs over us. Violence and death. Without end. It's not that we've forgotten how to approach the well in the right way: we've forgotten the well itself. The thing isn't even tragic: it's a bloody mess.' He finished his whisky.

The silence could not be defeated. It came in about them soft as velvet beyond the touch.

'I wonder,' he mused presently, 'if there's any of the well left – anywhere'.

'It's here now.'

'That's what we have come for to seek?'

'That's what I saw in you first.'

'How do you mean?'

'It was the hill air about you.'[139]

On his journey Peter participates in a number of events and eventually loses his footing, falls over a cliff, and survives by sucking the milk from a ewe. He has gone beyond empirical knowledge, has freed himself from the burden (amusingly symbolised by his rucksack) comprising the woes of the world (symbolised by his academic Chair in Ancient History). He knows that 'death was the presence that waited, the invisible companion'[140] and that its proximity can actually increase the awareness of life.

After probing the well of life Gunn turned to a consideration of primitive urges in *Bloodhunt* (1952), another psychological thriller with specifically Gunnian qualities. This one is fitted out with Christian symbolism. A pregnant girl is abandoned by her seducer, who is then murdered by his rival, who is then pursued by the dead man's brother. It is an allegory constructed in the light of 'the story of Cain and the story of Christ'.[141] As the receiver of all the narrative information there is Old Sandy, retired seaman, who takes in the murderer and the pregnant girl who then gives birth to new life in his barn. The allegorical implications are clear enough as is Gunn's increasingly optimistic assumption that creativity is capable of triumphing over the ubiquitious force of destruction. In his final, valedictory performance as a novelist Gunn set out to place that destructive force in a profoundly healing context.

The Other Landscape (1954) covers the area between symbolism and actuality, discusses the power of art, invokes supernatural presences and observes that 'the final tragedy is the woman's, the creator's tragedy'.[142] It contains, in other words, all the items Gunn dedicated his creative lifetime to. A Highland-born anthropologist, Willie Urquhart, broods on an encounter whose impact transforms him from a detached observer into an initiate to the mystery of life. Urquhart is professionally attracted to the study of primitive impulses and only incidentally concerned with literature though this secondary interest leads him to the isolated home of the composer Douglas Menzies. Urquhart's friend David Townbee is the editor of the journal *Serpent* (a name whose significance will not escape Gunn's attentive readers); he has seen a stunningly powerful typescript written by Menzies and wants to know more about this man of mystery. Urquhart goes to the Highlands in search of Menzies. What he finds there changes his life.

Menzies is obviously in tune with a spiritual world, the world beyond external appearances. This world eludes the crude grasp of logic and is only hinted at by myth and symbol. As this subject is central to Gunn's development as a novelist it becomes intensely important to the outcome of the novel. Urquhart and Menzies discuss the nature of art with regard to Menzie's typescript which shows human beings at the mercy of a destructive tendency personified as the Wrecker:

> 'It might,' I said, 'be worth considering. The Wrecker's motif, for example. I found myself lost somewhere between symbolism and actuality. That may be your intention. The reader feels that the writer has experienced with an intense clarity of vision what he, the reader, can see only as – as –'
> 'As in a glass darkly.'
> I looked straight at him. 'Yes,' I said. I held his eyes and added, 'The degree of darkness being in inverse ratio to the intuitive insight . . .'
> He was extraordinarily expert in the use of the image . . . The obvious was no longer of any interest to him.
> Perhaps the simplest way for me would be to illustrate it from my own experience. For example, when I looked back over my shoulder at the little landscape of the two ruins and saw finally the dismembered rowan tree with its one arm thrust against the sky, I had a feeling of turning

away from a landscape behind the physical one I looked at. Analysis here can go on for ever and ad nauseam, but 'the other landscape' remains as at least a useful label. To put it naively for the moment, it stands for something.[143]

What the other landscape stands for, as will be apparent, is the eternal world the everyday world is a poor copy of. It is, to give a Gunnian mixture of modes, the Gospel According to Plato. Douglas Menzies is a metaphysical Scot who has gone beyond metaphysics and lived as though the other landscape was omnipresent. Menzies is therefore fair game for the Wrecker. He had written his piece 'Cliffs' to please his wife. Tragically it anticipated her death in childbirth, a catastrophe that confirms Menzies's account of the Wrecker's malicious habit of playing havoc with human lives. Menzies has nothing left but the extent of his vision; he is a man obsessed by his experience and haunted by his wife. Her spectral presence informs vivid passages of the book. The novel moves towards Menzies's death which illuminates life for Urquhart:

> Menzies' love for [his dead wife] Annabel was taken for granted, like the memory of a profound understanding, a warmth, a light. In the loneliness, the bleakness, it was there. It evoked the dark enigma of the Wrecker. It was never mentioned.
> Once when I glimpsed his face which in the ordinary sense showed no personal emotion at all yet was alive with interest, that refinement of the mask, I had an intuition of the bleakness, the loneliness, of the human condition that strips nakedness to the grey bone and is terrifying beyond all further insights of terror. What horror, what tragic meaningless horrors, the Wrecker works on man, from without – and from within.
> Against that darkness man has the light, the warmth, the other insight which love has fashioned for him as his sole weapon on the eternal quest. I saw rather than thought this. I thought of Annabel.[144]

That weapon is enough for Gunn. His monothematic, yet never monotonous work, is a tribute to 'the light, the warmth, the other insight'.

In the English novel there is, according to F. R. Leavis, a Great Tradition; in the indigenous Scottish novel there is nothing as definite as that though we are aware of a Grim Presence, the ghostly persistence of the frequently disastrous Scottish past. The Scottish house of fiction is haunted, which explains the abundance of grotesque characters and Gothic events. The writers so far discussed all felt the grim presence and dealt with it in various ways, thus helping to establish a modern tradition capable of coming to creative terms with the past. To change the image, they all raised the level of a literary reservoir that all Scottish writers dip into. The Scottish novel has developed by ranging between symbolism and realism, between the rural idyll and the industrial inferno. Always there are extremes, always options. Little wonder the Scottish house of fiction is tense. After *Green Shutters* any novel contaminated by kailyardism was dismissed and critical praise was reserved for books that opened more shutters on the national disgrace. The grim presence was held to be the epitome of artistry; entertainment was not, though, entirely forgotten.

22. ENTERTAINING DOCTORS: DOYLE AND CRONIN

The distinction between the artist and the entertainer is a Scottish schism that has resulted in an excessively moralistic art and an extremely idiotic level of entertainment. Scots have seldom been able to combine artistry and entertainment; writers who do so are rare and remarkable. Sir Arthur Conan Doyle (1859–1930) is rightly regarded as a great Scotsman of Irish origin. Doyle's alcoholic father, Charles, settled in Edinburgh in 1849 and earned his living as an assistant surveyor until his incarceration in a city asylum in 1879. Doyle virtually disowned him and sought non-paternal figures of authority. He studied medicine in Edinburgh and based his two most famous inventions on men he had observed in the capital: Sherlock Holmes, who first appeared in *A Study in Scarlet* (1887), was modelled on virtuoso diagnostician Dr Joseph Bell, surgeon at Edinburgh Infirmary; Professor Challenger, the irascible, temperamental scientist of *The Lost World* (1912) and *The Poison Belt* (1913), on Professor William Rutherford. Both men believed passionately in the endless possibilities of the empircal method of observation and experiment, such faith being a typically Scottish phenomenon owing its formulation to the elegant prose of David Hume. Another Doyle hero, immortalised in *The Exploits of Brigadier Gerard* (1895), possessed the mock-heroic panache that flashes back to Scott and Stevenson and forward to Linklater's Juan and George MacDonald Fraser's Flashman. Doyle's Scottishness is perhaps most readily revealed in his pursuit of the supernatural. He was easily persuaded of the existence of paranormal phenomena, going so far as to suspend his disbelief altogether and risk his credibility by writing *The Coming of the Fairies* (1922) in defence of photographs apparently faked by two Yorkshire girls. In 1926 he published *The History of Spiritualism*, a monument to wishful thinking.

Another Scottish doctor, A. J. Cronin (1896–1981), almost equalled Doyle in mass appeal. In 1930 Cronin's health broke down and, while convalescing on a farm near Inveraray, he wrote *Hatter's Castle* (1931). Full of the vindictive smalltown atmosphere and the pettiness of capitalism writ small, it gives an extended account of that favourite Scottish villain – the domestic tyrant. He goes back to Stevenson's *Weir of Hermiston*, of course, but Cronin's James Brodie is really a grotesque version of George Douglas Brown's John Gourlay. Anything Gourlay can do, Brodie can cap. He destroys his son, disowns his daughter (by turning her out into the snow when he discovers she is pregnant), invites the wrath of his business rival and hits the bottle. He get all he asks for from life. Brodie is Gourlay made even more malicious. One man is a hatter and the other a carrier but they both attempt to be monarchs of all they survey before realising that their vision is limited by the materialist walls they construct around themselves. Compared to Brown's *The House with the Green Shutters*, Cronin's *Hatter's Castle* is too outrageously melodramatic to be immortal. It shows the basic difference between realism and naturalism: Brown's book digs into the reality behind the public front of his characters; Cronin meticulously describes the surface. Brown's book is a literary masterpiece; Cronin's was an international bestseller. Another Cronin novel, *The Citadel* (1937), went through twelve impressions in its first five months of existence. It describes how a doctor in a mining village listens to the siren voices of Harley Street. From this novel I give an example of Cronin's copybook style which has been forged by many an aspiring bestseller. It is clear to the point of transparency, effective but undemanding. Here is the description of Ida Sherrington who runs a fashionable nursing-home:

> She was short, stout and extremely full blooded. But her bright red face was so thickly covered with powder the result was a mauve complexion almost the colour of her uniform. She had a look of coarse bustling vitality, of knowing humour, of pluck. Her teeth were false and ill-fitting. Her hair was grizzled. Somehow, it was easy to suspect her of a strong vocabulary, to imagine her performing admirably as the keeper of a second-rate night club.[145]

That is precise with the rigidity of a studio photograph.

Scotland has always had more than its fair share of best-selling authors and the Scottish novel has severely tested Scotsmen on the make. Sir Walter Scott financed an aristocratic lifestyle on the proceeds of novels he could write quickly: *Guy Mannering* (1815) was written in six weeks and the first edition of 2,000 copies sold out in a day. At the present time Scots continue to make a profitable appearance in bestselling charts: George MacDonald Fraser's *Flash* series (which purport to be the personal papers of Harry Flashman, the bully of *Tom Brown's Schooldays*, and come complete with fake editorial apparatus) satisfy a public appetite for costume drama; James Herriot's *Vet* books, written in a homelier version of Cronin's copybook prose, are consistently successful (in print and various cinematic and televisual translations); Alistair MacLean made the *Guinness Book of Records* as the man who 'between 1955 and 1978 wrote 35 books of which the sales of 18 have exceeded a million copies and 13 have been filmed'[146]; and Ian Fleming, who had Scottish connections, sent James Bond to school in Scotland, a fact which endeared 007 to his boss, M. This spectacle of success, this pursuit of economic excellence, would have greatly impressed John Buchan who, as a young man, compiled a list of Things to Be Done and then set about doing them. From a literary point of view Buchan is the best of the bestsellers.

23. JOHN BUCHAN AND THE HURRIED JOURNEY

Born in Perth in 1875, the son of a Free Church minister who was called (in 1888) to the John Knox Free Church in the Glasgow Gorbals, Buchan was able to contrast the industrial inferno of Glasgow and, later, the smalltown atmosphere of Kirkcaldy (where he attended the burgh school when his father was minister at Pathhead Free Church) with the rural idyll of Broughton Green, Peeblesshire, where he summer holidayed annually with his maternal grandparents. In his own way the boy Buchan was a small-scale hero with a constantly shifting outlook. At least this is how he was seen by his sister Anna who grew up to be the romance writer O. Douglas:

> Brother John was the natural leader in the numerous adventures of the minister's family . . . From the beginning John was destined to be Anna's hero. John was born to lead, was infinite in resource and knew more than any other boy knew. Moreover, did he not have a scar on his head as a result of an accident which nearly killed him?[147]

Unlike Buchan's prose the question is rhetorical. Buchan won a classical scholarship to Oxford and, while still a student, published *Sir Quixote of the Moors* (1895), *Scholar-Gipsies* (1896), *John Burnet of Barns* (1898), *Brasenose College* (1898) and *Grey Weather* (1899). For this he appeared in the 1898 edition of *Who's Who* as a professional undergraduate. In 1901 he went, at the invitation of Lord Milner, to South Africa which provided local colour for *Prester John* (1910) and introduced him to the type of man Richard Hannay became. When he returned to London in 1903 he earned his living as a barrister, then supplemented this by joining Nelson's, the publishers. In 1912 he became ill as the result of a duodenal ulcer and, while resting at Broadstairs, produced his own 'shocker', *The Thirty-Nine Steps* (1915). During the war he became a director of Nelson's and made himself responsible for *Nelson's History of the War* (1915–19).

Buchan's career moved steadily towards the aims he had mapped out for himself. As an admirer and (in 1932) biographer of Scott he was aware of the Scottish precedent for the kind of life he led: the busy establishment man who could turn out bestsellers in his spare time. He became Director of Intelligence in the new Ministry of Information in 1918, a director of Reuters in 1919, a member of Parliament in 1927, High Commissioner to the General Assembly of the Church of Scotland in 1933. In 1935, as the culmination of his career as public figure, he became, as Lord Tweedsmuir, Governor-General of Canada. In this capacity he died, from cerebral thrombosis, in 1940.

Given such a crowded life one might have expected Buchan's books to betray hasty composition. No so. He was a natural writer, a stylist who admired Pater and adored Stevenson. He could sustain a narrative pace magnificently and had a marvellous ability to convey an exact sense of place. Here, from *John Barnet of Burns* (published, remember, when Buchan was in his early twenties) is the first-personal description of the house of Barns:

> The house of Barns stands on a green knoll above the Tweed, half-away between the village of Stobo and the town of Peebles. Tweed here is no great rolling river, but a shallow, prattling stream, and just below the house it winds around a small islet, where I loved to go and fish; for it was an adventure to reach the place, since a treacherous pool lay not a yard below it. The dwelling was white and square, with a beacon tower on the top, which once flashed the light from Neidpath to Drochil when the English came over the Border. It had not been used for half a hundred years, but a brazier still stood there, and a pile of rotten logs, grim momentoes of elder feuds. This also was a haunt of mine, for jackdaws and owls built in the corners, and it was choice fun of a spring morning to search for eggs at the risk of my worthless life.[148]

This is a favourite Buchan situation: an ostensibly peaceful place with uneasy connotations (elder feuds); a personal diffidence ('my worthless life'), and a love of the open air and gratuitous adventure. The same formula was to carry Buchan through all his books.

For Buchan action is the antidote to boredom, which is the greatest of all sins. Nothing is more destructive. At the opening of *The Thirty-Nine Steps* Richard Hannay is positively aching for action. He is back in the Old Country after a testing time in South Africa; he is appalled by the complacency of the average Englishman. Cleverly conveying the oppressive weight from Hannay's sturdy shoulders to the printed page, Buchan lets his get-up-and-go hero unburden himself:

> Here was I, thirty-seven years old, sound in wind and limb, with enough money to have a good time, yawning my head off all day. I had just about settled to clear out and get back to the veld, for I was the best bored man in the United Kingdom.[149]

Hannay is rescued from the enforced ennui when Scudder enters his life as if on cue. Subsequently he saves Britain from a fiendish German plot and is himself revitalised – the Buchan hero is euphoric on the move. The same pattern runs through Buchan's popular books: first comes boredom; then a dramatic development; then the chase; then the neat solution. *John Macnab* (1925) opens with the collective boredom of Sir Edward Leithen, Palliser-Yeates, and Lord Lamancha; as an antidote to their soul-destroying enervation they invent the eponymous protagonist and defy Highland landlords to apprehend him. Buchan's heroes all respond, like John Burnet of Barns, to 'the impulses of high passion, the glory of the chase, the stirring of the heart'.[150] And the greatest of these is the glory of the chase.

In his posthumously published autobiography, *Memory Hold-The-Door* (1941), Buchan reflected on his life but had very little to say about himself as a man of letters. What he did say was succinct and to the point:

> I suppose I was a natural story-teller . . . I generally thought of a character or two, and then of a set of incidents, and the question was how my people would behave. They had the knack of just squeezing out of unpleasant places and of bringing their doings to a rousing climax.
>
> I was especially fascinated by the notion of hurried journeys. In the great romances of literature they provide some of the chief dramatic moments, and since the theme is common to Homer and the penny reciter it must appeal to a very ancient instinct in human nature. We live our lives under the twin categories of time and space, and when the two come into conflict we get the great moment. Whether failure or success is the result, life is sharpened, intensified, idealised. A long journey, even with the most lofty purpose, may be a dull thing to read of if it is made at leisure; but a hundred yards may be a breathless business if only a few seconds are granted to complete it.[151]

Buchan's purpose is to shock the reader into accepting a bizarre situation then to take him on a breathless journey which will end in a triumph for decency. All Buchan's heroes are decent chaps. Hannay – of *The Thirty-Nine Steps, Greenmantle* (1916), *Mr Standfast* (1919), *The Three Hostages* (1924) and *The Island of Sheep* (1936) – is a solid Scotsman who has spent most of his life on the make in South Africa as a speculator and copper-engineer. He is ready to accept the call in the name of duty, and goes on to save Britain and the Near East; and to expose villains (stage villains really) like Moxon Ivery and Dominick Medina. Sir Edward Leithan – first seen in the story 'Space' in *The Moon Endureth* (1912), then in *The Power-House* (1913), *John Macnab* (1925) *The Dancing Floor* (1926), *The Gap in the Curtain* (1932) and *Sick Heart River* (1941) – is a Scot who goes to Eton, is called to the Bar, enters Parliament and rises to the position of Attorney General. Though no man of physical action, like Hannay, he too stands for decency and, close to death, penetrates the Canadian North in search of a fugitive and the meaning of his own life. Dickson McCunn – of *Huntingtower* (1922), *Castle Gay* (1930) and *The House of the Four Winds* (1935) – is a retired Glasgow grocer who prefers adventure, in the name of decency naturally, to affluent inactivity. Then there are the secondary characters like Sandy Arbuthnot, who assists Hannay; Peter Pienaar, Hannay's best friend; Leithen's friends Lord Lamancha and Sir Archibald Roylance; and the Gorbals Die-hards who helped McCunn in *Huntingtower* and who were based on a Sunday School class of boys Buchan had taught in Glasgow.

In *Prester John*, Laputa says to Crawfurd: 'There is no leader anywhere . . . And I am dying'.[152] The image of the Lost Leader is important to Buchan: Hannay, Leithen and McCunn are not temperamentally inclined to be leaders but are impelled to act in the absence of a strong, morally impeccable leader. There is some truth in what Anna said about her brother's popular books: 'Those books were a great deal more than mere thrillers. They struck a note of poetry and high courage which set them above other contemporary work in that field.'[153] Buchan wrote what he regarded as more serious works such as *The Path of the King* (1921) and, more impressively, *Witch Wood* (1927) in which he contrasted the restraints of Calvinism with the emotive power of paganism. These selfconsciously literary works did not have the appeal of the popular works. In his final novel, *Sick Heart River*, he articulated the obvious truth that for him an adventure was a test of personal faith. Terminally ill from tuberculosis, Leithen sets out on his last adventure. The novel was inspired by a tour Governor-General Buchan made in 1937 down the Mackenzie River to the Arctic Ocean; when the book appeared posthumously it therefore seemed both true to life and tolerant of death. Leithen comes to a conclusion like this:

> He was facing, too, the challenge of Death . . . Leithen's new-found mission for life gave him a happy retrospect over his own career . . . The North had not frozen him, but had melted the ice in his heart . . . The cold infernal North magnified instead of dwarfing humanity. What a marvel was this clot of vivified dust! . . . The universe seemed to spread itself before him in immense distance lit and dominated by a divine spark which was man. An inconsiderable planet, a speck in the infinite stellar spaces; most of it salt water; the bulk of the land rock and desert and astral and boreal ice; interspersed mud, the detritus of aeons, with a thin coverlet of grass and trees – that vegetable world on which every living thing was in the last resort a parasite! Man, precariously perched on this rotating scrap-heap, yet so much master of it that he could mould it to his transient uses and, while struggling to live, could entertain thoughts and dreams beyond the bounds of time and space! Man so weak and yet so great, the chief handiwork of the Power that had hung the stars in the firmament . . . Most men had their lives taken from them. It was his privilege to *give* his, to offer it freely and joyfully in one last effort of manhood.[154]

24. NEIL MUNRO: RECLAIMING THE KAILYARD

Buchan was a man who valued most highly the writing his public largely rejected; a similar irony applied to Neil Munro (1864 – 1930), whose historical novels Buchan greatly admired and which were once put on a par with the best of Stevenson and Scott before the public dropped them in favour of his low comedy characters. Munro was born in Inveraray, Argyllshire, and never relinquished his emotional hold on his native territory. Despite the appeal of the losing side in history, Munro managed to weave romance around the frequently victorious Clan Campbell version of Scottish affairs. Munro himself was born without any obvious advantages. As a child, indeed, he had his fair share of domestic strain since he did not know his father though he knew who his father was. In a letter of 10 March 1921 to Lynn Doyle he wrote: 'I fancy I shall never write the story of my own childhood, though there were tragic and pathetic elements in it which would make a dozen novels of the grimy sort now in vogue. I sought escape from them in the imagination for so long, and so ardently, that I couldn't help becoming a romancer in the end.'[155] Some of the pathos found its way into his novels of contemporary life for in these Munro rambles in the manner of Barrie and reclaims the kailyard as his own property. *Gilian the Dreamer* (1899) is the semi-autobiographical story of a country boy growing up in Inveraray where he is cared for by an elderly spinster. He is ridiculed by the town boys for his gauche rural ways and generally treated as an outsider. To realise how completely Munro cultivated the kailyard manner we need only compare the opening of Brown's *Green Shutters* (see p. 111) with a passage in Munro's *The Daft Days* (1907) describing a small town waking up:

> The burgh town turned on its pillows, drew up its feet from the
> bed-bottles, last night hot, now turned to chilly stone, rubbed its eyes,
> and knew by that bell it was the daftest of the daft days come. It cast a
> merry spell on the community; it tickled them even in their cosy beds.
> 'Wanton Wully's on the ran-dan!' said the folk, and rose quickly, and ran
> to pull aside screens and blinds to look out into the dark on
> window-ledges cushioned deep in snow.[156]

Munro's literary earnings increased as he progressively found his feet as a lad o pairts in Glasgow; he was a fluent journalist and eventually edited the *Glasgow Evening News*. He found he could turn his journalistic hand to the mass production of entertaining copy, providing readers with a low kind of comedy that further reduced Scottish stereotypes to absurd proportions. As the pseudonymous Hugh Foulis, Munro gave birth to daft creatures like the waiter *Erchie* (1904) and the commercial traveller Jimmie Swan (1917). He also wrote, to the endless amusement of the public, about the puffer 'The Vital Spark' and its eccentric crew comprising Para Handy, Dougie, Mcphail, Tar, Sunny Jim and Hurricane Jack. The stories strengthened a comic tradition that is still going strong (for example, in the kailyardish *Sunday Post* with its comic strip immortals 'The Broons' and 'Oor Wullie'). The figure of Para Handy himself, with his Gaelic-inflected broken Scots, is ridiculous and thus extremely appealing to Lowland Scots: 'If you never saw the *Fital Spark*, she is aal hold, with the boiler behind, four men and a derrick, and a water-butt and a pan loaf in the fo'c'sle. Oh man! she wass the beauty! She was chust sublime.'[157]

Munro's kailyardish novels – *Gilian the Dreamer*, *The Daft Days*, *Fancy Farm* (1910) – are but dimly remembered now. His three historical romances, *John Splendid* (1898), *Doom Castle* (1901), *The New Road* (1914), keep up a vastly superior artistic tone. Munro shows his paces as an enthusiastic storyteller who keeps romance alive by using a minimum of characterisation and a maximum of local colour with period detail. The characters in his serious novels, in other words, are as stereotypical as his other characters. The difference is in the density of detail in the serious novels; the highly particularised settings. *John Splendid* is narrated by Elrigmore, an educated Gael who intones his quaintly archaic English like a pibroch; Archibald, Marquis of Argyll (or Argile as the novel spells it) is the Clan Campbell figure of authority; John Splendid is Argile's kinsman and silver-mine manager. The three respond in their various ways to Montrose's war on Lorn. There is much action but the quality of the novel is most revealingly evident in the sense of place as in this description of market-day in Inneraora:

> The market-day came on the morning after the day John Splendid and I [i.e. Elrigmore the narrator] foregathered with my Lord Archibald . . .
> All day the town hummed with Gaelic and the round bellowing of cattle. It was clear warm weather, never a breath of wind to stir the gilding trees behind the burgh. At ebb-tide the sea-beach whitened and smoked in the sun, and the hot air quivered over the stones and the crisping wrack. In such a season the bustling town in the heart of the stern Highlands seemed a fever spot . . . A constant stream of men passed in and out at the changehouse closes and about the Fisherland tenements, where seafarers and drovers together sang the maddest love-ditties in the voices of roaring bulls; beating the while with their feet on the floor in our foolish Gaelic fashion . . .[158]

Munro's historical imagination seems to come alive in the streets of his boyhood town.

Doom Castle is not so much a historical novel as a history-tinted fairy tale showing a baronial version of the domestic tyrant who, by keeping his daughter locked up, makes her an irresistibly attractive damsel in distress. *The New Road* outlines the adventures experienced by Aeneas Macmaster in his odyssey after his inheritance. It is also, as the title suggests, about the new road the Highlander must take, for General Wade's network of roads and bridges was expressly designed to open up the Highlands and bring recalcitrant clansmen under control. Clan Campbell's winning instinct tells it to follow the new road that will make Scotland a united market. All this is seen by Aeneas's natural ally, the loveable Highland rogue Ninian MacGregor Campbell:

> 'George Wade's red sodgers, as ye ken,' said Ninian, 'have been for years at the makin' o' the Big Road that is goin' to put the branks upon the Hielanman – a bonny job for sodgers! It's killin', as ye might say, the goose that lays the golden eggs, for, wi' this road across Druim-Albyn, fighting will be by wi'tin the Hielands and the trade o' war will stop. But that's the way of it – the Road is cut already through from Crieff to nearly Lovat's country; I trudged a bit o' the lower part o' it myself last summer; most deplorable! – the look o' things completely spoiled, and walkin' levelled to a thing that even cripples could enjoy. A body might as well be on the streets! I'm tellin' you that Road is goin' to be a rut that, once it's hammered deep enough, will be the poor Gael's grave!'[159]

25. COMPTON MACKENZIE AND HEROIC FARCE

Neil Munro's attempt to reclaim the kailyard was doomed – as the rapid decline in his reputation suggests. Partly through the sustained pressure of successive fictional performances Scotland was acquiring a new image. The Ossianism of the eighteenth century, Scott's historical romanticism, the kailyard and the Celtic Twilight: all these tendencies dissolved into a new image of Scotland as a sturdy country capable of a heroic resurrection. The new century encouraged novelty and informed the novel with a sense of change. It was possible for a writer to take Scotland as a suitable stage on which to perform as a larger-than-life figure. R. B. Cunninghame Graham (1852–1936), a masterly storyteller and dazzling personality, seemed the very picture of the heroic Scotsman; Compton Mackenzie had almost as much panache and even more staying-power as a writer. He managed to participate in modern Scotland as both intellectual and entertainer. What is more, his humour persuaded Scots to laugh at their foibles; it was healing humour, not bilious ridicule. Mackenzie saw himself as a hero in a basically farcical world. There was a positive side to his persona. Scottish history had become such a deadly serious business that the national penchant for grimness had become an obstacle in the way of further progress. Mackenzie felt it was possible to see history as both tragedy and farce; as a writer it was his custom to divide his work into serious and farcical compartments. Yet his best work integrated the heroic and the farcical in an affirmative manner. As master of the heroic farce Mackenzie could both amaze and amuse the country he had come to love.

Like Buchan and Munro, Compton Mackenzie wrote both light and heavy fiction; made his fortune with one and his critical reputation with the other. He commenced his career as a promising and daring young novelist and ended up as a household name best known for his comic depiction of the Highlands and Islands. Mackenzie's astonishingly full life is recalled in loving detail in ten octaves of *My Life and Times* (1963–71) from which it is easy enough to gather that the author was an exceedingly vain man who preserved every page he wrote, however ephemeral. For the most part the octaves sound the same tune and Mackenzie plays it not by ear but with recourse to letters to and from publishers and colleagues. He was born (as Edward Montague Compton) in 1883 in a histrionic household: both parents were theatrical and his sister, Fay Compton, became a leading actress and the first to play the leads in two J. M. Barrie plays (the title role in *Mary Rose* in 1920 and Phoebe Throssel in *Quality Street* in 1921). Mackenzie took the world as his stage and always loved to be at the centre of things. Literature attracted him because he was so completely in control of every aspect of the production and could make his own life the subject of prolonged study. His serious writing is almost always autobiographical; his comic work, especially the farces, tends to be inspired invention.

Mackenzie was born in West Hartlepool and educated at St Paul's and Magdalen College, Oxford. At one time he intended to become a lawyer but became a professional writer instead. *The Passionate Elopement* (1911) was his debut as a novelist. *Carnival* (1912) was a bestseller. It told, in amusing and sometimes melodramatic incidents, the fortunes of the First Line of Boys in the corps de ballet at the Orient Palace of Varieties. A sequel, *Figure of Eight* (1936), appeared almost quarter of a century later which testifies to Mackenzie's ability to retain in his mind every aspect of a story. Throughout his life he was inordinately proud of his prodigious memory.

The publication of *Sinister Street* in 1913 really marked the beginning of Mackenzie's career as a literary celebrity. The book was highly publicised as a result of a decision by the circulating libraries to restrict the availability of the novel. Mackenzie's letter of protest appeared on the front page of the *Daily Mail*. He had become an issue. Mackenzie's big promotional break was fortuitous; his literary fortune was, however, well deserved. Ford Madox Ford reviewed the book as a work of genius. It is not difficult to see why. The educational progress of Michael Fane is delicately conveyed. Mackenzie's prose has an aesthetic fluency but avoids ninetyish decadence by virtue of its precision. Mackenzie did not blur any scene; he focused exactly. Another factor in the book's favour is the knowledgeability, for the narrative has the right tone of inside information. While at Oxford, Mackenzie himself had joined the Oxford University Dramatic Society. Here Michael Fane broods on its significance:

> The frequenters of the O.U.D.S. were always very definitely Oxford undergraduates, but they lacked the serenity of Oxford, and seemed already to have planted a foot in London. The big modern room over the big cheap shop was a restless place, and its pretentiousness and modernity were tinged with Thespianism. Scarcely ever did the Academic Muse enter the O.U.D.S., Michael thought. She must greatly dislike Thespianism with all that it connoted of mildewed statuary in an English garden. Yet it would be possible to transmute the O.U.D.S., he dreamed. It had the advantage of a limited membership. It might easily become a grove where Apollo and Athene could converse without quarrelling. Therefore he continued to frequent its halls.[160]

Likewise there was always a touch of Thespianism about Mackenzie since every action he contemplated was weighed for its effect. His genuine panache had its literary equivalent in a mannered prose full of flourish. Although he was to gravitate towards Scottish themes, Mackenzie eschewed the possibilities of Scottish realism and was not at all inclined to symbolism. He was attracted to the traditional English novel of middle and upperclass life, though he was not averse to innovation. His mild exploration of sexuality was daring in its period and *Sinister Street* was frank enough to impress Henry James, who wrote to tell the young author he had emancipated the English novel. Mackenzie himself realised that 'Henry James's congratulations were premature for in the spring of 1915 D. H. Lawrence's book *Women in Love* was suppressed by the police'.[161]

Once he had created a character Mackenzie liked to cling onto him or her and he always wanted to amass enough experience for a large-scale, even epic work of fiction. *Sinister Street* was conceived as the first step in such a work:

> My original plan was to take the subsidiary characters of *Sinister Street*, one after another, and make them principals in other books. I struck to this idea, as in *Guy and Pauline* [1914], *Sylvia Scarlett*, and *The Vanity Girl* [1920], until I was compelled to recognize that the First World War had smashed the series of linked novels I intended to call *The Theatre of Youth*, because I should never be able to escape from it. The First World

War as a *deus ex machina* would soon have become intolerable to myself and to my readers.[162]

Sylvia Scarlett (whose name was suggested by a novel Stevenson planned to write about a heroine named Sophia Scarlett) was too much of a character to disown. In *Sinister Street* her natural gaiety is a welcome contrast to Michael's moodiness. In the sequel, initially published in two parts as *The Early Life and Adventures of Sylvia Scarlett* (1918) and *Sylvia and Michael* (1919), Sylvia gets on with her career as a variety artiste and ends up in the arms of Michael. The final love duet shows the essentially stagey artificiality of Mackenzie's writing. He was able to extend his material effortlessly because the characters lent themselves so readily to utterly contrived situations:

> Then suddenly [Michael] turned to Sylvia and took her hand. 'My dear, when I dragged you up the beach yesterday I thought you were dead, and I cursed myself for a coward because I had let you die without telling you. Sylvia, this adventure of ours, need it ever stop?'
> 'Everything comes to an end,' she sighed.
> 'Except one thing – and that sets all the rest going again.'
> 'What is your magic key?'
> 'Sylvia, I'm afraid to ask you to marry me, but will you?'
> She stared at him; then she saw his eyes, and for a long while she was crying in his arms with happiness.[163]

Mackenzie's own life can only be fully appreciated as a testing ground for his fiction. He had a flair for the theatrical gesture and a love of the exotic. In 1914 he was received into the Roman Catholic Church and, on the outbreak of the First World War, attemped unsuccessfully to get a commission in the Seaforth Highlanders. However, General Ian Hamilton had read the second volume of *Sinister Street* and was sympathetic to Mackenzie's earnest desire to aid the war effort. Mackenzie first served in the Dardanelles, as described in *Gallipoli Memories* (1928); then headed the British Aegean Intelligence Service, as described in *Extremes Meet* (1928). In Capri (where he wrote *Sylvia Scarlett*) he mingled with Norman Douglas and D. H. Lawrence who duly satirised Mackenzie in the story 'The Man who Loved Islands'. Eventually he settled in the little Hebridean island of Barra and helped found the National Party of Scotland in 1928. Catholicism and Scottish Nationalism were to be the causes closest to Mackenzie's heart. His attachment to Scottish Nationalism was an emotional matter, as he explained in his Rectorial Address at Glasgow University in 1932. Mackenzie described how, at the age of eight, he travelled northwards alone and crossed the border into Scotland:

> It happened that soon after I came possessed of this talisman [i.e. Scott's *Tales of a Grandfather*] to live in the past of that race from which I

sprung I travelled northward alone. It was near dusk on an evening of earliest Spring. Somebody in the railway-carriage announced that we were crossing the border, and I craned my head out of the window to enjoy the magical sensation. Down the long train came a faint sound of cheering, and from windows far ahead I could see hats being waved. An austere landscape in the fast-fading dusk, a stream of flamy smoke from an engine, a few cheers ringing thinly above the roar of a train, a waving of hats: not much perhaps, but enough for a child of eight to sit back again in a dim railway-carriage and dream over, his heart blazoned like a herald's tabard with the bright symbols of his country's life, his heart draped like a hatchment with the sombre memories of defeat upon defeat. Thence onwards I lived secretly in the past of my country . . .[164]

That incident, like other important events in Mackenzie's life, reappeared as fiction; it occurs in the first Book of *The East Wind of Love*.

In scope *The Four Winds of Love* (1937–45) shapes up as Mackenzie's premeditated fictional masterpiece; it is a project even grander than the projected sequence on *The Theatre of Youth*. It amounts to around one million words of narration, though it was originally conceived on a more modest and manageable scale. On 29 June 1932 Mackenzie wrote to Newman Flower, giving the thematic outline of his 'next novel':

> *The Four Winds of Love* is intended to be a very long novel, and will consist of four love stories and four philosophies of love and four decades of a man's life. The problem will be how to finance myself while it is being written, because if I write a novel of probably more than 200,000 words, I don't see how it can be ready for you to publish before next Spring.[165]

Each wind was to have a season and a setting to itself: thus Spring and a Polish visit for the East; Summer in Italy and Greece for the South; Autumn in America, Ireland and Cornwall for the West; and Winter and Scotland for the North. So although the novel is massive the story is surprisingly simple, a monumental tribute to Mackenzie's ability to spin out a story until the subject is exhausted. The hero of the sequence is, like Mackenzie himself, a man of intellect and action. In *The East Wind of Love*, covering the period 1900–11, he endures his expensive education until he can contrive an escape from it; in *The South Wind of Love*, covering 1912–17, he becomes a secret agent in the Aegean and enjoys the subterfuge and possession of power; in *The West Wind of Love*, covering 1918–22, he watches the development of nationalism in Europe and buys a Hebridean island to apply the lessons he has learned to his homeland; in *The North Wind of Love*, covering 1930–39, he is a Scottish Nationalist leader watching the rise of a dangerously militant nationalism in Germany.

The hero of *Four Winds* is a Juanesque *Übermensch*, John Pendarves Ogilvie. He is nicknamed 'Judge' because of his initials (J. P.) and, when we first see him in *The East Wind of Love*, he is a seventeen-year-old schoolboy in the Classical Lower Sixth at St James's School, London. It is 1900, the beginning of a new century and Mackenzie's purpose is to show the gradual development of a flawed new world. Ogilvie inherits a talent for friendship and chooses companions who have both personality and representative gifts: Edward Fitzgerald is a familiar figure, the personification of Irish nationalism; Emil Stern, likewise, stands for the archetypal Jew – brilliant and prone to persecution. Ogilvie detests school and tells Stern why he abominates institutions: 'I've been at this penal servitude for eight and a half years. No wonder criminals are comparatively rare from the public schools. We learn what prison is like in time to avoid it.'[166] Ogilvie's father is Alexander Ogilvie, a son of the Manse and successful barrister about to take silk; Ogilvie's mother, Athene Pendarves, died when he was eight but her significance lingers on since she was the daughter of a Cornish squire and thus an important link with a rich Celtic heritage. Ogilvie longs for adventure and is delighted when his father (contemplating a second marriage) allows him to leave school and find himself in Switzerland. There he loses his money gambling and, at a low ebb, is saved by his greatest gift: Ogilvie is irresistibly attractive to all who come in contact with him. Cissie, a thirty-two-year-old nightclub singer with a heart of gold, saves him and he decides to take a moral stand and substitute prudence for passion: 'For many years to come John was to blame the cautious decision he took that summer evening in 1900 for every surrender he made thereafter to prudence and common sense, those two withered virgins of the moral code.'[167] In Cissie's nightclub Ogilvie meets the delicious Odette, who takes him home to her bed. Rather wiser in the ways of the world he moves to Paris, meets up with the Sterns and faces the fact that as much as Emil adores him so does Emil's mother, Miriam. The Ogilvie charm is not to be denied. Ogilvie has to leave Paris; on the train taking him home he meets Torquil Macleod, 10th of Ardvore in Assynt. Ardovre suggests that he and Ogilvie are related as Ogilvie's great-grandfather married a Macleod of Assynt. This chance encounter leads to an invitation to Ogilvie to visit Assynt and thus discover his Scottish roots. Ogilvie duly responds to the spectacle of romantic Scotland:

John [remembered] the first sight of Suilven standing up in the west like a huge grape-dark hand, miles away above the desolate moorland. What were the mountains of Switzerland compared with that shape of stone solitary as a mammoth upon the edge of the landscape? Huddled parvenus. His first sight of the Laird of Ardvore standing by the inn-door when the coach pulled up was not less memorable. That beaky-nosed bearded old man in faded kilt was autochthonous like Ben More Assynt itself.[168]

Going back south after his sojourn in Assynt he hears of the death of Queen Victoria and, fortuitously meeting Fitzgerald in the London crowd, goes to an Irish pub to drink a toast to the passing of an era.

In the carefully considered *East Wind* are all the elements of the subsequent saga. Ogilvie's eloquence, appeal and serendipity are established; it is inevitable that such a character will play a conspicuous part in the making of the new century. Although the *Four Winds* is generally contrasted with Mackenzie's slighter works the writing is not dramatically different, just more sprawling. In *Four Winds* Mackenzie brought all his talents, comic and serious, to bear on the portrayal of a personality as dashing as his own. One of the delights of the sequence is the intrusion of comic scenes into ostensibly serious situations. Mackenzie allowed himself this licence rather than let the sequence become unbearably ponderous or pompous. At one stage of the narrative Ogilvie falls for the charming Connie Fenwick and meets her father, who describes himself as a Jacobite and belongs to the ludicrous West London Legitimist League. Mackenzie's description of this incongruous gathering is as deliciously witty as anything in the series of farcical novels that made his a household name:

> To the majority of the young men present there clung an air rather of thwarted femininity than of thwarted political hopes. Nothing could have been less like the grave and gallant heroes of Jacobite romance than these wriggling giggling epicenes, most of whom were wearing high double-breasted waistcoats buttoning in a V, the mark at this date of a vaulting fashion which had overleapt itself. These young men made swans' necks of their arms while they chattered to one another in the too utterly utter style which was introduced in the early 'eighties and has survived to the present day with merely occasional changes in the laudatory adjective to mark the passing vogue. In distinction from the elegance of the young men most of the women present looked as if they had been dragged through a couple of hedges before they reached Gladwyn Road. Indeed, some of the older ones looked as if they had been dragged through the Maze at Hampton Court as well.[169]

Ogilvie's career is intertwined with the women in his life: he loves Connie Fenwick and Rose Medlicott and Miriam Stern; he has a mistress, Zoe, who is drowned; and he marries, first, the American Athene (*South Wind*), who gives him a daughter Corinna, then the Greek poetess Euphrosyne (*North Wind*) who coins couplets like

> Eyes which you found crystalline
> Will not seem opaque to mine.

Corinna is an important figure who ends by planning to marry Sebastian Stern, musical son of Emil Stern's virtuoso violinist brother Julius. The happy ending of the sequence is retrospectively ironical for we know that a second World War is about to engulf the world. Ogilvie is no conventional Don Juan, his greatest flirtation is with ideas, and collectively the *Four Winds* comprise an ideological romance. All the isms are present: nationalism, communism (as experienced by Emil Stern), fascism (which initially attracts Ogilvie himself). Ogilvie's dream is of a world united by romantic aspiration. He explains, to a friend, the gist of his vision:

> 'I had a short talk with De Valera, and I was rather depressed to find how completely uninterested he was by the possibility of a Scottish revival. True, he may have thought rightly that I was inviting him to speculate about an impossibility . . .But, Mazy, don't you think his vision of Ireland would be enriched by the prospect of what I'll have to call Pan-Celticism? I don't believe that Ireland alone can sustain itself like Andorra. Yet, if Ireland, Scotland, Wales, Cornwall, and Brittany could form a Celtic federation, with regional autonomy, it would genuinely weigh in the balance against Pan-Americanism or Pan-Germanism or Pan-Slavism.'[170]

Mackenzie means us to take this suggestion seriously. Whereas Gibbon wrote realistically with ideological overtones, Mackenzie writes romantically with perfectly serious intentions. Mackenzie's friend Hugh MacDiarmid had a Pan-Celtic proposal 'to get rid of the English Ascendancy and work for the establishment of Workers' Republics in Scotland, Ireland, Wales and Cornwall, and, indeed, make a sort of Celtic Union of Socialist Soviet Republics'.[171] Ogilvie is an accomplished playright who sees the world in theatrical terms and imagines, at his most omniscient moments, he can manipulate history like the plot of one of his fashionable plays. His insular paradise of Tigh nan Ron encourages him to dream his dreams and he has to rediscover himself and the world he plays his part in. He is in tune with the world so long as art has its due status and can come to terms with international affairs so long as they conform to creative principles; such thoughts come to him when listening to Julius Stern playing Beethoven's Sonata in F major.

Mackenzie's expansive nature easily filled *The Four Winds of Love* with incident and character – and humour. Having conceived his magnum opus and seen the thing through, Mackenzie was entitled to rest on his laurels. He did nothing of the kind even when another World War came along to interfere with his peace of mind. During the war Mackenzie began a series of interconnected comic novels which he referred to dismissively as farces. The public adored them and Mackenzie became known as a comic rather than a serious writer, the author of *Whisky Galore* (1947) rather than of *The Four Winds of Love*. Two of the best farces illustrate Mackenzie's appeal. *The Monarch of the Glen* appeared in 1941 with Europe, and the Western world, at war; but the combat described by Mackenzie takes place at Glenbogle Castle, Inverness-shire, ancestral home of old Donald MacDonald, 23rd of Ben Nevis. Harrow-educated Ben

Nevis is infatuated with the old clan ideals (so far as he is able to understand them) and inspired by the heroic deeds of his ancestor Hector. His immediate clan is formidable: two Amazonian daughters (Catriona and Mary), three sons (Hector, Murdoch, Iain) and his English wife, Trixie, whose money keeps Ben Nevis in style.

Ben Nevis meets an American millionaire, Chester Royde Jr, and invites him home in the hope (forlorn as it happens) that there might be a match between Chester's sister Myrtle and Ben Nevis's son Hector. Thus the scene is set for the preposterous events that converge on Glenbogle Castle. The mood is mock-heroic as Mackenzie creates a whole host of ridiculous characters and some sympathetic caricatures. For example, Royde's wife, Carrie, is a MacDonald by birth and has dreamed of Scotland since childhood: 'As a girl Caroline Macdonald had suffered from the Lone Sheiling complex...She had repined at not having been christened Flora, but had derived a measure of consolation from the thought that Caroline was the feminine of Charles...'[172] Ben Nevis's land is invaded by members of the National Union of Hikers and by members of the Scottish Brotherhood of Action. At the climax of the farce the two forces fight a battle over Ben Nevis. The portrait of Ben Nevis is the best thing in the book; he is so ridiculously pompous that the Muckle Hart of Ben Glass (the Monarch of the Glen) laughs at him. Ben Nevis is a comic Scotsman around whom the others gather because he conforms to their image of a Scotsman. He is reckless, stupid, reactionary and ludicrous. The humour is not directed at Scotland but at the tourist travesty of Scotland.

Ben Nevis's best friend in *The Monarch of the Glen*, Hugh Cameron of Kilwhillie, reappears in *Hunting the Fairies* (1949). Three years have passed since the events described in *Monarch* and Kilwhillie is about to celebrate his fiftieth birthday. From Carrie Royde he receives a request to accommodate Mrs 'Yu-Yu' Urquhart-Unwin, President of the Ossianic Society of Boston, plus daughter Deirdre. Yu-Yu is in the business of hunting fairies and other Scottish phenomena like the Loch Ness Monster and the astral presence of dead bards such as Ossian. As Ben Nevis is Kilwhinnie's foil, so Mrs Linda Wolfingham (a Campbell by birth) is Yu-Yu's. The two Americans try to score off each other in a protracted mock-heroic contest which tests even their credulousness to the limit. Into this farce comes a love interest, for Kilwhinnie has fallen for Deirdre, thirty years his junior. His passion comes to nothing and Kilwhinnie contents himself with the delights of the Glorious Twelfth. Like *Monarch*, this book derives much of its humour from the fact that the characters who advertise their Scottishness (Harrow-educated Ben Nevis and Winchester-educated Kilwhinnie) are Blimpish figures whereas the inhabitants of the New World have more Highland spirit than the native Scots.

Mackenzie derived a comfortable living from his work and spent summers in Edinburgh (where he held court as a Grand Old Man) and winters in the south of France. He was never again to attempt a novel on the scale of *The Four Winds of Love* but his massive autobiography made up for that in terms of scale. Not, alas, in terms of quality for the work is basically an exercise in regurgitation. Still, he remained alert and was always able to create a novel out of the slimmest of opportunities. Some insight into this facility is given by the politician Tom Driberg. During a blackout in the Second World War an Edinburgh policeman caught Driberg in homosexual embrace with a Norwegian sailor in Princes Street Gardens. When the policeman discovered Driberg's journalistic identity – he wrote the celebrated William Hickey column – he turned a blind eye to the incident. Driberg explains:

> When I got back to London next day, I was able to describe the incident, almost as a joke, to at least two friends, Harold Nicolson and Bob Boothby. One of them, I think Bob, subsequently recounted it to Compton Mackenzie. Either Mackenzie had started on, or this anecdote gave him the idea for, a novel called *Thin Ice*, about the precarious life of a homosexual politican – and in particular including a passage that was clearly to me, based on my Edinburgh experience.[173]

The novel Mackenzie made of that anecdote, *Thin Ice* (1956), is one of his most perceptive performances; it is short and to the point, a short story in the context of Mackenzie's output. I have the feeling that Mackenzie could turn out a novel about almost anything, that he needed only a notion to carry it through hundreds of pages of vigorous prose. His literary hero was Sir Walter Scott and his productivity surpassed even that of the Wizard of the North. When Mackenzie died in 1972 the news made the front pages. His body was taken to Barra and the piper in attendance for the last ritual died. It was the sort of incident that Mackenzie could have made much of; a final dramatic gesture. So far as the general public was concerned he was the Grand Old Man of Scottish letters and it was a role he relished and played to perfection.

26. ERIC LINKLATER: MOCKING THE HEROIC

In the dedication to the first volume of *The Four Winds of Love* Mackenzie addressed Eric Linklater (1899–1974) as follows: 'I have chosen a junior contemporary for whose existing work I have a secure admiration and in whose future work I have an equally secure confidence'.[174] There spoke the master. Yet when these words were written, in 1936, Linklater was no neophyte but a novelist whose solid reputation was built on *White-Maa's Saga* (1929), *Poet's Pub* (1929), *Juan in America* (1931), *The Men of Ness* (1932), *Magnus Merriman* (1934) and *Ripeness Is All* (1935). His major work was already behind him for he had written a picaresque classic and some wildly funny books in which his sense of fun was controlled by a strictly functional and absolutely precise prose style. After the Second World War, during which he was partly responsible for the defence of his adopted Orkney, Linklater published nothing to equal *Juan in America* but varied themes he was already familiar with. Of his later work the most endurable titles are *Private Angelo* (1946), *Laxdale Hall* (1951), *Position at Noon* (1958) and *The Merry Muse* (1959).

Whereas Mackenzie enjoyed his sublime moments, Linklater was always on the lookout for the ridiculous. Whereas Mackenzie occasionally resorted to a mock-heroic mood, Linklater applied the method with a view to reducing life to a ripple of laughter. Linklater liked to cultivate a devil-may-care public persona; like Mackenzie he became a household name, a professional writer the public identified with. He was no aesthetic longhair but a prematurely bald egghead with the common touch. He was soldier, scholar, journalist, traveller, writer. Still, his professional pride made him something of an armchair activist whose every excursion was turned into good, readable copy. He boasted of the range of his experience and wrote three essays in autobiography about his eventful life: *The Man on My Back* (1941), *A Year of Space* (1953) and *Fanfare for a Tin Hat* (1970). As he came towards the end of his life he fanfared patriotically:

> I still live in Scotland, and though, many years ago, my impulse to do so was obscured by a sense of duty – I felt that Scottish writers should live in the land to which they belonged – that sense has long since evaporated, and I live where I do in the pure light of self-indulgence. I have seen much of the world, but no part of it has so constantly and consistently pleased my eyes as the northern counties of Scotland; and throughout my life my eyes have been my primary instrument of pleasure.[175]

Although he is always identified with Orkney, Linklater was actually born in Penarth, Wales. However, his paternal ancesters were Orcadian and his mother, a spirited English woman, fell in love with Orkney. Linklater subsequently discovered, to his delight, 'that I had been conceived in Orkney'.[176] Many of his novels were conceived there or thereabouts. *White-Maa's Saga* takes Peter Flett from Inverdoon (Aberdeen, where Linklater studied, first, medicine then literature) to Orkney where he finds love and a suitable challenge. In *Poet's Pub* the plot is more inventive and absurd. Mr Saturday Keith, former Oxford Rowing Blue and celebrated poet, manages The Pelican Inn on behalf of Lady Mercy Cotton who owns it and Cotton's Beer besides. There is a kidnap, a missing manuscript, and a frenetic denouement. The book is full of promise which frequently materialises in mock-heroic incidents. Linklater's third novel, *Juan in America*, easily surpasses the first two; it is a comic masterpiece and the book its author is likely to be remembered by.

Having been in Europe for the war and in India for experience (he was assistant editor and leader-writer on *The Times of India* in Bombay) Linklater worked his way into a job at Aberdeen university; thus equipped he applied successfully for a Commonwealth Fellowship and spent the years 1928–30 in the USA. There he conceived and executed the novel:

> I spent my second winter at the University of California . . . I was . . . able to begin a novel which, for some months past, had been taking shape in my mind. It was to be called *Juan in America*, and its pedigree was by Byron out of the United States; or if not Byron himself, his statue outside the Aberdeen Grammar School. As originally conceived, it was to have been written in verse – Byronic stanzas – but having begun to take pleasure in the looser and more variable rhythms of prose, and flinching when it came to the point of finding thirty thousand rhymes, I unhorsed the infant poem in its first canto and bade it walk.[177]

Linklater has got to be joking; there is no evidence that he was ever anything but pedestrian as poet and no chance that he could have out-Byroned Byron. As a writer of fast-moving mock-heroic prose, however, he commands a class of his own and Juan is at the top of that class.

Linklater's Juan is born in 1905, the third child of Sir Hildebrand Motley and his American cousin Charlotte. He is conceived in England but the pregnant Charlotte escapes to Spain before returning to give birth to Juan. The child is a descendent of Young Jack Motley, the child of Byron's Don Juan and the Duchess of Fitz-Fulke. From the beginning he behaves like the picaro he is destined to be. He is sent down from Cambridge after an affair with the daughter of the Chapel clerk; diplomatically he is sent to Australia with a Motley relative. After two years Juan arrives in New York to attend Motley College, an institution endowed by Charlotte's father. Here, in the proverbial land of the free, the adventure really begins:

> The life of America was spread over so vast an area, and was everywhere so vigorous, that any number of strange and sinister interludes could be enacted without upsetting the national equilibrium. Those miraculously united states with their wild harmonious names – Utah, Wisconsin, Oregon, Kentucky – were the home not only of Republicans and Democrats but of peacocks and mandrills. Gold and ivory were in their houses as well as rocking-chairs and motor cars. Fantasy lived there, satyrs walked in the woods, and millionaires built with the large and unstudied imagination of Haround al-Raschid. America was the last home of romance and anything could happen there . . .[178]

That fairly outlines the territory Linklater explores in the book. Juan is in a world where fantasy and fact are interchangeable.

There is no neat plot, as such, in Linklater's fantasy; things just happen to Juan as he links up with the most improbable people. America is under the influence of Prohibition so Juan, naturally, becomes involved with the gangsters of whom the most powerful is Red-eye Rod Gehenna. Red-eye descends, like a monarch, on Chicago where Juan hopes to find a girl dressed in black who just happens to be Red-eye's daughter. Although Lalange is his American dream-girl there are many distractions to compensate for her initial inaccessibility. Juan disappoints the daughter of Motley College's football coach and decides to move on. He becomes a bootlegger, working for The King of Diamonds; he works in a drugstore; he meets Olympia, the Unique Operacrobat; he has a love-affair with Lalange, his dark lady. When Red-eye discovers that Juan has dallied with his daughter he decides to have him killed. Juan is trussed up and put to sea in a canoe, only to be rescued by a poor little rich boy. Juan looks at life in the Deep South before going to Hollywood to work as an extra for Tantamount Studios. Here he rescues a film star from drowning and, through her, obtains an introduction to Dr Julius Salvator, founder of a philosophical cult of pure, selfish sensation. Juan's interest in Dr Salvator is entirely due to the proximity of a beautiful Chinese girl, Kuo Kuo. At the end of the novel Juan is, once more, in pursuit of a female. He is determined to find Kuo Kuo who has joined Dr Salvator's School of Thoughtlessness Nudist Colony at Arroyo Beach in California. And this is where he, naked and ashamed, finds her in the first chapter of a sequel *Juan in China* (1937).

In the First World War, Linklater was 'hit on the head by a German bullet.'[179] The experience of close contact with death did not unnerve him but it gave him an extreme distaste for the pretensions of humanity. His is a black comedy, dedicated to the proposition that the human race is hardly worth running. What makes life worthwhile is the spectacle of the astonishing individual. As a species mankind merely adds up to the pitiable sum of its exposed parts. When Juan is travelling by train from New York to Chicago there is an unforgettable glimpse of humanity caught short with its trousers down:

> Privacy's the thing. For some of us look respectable when we're fully clad, and a few bear studying naked, but none, man or woman, looks anything but pitiable half-way between bare skin and broadcloth. Shirt-tails, sock-suspenders, armour-plating for ruined belly-walls, bandages to support this and that, moulds that a pair of breasts may be stuffed into and empty cups for no breasts at all; long drawers wrinkling down the scrawny legs of old men, and short drawers on the fat thighs of middle-aged men; ringlets of red crushed flesh above women's knees where their garters clipt; vests that stick slightly to a man's hot chest and

coyly repeat his umbilical dimple – these may not be shown. These are
shameful things. These are the deformities of our wardrobes and
conspirators with our corporeal frailty. These are ludicrous, these wake
laughter, and laughter is destructive.[180]

Destructive laughter is what Linklater's black comedy suggests. He
is capable of a Swiftian disgust for the brazen mask mankind draws
over its imperfections. Linklater pulls back the mask to reveal the
individual who then – at his or her most vulnerable – deserves
perhaps a little sympathy. Linklater's work can be cruel and the end
of the cruelty is to encourage the reader to distrust pomposity and
posturing. Linklater actually refined, to a literary art, the Scottish
supposition that dignity is deceit in disguise. Nobody, in other
words, is to be trusted.

That scepticism is to be applied equally to the heroes of history or
the pioneers of tomorrow. Having toured America with Don Juan,
Linklater turned to the Viking period in *The Men of Ness* (1932).
Like Neil Gunn, whose *Sun Circle* appeared the year after Linklater's Viking novel, and (much later) George Mackay Brown, Linklater found readymade narrative material in the *Orkneyinga Saga* (a
thirteenth-century work composed and compiled in Iceland). In cutting the Vikings down to suitably human proportions Linklater also
reduced his prose style to a descriptive standstill by theoretically letting actions speak louder than words. In *Magnus Merriman* (1934)
he was back to his satirical and speculative best.

Magnus Merriman has the Christian name of a saint and the surname of a sinner (as the narrow disciples of Knox made merriment
synonymous with sin). To confound matters he is an Orkneyman
with literary ambitions to conquer the world. He is uninhibited
enough to make an idiot of himself regularly so that the novel becomes a portrait of the Scottish artist as a spectacle. Linklater had
great fun taking Don Juan to America; in *Magnus Merriman* he
brings Don Quixote to Scotland. The big set-pieces incorporated
into the novel make great mock-heroic battles and the discussion of
ideology gives Linklater ample scope for satire. In mocking Magnus,
Linklater is also laughing at his own fallibility for the novel is an extension of reality. In his Admonition to the reader Linklater tells us
that the book is no *roman-à-clef*. However, it cites real people like
R. B. Cunninghame Graham and Compton Mackenzie while the
poet Hugh Skene is a splendidly pugnacious portrait of Hugh Mac-
Diarmid (as the original acknowledged in *Lucky Poet*). Linklater
contested a parliamentary by-election in East Fife in 1933 on behalf
of the National Party of Scotland; he later recalled that the election
'was full of comedy'[181] There are other similarities between Merriman and Linklater. Magnus was born in 1897 in Orkney; two years
later, as we have seen, Linklater was conceived in Orkney. Both
Merriman and Linklater enlisted in a Territorial Battalion of the

Gordon Highlanders, saw action in France, then settled into Inverdoon (Aberdeen) University. Both had an early success with a best-
selling novel. There the resemblance begins to end.

The novel itself begins and ends in Orkney. Magnus, who has a
monstrous ego, leaves his native island for the delights of the wider
world but is finally brought down to earth by an Orkney earth-
mother. He ends up contemplating the kailyard or, rather, cowshed.
This is, of course, the logic of his belief in a world of autonomous
units. Linklater took seriously the case for what he called 'small
nationalism'[182] but could (and how could a humourist fail to) see the
inescapable conclusion that independence logically extended to each
bit of land a man claimed as his own. Behind this comic conclusion
there is a serious point, for Linklater had seen, as a soldier, the
terrible consequences of wars waged in the name of nationalism:
'Kings had fallen and nations perished, armies had withered and
cities been ruined for this and this alone: that poor men in stinking
pubs might have great wealth of memory.'[183] The same contempt
for the destructive consequences of the heroic posture informs Linklater's Second World War satire *Private Angelo* (1946) in which the
eoponymous protagonist learns that his constitutional cowardice is a
useful aid to survival.

Laxdale Hall (1951) opens in the manner of one of Mackenzie's
Ben Nevis farces. In a largely depopulated Highland parish a crisis
involves the coming-together of natives, incomers and outsiders.
Each character in the book embodies a Jonsonian humour: General
Matheson stands for military honour, his daughter Catriona for
Highland pride, socialist millionaire Sam Pettigrew for bureaucratic
idiocy, village shopkeeper Nicholas McLeod for adventure. Laxdale
itself is a village with little to recommend it but natural beauty and
Laxdale Hall stands out in this landscape like an alien presence. It is
a classical construction that contrasts with its romantic background;
Linklater is in his own element of uncertainty. Like Olaf Swanson,
the novel's token novelist, Linklater's 'regard for good form is
lavished on every page'.[184] His exposition is not only direct but
methodical as he patiently sets up the rural scene then threatens its
peace with three well-defined disturbances: first, the coming of a
parliamentary delegation led by the officious Pettigrew, profit-
motivated prophet of Socialism Plus; second, the offensive invasion
of the parish by a gang of Glaswegian poachers who have the
General's gamekeeper in their service; third, the production, by
Catriona, of the *Bacchanals* of Euripides, a play demonstrating that
'you can't ignore nature without nature having its revenge'.[185]

As rehearsals of the play progress under the attentive direction of
resident Greek scholar Mr Crantit, the classical tragedy repeats itself as parochial farce. In the Euripidean play King Pentheus
offends the Theban women by his killjoy policies and pays the price;

187

in little Laxdale, Pettigrew provokes the wrath of the Highland women by his indifference to the Scottish Sabbath. When he goes for a swim the women pursue him and take a terrible revenge (and remember Juan's terrible vision of a trouserless humanity). The scene is witnessed from afar by the novelist Swanson:

> Above the mill, on the far bank of the mill-dam, grew an immense and ancient willow tree with a bifurcating trunk. At a height of five or six feet one arm leaned earthwards and grew parallel with the ground, while the other, inclining a little to the opposite direction, soared to a high cupola of pendant leaves. – And while they stood, and stared, the naked figure of a man climbed desperately from the lower limb to the bending branches of the upright trunk, and on the bank below him some thirty or forty women, most of them elderly, stood and howled their anger. In the forefront of their array was Mrs McKellaig, shouting abuse, and waving at the naked man what looked, from a distance, like a human leg.[186]

The novel is Linklater a bit below his best. The characters are too close too caricature for comfort: for example, the local minister is provided with a two-handed sword to underline his Knoxian identity.

Inevitably perhaps Linklater's later work failed to live up to the standards he had set himself in his first half-dozen novels (*White-Maa's Saga, Poet's Pub, Juan in America, The Men of Ness, Magnus Merriman, Ripeness is All*). Unable to maintain the *enfant terrible* enthusiasm he succumbed to middle- and old-age and it showed in the themes of his later novels. *Roll of Honour* (1961), for example, is a study of defeatism. Andrew Birnie is a retired schoolmaster living in Inverdoon. He lives comfortably in his regulated way: he has his golf, his walks, his set periods for reading *The Times*. His life is arranged like a school timetable. As the novel opens he is startled to discover in the obituary column the announcement of the death of his old headmaster James Gilmour at the age of ninety. This stirs memories and Birnie takes down the two-volume Roll of Honour listing the names of Old Boys who fell in two World Wars. In a rhythmically stiff free-verse, Birnie recalls the pupils Old Gilmour groomed for premature death. As Birnie reflects on the loss of life he considers his own life which has amounted to very little. He has lost his position in the school (after resigning as an angry gesture against the governors who failed to appoint him rector in succession to Old Gilmour) and has lost his wife (who left him after his resignation).

A letter comes to Birnie from Simon Kyle who wants to have Old Gilmour's ashes buried in consecrated ground in the School Garden. Kyle thinks Birnie can help him. Kyle is (in contrast to Birnie) a successful novelist, a twice-married man-of-action, so Birnie gets in an extra bottle of whisky before receiving Kyle at home. He is then subjected to a traumatic tale about Old Gilmour. It transpires that

Old Gilmour's son Hector was an ignoble chip off the old block. He died in Spain (from drink-induced illness rather than fighting for the Republicans) and left behind a bastard son called Rowley. When Rowley turns out to be made in the image of his father there is tragedy in store for Old Gilmour for Rowley becomes a pop star then works as bait for homosexuals. He is apprehended and sent to Borstal. It is all too much for Old Gilmour as Kyle explains: 'I found him, one evening, crying over a photograph of the boy: he was the spit and image of his father . . .And next morning, when I took a cup of tea up to the old man, he couldn't talk, and he couldn't hold the cup. He'd had a stroke of some sort . . .he was dead by the end of the week.'[187] This revelation changes Birnie, who becomes brave enough to break his habits. As the book closes he begins to experiment with solitary whisky-drinking and, in a stupor, knock over his Victorian books before falling to sleep on them: 'Then he awoke, in momentary panic, having dreamt that he was late for an appointment with Old Gilmour; but when he saw what time it was, he was reassured . . .he had no need now to be afraid of Old Gilmour . . .'[188] Basically the novel is about a tiresome man whose sudden insight into his boring life hardly saves the day: 'The life he knew had blossomed like a great garden with brave young men; and in his own allotment he had learnt how to enjoy life by keeping his allotment small and private'.[189] What purports to be a poignant story is really a dull one. Without his wicked sense of fun and distrust of emotion Linklater is reduced to a totally out-of-character sentimentality. It shows in the style: the use of free verse for Birnie's interior monologue is clumsy and contrived; as is the use of formal dialogue for the encounter between Kyle and Birnie. Unlike Birnie, however, Linklater could look back in admiration of the promise he kept early in his life. Three final novels – *Husband of Delilah* (1962), *A Man Over Forty* (1963), *A Terrible Freedom* (1966) – showed Linklater in full command of his narrative faculties but lacking the coruscant wit of his youth.

27. DOUGLAS, LINDSAY, MACPHERSON: THREE OUTSIDERS

Like Gunn and Mackenzie, Linklater achieved an oeuvre. This is still the exception in Scotland, for Scottish fiction is stronger on novels than novelists. The masterbuilders who construct a solid body of work are rare and we have become accustomed to associate Scottish novelists with one novel: to a list that includes George Douglas Brown's *The House with the Green Shutters* and J. Mac-

Dougall Hay's *Gillespie* we could add Norman Douglas's *South Wind* (1917), David Lindsay's *A Voyage to Arcturus* (1920) and Ian Macpherson's *Wild Harbour* (1936). It is usually only the specialist who thinks of Douglas, Lindsay and Macpherson as other than one-novel novelists. The concentration on the single novel is not to be taken as an insult to the writers involved but a tribute to the novels so honoured.

One of the signs of a cohesive national literary idiom is the extent some writers go to avoid it in the interests of originality. There is little doubt that Douglas, Lindsay and Macpherson regarded themselves as outsiders who had to search for a personal aesthetic salvation by avoiding the stereotypes of fictional realism. George Douglas Brown had set such an emphatic precedent that subsequent Scottish novelists had responded to his work either positively or negatively. Their work was defined in relation to *Green Shutters*; even those, like Mackenzie and Linklater, who ventured into farce preserved a realist texture to their prose. Douglas, Lindsay and Macpherson had in common a desire to transcend national limitations and the novels their names live by attempted to challenge the supremacy of realism. Of course it is impossible to avoid certain national characteristics and Douglas the aesthete, Lindsay the mystic and Macpherson the prophet all practised an art coloured by Scottish psychology.

Norman Douglas (1868–1952) was born at Tilquhillie, on Deeside, of distinguished Scottish and Germany ancestry. He worked for the Foreign Office and served in the diplomatic corps at St Petersburg from 1894 to 1896. He found his spiritual home when he travelled in Italy and eventually settled in Capri (where he came into contact with Compton Mackenzie and D. H. Lawrence). He made his early reputation with an Italian travel book, *Siren Land* (1911), and made the travel book his speciality: *Fountains in the Sand* (1911), *Old Calabria* (1915), *Alone* (1921), *Together* (1923). He also wrote autobiography, *Looking Back* (1933), and gathered together some personal essays in *Late Harvest* (1946). Although most of his life was spent away from Scotland, Hugh MacDiarmid described him in 1953 as 'one of the greatest Scottish writers of the last hundred years, born of old Scottish stock'.[190] This judgement was based on the novel *South Wind* which is a magnificent achievement.

Douglas seems to have had the mind of a scholar and sensibility of a sybarite; he remarked, in *Late Harvest*, that 'I should prefer to be labelled Epicurean rather than hedonist, though it may seem hard in some cases to draw the line beween them'.[191] The distinction he drew was between Epicurean pleasures of the mind and hedonistic pleasures of the body. Douglas loved to indulge his intellect and artistry. His seductively descriptive prose is drenched in sensuous images; he luxuriates in details and drops esoteric facts like famous names. *South Wind* hangs a whole attitude to life on a slim narrative peg. Thomas Heard, Bishop of Bampopo in Africa, breaks his journey to England by stopping off on the island of Nepenthe. Heard's first glimpse of it contains many of the insinuations that will be taken up in the novel (the nebulosity of the place, the influence of the sirocco, the sense of other-worldliness). Douglas paints a word-picture of a lost paradise:

> Viewed from the clammy deck on this bright morning, the island of Nepenthe resembled a cloud. It was a silvery speck upon that limitless expanse of blue sea and sky. A south wind breathed over the Mediterranean waters, drawing up their moisture which lay couched in thick mists about its flanks and uplands. The comely outlines were barely suggested through a veil of fog. An air of unreality hung about the place. Could this be an island? A veritable island of rocks and vineyards and houses – this pallid apparition? It looked like some snowy sea-bird resting upon the waves; a sea-bird or a cloud; one of those lonely clouds that stray from their fellows and drift about in wayward fashion at the bidding of every breeze.[192]

Nepenthe is truly another world for Heard. It has its own saint, Dodekanus, whose thigh-bone is preserved in a silver statue in the island's principal church. Nevertheless the climate is unmistakably pagan. As Heard discovers, the inhabitants of the island are eccentric, endlessly amusing, and shrouded in a mystery of their own making. The whole book, in fact, is a black comedy illuminated by Douglas's aesthetic wit. There is the Alpha and Omega Club as the noisy centre of social life – this shrine to alcoholic excess is a pagan place of worship. The island has its own atmosphere of abandon and those who breathe this atmosphere are conditioned by it. Douglas had a definite plan in writing the novel: '*South Wind* was the result of my craving to escape from the wearisome actualities of life. To picture yourself living in a society of such instability, of such "jovial immoderation" and "frolicsome perversity" that even a respectable bishop can be persuaded to approve of a murder – this was my aim.'[193]

Those who live in Nepenthe are remarkable creatures. There is the ersatz Duchess; there is Ernest Eaves who spends his life annotating a book on the antiquities of the island; Commissioner Freddy Parker who epitomises seediness; Judge Malipizzo who is completely and utterly corruptible; the embarrassingly alcoholic Miss Wilberforce; Heard's elusive cousin Mrs Meadows; the flashy, overdressed Mr Muhlen; the obese priest Don Francesco; the handsome young Denis Phipps; the self-styled Messiah Bazhakuloff who limits his disciples to the Sacred Number 63 and calls them Little White Cows; and the rich Scotsman Mr Keith. Keith only visited Nepenthe a few weeks each year, we are told, and left when the cicada came. His heart was in the Highlands:

Northwards!

To his little place in the Highlands, at first. The meagre soil and parsimonious culture, the reasonable discourse of the people, their wholesome disputatiousness, acted as a kind of purge or tonic after all this Southern exuberance. Scotland chastened him; its rocks and tawny glinting waters and bleak purple uplands rectified his perspective. He called to mind the sensuous melancholy of the birches, the foxgloves, the hedgerows smothered in dog-roses; he remembered the nights, full of fairy-like suggestions and odours of earth and budding leaves – those wonderful nights with their silvery radiance, calm and benignant, streaming upwards from the luminous North.[194]

That is a rare view of Scotland as a cure for euphoria; to the pagan Mr Keith his native land is appropriately chilling.

South Wind brings the sirocco to bear on the strange characters of Nepenthe. The islanders converse on the most arcane topics and cordially despise intrusions into their set way of life. Judge Malipizzo, for example, detests the Russian colony on the island and bides his time to get rid of them. His opportunity arises when the Little White Cows misunderstand the Messiah's latest Revelation. He, in his strictly finite wisdom, has decided that the flesh and blood of warm-blooded beasts is Abomination to Little White Cows (an injunction that allowed Messiah Bazhakuloff to continue to eat fish); the Little White Cows take this to mean that everything deriving from dead beasts is Abomination to Little White Cows. Thus they could touch little, a situation that 'gave them what all religious people require – something to torment themselves with'.[195] One Little White Cow buys a packet of cigarettes (permissible) but is shocked to discover that the box of matches sold to him contains wax derived from the fat of dead animals:

> it was the Abomination, the Unclean Thing. Devout, and gifted with the hot impulse of youth, he acted precisely as he would have acted in Russia under a similar provocation. With a third gesture, one of abhorrence and ungovernable fury, he threw the box in the tobacconist's face.[196]

The resulting battle has epic proportions and involves the Little White Cows and the militia. The episode could have been a brilliant short story (and Douglas began as a short story writer, collaborating with his wife on *Unprofessional Tales* in 1911) but Douglas's artistic triumph is to integrate each part of the novel to the whole so that the various major scenes blend into a total image of an island with a personality of its own.

The characterisation, too, is exquisitely done. Mr Eames, for instance, is irresistible. He is absolutely dedicated to his scholarly work yet attracts the sort of gossip that sweeps round the island like the sirocco. The following passage conveys the stunning virtuosity of Douglas's prose:

It was not true to say of Mr Eames that he lived on Nepenthe because he was wanted by the London police for something that happened in Richmond Park, that his real name was not Eames at all but Daniels – the notorious Hodgson Daniels, you know, who was mixed up in the Lotus Club scandal, that he was the local representative of an international gang of white-slave traffickers who had affiliated offices in every part of the world, that he was not a man at all but an old boarding-house keeper who had very good reasons for assuming the male disguise, that he was a morphinomaniac, a defrocked Baptist minister, a pawnbroker out of work, a fire-worshipper, a Transylvanian, a bank clerk who had had a fall, a decayed jockey who disgraced himself at a subsequent period in connexion with some East End mission for reforming the boys of Bermondsey and then, after pawning his mother's jewellery, writing anonymous threatening letters to society ladies about their husbands and vice-versa, trying to blackmail three Cabinet Ministers and tricking poor servant-girls out of their hard-earned wages by the sale of sham Bibles, was luckily run to earth in Piccadilly Circus, after an exciting chase, with a forty-pound salmon under his arm which he had been seen to lift from the window of a Bond Street fishmonger.

All these things, and a good many more, had been said. Eames knew it. Kind friends had seen to that.[197]

The inventive power raises the old Scottish love of cataloguing to a fine art. The story is secondary to the brilliant effects Douglas creates. Heard witnesses a murder: his cousin Mrs Meadows pushes the odious blackmailer Muhlen off a cliff. Heard, once burdened by a conventional Christian conscience, ignores the criminal implications of the act and regards it as an example of natural justice. The island has transformed him as it transforms all who visit it through the medium of Douglas's multicoloured prose.

David Lindsay was a more prolific novelist than Douglas. He published five novels in his lifetime – *A Voyage to Arcturus*, *The Haunted Woman* (1922), *Sphinx* (1923), *The Adventures of Monsieur de Mailly* (1926), *Devil's Tor* (1932). *The Violet Apple* and *The Witch* were published posthumously in 1976. Lindsay's name is conspicuously absent from standard critical books on the novel and it took a collective study by J. B. Pick, Colin Wilson and E. H. Visiak to arouse interest in the man. In 1981 a Frenchman, Bernard Sellin, published the first thorough study of Lindsay as man and writer. Sellin's book began life as a doctoral thesis and this academic genesis shows in the time it takes for the Frenchman to convey the spirit of Lindsay's work. At first Sellin emphasises the unusual aspects of Lindsay, describing him as 'a self-taught person who...was to have much need of guidance...University would not only have enabled him to extend the field of his knowledge, but would also have directed him towards a sound critical basis, and to great writers, both English and foreign'.[198] I wonder. Lindsay the autodidact seems to have gravitated towards the authors who could teach him most. From Scott he learned how to objectify experience and from George MacDonald how to render fantasy in a realistic way. Lindsay was a Scottish writer with an excellent working knowledge of the Scottish literary tradition. It should be noted that the voyage to Arcturus begins in Scotland with the hero in possession of 'an uncorked bottle of first-class Scotch whisky'.[199]

Lindsay was born in 1876 in suburban London; his father worked in the City then suddenly emigrated to Canada, leaving his wife with no financial support and three children to care for. As a child Lindsay was frequently taken to visit an uncle who lived near Jedburgh. He thus became acquainted with Scotland as a visitor rather than a native. He worked in a London insurance broker's office from 1894 to 1916 and during the First World War he served in an administrative capacity and married a girl some twenty years his junior. After the war Lindsay moved to Cornwall and set himself up as a fulltime writer. He was a difficult man to live with and preferred solitude to conversation. When he moved to Hove in 1938 his wife had to take in paying guests and Lindsay was even more inclined to keep his own company. In 1945 he suffered from an infected abscess on a tooth and refused to seek medical help. As a result he died of carcinoma of the mouth and gangrene of the lower lip. It was an agonising end for a man who had already had his unfair share of intellectual anguish.

So much for the man; the writer was a more complicated creature. Even Lindsay's most fervent admirers find his prose style lamentable. Colin Wilson refers to Lindsay's 'hopelessly amateurish'[200] style; Victor Gollancz, who reprinted *Arcturus* in 1946, thought Lindsay 'wrote abominably'[201]; and Bernard Sellin contends that 'the tragedy of Lindsay, and it was indeed a tragedy, was that he was not a born writer'[202]. We are faced with the paradox of Lindsay: how could a man lacking literary fluency nevertheless influence a man like C. S. Lewis, inspire a man like Colin Wilson, and eventually become the object of undergraduate veneration in the USA? Sellin's solution is to argue that Lindsay's greatest contribution to literature derived from the quality of his thought; although Lindsay found it difficult to construct a smooth narrative his implausible plots contained forceful ideas and so 'David Lindsay is an ideologist rather than a philosopher'.[203] The ideological message, paraphrased, amounts to this: 'Life is mediocre, vulgar, made up of false pretences and trickery. It is not worthwhile to be alive, unless there exists another world, supernatural and superior, to which it serves as a necessary introduction.'[204]

Lindsay was, by temperament and circumstance, a committed pessimist. He responded to the writings of Schopenhauer and wrote, in the *Philosophical Notes* preserved in the National Library of Scotland, 'One must not regard the world merely as a home of illusions; but as being *rotten* with illusion from the top to bottom; not a sound piece anywhere, but all springs, glasses and traps throughout'.[205] There was, fortunately, an answer to this enervating attitude. Music, especially the symphonic music of Beethoven, had revealed a transcendent world to Lindsay and his ambition was to provide a glimpse of the Sublime in his writing. He took from Plato the notion of the everyday world as an imperfect copy of an ideal world accessible to the artistic imagination; and from Nietzsche the supposition that the man of genius can impose his will on the world. Now this ideology sounds suspiciously like wishful thinking. In life, Lindsay was a loner who could not abide the company of others. He was, in his own judgement, a financial failure; he was also an intensely shy man intimidated by the power of female sexuality. His life was a struggle and it is hardly surprising that he compensated by formulating an ideology insisting on the existence of a spiritual dimension he could enter. In *Arcturus*, Maskull speaks for Lindsay in the following passage:

> This world of yours . . .doesn't give me the slightest impression of a dream, or an illusion, or anything of that sort. I know it's really here at this moment, and it's exactly as we're seeing it, you and I. Yet it's false. It's false in this sense . . .Side by side with it another world exists, and that other world is the true one, and this one is all false and deceitful, to the very core.[206]

There had to be a meaning to life and Lindsay felt he had found that meaning in the spiritual world inhabited by the hypersensitive artist. To practice his art, Lindsay had sacrificed a safe job and endured hardship and humiliation. It had to be worth it somehow. Lindsay therefore denied the values of the everyday world and tried to keep in contact with the ideal world. His writing reflected his intensions and he accurately defined his own style as being 'a blend of common and supernatural life'.[207]

A Voyage to Arcturus was published in 1920 and sold 596 copies: on its first appearance the book made hardly any impact at all. It is a peculiar novel, a very Scottish novel in its obsession with morality and duty. The voyage itself begins in Scotland – at Starkness Observatory – and before the voyagers leave earth they hear a wailing sound which turns out to be 'A Scottish spirit trying to reproduce the bagpipes of its earth-life – in honour of our departure.'[208] Lindsay was conditioned, under the influence of his father, in the ways of Calvinism; *Arcturus* reflects this early indoctrination. Ostensibly the book is a work of science fiction but it soon resolves itself into a discussion on the nature of pleasure and pain. On Arcturus there is even a bare country called Sant that sounds like a Calvinist vision of Scotland: 'In Sant all is icy selfishness, a living death. They hate pleasure, and hatred is the greatest pleasure to them.'[209]

A Voyage to Arcturus opens with a seance in Hampstead. Backhouse, the medium, explains his method as the penetration of dreams: 'I dream with open eyes and others see my dream.'[210] This is the technique of *Arcturus*, for Lindsay sets up a dream world then questions its moral assumptions. Into the seance come Maskull and Nightspore who, it will be revealed in the novel, are the day and night of the same divided personality (hence yet another variation on the Jekyll and Hyde theme). Backhouse achieves, as promised, the materialisation of a youth. At this point a third character, Krag, rushes in and confronts the youth. He then twists the neck of the apparition:

> A faint, unearthly shriek sounded, and the body fell in a heap to the floor. Its face was uppermost. The guests were unutterably shocked to observe that its expression had changed from the mysterious but fascinating smile to a vulgar, sordid, bestial grin, which cast a cold shadow of moral nastiness into every heart. The transformation was accompanied by a sickening stench of the graveyard.[211]

This vulgar, sordid, bestial grin is 'Crystalman's expression'[212] and it appears at the moment of death throughout the book. E. H. Visiak, who knew Lindsay, felt the significance of *Arcturus* was dogmatically Christian with Crystalman representing Satan. On this logic two other important figures can be seen as representative: Muspel must be God just as Krag must be the Redeemer. It is Krag's intention to set Maskull on an odyssey to find the source of Muspel's light. This journey is to take Maskull to Tormance, the planet of the double star Arcturus. They leave from Starkness Observatory by means of a crystal torpedo fuelled by back-rays (which take light back to its source). Before leaving, Maskull finds the bottle of whisky and begins to polish it off. He is, therefore, intoxicated with the alcoholic spirit of Scotland before underaking his hallucinatory dream-journey. It is a journey across fantastic landscapes alive with other-worldly creatures. In order to cope with it all Maskull is progressively equipped with new sense organs so he will be at home in the hostile environment. Tormance is described in hallucinatory terms:

> Maskull now began to see strange specimens of vegetable life. What looked like a small patch of purple grass, about five feet square, was moving across the sand in their direction. When it came near enough he perceived that it was not grass; there were no blades, but only purple roots. The roots were revolving, for each small plant in the whole patch, like the spokes of a rimless wheel. They were alternately plunged in the sand, and withdrawn from it, and by this means the plant proceeded forward.[213]

To match the flora there are equally unlikely specimens of animal life. No wonder Maskull asks 'Am I dreaming, or awake?'[214] Lindsay is intent on evoking the alternative world accessible to the artist. Although Lindsay observes some of the conventions of science fiction his intention was not to create an escapist fantasy but to explore moral issues. Maskull specifically states that he has 'A moral aim'[215]. While, at first sight, Tormance seems a more perfect world than earth it soon becomes apparent that it is a world haunted by the Satanic Crystalman, a world where the pursuit of pleasure has diabolic consequences. Maskull himself becomes a killer on Tormance: he kills Oceaxe's lover Crimtyphon; he executes Spadevil, a Calvinistic figure; and he kills Crimtyphon's mistress Tydomin. He has come to Tormance as a Promethean figure in search of 'Muspel-fire'[216] and achieves a resurrection for when he dies his place is taken by his alter ego Nightspore. The world made by Surtur (also called Shaping, hence the creative impulse) is a world that involves clear moral choices. One can choose the pleasure-principle and worship Crystalman; or one can choose spiritual duty and worship Muspel, the divine light. Nightspore realises this at the end of the book:

> The truth forced itself on him in all its cold, brutal reality. Muspel was no all-powerful Universe, tolerating from pure indifference the existence side by side with it of another false world, which had no right to be . . .Muspel was fighting for its life . . .against all that is most shameful and frightful – against sin masquerading as eternal beauty, against baseness masquerading as nature, against the Devil masquerading as God . . .Now he understood everything. The moral combat was no mock one, no Valhalla, where warriors are cut to pieces by day and feast by night; but a grim death-struggle in which what is worse than death – namely, spiritual death – inevitably awaited the vanquished of Muspel.[217]

Awed by his insight into the moral battlefield that is the universe, Nightspore feels that he is fighting a losing battle. Krag, however, tells him differently:

> 'I am the stronger and the mightier. Crystalman's Empire is but a shadow on the face of Muspel. But nothing will be done without the bloodiest blows . . .What do you mean to do?'
> Nightspore looked at him strangely.
> 'Are you not Surtur, Krag?'
> 'Yes.'
> 'Yes,' said Nightspore in a slow voice, without surprise. 'But what is your name on Earth?'
> 'It is Pain.'
> 'That, too, I must have known.'
> He was silent for a few minutes; then he stepped quietly on to the raft. Krag pushed off, and they proceeded into the darkness.[218]

Suffering, Lindsay suggests, has its own rewards. Thus the book ends on a bleak moral note. Lindsay is inviting the reader to go beyond the pleasure-principle to a deeper world of duty and spiritual health whereby the Muspel-light may be glimpsed. In this sense the book has more in common with, say, Hogg's *Justified Sinner* than a fantasy by Jules Verne. The moralistic message of truth through spiritual trial is a forbidding one and we realise that Lindsay has composed an extraordinarily inventive allegory on the basis of Calvinist theology.

Ian Macpherson's *Wild Harbour* (1936) falls into the category of one-off modern Scottish classics. In an introduction to a reprint of the book Donald Campbell argues that 'the early death of Ian Macpherson presented [Scottish] Literature with the severest loss that it has so far had to endure.'[219] So much for George Douglas Brown, Lewis Grassic Gibbon and the other marvellous boys who provide Scotlit with its many glorious might-have-been moments. Still, it is possible to see how Macpherson's novel could arouse great enthusiasm. *Wild Harbour* is a novel prophesying war. It appeared during the 1930s and assumed that the Second World War would begin in 1944. Now the writing, particularly the poetry, of the 1930s is consistently apocalyptic in tone so Macpherson's martial projection is fairly typical of the time. In *The Gas War of 1940*, published in 1931, 'Miles' (S. Southwold) imagined hostilities commencing on 3 September 1940: 'Alsace and Lorraine were invaded after punishment from a German air-fleet that left alive a mere handful of their people.'[220] Macpherson's individual contribution to the prophetic genre of the 1930s was to describe what might happen should a couple refuse to participate in the war and, instead, take to the supposedly romantic hills of Scotland.

Scotland's most successful escapist was Bonnie Prince Charlie whose name is quickly, and significantly, introduced into Macpherson's narrative. Hugh and Terry, the husband-and-wife team who decide to opt out of the conflict, find a cave to covet: '"Would this be one of Prince Charlie's caves?" Terry wanted to know. "He passed this way to Benalder," I told her, "so no doubt it would be a Prince Charlie cave if people knew about it."'[221] In order to survive in the cave, Hugh, the narrator, has to show himself a cunning hunter and throughout the book there is enough gun fetishism to satisfy as Ian Fleming fan:

I had a B.S.A. single shot .22 with Martinix action which had often killed a hare at nearly two hundred yards. It had leaf sights for fifty, a hundred, and two hundred yards. I made sure that I got non-fouling rust-preventing ammunition for the .22. The barrel would never rust, nor would it require cleaning . . . The .303 was an old long Lee-Enfield. I had 500 rounds for it, and I had filed away the noses of the steel-jacketed bullets to make sure that they would spread and kill.[222]

The big set-pieces in the novel describe the various scenes as Hugh shoots his way to survival. He is no pacifist, clearly, but opposes military service because the conduct of war has become unbearably sordid: 'Oh, I'd fight all right, I'm no pacifist when it comes to defending my own right, but I'll not fight in any bloody stupid war. War's not fun any longer; it's murder, and I'm not a murderer.'[223] The accuracy of that statement is to be severely tested during the bitter finale of the book when Terry is shot and Hugh is obliged to exchange his theory for action of the most drastic kind. The bloody end of the novel implies that there is no escape from modern civilisation; that it will contaminate all unfortunate enough to be born in an appallingly troubled time.

Much of the tension in the book is provided by the inconsistency of Hugh's heavily opinionated position. Obviously there is something philsophically fascist about slaughtering beasts with relish then refusing to kill the inhabitants of another country threatening one's territorial integrity. The great strength of the book, in fact, derives from the authentic sound of the huntin' and shootin'. As antiwar troglodytes Hugh and Terry are shadowy figures and the novel only comes properly alive when Macpherson's prose explodes into violence:

> I dropped my rifle as I went towards my enemy. His wavering rifle fired from the hip. I saw it vomit flame before the bullet struck my breast with a force like a hammer blow. In a blur I saw him tumble backwards. I stood alone on the hill-top in the light of the rising sun, staggering like a drunk man, vomiting blood. The deep-ranked peaks climbed out of the morning to circle me around.[224]

Macpherson, who wrote three other novels before his death in 1944 in a motorcycle accident, spent almost all his life in rural Scotland and this familiarity with an emotionally loaded landscape carries him through the flattish stretches of a difficult novel. Stylistically the book is a conversation-piece frequently interrupted by bursts of action. There are no Eliotic objective correlatives but Macpherson has an appealing penchant for epic similes, like this one:

> We slept when we had eaten; like swimmers who have barely escaped with their lives and lie on the shore of the flood that almost swept them away and do not care whether the waters against which they struggled in despair now drag them back, we were overcome with lassitude of mind and body.[225]

Wild Harbour is a fascinating, if flawed, book and qualifies as an important Scottish novel.

28.   FIONN Mac COLLA AND CELTIC CULTURE

The fact that Douglas, Lindsay and Macpherson have been largely ignored in Scotland does not follow from the paucity of Scottish subjects in their novels. It is more likely that their sheer intellectuality intimidated the Scottish reading public. Scottishness alone does not give a book popular appeal or critical status, for the Scots are notoriously mean with praise and reluctant to recognise native talent. Although his work was wholeheartedly Scottish, Fionn Mac Colla was always kept on the sidelines by a consensus of critical indifference. MacDiarmid praised Mac Colla and offended Neil Gunn by championing the author of *The Albannach* (1932) as the authentic voice of the Scottish Highlands; Gunn, of course, regarded the Scottish Highlands as his own territory. During his lifetime Mac Colla published two major novels, fragments of a third novel, and *At the Sign of the Clenched Fist* (1967), a blistering attack on Knoxian negativity. He died in 1975 at the age of sixty-nine, a neglected and justifiably bitter man. His autobiography, *Too Long in this Condition* (1975), came out a month after his death. Mac Colla had few favours from fortune.

He was born Tom Macdonald, brought up in Montrose as a Plymouth Brother and grew to detest the religion of Knox and to believe that the glory of Scotland lay in the Gaelic past which, he insisted, had been obliterated by genocide. His continual assault on the Kirk did not endear him to the majority of Scottish readers and the fiercely intellectual, argumentative tone of his novels made him a difficult product for publishers to market. His personal convictions allowed him to be as theologically obsessive as any kailyard novelist and he was occasionally willing to sacrifice his splendid gifts for narrative and character-creation on the altar of his anti-Calvinist concerns. He was, for all that, an outstanding modern novelist with a uniquely troubled tone. The failure of his countrymen to make room for both Gunn and Mac Colla really speaks for itself.

As a writer of fiction Mac Colla was especially interested in psychological tension and cultural confrontations. *The Albannach* (1932) portrays a man saved from despair by his recovery of the Gaelic consciousness. *And the Cock Crew* (1945), Mac Colla's masterpiece among his novels, presents a parish minister whose Calvinist conscience persuades him to betray his people (hence the biblical title). On these two novels alone Mac Colla deserves to be judged as an incisive stylist and a novelist of real insight though I think MacDiarmid somewhat overstated the case when he wrote that the death of Mac Colla was a greater loss to Scottish literature 'than the deaths of Compton Mackenzie, Neil Gunn, Eric Linklater, George Scott Moncrieff put together'.[226] *And the Cock Crew* is on a level with the masterwork of Mackenzie and Gunn and Linklater. It is a novel of considerable austerity, dealing with the Highlands in its most desolate period. It has, moreover, a negative protagonist. With its oblique flashes of insight into the Gaelic past it conveys, with dignity, the tragic loss of the way of life that was Gaelic culture (as conceived by Mac Colla).

Basically Mac Colla believes that the destruction of Gaelic culture was not merely a national disaster for Scotland but an international loss. As he says in his philosophical manifesto, *At the Sign of the Clenched Fist*:

> had the community retained, as it had in Gaelic, a language of immense strength and resources potentially equal to any other, and of unsurpassed mellifluence . . . then the community of Albannaich instead of falling to the condition of 'the greatest cultural desert in Europe', would *necessarily* have developed into a veritable oasis of unexcelled fertility and of vast extent in the area of the human spirit.[227]

However extravagant this notion may seem, there is no doubt that it informed Mac Colla's work with a sense of urgency. Mac Colla is adamant that Presbyterianism – with its deification of negativity, its denial of creativity, its rejection of expansive spiritual qualities – gave the Lowlanders the ideological justification for their genocidal treatment of the Highlands. Mac Colla further believes that the Presbyterian theological conquest of Scotland was not historically inevitable but implemented by individuals. Hence in *And the Cock Crew* we are dealing with the activities of men, not embodied ideas, and we are encouraged to judge these activities. It could hardly be otherwise for an author who firmly believes that 'what the reformation did was to snuff out what must otherwise have developed into the most brilliant national culture in history'.[228]

The protagonist of *And the Cock Crew* is Maighstir Sachairi Wiseman, the forty-seven-year-old Protestant minister of Gleann Luachrach. The action of the novel is Maighstir Sachairi's relationship with his human flock and his attitude to the attempts of the Lowland establishment to replace them with sheep. As befits his position of fictional prominence Maighstir Sachairi makes a dramatic first appearance in the novel. The people of the Gleann have been summoned to Dun Eachain by Master Byars, the Factor–an oppressive bogeyman known to the Highlanders as the Black Foreigner. Seeing the English redcoats the Highlanders anticipate a massacre and word goes round that this is the punishment of God for accumulated sins. While the Factor interrogates the Highlanders the people of the Gleann shudder in their collective impotence, ready for the expected violent assault. Suddenly, however, things are changed:

> But at this point something very unexpected occurred . . . Every head turned, necks were craned. A kind of swirling movement was going on there and this swirl began to travel forward through the crowd. There could be no doubt about it, an angry voice was making its way to the front! . . . . It was a strong-looking reddish man, wearing his bonnet. He was about the middle-size, but looked both larger and redder because he was buzzing with rage.[229]

This is Maighstir Sachairi and it is immediately obvious that the Factor is as much in awe of him as the people are. He is 'a king, nae less, in [his] ain parish'[230] And as befits a parochial monarch Maighstir Sachairi soon takes control of the situation. He accuses the Factor of trying to provoke a bloody confrontation for his own nefarious ends. Far from being the will of God, he says, the actions of the Factor are the oppressions of men. Then Maighstir Sachairi announces his credo:

> I am Sachairi Wiseman, the servant of Jesus Christ, not of men. He has given into my care the orphan and the defenceless. In the day of bloody men *I* will be their protector![231]

Thus in the first major scene of the novel Fionn Mac Colla has shown us a grotesquely vulnerable group of Highlanders so accustomed to viciousness that they cower before the enemy they once routed. They are totally dependent on the protection of one man. However so far Maighstir Sachairi seems a worthy champion, a fearless fighter, an eloquent and imposing person who will openly declare: '*I* will be their protector'. In order to demonstrate their need for such a protector Mac Colla has to give us some idea of the worth of the Highlanders. Maighstir Sachairi, for all his raw and impulsive bravado, is soon to emerge as a theologically arid type; a man with a closed mind, but still a man in search of abstract perfection. He is, therefore, almost a symptom of the decline of the Highlands, of the passing of the Clan system. He is attracted to the parish, not out of sympathy with the people, but because of what he believes to be an organically complete, philosophically perfect way of life.

> The life of the glenpeople was a living whole, for it revolved about its own axis and its centre was within itself; the mind could consider it in isolation from adjacent regions and see it satisfyingly, as unity. But given over to sheep and shepherding the life of the district would be meaningless by itself, its centre would lie outside it far away in the woolmarkets and factories of the south; it would decline at once from an intelligible whole and become no more than an insignificant and not even necessary point on the circumference of a life centred elsewhere.[232]

As long as Maighstir Sachairi can believe in this little Eden he is happy, but the very contentment he feels forces him to regress into the Presbyterian obsession with sin:

> ... he had been seeking the satisfaction of an inner craving of his mind for harmonies, for the beauty shed by intelligibility in created forms. And as the natural man is in Sin, and the natural mind seeks what is contrary to God, *he had been sinning*. All those years.[233]

The theme of betrayal is implicit in the title of the novel, and it occurs several times: Maighstir Sachairi betrays the people of the Gleann; Maighstir Sachairi's own servant betrays him; and Lowland commercial interests (the Black Foreigner) betray the concept of one Scottish nation. There is betrayal too in the weary diffidence of the Highlanders. They are a group of broken men ready to toady for favours to Maighstir Sachairi. There is therefore a sense of doom from the beginning of the novel, a realisation that the culturally deprived are being led to their destruction by the theologically blind.

Nothing of the old spirit has survived Culloden. The waves of terrorism have had their intended impact. So, the reader might ask, who is there in the novel to sympathise with? Well, Fearchar the Poet for one. Though he is offstage for most of the novel (before his extended dialogue with Maighstir Sachairi at the end) he is represented as the agent of joy and creativity. And there is the past. With considerable subtlety Fionn Mac Colla gives us the traditional gaiety of the Gaelic people through the gloomy cogitations of Maighstir Sachairi:

> Twenty years before, Maighstir Sachairi came to Gleann Luachrach a young man of twenty-seven, full of zeal for the service of God. He found it given over to vanity; singing and dancing, contests of wit or manly prowess, were the principal enjoyment of the people. But his zeal was not little. Any man that was for the Devil's amusements found his flinty face never relaxed against him. He did not spare his flesh. He was so active on the foot of duty that he seemed to be everywhere at once; breathing out anathemas, exhorting, pleading, thundering. In the end he had them on their knees weeping and crying to God to avert the visitation of His wrath. The Holy Ghost swept through Gleann Luachrach with the sough of the whirlwind, so that any that were without the changed heart hid their faces and kept peace. Even Fearchar the Poet had been confounded and silenced.[234]

That, then, is the achievement of one Presbyterian minister: to consciously strive for the expulsion of joy. We see at once why the people of the Gleann are so weak and timid: they are the creation of Maighstir Sachairi. In St Matthew's Gopel Christ says 'Before the cock crow, thou shalt deny me thrice.' Maighstir Sachairi has literally *denied* his parishioners for twenty miserable, bibleblack years.

In *And the Cock Crew* there is no elemental force guiding events. There are only 'the actors in the drama.'[235] There is the cynical avaricious Black Foreigner, the presence of an army of occupation, and Maighstir Sachairi reduced to theological introspection by the dogma of a religion that stresses innate good and evil. For Maighstir Sachairi comes to believe that history *is* made by an impersonal force – God – and that it is possibly His wish that has cleared the Highlands of its Gaelic non-elect. Mac Colla is sure that 'history is made by man and only by man, acted upon at every moment by whatever is in fact acting upon or motivating him'.[236] In *And the Cock Crew* he shows one man, Maighstir Sachairi, activated (or rather de-activated) by Reformation doctrine to such an extent that 'he could not put his hand to his mouth without a moral struggle and a smart of conscience'.[237]

Thus Mac Colla's evocation of the naysaying theology that meant spiritual death to much of Scotland is in itself negative. Nowhere does he offer any hope of a Gaelic renaissance in the novel. There is only the prospect of yet more atrophy as the forces represented by Presbyterianism and Lowland commerce destroy the life of the Gleann people and Maighstir Sachairi himself. Such a novel could have been entirely bleak and it is only through imaginative skill that Mac Colla saves the novel in several key scenes.

At the end of the book there is catastrophe. The people are to be driven out and their houses burned. After some meaningless gestures at resistance the people go to Maighstir Sachairi for help but he denies them, feeling they deserve the judgement of God. Ironically, Maighstir Sachairi is fatally wounded when he and his horse are stampeded over a precipice in an attempt to save the Black Foreigner being trampled to death by cattle. The descriptive presentation of this and the subsequent glimpse of Maighstir Sachairi's early life are poignantly handled. Mac Colla impresses with this novel which is as deeply felt as any modern Scottish work of art and it is unfortunate that he turned increasingly to polemic at the expense of his fiction. At Mac Colla's death there were three unpublished novels among his papers: two of them (*Move Up John* and *The Ministers*) were written in the 1940s; another, *Facing the Muzhik*, dates from the 1950s. *The Ministers* was posthumously published in 1979 and shows that Mac Colla was not confined to the didactic manner of *The Albannach* and *And the Cock Crew*. *The Ministers* shows a more mellow Mac Colla though the characteristic touches remain.

The novel opens evocatively at the ocean's edge in the north-west of Scotland. Ewen MacRury, the young minister of Mellonudrigill, is in one of his visionary moods and this is the beginning of all his troubles. For gentle Ewen does not conform to the requirements of his parishioners, who are accustomed to the Knoxian tradition of thunderous pulpit indignation. Appalled at his innovation of taking some services in English instead of Gaelic, the locals take their complaints to a higher authority and once they have set the wheels of prejudice in motion there is no stopping them. Every supposed flaw in Ewen's character is exaggerated by the forces of malicious gossip (it is significant that *The House With The Green Shutters* is cited in the text) so that 'In the end they got to thinking of the minister as a necromancer, a dealer in black arts, sitting up there in his study raising the Devil – when he wasn't (this in broad whispers with a look towards the children) gaping at flesh in his legendary pictures.'[238]

The outcome of this wicked persecution of a man who deviates from the presbyterian norm is a full-scale examination of Ewen by his fellow ministers in a grandiose set-piece that owes something to the trial in Shaw's *St Joan*. Like Joan, Ewen is in trouble because of his visions which seem altogether too Christ-like for the pragmatic kirkianity of his superiors. Ewen is able to explain his transcendental experiences to the satisfaction of the reader but not to the expectations of the presbyterian elect. The final solution of his problem is both hilarious and satirically pointed.

In arranging his material Mac Colla achieves great depth by the use of the multiple viewpoint. Ewen's activities as seen by Mac Colla are one thing; as seen by his characters something altogether more sinister. The extended group-portrait of a malevolence of ministers is probably the finest thing in the novel though the supporting characters are sensitively drawn: the obnoxious gardener who regards himself as the guardian of public morality; the trendy ministerial colleague whose blandness conceals treachery; the maid with 'her arms folded high on her problematical bosom in the attitude of a veteran returning from the conversational wars'.[239]

On the evidence of this novel Mac Colla's gift for fictional recreations of ironically Scottish situations is considerable. Unfortunately, irony intervened in his own life for this most urgent of writers could not find a publisher to champion his work, and had either to pay printers to bring out his books or contemplate the remote possibility of a creative life after physical death. Mac Colla bitterly resented his status as a writer with unpublished manuscripts on his hands when he felt Scotland would benefit from the appearance of his work in print.

29. THE REFLECTIVE NOVEL: JENKINS AND URQUHART

Mac Colla's work simmers with indignation as he sits in judgement on his characters. His is the avenging God's-eye-view; he is the artist as moralist, aware that his is an unfashionable approach to fiction. A more conventional attitude results in what we might call the reflective novel since the protagonists reflect a carefully delineated ambiance. In the reflective novel a morally neutral narrator introduces characters from a closely observed environment. In England such a method would pass as naturalism but the Scottish nature is such that morality is never entirely absent and fictional characters never completely escape the clutches of their creators. As the behavioural psychologist considers the individual a mass of conditioned reflexes so the Scottish reflective novelist portrays the individual as a creature of habits acquired in Scotland. In the novels of

Robin Jenkins and Fred Urquhart we encounter characters conditioned by Scotland's physical shape and reluctantly metaphysical
climate. The influential environment intrudes; it plays an active part
in the events that occur.

Robin Jenkins has made it his creative business to study characters in a morally oppressive environment. He was born in Cambus-
lang, Lanarkshire, in 1912 and has made a living by teaching at
home and abroad (Kabul, Barcelona and Sabah). Although his
work is moralistic he has a deft way with characters and a capacity
to control explosive action. Jenkins's work makes an exhibition of
its Scottishness; his subject matter gives an image of Scotland as a
country distorted by religiosity and worn down by its own debatable
past. *The Thistle and the Grail* (1954) examines football as a surrogate for religion; *The Cone-Gatherers* (1955) shows the Scottish side
of homicidal violence; *The Missionaries* (1957) looks at religious
bigotry; and *A Very Scotch Affair* (1968) touches on Scottish sexual
inhibitions. Jenkins is very much a selfconsciously Scottish writer,
although he has used exotic settings. His Scotocentric idiom is
perhaps best illustrated by a superlative short story, 'Imelda and the
Miserly Scot', which appeared in the collection *A Far Cry from
Bowmore* (1973). It is a portrait of the Scot as stereotype. Andrew
McAndrick, a thirty-six-year-old Paisley man, is Api's dentist. He is
also the former colony's most accomplished womaniser. One evening he appears with his latest conquest, an astonishingly beautiful
Asian girl. To Andrew she is a sex object he can flash around, a
possession; a brainless beauty. Though she is initially submissive she
gradually asserts her independence (as Api did in breaking away
from its colonial status). When he attempts to subdue her she
defends herself with a blowpipe:

> It was aimed at him. Before he could yell or put up his hands as a shield,
> she charged at him, with a strange bounding action no doubt inherited
> from ancestors used to hopping over logs and roots, and drove the sharp
> point past his Api Yacht Club tie, gold sails on black ground, through his
> white shirt of finest Hong Kong cotton, and into his belly made,
> thirty-six years ago, in far-off Scotland. He was too young to die, he
> thought.[240]

Everything comes back to Scotland in a Jenkins work. The Scotocentric approach informs his stories and his novels.

A Toast to the Lord (1972) is set in Ardhallow, a small resort on
the Clyde. The community, quite literally, live with the threat of the
nuclear bomb as the USS *Perseus* is anchored in Loch Hallow with
Polaris submarines in attendance. That is the shape of the big world.
Locally things seem more normal. The novel is dominated by two
families, the Plenderleiths and the Tolmies. The Rev Robert Plenderleith, minister of St Aidan's kirk, is a widower engaged to Eli-

zabeth Greenloaming – the richest woman in Ardhallow and owner of the biggest hotel. As the novel opens Plenderleith's daughter Dora is returning from teachers' training college in the company of fellow graduate Agnes Tolmie. Though introduced as small, unattractive and sex-starved it is Agnes who will dominate the action of the book. Agnes watches Dora's sister Ann stage a one-woman protest against the American presence:

> Then Agnes noticed him, the young American at the front, being stopped by Ann. Pale and earnest, he was the kind of lover she had often imagined. Her breasts itched. She gasped. This had happened before whenever she had seen a man she fancied, but never so violently as now. She knew the Lord had at last acted. She looked up at the sky. Never had gulls been so beautiful, so perfect, so emblematic of the Lord's power.[241]

Agnes has a religious faith so fundamental and dogmatic that she regards every action as evidence of God's intervention. She is besotted with religion. She is a product of Scotland's theocratic state of mind.

Luke Dilworth, the American sailor, is attracted to Ann and impressed by her political fervour. However, Agnes has chosen him as her future husband and is determined to get her way – with God's assistance. Her task is made that much easier by Luke's personal naivety and his own religiosity: he constantly questions the morality of nuclear weapons and plagues the ship's chaplain with agonising doubts about the Christian attitude to war. Thus we have characters who represent varying degrees of commitment to Christianity: there is the casual approach of the ship's chaplain, the pragmatic attitude of Rev Plenderleith, the evangelical mission of Ann Plenderleith, the absolute certainty of Agnes Tolmie, and the twisted doctrinaire faith of Agnes's father. William Tolmie is the founder of the local branch of the Church of Christ the Master and has brought up Agnes in this narrow doctrine. He is an appropriately miserable man:

> For over thirty-five years, since his acknowledgement at the age of ten of the Lord as his Saviour, Mr Tolmie had prayed, read the Bible, preached, and believed more than any other man in Scotland. He should have been rewarded with the Lord's shining approval; instead, there had been a long eclipse until now only the darkness of rejection remained. That terrible judgement he had accepted without complaint.[242]

Tolmie's fanaticism and grim outlook is difficult to live with and Tolmie's wife, Isa, is worn out with his ways.

In accordance with her grand design, Agnes finds Luke a home near to her. While she pursues him, Luke pursues his interest in Ann which means taking on Ann's various good causes including her friendship with a foundling called Tommy Springburn (because found on the doorstep of a police station in Glasgow's Springburn). Having assembled his cast of characters Jenkins now constructs his novel round a series of violent, unpredictable moments. Scots, by this reckoning, live with pressure until they can bear it no longer. Agnes imposes herself on Ann, Luke and Tommy for a day in the country. When they see three teenage boys uprooting a young tree Ann, the crusading spirit, screams her protest. Luke is terrified:

> One of the boys was as big as and stronger than Luke; the other two were tough and violent. They were from Glasgow. They could have knives. Two had heavy sticks, one an iron bar.[243]

The vandal with the iron bar strikes and kills Ann's dog which precipitates her nervous breakdown and gives Agnes, witness to Luke's cowardice, power over the American. Luke finds Agnes's persistence distasteful and tells her so; Agnes takes a counter-offensive. She lets herself be picked up by an American sailor who makes sordid love to her on some waste ground. Then, convinced the act will result in conception, she breaks into Luke's room and virtually rapes him. She is sure any child can be attributed to Luke.

When Agnes's pregnancy is confirmed, Luke determines to do his moral duty and marry her even though he cannot fall in love with her. One ominous evening everything comes to a violent resolution. Agnes's mother dies and Luke goes home to find his landlady dead. He hears a visitor at the door. It is Agnes's father who has disowned Agnes to show his disapproval of premarital sex. Luke is surprised by the visit, yet also relieved, for Tolmie is holding a bunch of flowers. Taking this as peace offering, Luke is unprepared for what happens next:

> Agnes and Luke would get married, the baby would be born, and Mr Tolmie, as its grandfather, would be able to feel as he held it in his arms that, whatever disappointments he had suffered, this gift of a child was consolation.
> Then the man in the black hat stepped forward. It was Mr Tolmie. Amidst the flowers was a hatchet. He began to strike out madly.[244]

After murdering Luke, Tolmie kills himself. Thus in one evening, in a quiet Scottish coastal resort, we have 'the hell of murder, suicide and cancerous death'.[245] It is followed by the disappearance of Tommy Springburn who is later found dead, his body mutilated by crows and foxes. Despite all this Agnes's faith is stronger than ever. She is a model teacher and the children adore her; her assurance prevents the townspeople from turning against her. So the novel ends with Agnes pregnant and minus a husband, a father and a mother. Still, she is triumphantly sure that the whole situation is God's work. Doubt never crosses her closed mind. She is the true fanatic who endures by testing the endurance of others.[246]

In contrast to the *Green Shutters*-type drama that erupts in *A*

Toast to the Lord, the action of *A Would-Be Saint* (1978) is minimal, the burden of the novel being carried by a man's conscience which is microscopically examined as the book develops. It traces the life of Gavin Hamilton from 1918 (when he is eight) to 1946. Gavin lives in Auchengillan, a Lanarkshire mining community, with his mother; his father is away fighting in the Great War. In his father's absence Gavin is guided by his mother's narrow moral code. He begins to shine with good deeds, like a saint. When he hears the news of his father's death he takes it in his saintly stride. Everything, he is sure, conforms to a divine plan.

Through natural ability Gavin wins a place at Cadzow Academy where he shines as a scholar, a person, and a football player. He attracts a rich Jewish girl, Rachel Hallad; and befriends a poor boy, Douglas McIntyre, who has to leave the academy on the death of his father. Gavin feels the loss of McIntyre keenly as he continues to shoulder the pains of the world. In 1926, during school hours, he learns that his mother has died of a stroke. His future is placed in the hands of his vindictive grandmother who takes him away from the Academy because she resents its superior image; reluctantly, Gavin sacrifices a brilliant academic future and becomes a clerk in the office of a lawyer whose daughter, Julia Bannatyne, falls in love with him if not his air of sanctity:

> He wanted to remain poor and humble; yet he struck her as being dangerously ambitious in a spiritual sense. He acted as if the goodwill of everyone was important to him; yet he could be so self-sufficient that she herself often felt excluded. He did good deeds; but she sometimes wondered if he did them out of pure compassion and not out of a wish to show up the selfishness of others, including herself.[247]

Gavin continues to impress everyone with his astonishing prowess at football, a skill that could make him a modern icon if not a saint. Julia, now walking out with him, is afraid that 'one day he would commit some act of utterly irresponsible and ruinous goodness'.[248] He does. As his religiosity grows more intense he decides to give up football because 'Football had taken the place of religion in Scotland'.[249] He takes in, and is taken in by, a prostitute and thus loses Julia. On the outbreak of the Second World War he decides to become a conscientious objector.

Gavin has made a decision; the book now tests his faith in the light of that decision. He is exempted from military service on condition that he works in forestry and goes to Ardmore Forest in Argyll where he is surrounded by COs whose motives are suspect; his own priority is to avoid being beholden to anyone who supports the war. Although his fellow COs think, initially, that Gavin is too good to be true they gradually respect his sincerity. He is willing to pursue his saintliness to extremes: he hands over his wages to a tramp, a prelude to his renunciation of his inheritance (so that he gives away the property and the £2,000 his grandparents left him). Finally Gavin's acts earn him the respect of the local people but his diffidence is so deliberate he is taken as a plaster saint and not the genuine article. Ironically, Gavin is a dedicated Christian in a society that pays only lip-service to Christianity. Therefore the ultimate sacrifice is denied to him. Jenkins's tentative canonisation of Gavin is a comment on the shaky spiritual level of contemporary Scotland.

Jenkins puts a moral interpretation on the quality of Scottish life; he is a novelist who searches for evidence of the soul. Jenkins's contemporary Fred Urquhart concentrates on the exterior of his characters who are revealed by words rather than actions. Urquhart's ear for dialogue, especially Scots dialect, is unsurpassed in modern Scottish writing and it is matched by a mastery of descriptive detail and a command of understatement. Whereas Jenkins searches the Scottish west coast for his material, Urquhart works over scenes associated with his native east coast (the difference between west coast and east coast life being yet another typically Scottish division to contend with). Urquhart nevertheless gives himself creative *Lebensraum* since he is equally at home with agricultural or industrial settings.

Urquhart was born in Edinburgh in 1912, the son of a chauffeur who features as the character Jim Lovat in the *Palace of Green Days* (1979): 'Daddy was great fun when they were wee. He was forever playing games and singing daft songs. He pretty well let them wind him round their little fingers.'[250] *Palace of Green Days* recalls the years 1918 to 1925 when Fred's father's work took him to various homes of the gentry before returning to Edinburgh. Fred won a bursary to go to Stranraer High School and Edinburgh's Broughton Secondary School. He disliked Broughton and left at the age of fifteen to work in J.B. Cairns's bookshop, near Edinburgh University. Though he 'hated being a bookseller'[251] he stuck at the job for seven years and dreamed of being a writer: 'It was, I like to think, a better grounding for a writer than any university. Although I hated the long hours, the monotony and the poor pay, I suppose those years in the bookshop helped to develop me as a writer.'[252]

Subsequently he worked as a literary agent in London, as a reader for M G M and London scout for Walt Disney, and as a reader and editor for Cassell. All the time he was establishing himself as a writer. His first novel, *Time Will Knit*, was published in 1938. Although it was set in Scotland the main influence was an experimental English one: 'I was greatly influenced by Mrs Woolf at that time, and my one desire was to write "inner monologues" in Scots.'[253] The novel is structured so that the 'Plain' narrative of an American, Spike, alternates with the 'Purl' monologues of the Scottish characters. Spike has come, in 1929, to stay with relatives and observes the atrophy of the community in Harrisfield, a small town near Edinburgh. The Scots is nowhere near as rich as it is in the short stories and the inner monologues are anglicised so that Spike's grandmother Mirren can tell herself with some affectation: 'You can't rear seven children in a three-roomed cottage on thirty shillings a week without finding out that life isn't a bed of roses.'[254]

Urquhart's second novel, *The Ferret Was Abraham's Daughter* (1949), retraces the terrain of the first and introduces the daydreamer Bessie Hipkiss whose escapist fantasies cannot compensate for the reality of urban squalor. *Jezebel's Dust* (1951), a sequel, takes up the story after Bessie (the Ferret) has run away from her father and stepmother to work for the snobbish Edinburgh landlady Mrs Irvine. Bessie has changed her surname to Campbell (her mother's maiden name) but her friend Lily (the eponymous Jezebel) will have none of this:

> 'You and your daft notions!' Lily jeered. 'Hipkiss you were born and Hipkiss you'll die – unless ye get married, of course. Which I very much doubt, if ye keep goin' at the rate ye're goin' at. Terrified even to wink at a felly. I don't know what's come ower ye lately, Ferret.'[255]

Into the humdrum lives of the two girls come two Polish soldiers: Klosowski, a masochist, who seduces Lily; and Rolewicz, who marries Bessie and is then killed on duty in North Africa. When the scene moves from Edinburgh to London melodrama takes over from realism: Lily stabs yet another Pole and Bessie becomes a GI bride as a prelude to becoming a respectable American matron. In these novels I feel the intricate plots are inconvenient pegs for Urquhart to hang his brilliant dialogue on. The characters are what they say. Here, from *Jezebel's Dust*, is the hardbitten, street-wise Lily again:

> 'Lookit that Raf felly with the wallopin' walrus moustache!' Lily nudged Bessie with her knee. 'Across in that corner with the wee pug-nosed bitch in pink. Lookit the way he's gazin' at her, as if he could eat her. My God, he's welcome to her, too. He'll get indigestion if he doesnie watch out. She should ken better than wear pink with that sallow complexion.'[256]

It is appropriate that Urquhart's talent for orchestrating dialogue should find its finest expression in the short story. 'The Dying Stallion' uses the horse as a symbol of vitality to point up the onset of impotence in an old man who has been a bit of a stallion in his youth. 'Gentlemen, The Queen' is a surrealistic fantasy set in a pub patronised by bizarre characters who indulge in make-believe. 'Maggie Logie and the National Health' is possibly the funniest story ever written by a Scotsman. Maggie, inspired by the benefits of the NHS, makes up her mind 'that she must get her money's worth.'[257] She plagues her doctor with requests for treatment until 'the cupboard in Maggie's back bedroom was filled to overflowing with full, near-full and half-empty bottles of coloured water, as well as with boxes of pills of all shapes and colours.'[258] This is not enough so she has her teeth out, cuts her hair off, and works out a way to get a free gammy leg – with disastrous results.

Perhaps Urquhart's finest story is a sad one, 'The Bike', which displays most of the characteristics of his repertoire: his insight into female psychology, his ability to construct a grand theme on a simple anecdote, his authentic use of Scottish dialogue, and his emphasis on the way dreams are defeated by hostile circumstances. Annie, a worker in a warehouse, buys a bike and it becomes her most treasured possession, a symbol of escape from her dull environment: 'Here was something of her own . . . Her heart sang with exhilaration and proud accomplishment.'[259] Inevitably her dream-bike is destroyed by antisocial individuals and Urquhart concludes the story with a paragraph that speaks volumes: 'But Annie knew that even if she got another bike it would never be the same. She would always remember Charlie's derisive grin as he looked down at the broken frame, and his scornful words. She knew that something more than her bike had been broken. Nothing would ever be the same again.'[260]

30. RURAL REALISM: TOULMIN AND KESSON

Any novelist who uses Scots dialect for a serious, rather than a comic, purpose is likely to be linked with the achievement of Lewis Grassic Gibbon. Urquhart, who has been categorised as a disciple of Gibbon, resents the implication that his fiction is stylistically derivative. In fact he did not read Gibbon's great work until 1939 when Tom Scott gave him a copy of *Cloud Howe*. Then, during the Second World War, he went to live in Kincardineshire and 'living about ten miles from Leslie Mitchell's birthplace . . . I naturally listened to the local speech and the farm stories grew. So I don't really feel I'm a follower – though, of course, I have covered the same ground in many stories.'[261] Yet Gibbon's influence is inescapable for any writer who attempts to reproduce in prose the ancient, agricultural rhythms of Scotland. It is an option most obviously open to those with the opportunity to experience the rhythms at first hand. It comprises a still-living tradition of unabashedly lyrical prose, an affirmative alternative to the kailyard concept of the countryside. It was used by James Barke (1905–58) in his *The Land of the Leal* (1939) and with even greater impact in his massive Burnsian novel-sequence *Immortal Memory*, comprising *The Wind that Shakes the Barley* (1946), *The Song in the Green Thorn Tree* (1947), *The Wonder of all the Gay World* (1949), *The Crest of the Broken Wave* (1953) and *The Well of the Silent Harp* (1954).

Gibbon's greatest disciple (and the term is not meant pejorative-
ly) is David Toulmin who was born John Reid in Rathen, Aberdeenshire, in 1913. He left school at fourteen and was a farmworker
for the next forty-four years. At the age of fifty-eight Toulmin took
up landscape gardening and settled in Aberdeen where he became
something of a celebrity when his story-collection *Hard Shining
Corn* (1972) established him as a prose lyricist of great sensuous
gifts. Toulmin's novel *Blown Seed* (1976) is already recognised as a
classic of its kind. It is a love story; more accurately a lust story. It
features the working folk who are usually relegated to background
significance in romantic fiction. Toulmin's characters are as moody
as the seasons and endure like the earth. He is able to make his romance rugged with realism. The novel revolves round the figure of
Helen who is introduced in Toulmin's best prose:

> Now she was twenty-one. She had laboured in her father's fields and
> sweated in his byres; doing a man's work to save him paying wages . . . In
> the early hours of spring mornings she gathered weeds and stones from
> the harrowed furrows, a mantle of white frost still on the ground,
> awaiting the warmth of the rising sun. She had gone to school with cow
> dung caked on her shoes and with chaff in her tousled hair, because she
> never had time to rig herself, and the bairns of gentler folk jeered at her
> untidiness. While they were still in bed she was up milking the kye and
> mucking out the byre, with scarcely time left to take her breakfast.[262]

As the vivid description demonstrates, Helen is more substantial
than the heroines of conventional romance; Toulmin is creating a
fictional climate suitable for convincingly flesh-and-blood creatures
like Helen (or Chris Guthrie before her). Another writer who re-
news the Gibbon-orientated rural realism is Jessie Kesson who came
to feel, however, that Gibbon's 'attitude to the land and landscape
was too emotional'.[263] Her own attitude is more objective as her
autobiographical novel *The White Bird Passes* (1958) shows. It recreates the details of an exact place (Elgin) and an exacting period
(the 1920s) and does so in a language that is remarkable for its verbal economy. The autobiographical tale Jessie Kesson has to tell is,
on one level, a grim saga of bureaucratic brutality but she lifts it to a
more rarefied level by the vivacity of her writing. When the Vigil-
ance Officer wrenches the young heroine from her own home to an
institutional home in Aberdeenshire the new scene is set with a
metaphorical precision:

> Skeyne never had the colour of its sound. It lay on the threshold of
> Deeside, a doormat against which hurrying tourists wiped their feet,
> their eyes straining ever forwards towards the greater glories of the Moor
> of Dinnet and Lochnagar.[264]

The book opens in Elgin or, rather, a back street of Elgin called
Our Lady's Lane. 'The Lane,' Jessie Kesson tells us, 'was the world.

And, being so, ever willing to offer up some new distraction.'[265] It is this world that Janie tries to make sense of as she grows up in the somewhat red light cast by her mother Liza and in the shadow left by a father she has never seen. By the use of her imagination Janie compensates for the missing parts of her life; in other words, like the other children, she lies about her circumstances. 'So, Janie, perforce, had given life to a new Father. And death too. Death eliminated awkward questions to which Janie hadn't got the answer.'[266] She even concocts a neat little grave for her newly-created Father, with the motto 'Asleep in Jesus' on his stone. Jessie Kesson avoids sentimentality by stressing the raw vitality of a way of life. Thus some of her colourful characters – like O'Casey's slum characters – are presented as natural lords, or ladies, of language. Annie Frigg, for example, habitually persuades the children of the Lane to run her errands with the promise of great gifts: 'I've got something for you. A great big ball. All the colours of the rainbow it is. Blue, red, green, and yellow . . . It will never burst.'[267]

Too much of that kind of forced charm would have resulted in a false glamour. Jessie Kesson, who has presumably seen it all, juxtaposes the moments of nostalgia with instances of sickening violence. When two of the women, Battleaxe and Poll, have a fight one of them ends up having ten stiches in Casualty. 'Through the sawdust Janie still saw the blood, a small, dark loch submerged between cobbles that had become mountains.'[268] On another occasion Mysie Walsh hangs herself and we are spared none of the details: 'Her face black. Her tongue swollen twice the size of your fist. And a lump of cheese fit to choke her on its own stuck in her gullet.'[269] It would seem that suicide was the one certain means of escape from the Lane.

Janie herself escapes by a different route and it involves a considerable amount of psychological pain. Although many of the women of the Lane are prostitutes Janie's mother, Liza, has the misfortune to attract the attention of the authorities who track her down to the Diddle Doddle (poorhouse) and bring her to what passes for justice. Janie, not yet nine, faces the prospect of institutional life for the next eight years. Her efforts to survive in the orphanage take up the second half of the book. There is one poignant moment when Liza comes from the Lane to see her daughter. Her appearance suggests insobriety but Janie is quick to leap to her defence: ' "My Mam wasn't drunk." Janie brought out the name of Liza's illness triumphantly, completely vindicating the shameful accusation of drunkenness. "She's got an illness called chronic syphilis. That's what made her stagger. And that's what made her white and not bonnie any more." '[270]

The exploration of childhood is a common enough theme in Scottish literature but Jessie Kesson brought some new variations to it. For one thing she invested a difficult life with dignity; for another, she resisted the temptation to over-sugar the narrative pill and made the general reader swallow some unpalatable facts of life.

Jessie Kesson is a woman adamant about her own identity. In general terms, Scottish women novelists do not constitute a recognisable group though they share a female capacity for tolerance and can be surprisingly patient with recalcitrant male characters. They often have a light artistic touch so that even when the subject matter is earthy, as it is in *The White Bird Passes*, the idiomatic dialogue is counterpointed with a verbally delicate narrative. The exception to this rule is Anne Smith whose *The Magic Glass* (1981) is ruggedly realistic in both subject and style. (If there is a distinct Scottish genre that examines the young girl's transition from innocence to experience then Kesson and Smith are in control of it.)

31. WOMEN AND HISTORY: PLAIDY, MITCHISON, DUNNETT

Writing of the pre-eminence of women in historical fiction, Anthony Burgess argued: 'This feminine boldness may spring from a conviction that life does not change very much, and that to walk into history is merely to open an alternative door to the present'.[271] In Scotland, historical fiction tends to be produced with an energy that would overwhelm an industry. Jean Plaidy and Nigel Tranter have each covered, in staggering detail, celebrated stretches of Scottish history. In a woman's world Tranter is the odd man out. His style is journalistically informative, his manner is objective, and he excels in setting up spectacular scenes so that the climax comes as no particular surprise. In the second volume of his Robert the Bruce trilogy, *The Path of the Hero King* (1970), Tranter gives a matter-of-factual account of Bannockburn:

> In all the excitement and confusion, it was some time before Bruce realised that they were not being showered with arrows. He could not pause in this undignified plunging amidst other jostling bodies, but he did make darting glances to the left. And there, on the higher ground, he could see Keith's banner flying bravely, and horsemen hacking and swiping at fleeing archers in every direction. The King's sigh of relief was only metaphorical, but very genuine. He knew now that this battle could indeed be won.[272]

Jean Plaidy's approach is less subdued and much more subjective. She is a literary phenomenon, an industry in her own right. She has tried to recast popular history with empathetically attractive characters and seems on intimate terms with historical celebrities, particularly in her Mary Queen of Scots Series and her Stuart Saga.

A more obviously intellectual woman, Naomi Mitchison, writes historical novels with a contemporary relevance. Mitchison is an extraordinary personality, as colourful as any of her fictional characters. She was born in Edinburgh in 1897, daughter of the Oxford physiologist J. S. Haldane; her older brother was J. B. S. Haldane, the controversial geneticist. Her background combined economic privilege and radical unrest. She became every inch an upper-class rebel, espousing feminism and socialism and marrying (in 1916) G. R. Mitchison, later Lord Mitchison. Her novels reflect her abiding interest in current affairs and she tends to treat the past as an adumbration of the present. In her autobiographical essay *You May Well Ask* (1979) she claimed to be an innovator:

> That first novel [*The Conquered*] has echoes of Kipling. In later books there are echoes of D. H. Lawrence. But I was developing a style of my own. Oddly enough I was the first to see that one could write historical novels in a modern idiom: in fact it was the only way I could write them. Now everybody does, so it is no longer interesting.[273]

The ability to convey the consequences of historical action is Mitchison's greatest asset. By way of illustration I cite a passage from *Cloud Cuckoo Land* (1925). Young Cyrus is the son of Cyrus, the founder of the Persian empire, and the novel examines the way his struggle for supremacy will involve the Greek people. In this passage the movement of Young Cyrus's mind is expressed with idiomatic pace:

> Cyrus did most of the talking; he was anxious and excited, and for a little the Spartans wondered if he was drunk. But it was only that he had got a message to say his father was very ill and bade him come to Media to see him; and now he was beginning to think of the succession – his brother against him – the Satraps, Tissaphernes worst of all – oh what a tussle it would be, and what a prize! In the meantime he must keep the balance here; it would be terrible if things went back while he was gone, Athens got command of the sea again, threatened Ionia and Egypt! 'Lysander!' he said. 'Oh, Lysander, what will you do while I'm gone.'[274]

Although the novel is one of her most evocative, Mitchison has said: 'I had not been to Greece when I wrote *Cloud Cuckoo Land*, but when I got there it was as I had intended it to be '.[275]

That throwaway remark is revealing for it reminds us that Mitchison's primary source is booklore so her descriptive work is an imaginative projection. And her imagination has been fuelled by an immense amount of reading. For all her political activism (she helped her husband in his career as Labour MP and herself served on Argyll County Council) she remains a very cerebral writer interested in establishing themes that will move modern readers. Her first novel, *The Conquered* (1923), sees the victims of Roman imperialism in terms of the English oppression of the Irish; in *The Corn King and the Spring Queen* (1930), Tarrik and Erif Der attempt

216

to demythologise themselves in the interests of the Scythian people; *The Blood of the Martyrs* (1939) brings the contemporary European situation to bear on the plight of the early Christians; *The Bull Calves* (1947) uses the marriage of William McIntosh and Kirsty Haldane to suggest what all Scotland had in common in the eighteenth century. She has always remained astonishingly alert and is one of the few Scottish writers to write convincing science fiction, composing the *Memoirs of a Space Woman* (1962) and coming to terms with clones in *Solution Three* (1975).

Dorothy Dunnett's sequence of historical novels based round the fictional Francis Crawford of Lymond establish her as a perfectionist in a genre that is open to sentimental abuse. She expertly weaves historical fact with fictions; places Crawford in extreme situations as he travels from Scotland in search of excitement. Crawford is a historical hardman, a tough mercenary leader who retains some principles (like loyalty) in the six novels comprising his story: *The Game of Kings* (1961), *Queen's Play* (1964), *The Disorderly Knights* (1966), *Pawn in Frankincense* (1969), *The Ringed Castle* (1971), and *Checkmate* (1975). Although told on an epic scale Crawford's life is contained by his nationality and events always bring him back to Scotland. Dunnett's grasp of history is sound and her ability to examine her central character substantial. She keeps up the reader's interest by introducing sufficient data to control her penchant for purple prose. In *The Ringed Castle*, Danny Hislop, one of eight mercenaries summoned to Moscow by Lymond, describes the leader as gorgeous. The same epithet could be applied to Dunnett's prose as three passages from the novel will demonstrate. First, the description of Crawford's new mistress Kiaya Khátun, former head of the Sultan's harem:

> Her hair shone and glittered like coal: her brushed eyebrows gleamed above the moist coffee shells of her lids. Her nose was Greek and short; her warm cheekbones and brow a smooth sun-ripened olive. In Stamboul she had been tinted and gemmed like a Persian painting.[276]

Second, Crawford's first appearance to the eight mercenaries:

> For a moment Lymond remained there, surveying them. His eight officers, staring edgily back, saw a delicate-looking gentleman in a pretty paned and pinked tunic with the finest voile shirt and a link-belt of Italian enamel work. A man whose yellow hair, dry and light and unevenly tipped, eclipsed the sunlight behind him . . .[277]

Third, Crawford's encounter with Kiaya Khátun before his audience with the Tsar:

> He wore a doublet her tailor had fashioned for him from woven Indian silks of all colours; and over it a sleeveless coat cut with cunning, the seed pearls glimmering as he moved in the warm morning sun. She came

to meet him and considered him standing in silence, while he watched her with unmoved, cornflower eyes. 'The word,' he said 'is gorgeous.'[278]

All the novels contain hyperbolic descriptions and prose that some-times approaches costume-catalogue copy. The result is to bathe Crawford's mercenary career in a warm glow conveyed by the rich texture of the diction. Whereas Naomi Mitchison stresses the con-temporaneity of her historical fiction, Dorothy Dunnett lets the read-er relax and lean back into the warmth of her cushioned prose.

32. JANE DUNCAN: A WOMAN IN A MAN'S WORLD

The English novel was arguably invented by a woman, Aphra Behn, whose works appeared long before Defoe and Fielding had thought of (respectively) *Robinson Crusoe* (1719) and *Pamela* (1740). The Scottish novel is a man-made creation that generally presents a world dominated by the oppressive figure of the domestic tyrant whose tolerance of women is virtually nonexistent. It is instructive to consider how Scotswomen have dealt with the realist tradition of the novel. They have either tested their strength by observing the masculine rules of realism; or they have attempted a total contrast in style. We can read into the results by comparing two Scottish women novelists. Jane Duncan put her heroine into a man's world and essayed the realist novel. Muriel Spark found realism ultimately inadequate for her needs and created instead an enigmatic alterna-tive – a world of endlessly mysterious femininity.

Jane Duncan (1910–76) introduced Reachfar, the centre of her imaginative world and link binding nineteen related novels, in *My Friends the Miss Boyds* (1959). Ostensibly a hilltop croft in Ross-shire where the narrator, Janet, was raised it is also a symbol of the childhood idyll of innocence. As the first Friends novel has it, 'Reachfar was the one unchanging place in a world of constant change'.[279] The most potent use of the Reachfar image comes, I think, in what is arguably Duncan's most powerful and mature novel, *My Friend Sashie* (1972). Although it has an exotic setting it draws on many quintessentially Scottish themes. It has deeply mov-ing moments and stretches of sentiment. It is both personal and archetypal.

In fact Jane Duncan's husband died in Jamaica in 1958; in fiction Janet's husband Twice (so called because named Alexander Alexan-der) has died in the West Indian island of St Jago in 1958. It would be unwise to press an autobiographical element because Janet is never simply a self-portrait of the artist. Yet the novel has emotional depth because Duncan drew, as never before, on her personal reserves. To externalise her own predicament Duncan used the indigenous traditions of the Scottish novel. Of course there is 'duality of personality'.[280] Janet, blaming herself for causing Twice's death, reflects on her selfishness in cultivating her own literary ambitions at the expense of her husband. She reflects on her ability to perform routine tasks when necessary:

> In retrospect, I can see that I was living an extraordinary double life at this time, one side of it being the practical life of day-to-day, filled with trivial matters that required my attention, the other side being a perpetual flight from myself and life, a flight often aided by the means that came most readily to hand, which was alcohol.[281]

Convinced she has descended to the depths of alcoholic despair Janet leaves the house she shared with Twice and moves to the Great House of Paradise to become personal companion to Madame Dulac, a blind nonagenarian. Madame Dulac and her son Sir Ian are preposterous figures from an improbable past; they still believe that nothing has changed since the days when their class lorded it over the natives. Janet's move to the Great House is opposed by another extraordinary character: Sashie de Marnay, who is devoted to Janet and convinced that the Great House represents lunacy. When he first appears Sashie is presented as an unlikely hero:

> Both his legs were artificial, the result of his service in the Air Force during the 1939–45 war, so that he could walk only in a mincing unnatural fashion but Sashie regarded his disability as his own private affair and he concealed it by exaggerating it. He had adopted and dramatised all the mannerisms accepted by the conventional minds as peculiar to the homosexual to the point, almost, of caricature . . .[282]

Duncan charges her narrative (which branches off to describe the shattering impact on Madame Dulac of her grandson's marriage to a Chinese girl) with a Scottish energy. First, she emphasises the symbolism. One symbol in particular increases in importance with the deterioration of Janet. It is 'a long black, metal trunk like a coffin, with the words: "Major A. Alexander, R. E. M. E." in white paint on its lid'.[283] This trunk contains the manuscripts of Janet's novels and is identified with guilt since she believes her literary success killed Twice:

> The black trunk and the black guilt in my mind became merged into one, for the trunk contained the novels that I had written against the wishes of Twice. It was on the day when I had told him of the acceptance of one of these novels by a publisher that he had decided not to live any more.[284]

Although Janet wishes to destroy the trunk and its guilty contents, her friend Sashie has it taken to his home at Silver Beach. After the death of Madame Dulac (from a stroke caused by distress at her grandson's marriage) Janet is persuaded to join Sashie at Silver Beach. In the presence of the trunk and under the influence of alcohol her mind snaps with results that come out of *Green Shutters* by way of *Gillespie*:

> I staggered towards the trunk, whisky bottle in one hand, matches in the other and knelt on the floor, fumbling as I disengaged the key-ring from the steel handle. Suddenly, Sashie was beside me and I sprang up, raising the whisky bottle like a club above my head. I was taller than Sashie and I knew that I might kill him if I brought that bottle down on his head but I did not care. But as I tensed my arm to strike the downward blow, Sashie reached up almost casually, took my upheld wrist in a grip like a vice and although I exerted all my strength, a frenzied strength, against him, he forced my arm down and down until the bottle was standing on the lid of the trunk, where he forced my fingers to relax their grip on its neck.[285]

Sashie's part in Janet's rehabilitation makes him the proverbial friend in need. Whereas a Douglas Brown or MacDougall Hay would have reached out for tragedy and catastrophe, Jane Duncan avoids the ultimate issues by devoting the second half of the book to a description of how Sashie makes a successful novelist out of Janet, now dried out and unbearably efficient.

In her crisis Janet goes back, imaginatively, to Reachfar (as an Interlude makes clear). Thus the adult woman can only survive by repossessing her childhood happiness. This theme, sounded so often in Scottish fiction, is revealingly reassuring to Jane Duncan. Reachfar represents reality; in other words, the memory of childhood becomes more important than the acceptance of maturity. Up to the end of the Interlude, *My Friend Sashie* is so arranged as to make it an identikit Scottish novel with all the features present: it has dual personality, alcoholism, loss, defeatism, and a climactic act of violence which, in this case, is avoided. Part Two shows Jane Duncan reverting to the conventions of the popular novel and there is even a surprise ending to show that legless Sashie had once been a ballet dancer which leaves Janet brooding on the thought that she was helped by a man who concealed the fact that he needed help. The inability to see the story through to a realistic conclusion vitiates Jane Duncan's fiction. It represents a reliance on fairytale evasions and her work, as a whole, fails to integrate the conventions of realism and romantic escapism she puts to such excellent incidental use.

33. MURIEL SPARK: THE STYLE IS THE WOMAN

Muriel Spark is an accomplished artist, a writer who fully deserves her international reputation. She was born in Edinburgh in 1918, and educated at James Gillespie's School (fictionalised as Marcia Blaine School in *The Prime of Miss Jean Brodie*). After some time in Central Africa she worked, during the Second World War, in the Political Intelligence Department of the Foreign Office. She began as a *bellelettriste* then, after her conversion to Catholicism in 1954, became a novelist with an elegant turn of phrase and an elliptical technique that owed something to Firbank (also an influence on Spark's admirer Allan Massie). She settled in Rome, acknowledging, interestingly, that 'Edinburgh is the place that I, a constitutional exile, am essentially exiled from'.[286] Spark's fiction explores internal psychological divisions and external social divisiveness with equal enthusiasm. Her own inheritance was divided between Scottishness and Jewishness and she accepts the influence of her early environment:

> I am certainly a writer of Scottish formation and of course think of myself as such. I think to describe myself as a 'Scottish Writer' might be ambiguous as one wouldn't know if 'Scottish' applied to the writer or the writing. Then there is the complicated question of whether people of mixed inheritance, like myself, can call themselves Scottish. Some Scots deny it. But Edinburgh where I was born and my father was born has definitely had an affect on my mind, my prose style and my ways of thought.[287]

Although she is a stylist of unbounded vitality she dwells on morbid themes with a neo-Gothic relish and a surrealistic flair. *The Comforters* (1957) has a heroine in a hospital ward; *Robinson* (1958) projects an island that sustains hopes of life after death; *Memento Mori* (1959) connects geriatrics with a telephonic presence that urges death on them; *The Ballad of Peckham Rye* (1960) introduces a Scottish devil to the contemporary world. After these performances Spark surprised herself and her readers with the impact of her fictional return to Edinburgh: *The Prime of Miss Jean Brodie* was originally issued by *The New Yorker* in 1961. It was an instant success and has remained in the public consciousness as a representative story of the twentieth century. Miss Jean Brodie lives on and has appeared on stage, in the cinema, in a television series and has tempted actresses as sensitive as – respectively – Vanessa Redgrave, Maggie Smith and Geraldine McEwan.

    The Prime of Miss Jean Brodie is a study of the closed mind; the elitist mentality that powers the body of Miss Jean Brodie. Jean believes in the principle of leadership and the Calvinist doctrine of the elect. When Sandy Stranger, member of the Brodie set, muses on Edinburgh she realises that Calvinism is built into the city and she aches for its influence:

> In fact, it was the religion of Calvin of which Sandy felt deprived, or rather a specified recognition of it. She desired this birthright; something definite to reject. It pervaded the place in proportion as it was unacknowledged . . . Sandy was unable to formulate these exciting propositions; nevertheless she experienced them in the air she breathed, she sensed them in the curiously defiant way in which the people she knew broke the Sabbath, and she smelt them in the excesses of Miss Brodie in her prime . . . In this oblique way, she began to sense what went to the makings of Miss Brodie who had elected herself to grace in so particular a way and with more exotic suicidal enchantment than if she had simply taken to drink like other spinsters who couldn't stand it any more.[288]

Miss Brodie's heroes are Mussolini, Franco and Hitler and she believes women should be dedicated. Although 'in many ways Miss Brodie was an Edinburgh spinster of the deepest dye'[289] her closed mind contains fascinating fantasies. She intends to live vicariously through her set of selected disciples, her élite and her elect, for 'all my pupils are the crème de la crème'[290] and 'Give me a girl at an impressionable age, and she is mine for life'.[291] Sandy Stranger, the most reflective of the disciples, realises the truth about the self-styled leader: 'it occurred to Sandy, there at the end of the Middle Meadow Walk, that the Brodie set was Miss Brodie's fascisti'.[292]

Like many other Scots, Miss Brodie is full of contradictions. She idolises the fascists yet is against the team spirit; she speaks of love and freedom yet sleeps with the dreary Mr Lowther and denies herself to one-armed Mr Lloyd because he is married; she loves Rome and the Italians yet she is against the Church of Rome: 'Her disapproval of the Church of Rome was based on her assertions that it was a church of superstition and that only people who did not want to think for themselves were Roman Catholics'.[293] With frequent time-shifts the novel closes in on the action, usually seen through Sandy Stranger's eyes. Sandy is a dreamer who becomes Miss Brodie's Judas. She is a romantic who has imaginary conversations with fictional characters like Alan Breck and great artists like Pavlova. With her friend Jenny Gray she concocts a romantic tale around Jean Brodie's love affair with Hugh Carruthers (who died at Flanders). Sandy's romanticism is disappointed by the facts of life and she becomes a nun with novelty value because of a strange psychological treatise on 'The Transfiguration of the Commonplace'. She grows out of Miss Brodie who falls from grace when she becomes ridiculous rather than sublime. Judas-like, Sandy reports to the headmistress that it was Miss Brodie who persuaded Joyce Emily to go to her farcically ironical death in Franco's Spain. Sandy brings her judgement to bear on Miss Brodie who is found wanting:

> She thinks she is Providence, thought Sandy, she thinks she is the God of Calvin, she sees the beginning and the end.[294]

Sandy also tells the scheming headmistress that Miss Brodie is 'a born Fascist'[295] Later she reflects on the implications when she hears that, as a result of her report to the headmistress about Miss Brodie, Jean has been forced to retire on the grounds that she had been teaching Fascism. Sandy, who has been Miss Brodie's proxy in bed with Mr Lloyd, has become Sister Helena of the Catholic Church 'in whose ranks she had found quite a number of Fascists much less agreeable than Miss Brodie'.[296]

The novel creates its own claustrophobically close world in which the characters move with moralistic deliberation. It is a real world whose hoped-for ethical purity is destroyed by internal division and external threat. It creaks with contradictions native to Edinburgh. For example, the privileged girls who attend Marcia Blaine School are out walking when they are confronted with a sight that shows them their less fortunate fellow citizens:

> They had come to the end of Lauriston Place, past the fire station, where they were to get on a tram-car to go to tea with Miss Brodie in her flat at Churchhill. A very long queue of men lined this part of the street. They were without collars, in shabby suits. They were talking and spitting and smoking little bits of cigarette held between middle finger and thumb.
> 'We shall cross here,' said Miss Brodie and herded the set across the road.
> Monica Douglas whispered, 'They are the Idle.'
> 'In England they are called the Unemployed. They are waiting to get their dole from the labour bureau,' said Miss Brodie. 'You must all pray for the Unemployed and their families, I will write you out the special prayer for them . . . Sometimes they go and spend their dole on drink before they go home, and their children starve. They are our brothers, Sandy, stop staring at once. In Italy the unemployment problem has been solved.'[297]

Spark is a virtuoso who can create a mood out of a few juxtapositions and can create, in Miss Brodie, a vulnerable character sturdy enough to stand supreme in a physically small novel that expands imaginatively to contain religious tension, class conflict, international politics, civil war and unemployment. Such concision is rare in the Scottish novel but this densely packed prose is Spark's special concern.

Having dealt with Jean Brodie's girls, Spark turned to another claustrophobically female world in *The Girls of Slender Means* (1963). The girls are members of the May of Teck Club and they have their romantic dreams to amuse them. However, the time is

1945 and there is a bomb in the garden; when this symbol of the twentieth century explodes it destroys the world the girls believed in. Spark frequently portrays women who are denied privacy by the pressures of a troubled world. *The Mandelbaum Gate* (1965) is, for Spark, a big novel with a heroine whose ethnic and ethical characteristics are similar to those of the author. Like Spark, Barbara Vaughan is partly Jewish and a convert to Catholicism. She is also acutely aware of divisions since she has come to Jerusalem whose two sections are separated by the titular gate. There is endless activity rather than steady action and the point of the book is to emphasise what Jerusalem really stands for in symbolic terms. Next came *The Public Image* (1968), about an actress tough enough to survive in Rome, and Spark was ready for a prolonged raid on the area she knows best. She is at her best in evoking the mysterious and enigmatic quality of everyday life. In three consecutive and thematically related novels – *The Driver's Seat* (1970), *Not to Disturb* (1971), *The Hothouse by the East River* (1973) – Spark set out to make inroads into the everyday strangeness of the modern world. In this world language is more of a barrier than a bridge so characters use words to protect, rather than to reveal, themselves. All three novels are written in the present tense and Spark must have had both senses of the word 'tense' in mind, for the books are as full of tension as they are of immediacy. They explore the interdependence of fact and fantasy and exhibit a surrealistic ambiguity, a dreamlike continuity, an element of menacing uncertainty. In the traditional novel the novelist knows all: in the first of Spark's three experimental novels the novelist is sometimes at a loss for words, for 'Who knows her thoughts? Who can tell?'[298]

The Driver's Seat is the study of a willing sacrificial victim. Lise, a thirty-four-year-old office worker, flies south to get herself killed and to ·make the crime as spectacular as possible. She prepares for the sacrifice. In order to attract the maximum amount of attention she dresses in a bizarre outfit: red and white striped coat; purple, orange and blue skirt; a yellow top. This provokes the hilarity of onlookers who, when the events of the novel are over, will become witnesses with good cause to remember this particular victim. Lise is conspicuous by her colourful presence. She is obsessively in search of a man who is, to use her favourite expression, her type. In order to drive home the macabre nature of the narrative Spark elevates prolepsis to a stylistic principle. Chapter Three begins by giving the game away, so depriving the reader of a major element of suspense:

> She will be found tomorrow morning dead from multiple stab-wounds, her wrists bound with a silk scarf and her ankles bound with a man's necktie, in the grounds of an empty villa, in a park of the foreign city to which she is travelling on the flight now boarding at Gate 14.[299]

Immediately, then, Lise chooses her murderer, a rosy-faced young businessman who is clearly her type. For the remainder of the book he is conspicuous by his absence; he then reappears for the bloody climax the book has been inexorably moving towards. At first the man is frightened by Lise's attentions and when she sits near him on the plane he moves. She talks instead to Bill, a food faddist about to set up a macrobiotic establishment – the Yin-Yang Young centre – in Naples. He explains to Lise that his macrobiotic style demands an orgasm a day and wonders if she will oblige him that evening. As he takes her to her hotel in a taxi he makes a pass at her and spills his macrobiotic seed on the floor; this sexual metaphor is at once comic and revealing. Lise, it seems, is not interested in passive sexuality.

Lise's odyssey through the resort is both bizarre and believable. She meets an old lady, Mrs Fiedke, waiting for her nephew who is (so she affirms) Lise's type. Lise helps Mrs Fiedke choose a paper-knife as a present for the nephew and Spark's detailed dwelling on the potential weapon underlines its importance. At Mrs Fiedke's suggestion Lise looks after the knife; she then walks into a student demonstration and is accidently knocked down. Thinking her a political demonstrator a garage proprietor curses her. Subsequently he apologises and offers to give her a lift back to her hotel. It is impressed on the reader that Lise is deliberately arousing the expectations of men so she can reject them. The garage proprietor attempts to seduce her but she escapes from his clumsy clutches and makes off with his car. Thus she assumes the driver's seat to proclaim that in a deterministic universe she will nevertheless choose her own destiny. When Lise keeps her date with the macrobiotic evangelist there is a repetition of the seductive routine. Lise makes such a fuss that Bill is taken away with the police and, once more, takes the driver's seat. Eventually her dream-cum-nightmare comes true and she finds her perfect homicidal type. He is the man on the plane; he is also, fortuitously, Mrs Fiedke's nephew. Lise has to present him with the knife although she knows, intuitively, that he is a sex maniac recently charged with attempted murder. She will help him succeed in his vocation. She persuades him to come with her in the car and, in the driver's seat, takes him to the park. She instructs him exactly how to kill her and he carries out every instruction but one. Lise asks him to eschew sex but Spark's pun on 'plunges' makes it plain that he ignores her request.

> 'I don't want any sex,' she shouts. 'You can have it afterwards. Tie my feet and kill, that's all. They will come and sweep it up in the morning.'
> All the same, he plunges into her, with the knife poised high.
> 'Kill me,' she says, and repeats it in four languages.
> As the knife descends to her throat she screams, evidently perceiving how final is finality. She screams and then her throat gurgles while he stabs with a turn of his wrist exactly as she instructed. Then he stabs wherever he likes and stands up, staring at what he has done. He stands staring for a while and then, having started to turn away, he hesitates as

if he had forgotten something of her bidding. Suddenly he wrenches off his necktie and bends to tie her ankles together with it.[300]

The allegory has sexual presence and feminist overtones; it also condemns, by incidental detail, the values of the consumer society.

The second of the first-personal sequence, *Not to Disturb*, is another portrayal of people who simply go through the motions of living. People who exist without emotions. It relies, like *The Driver's Seat*, on prolepsis, Lister, butler to the Baron and Baroness Klopstock, stage-manages the aftermath of a violent event: the suicide of the Baron after he has murdered the Baroness and her lover Victor Passerat. Lister has arranged a press conference, sold the movie rights of the sensational story, and has a cinematographer and sound-track man on hand. The cinematographer, Mr Samuel, thinks the whole plot a 'first-rate movie script'[301]; certainly there is a Gothic atmosphere, a symbolic storm and a cast of eccentrics including the Baron's imbecile brother who is kept in the attic. Spark is conjuring up a zany deterministic world that is uncomfortably close to the world we all live in. As the novel moves on Lister explains that, though the Baron has yet to actually accomplish the events, the direction of the plot is a foregone conclusion: 'To all intents and purposes, they're already dead although as a matter of banal fact, the night's business has still to accomplish itself.'[302] As a matter of creative fact, of course, everything in a particular fiction is decided and Spark seems to be playing conceptual games with the notion of the novelist as surrogate God and solipsistic creator. Spark makes the reader aware of the structural act of making a novel wherein nature (and life) is made to copy art. At one point Lister dismisses two incidental characters because he feels they do not fit into the story.

The story, though, has happened before the novel gets underway. There is no element of suspense, simply a situation and its inevitable development. Spark uses this situation as a stage for the exercise of her ironic wit and surrealistic sense of fun. At an important point in the narrative it transpires that Heloise, a maid, is (probably) pregnant by the imbecile in the attic. A Reverend is summoned to marry the couple, thus ensuring that the Klopstock family fortune will remain in the capable hands of the servants. The entry of the imbecile is a marvellously macabre parody of the Gothic manner:

> The zestful cretin's eyes fall first on Irene [the maid]. He neighs jubilantly through his large teeth and shakes his long white wavy hair. He wears a jump-suit of dark red velvet fastened from crotch to collar-bone with a zip-fastener. This zipper is secured at the neck by a tiny padlock which very likely has been taken, for the purpose, from one of the Baroness Klopstock's Hermès handbags.[303]

The title of the novel is itself ironic. The Baron has given orders that the servants have not to disturb him. They are more than disturbing. They are all-devouring. They package him and market him while he is still alive. The Baron is secondary to the action; the focal point of the book is Lister – a servant whose ingenuity makes Figaro look naive. Spark's novel is really an anti-novel – though it is intellectually provocative rather than artistically flashy. The literary experiment she is conducting is related to her research into the ways in which we deny life.

'One should live first, then die, not die then live; everything to its own time'.[304] That sentence is the moral spine that supports the pages of grotesque fantasy that comprises *The Hothouse by the East River*. Told, like the other two anti-novels, in the first person it concerns a group of ghosts who have been brought into collective consciousness by the restlessness of one of them – Paul Hazlett, a reluctant corpse whose 'heart knocks on the sides of the coffin'.[305] Paul lives in a posh New York apartment with his wife, Elsa, the central character. Elsa's shadow falls here, there and everywhere but the right place. She is insubstantial so her shadow has a life of its own. Paul and Elsa have two children, Pierre and Katerina, who participate in the novel. Other characters are Elsa's bosom friend Princess Xavier; Elsa's analyst Garven Bey; Paul's analyst Annie Armitage. This strange group pursue an eccentric lifestyle that seems entirely appropriate to New York.

Spark introduces a suspenseful element into the novel by staging an encounter between Elsa and Helmut Kiel, a double agent she last glimpsed in 1944. He has, she tells Paul, turned up in New York as a shoe salesman. Paul, whose investigations put Kiel in prison, is understandably alarmed. Or would be unless he could rationalise on the impossibility of it all. For he knows he and his wife were killed in St Pancras station in 1944 when a V-2 bomb fell directly on the train in which they were sitting. Constantly his mind flashes back to the wartime period when he and Elsa were engaged on intelligence work and when he suspected Elsa of having an affair with either Kiel or somebody as insignificant. The novel, then, explores the life Paul and Elsa might have enjoyed if they had settled in New York after the war, if they had had two children, if they had acquired enough money to live in comfort. It is a ghost story with darkly comic tones and the humour operates in a surrealistic mode. For example, Princess Xavier, we are informed, keeps a farm of sheep and silkworms. She habitually keeps the eggs of her silkworms warm by, literally, taking them to her bosom. Garven, the analyst, witnesses the result of this gestation:

> Garven screams. His eyes are on the Princess's bosom. He screams.
> Under the protective folds of her breasts the Princess, this very morning,
> has concealed for warmth and fear of the frost a precious new
> consignment of mulberry leaves bearing numerous eggs of silk-worms.
> These have hatched in the heat. The worms themselves now celebrate

life by wriggling upon Princess Xavier's breast and causing Garven to scream.[306]

Shortly after this Garven abandons his professional calling and becomes Elsa's manservant.

Elsa's behaviour passes as normal in New York where (Spark is inferring) contemporary urban life is as bizarre as any work of fiction. Elsa does exactly as the mood takes her. When she wants to make sure the shoe salesman is Kiel she goes to Zurich to have an affair with him and tells Paul, in a long-distance phonecall, 'I slept with him last night. I don't think he's Kiel.' [307] Appearance and reality, art and artifice, dissolve into each other in this book. Elsa returns to New York for her son Pierre's production of Barrie's *Peter Pan*. The novelty is in the casting as all the parts will be taken by sexagenarians to prove Pierre's contention that '*Peter Pan* is a very obscene play'. [308] Elsa causes a sensation at the premier of Pierre's production by throwing tomatoes at the cast: chaos follows but Elsa takes it in her stride. It seems the problem with New York is that there is no substantial difference between the ghosts and the supposedly living beings. This brings Spark back to the nature of the novel which can be either an artistic impression of reality (as in *Jean Brodie* and *The Mandelbaum Gate*) or an autonomous literary form that exhibits the author's inventive abilities (as with the three anti-novels). Paul and Elsa are, after all, only literary creations and hover between the reality the reader invests them with and the illusion the author plays with. Paul and Elsa watch the ghosts of friends who died with them in 1944 and are impressed.

'You would think they were alive,' says Elsa.
'One can't tell the difference,' Paul says.[309]

Finally, Elsa and Paul stand in front of their apartment block. A new block is to be built on the site of the old. A Rolls drives up, bearing some friendly ghosts, and Paul and Elsa decide to join them:

She turns to the car, he following her, watching as she moves how she trails her faithful and lithe cloud of unknowing across the pavement.[310]

The self-awareness of the three anti-novels reflects an aesthetic fascination with form, an interest the public may not share. After these experimental books Spark returned to more entertaining subjects though with her stylistic options open. *The Abbess of Crew* (1974), satirised American politics, particularly the Watergate Affair, by depicting the underhand ways of a Nixonian abbess; *The Takeover* (1976) effectively undermined the success-orientated superficialities of the 1970s; and *Loitering With Intent* (1981) offered, as heroine, the novelist Fleur Talbot whose creative credo corresponds to Spark's belief in the magical act of invention.

34. TALES OF TWO CITIES: EDINBURGH AND GLASGOW

In *The Prime of Miss Jean Brodie*, Spark showed two contrasting aspects of Scotland's capital. Another Edinburgh lady, Joan Lingard, studies the one-sided picture of Edinburgh that tourists treasure and visitors expect. Lingard was born in Edinburgh, left the city at the age of two to live in Belfast (which provided the background for her 1970 novel *The Lord on Our Side*), then resettled in Edinburgh when she was eighteen. Her novel *The Prevailing Wind* (1964) dwells on the image of Edinburgh as a city that values its cold, respectable front. Janet has returned to Edinburgh with her daughter Sally; as they arrive they feel the prevailing wind howling down the steps of Waverley Station. Janet feels inordinately vulnerable in Edinburgh and gets little emotional change out of her family and friends. Her family are offended by the fatherless condition of the child Sally; her friends either want to marry or mother Janet. Janet's father is a subdued version of the Scottish domestic tyrant who expects only obedience and unquestioning respect from his children. He is disappointed in Janet, the drifter of the family; delighted that Fiona, Janet's sister, is a respectable married woman.

Janet's only real friend is an enigmatic Indian, Khalil, himself an exile in an indifferent city. The book describes Janet's passivity which allows things to happen to her. Fiona loses her baby and blames Janet because Fiona's husband, Howard, spent the night, innocently, at Janet's flat. On Christmas day a crisis develops when Janet's father strikes Sally for a display of independence. Having fallen out with her father, Janet is plagued by guilt when he dies. The book then ends with a mild surprise: Sally is not the illegitimate child the Edinburghers took her to be since Janet was married to a man who was killed in a car crash shortly after their marriage. The Edinburghers are seen an hypocrites who tend to assume the worst. Joan Lingard conveys all this action in a low key and speaks, softly, for all the characters. Perhaps the most acutely observed character is Janet's mother, Agnes, who is offered as an archetypal product of Edinburgh:

> An Edinburgh lady who is loyal to her husband, who loves her children and worries over them during long sleepless nights, who goes faithfully to church, delivers its magazines along suburban roads, stands behind cake stalls with hands sticky from soft sweet icing and shiny red cherries, who works diligently sweeping the dirt from the corners of her house, whose tear-washed eyes betray a self-induced martyrdom of sadness; a wife and mother who has known what it is to be peacefully content with a fire at her feet and children sleeping in upstairs rooms but who has never known what it is to be wildly, deliriously happy and want to shout it out of every window up to the stars in the sky.[31]

Through novels like Lingard's *The Prevailing Wind* – and there are several of them, some as delicately written as Jeremy Bruce-Watt's New Town novel *The Captive Summer* (1979) – Edinburgh has become a mythical city of restraint and denial. However, it is convenient rather than entirely convincing to classify the capital as genteel. Such classification reflects the temperament and background of particular novelists rather than the character of the city, which has extensive no-go areas of squalor and economic distress. Still, the image endures and it is Glasgow and the west coast that have been principally associated with realism even though the rugged surface texture of west coast novels can conceal the soft centre of proletarian romanticism. Glasgow, Victorian Glasgow at least, provided a suitable setting for Guy McCrone's essentially sentimental saga of the Moorhouse family: the Wax Fruit Trilogy of 1947 comprising *Antimacassar City, The Philistines* and *The Puritans*. But the really lasting fictive image of Glasgow is of a vast slum, a frighteningly vicious place populated by gangsters, morally angelic hardmen, loyal but downtrodden wives, sluttish but well-meaning mistresses and domestic tyrants of all ages. The image was vividly present in Alexander McArthur's *No Mean City* (1935), which forever fixed the Gorbals in the public mind as an inferno unfit for human habitation; it was, with suitable alterations, represented in Edward Gaitens's Gorbals novel *Dance of the Apprentices* (1946), Hugh Munro's *The Clydesiders* (1961), and John Quigley's *The Golden Stream* (1970). These titles conform to stereotypical expectations, whereas one man, George Blake (1893–1961), at least attempted to explore the nuances of the industrial west of Scotland.

35. GEORGE BLAKE AND SOCIAL REALIST SENTIMENTS

Blake was destined for a career in law until the Second World War interrupted his studies at Glasgow University. He was wounded at Gallipoli and looked back on this period in *The Path of Glory* (1928), in which a Scottish insular innocent is buried alive in the trenches of Gallipoli. Blake later worked as a journalist, in Glasgow and London; during the Second World War he worked for the Ministry of Information in London, then went back to Glasgow. In his vigorous attack on *Barrie and the Kailyard School* (1951), Blake dimissed rural sentimentalism as a mode unworthy of modern Scotland. Blake was middle-class by birth and breeding but empathised with the working class and wanted to create, as an alternative to kailyardism and Celtic Twilightry, a Scottish socialist realism. In fact he created an admirable body of work that displayed all the best features of proletarian romanticism – a genre that puts in the place of the kailyard's lad o' pairts the working class lad o' talent struggling to overcome cultural underprivilege and an economically depressing background.

Like John Davidson before him, and Alan Sharp and Bill Bryden after him, Blake was a Greenock man. Greenock became the Garvel of his fiction and the image of the industrial community which, with all its internal tension, was ultimately derived from George Douglas Brown's Barbie. The story of Garvel, as effected by industrial revolution and European war, is told in terms of various groupings, including the shipbuilding Oliphant family, in a sequence of novels: *Late Harvest* (1938), *The Constant Star* (1945), *The Westering Sun* (1946), *The Paying Guest* (1949), *The Voyage Home* (1952),' *The Peacock Palace* (1958). In these novels Blake's own middle-class-consciousness intrudes so that he is capable of creating persuasive middle-class characters but accustomed to seeing the proletariat in generalised abstract terms. In *The Paying Guest*, for instance, Peter Oliphant Pomphrey is well described as a sympathetic simpleton; as 'a specimen of the middle class in decay'[312], a man who fills in the time on his hands with the same predictability that he fills in the football pools. He is, nonetheless, an individual as opposed to the people he watches in the main street of Garvel on a Saturday evening in 1946:

> Those slowly-tramping folk of an industrial region, every little group continually halting to stare into a shop window and exclaim at either the beauties it contained or the prices demanded, could not help on this one evening of their freedom regarding Olly as either an intruder or a freak, or both . . . In the face of these conditions Olly did not find it difficult to sustain the attitude of indifference proper to a person of breeding in the presence of the lower orders.[313]

In Blake's books, despite all his efforts, the bourgeois characters are individualised and the proletarian characters are representative specimens.

If Blake's heart was in the Garvel sequence, his head conceived other ideologically improving works. In *Mince Collop Close* (1923) he offered as heroine the slum girl Bella McFadyen and in *The Shipbuilders* (1935) – published the same year as *No Mean City* – he essayed an epic allegory on Clydeside.

The Shipbuilders begins with the dramatic sentence 'It was all over'.[314] Blake is punning on the pronoun, for 'It' is both the newly launched ship *Estramadura* and the prosperity of Pagan's Yard. The great days of shipbuilding are finished for Pagan's, as Leslie Pagan realises: there are are no orders on the books. Leslie, married to the aloof Englishwoman Blanche, is an individualised and well-meaning figure of affluence. He is the ideal boss, concerned about his men.

231

True to Blake's limitations, however, the employees are generalised types, 'rough innocents'[315] like Leslie's proletarian counterpart:

> Danny Shields, bow-legged, broad-shouldered riveter whom a hard life and four years of Gallipoli and Sinai and Palestine and Flanders had left with the heart and mind of a boy . . . Danny Shields, who had been [Leslie's] batman from the beginning of the war to its end and was his friend, bound to him by ties innumerable and strong . . . Above the relationships of master and man, officer and private, they had lived together every emergency of the masculine world; Danny Shields, ever with the desperate humour of the western Scot on his lips, the grin of inexhaustible mischief on his face, courage and steadfastness in his simple heart — a man.[316]

Between them Leslie and Danny draw on great reserves of decency yet this two-man effort does not save them from defeat at the hands of an increasingly indecent world. Capitalism ruthlessly discards inefficient working methods and the men who go with them; reluctantly, Leslie has to sell Pagan's Yard. In doing so he feels he has betrayed Danny whose name is sounded like a bell throughout the book. Blake tries to sustain the allegory by giving each fictional episode a symbolic significance and by emphasising that all the men are at the mercy of an impersonal force – capitalism – as devastating as any mythological fate. While Leslie searches his conscience Danny is brought down by professional pride and domestic circumstances for, in his fury, he lashes out drunkenly and ends up briefly in Barlinne Jail. Towards the end of the book Leslie, having sold out financially, tries to implement a scheme to bring discarded shipbuilders to a rural idyll in the English Downs. This escapist solution is rejected by Danny, the 'most moving symbol of the old life'[317], and the book ends with the parting of the old comrades. In bidding a fond farewell to Glasgow, Leslie salutes the city:

> It was his own city, for better or for worse. Never could he escape it. By no adjustment of the selfish mind; by no prepared indictment of its social deficiencies, its ugliness, its smugness, its sentimentality, its brutality, its dirtiness, its wetness, its greyness, grimness – by no elaboration of personal criticism could he escape its grip on him or his awareness of responsibility to it. A city that had had its day; a city built on exhausted coal-beds and empty shipyards; a city now of middle-men and Jews and pimps, eternally bemoaning over the coffee-cups what they called 'the drift South', rationalising their own inertia; a city living on a sordid past and selling its war-gotten War Loan to buy pesky and expensive motor cars . . . Very well! But a city that was still Glasgow, peopled by such as Danny Shields, the salt of the earth.[318]

From such excruciating sentimentality it can be seen that Blake's novel is naturalistic rather than realistic. It is shot through with technical imperfections, for the proletarian dialogue is stagey and artificial and the cloyingly unreal relationship between Leslie and

Danny is a false model of human harmony. Blake's book is remembered, though, for its ambitious attempt to portray men in a
contemporary industrial setting and for the way it helped soften
up the Scottish novel for subsequent expressions of proletarian
romanticism.

36. PROLETARIAN ROMANTICISM: SHARP, HIND, McILVANNEY

The genre of proletarian romanticism has been one of the strongest
influences on Scottish fiction for the last two decades. A typical
novel in the genre usually threatens the reader with a realistic prelude then dissolves into vast stretches of affirmative lyricism and
egotistical philosophising before ending on a heroic note of resignation. The bourgeois novel, with its attention to detail and emphasis
on behavioural norms, still gets written is Scotland but gets relatively little attention which accounts for the neglect of novelists as
perceptive as Elspeth Davie, whose atmospheric short stories are
almost equalled by the tone of the novels *Providings* (1965), *Creating a Scene* (1971), *Climbers on a Stair* (1978); or James Allan Ford,
whose *A Statue for a Public Place* (1965) and *A Judge of Men*
(1968) deal with, respectively, a civil servant (authentically as Ford
was a prominent Scottish civil servant) and a law lord (namely
Robert Falkland who embodies, powerfully, the negative virtues of
Scottish authoritarianism). Far more characteristic of relatively recent Scottish fiction is the work that deals with tough sensitives surviving in physically and culturally challenging surroundings. George
Friel (1910–75) produced several novelistic investigations into the
spiritual and economic atrophy characteristic of parts of Glasgow:
The Bank of Time (1959), *The Boy Who Wanted Peace* (1964),
Grace and Miss Partridge (1969), *Mr Alfred MA* (1972), *An Empty
House* (1975), While there are few novelists as compelling as Friel
there are others as combative: Cliff Hanley's *The Taste of Too
Much* (1960) deals with the school rather than the street life of Glas-
gow but the most memorable scene is a vivid description of corporal
punishment which, though derived from a similar scene in D. H.
Lawrence's *The Rainbow*, shows powerfully the way violence is in-
stitutionalised in Scotland. Stuart MacGregor's *The Myrtle and the
Ivy* (1967), Allan Campbell McLean's ritualistically violent *The
Glasshouse* (1969), and Alistair Mair's *The Ripening Time* (1970) all
explore the possibilities of proletarian romanticism. In three novels
in particular, however, the genre rises above its inbuilt limitations
and begins to come close to major areas of achievement. The novels

are Alan Sharp's *A Green Tree in Gedde* (1965), Archie Hind's *The Dear Green Place* (1966) and William McIlvanney's *Docherty* (1975).

Alan Sharp was born in Alyth in 1934 and adopted by a Greenock couple; his father worked in the shipyards by day and served in the Salvation Army by night. This parental combination of hard work and moral purpose was Sharp's adoptive inheritance and he later luxuriated in a verbal virtuosity that replaced grim morality with bohemian hedonism. Sharp left school at fourteen and spent the next four years working in the shipyards. After his national service he did a variety of odd jobs (some of them decidedly odd like being assistant to a Greenock private detective). He achieved a critical and commercial triumph with *A Green Tree in Gedde* which was announced as the first part of a trilogy: the middle part, *The Wind Shifts*, duly appeared in 1976 but then Sharp himself shifted from Scotland to Hollywood to enjoy the hedonistic lifestyle of a highly paid screenwriter. Sharp's financial dreams had come true and he had found his green tree in Beverly Hills. This richly rewarding life appealed to Sharp; much more than recognition as a Scottish novelist ever could. Looking back on his work he felt his fiction was impossibly ambitious and that 'I'd rather be happy and have my health than be a great writer'.[319] The intentions were encouragingly clear in the first place:

> I've always been a formalist, inasmuch as I always really wanted to write allegories, you know, multilayered pieces that work at this level and also at a higher level; the idea being that I would someday write a book such that if every other book in the world was destroyed, you could still reconstruct literature from this book. Everything would be in it – the compendium novel, as it were.[320]

The tacit assumption is that it might be possible to emulate Joyce's *Ulysses* which is, supremely, one of those 'multilayered pieces'. As Archie Hind modelled his first novel on Joyce's *A Portrait of the Artist as Young Man* and Sydney Goodsir Smith his only novel on *Finnegans Wake* (suitably cut down to size) Sharp went after the Joyce of *Ulysses*. Here is a sample of Sharp's Joycean style:

> [Cuffee] whorled his tongue till the tease made [Gerda] wince, and then shifting she swallowed him in unlappe. The smell of her, warm white bread. He kissbit up into the fold, blinded in dark nearness. Slipping down impatient for incus she reached the barb but he pulled her back, this time dragging down between her breasts, his mouth open the lip membrane pulling dryly over her belly, tongueing the sunken curl of the navel, perspiration bitter pitlet, down until the rough scrub above the bone caughts his mouth, wiry tangle, and she all the while reaching down to kiss his far below head.[321]

Sharp counterpoints that simulation of sexual ecstasy with gravely informative passages and impersonal narrative; the book studiously avoids setting into a prosaic monotone.

Thematically, too, the novel works by juxtaposition, the whole being the sum of three interdependent parts: Moseby's Book, Ruth's Book, Gibbon's and Cuffee's Book. John Moseby has been adopted into the middle class and is settling into a routine as a Glasgow University student, married with a three-year-old daughter. Like the other characters, Moseby is umbilically attached to an environment he longs to escape from. His best friend, Harry Gibbon, is a carpenter ponderously seeking the meaning of life. Harry inherits his exploratory mental habits from his great-uncle Robert Gibbon who came to Greenock and developed into a peripatetic preacher who prophesied a new world and partly populated it with his illegitimate children. Gibbon's message is one of earthly affirmation:

> It was from the outset apocalyptic, but its vision was not couched in traditional mystic terms, not the glittering hallucination of St John, rather the rural dream of a Langland. He spoke of the earth as a great mothering fecundity and of the humans who tended it as a blessed elect, yet made no attempt to glamorize the monotony and harshness of toil . . . After his meetings a dance was usually held and he joined in, spinning the girls until their hair flew in his face and their free breasts throbbed in their dresses and later in the hedgerows he held some willing one close as the sky swole enormous black and trembled with stars.[322]

Harry is raised on a book of great-uncle Robert's sermons (one of which suggests the title for the novel) and is forever quoting his saying 'if you don't go you can't go back'.[323]

While Moseby complicates his marital status by having an affair with a working-class girl, Cathie, Gibbon leaves Greenock for adventure and an answer to the questions that have been haunting him. He meets up with an army pal, Peter Cuffee who, apparently, is incestuously intimate with his sister Ruth – a theme also deployed in Kennaway's *Household Ghosts* and Angus Wolfe Murray's *The End of Something Nice* (1967) – and has graduated from precocious eroticism to obsessive sexuality. Cuffee leaves his studies at Manchester Art School and (like the heroes of the odyssey-obsessed American fiction Harry's homosexual poet-friend Kimber admires) they hit the road, intent on London and Paris, searching for a meaning to life. Cuffee seems to be a contemporary equivalent of the biblical Adam; certainly he is always seeking comfort in the arms of the nearest Eve. Gibbon, in long discussions with Cuffee and Kimber, comes to realise that the answer lies in formulating the right questions. The paradisal green tree is an internal affair.

Sharp implies that the restless search for the perfect place is a re-enactment of the ancient quest for spiritual perfection. At least

Moseby, considering Glasgow, understands that man-made cities obscure the 'old green eden' underneath:

> He had never really seen [Glasgow] before, [Moseby] realized. Not really, not clearly . . . Through its streets the mind might wander for ever and not come upon a single image of transcendence, buildings and more buildings, monuments that echoed buildings and buildings that echoed monuments. Green squares sewn into the city's monochrome, in which the old sit and watch their feet . . . A city demanding to be loved in default of alternative, allowing its sons and daughters no glimpse of the world beyond, preforming their minds to an acceptance of the human landscape as being of brick and stone, slate and cement, making such words as he had read almost incomprehensible, an alien rhetoric.
>
> It made him see something he had known but never quite focussed before. About Cathie and himself. That their affair was, in this new sense, Glaswegian, it had this incarcerated, airless aura to it, this unease that lay upon the city-dweller, that beyond what they had something unguessably better existed, that corroded the pleasures of the present without promising future recompense. Was it that yearning for the garden genesis, old green eden, wherever and whatever it has been? Was that why his room was green, why he liked to lie naked and let it swim around him, under the green aquarial light of the mnemonic tree of life.?[324]

That vision, born of the sight of Glasgow, should be compared with the Glasgow envisaged by George Blake and Archie Hind.

For Cuffee and his sister Ruth the tree of life is made in a sexual image; they, in their Englishness, are sure that eroticism is an antidote to the provincial respectability of the Knutsford their parents live in. The two Scots, Moseby and Harry Gibbon, have a more spiritual attitude: at the end of the novel Moseby realises his odyssey is about to begin, 'that he must leave, must go, escape, fly, find that freedom in which all life must be lived'.[325] It means leaving wife Edna and daughter Carol to take up the life that waits for him in *The Wind Shifts*. The burning desire to produce a magnum opus, a trilogy, deserted Sharp after the publication of the second volume. In *The Wind Shifts* Moseby comes to London, to share living accommodation with a friend (who turns out to be the Glasgow poet Eddie Linden in thin fictional disguise); he meets up with Ruth, and Cuffee shifts towards his inevitable and abruptly violent end. Sharp's style is restless as he himself shifts between the serious and the sensuous by breaking into stretches of fine writing.

Archie Hind, by contrast, tries to sustain a heightened prose style throughout his novel. Whereas Sharp attempts Joycean wordplay, Hind has learned from Joyce's *Portrait* the advantages of using leitmotif and meditating closely on all the implications of the story unfolding before the reader. *The Dear Green Place* is Archie Hind's portrait of the working man as would-be artist.

Hind was born in Glasgow in 1928, served in the RAMC in

Malaya and and Ceylon from 1946 to 1948, and worked at various
jobs. Like George Mackay Brown and Tom Scott, he studied under
Edwin Muir at Newbattle Abbey College. While working to support
a large family (three sons, two daughters) he produced a deeply felt
and carefully composed novel. It is evidently autobiographical. The
hero, Mat Craig, is 'a working-class boy'[326] in Glasgow. He day-
dreams of being an artist and spends sleepless nights trying to realise
this ambition. The novel describes how he is gradually worn down
by hostile circumstances and working-class assumptions of the worth
lessness of culture. The novel gives all the reasons why a working-
class Glaswegian cannot write a novel; the existence of *The Dear
Green Place* is a triumphant refutation of the argumentative logic of
book.

When we first come across Mat he is burning the midnight oil, or
its electrical equivalent. The world has gone to bed but Mat is doing
his best to be creative:

> In one of these council houses late on a September night there was a
> light still burning . . . Within the circle of light which the lamp cast on the
> surface of a table a man sat in the room, trying to write . . . He was
> crouched over the paper on the table holding the pen in his hand tightly;
> his left arm was circled around the paper giving him the cramped
> appearance of a dull and unwilling schoolboy at his desk. For a couple
> of hours – ever since the other people in the house had gone to bed – he
> had been sitting writing . . . Mat was 'burning the midnight oil'.[327]

The other people in the house constitute Mat's connection with supposedly real life. He has made a hypergamous marriage to Helen, a
middleclass girl, and they live in the council house rented by Mat's
parents. There is much banter in the family, especially between Mat
and brother Jake, a slaughterhouse worker; there is also a sense of
family togetherness especially at the festive season and the book
opens with the idea of Christmas slowly dawning on Glasgow. Mat
is a dreamer and his dreams of cultural splendour are vicarious and
essentially phoney. Helen shares these dreams:

> They had imagined a house of their own, Helen cooking fantastic meals,
> cosy nights by the fire, long slow evenings with the clock ticking slowly
> and Mat sitting writing, and their friends would all come and sit and eat
> open sandwiches, drinking coffee and talking; and music, listening to the
> Vienna Philharmonic under Furtwangler on the gramophone. Instead of
> the vicious knockout drinks like whisky and gin they would drink wine
> and there would be talk, witty, relaxed, and coruscating with ideas.[328]

Mat, with his Joycean epiphanies concerning the hidden spir-
ituality of life, has ambitions to realise the potential he is sure he
possesses. He cannot accept that his life will only amount to 'responsibility, a diploma in accountancy, a house up a tiled close in a
brownstone building and a good steady wage coming in every week,

in lieu of love'.[329] He has been brought up on the commonplaces of Clydeside radicalism and believes that the working class represents the voice of the socialist future. Thus he works on a magnum opus that will, he hopes, add eloquence to that voice so that the golden future is as celebrated as the golden age enjoyed by other classes. Mat believes, above all, in Glasgow as an industrial breeding ground of genius. He knows that the Gaelic name Gles Chu means 'the dear green place' and intends to celebrate its vitality:

> Gles Chu! Glasgow! The dear green place! Now a vehicular sclerosis, a congestion of activity! He felt for a cigarette in his pocket and the match which he lit flared bitterly in the cold air. The city about him seemed so real, the buildings, the bridge, the trams, the buses, so separate and hard and discrete and other . . . He leaned on the smooth granite parapet of the bridge easing the weight on his legs. Glasgow! Gles Chu! The dear green place! . . . A Calvinist, Protestant city . . . A city whose talents were all outward and acquisitive. Its huge mad Victorian megalomaniac art gallery full of acquired art, its literature dumb or in exile, its poetry a dull struggle in obscurity, its night life non-existent, its theatres unsupported, its Sundays sabbatarian, its secular life moderate and dull on the one hand and sordid, furtive and predatory on the other. Yet Mat had to admit that all this moved him in a way that art could only be secondary to; the foundries, steelworks, warehouses, railways, factories, ships, the great industrial and inventive exploits seemed to give it all a kind of charm, a feeling of energy and promise . . . A dirty filthy city. But with a kind of ample vitality which has created fame for her slums and her industry and given her moral and spiritual existence a tight ingrown wealth, like a human character, limited, but with a direct brutish strength, almost warm. Glasgow. Gles Chu![330]

Stunned with this vision of Glasgow as the dear green place, Mat becomes obsessed with the notion of writing a great novel: a book with the scope of Thomas Mann and the stylishness of Flaubert. Encouraged by Helen's belief in him he gives up his office job and begins on a more satisying existence, dividing his time between the mental demands of his writing and the physical demands of a job beside Jake in the slaughterhouse. The descriptions of the slaughterhouse are magnificently done, exhibiting a verbal power that relates to actual experience. As set-pieces they are unsurpassed by anything in recent Scottish fiction:

> When a beast was felled it was quickly pithed, the killer feeling for the hole in the skull and inserting the cane, pushing it down the spinal canal for about four feet, then working it in and out until the animal would thrash its legs about and its muscles would twitch and shudder. After he had pumped the cane in and out a few times the animal would be left lying absolutely slack and the killer would stand up between the animal's forelegs, kicking the top leg back with his heel so that the skin about the throat would be stretched tight. Then casually, usually while bantering away with his mate, he'd stroke the eight-inch sticking knife on his steel then bend down and, inserting the knife's point under the hide just

above the dewlap, he'd bare the flesh in a long forward stroke to beneath the chin. The flesh would then be stroked lightly with the edge of the blade until the killer could feel the warm pulse of the carotid; again he'd insert the point of his knife and slit the artery longitudinally, releasing the rich purple frothy blood into the waiting pan. After this the beast was hung for a while by a rope, hitched round a hind foot and slung on to the crane. When the blood had drained from the carcase it was lowered back down on the floor and turned on its back with its head twisted round and a loose foot wedged into the ridge of its spine to help prop it up. This was when the killer's job really began. While the head was being skinned by the benefit man the killer would remove the feet with his straight sticking knife. This was done quickly, the killer swiftly laying open the knee with a semi-circular cut and a flick of the knife which folded back the skin pad over the knee and exposed the white membrane over the joint; then he merely twisted the knee with his left hand and stroked the joint with his knife and the foot was off and flying through the air to join the pile of other feet lying outside the door of the room. Before the last foot had landed the long straight knife was being used to extend a slit in the hide, from the throat, over the dewlap and breast, down the middle of the broad flat belly, and back to the vent. The hide was then flayed with the curved skinning knife, from the forelegs, flank and rump of the animal and spread out leaving the flensed carcase all glistening and fresh with the hide attached now only to the tail, back and shoulders.[331]

Events overwhelm Mat. Helen becomes pregnant and Mat finds a flat for his family. His father is killed in an accident and Mat mourns for the way economic conditions waste the working-class life. Having sold two stories, Mat decides to give up his slaughterhouse work and concentrate entirely on his writing. He is appalled at the superficiality of the Glasgow literati he mixes with and humiliated by having to accept handouts from his family. He is sure that his failure is a failure of nerve related to his working-class consciousness. At the end of the novel Mat is sick, physically and spiritually. In Hind's fine and sensitive writing we can see the central assumption of proletarian romanticism: the working-class character is simply too good, morally, for the life he is obliged to lead by economic pressure. It is a theme worth a writer's while and was taken up, in a grandiose manner, in William McIlvanney's *Docherty* (1975). McIlvanney, a miner's son, was born in Kilmarnock in 1936. After attending Glasgow University he became a schoolteacher in Irvine. His novel *Remedy Is None* (1966), in which a student avenges what he takes to be his mother's betrayal of his dead father, was followed by *A Gift from Nessus* (1968) in which a salesman chooses self-assertion rather than death. Like his journalist brother Hugh, William McIlvanney is (to adapt a Disraelism) a rhetorician occasionally overcome by his own verbosity. He is fascinated by violence and the hardman image – as his detective thriller *Laidlaw* (1977) shows – and his writing dwells lovingly on physical confrontations. The hero of *Docherty* is a working-class hero; tough, tenacious and – in the goodness McIlvanney attributes to him – ultimately unfit for the life.

The novel opens in 1904 with the birth of Tam Docherty's fourth and final child, Conn. It is just after Christmas and hope is high even in the High Street of Graithnock, Ayrshire. Conn is symbolic of a new life. Tam, a miner, is sure of that:

> 'He'll never be ready fur the pits. No' this wan. He'll howk wi' his heid. Fur ideas.' He winked at the baby. 'Eh, Conn? Ah'm pittin his name doon fur Prime Minister. First thing in the moarnin'.[332]

Tam, though teak-tough, is not like the domestic tyrant of so many Scottish novels. He is rather, and in spite of himself and his lapsed Catholicism, a proletarian saint. He is a socialist, a potential saviour of his class. He is also the protective patriarch who adores his four children. He is, as one of the local says, 'a wee man but he makes a big shadda'.[333] Yet Tam is gradually martyred by the economic burden he (as a representative of his class) has to carry. Conn has, after all, to go into the pits which represents a major defeat: '[Tam] had fathered four children and all he had ever been able to give them was their personal set of shackles'.[334] The children cause him pain as well as pride: Mick loses an eye and a limb in the war and comes home to torment Tam; Kathleen marries a wife-beater; Angus gets a girl pregnant and is rejected by Tam for not doing the decent; and Conn becomes a carbon copy of his father as far as heroic toughness is concerned. Tam is, fundamentally, a fighter and is a match for any man (though not, it is implied, for any system which is what finally crushes him):

> He had believed himself capable of confronting any man or any situation and surviving intact . . . There were a lot of men he knew he couldn't beat. But there was nobody he wouldn't have fought. Similarly, there had been no situation he felt unable to face. From that pride radiated the force that had given his life any sense of purpose it possessed. He felt at least able to give his family the protection of himself and at the same time to pass on to them an awareness of the importance of themselves.[335]

Tam the radiant proletarian saint is thus set up for the final martyrdom. He emphasises his heroism casually by sorting out a nuisance in the High Street and conclusively by sacrificing himself that another might survive a pit collapse:

> While Conn whimpered with effort, the realisation of it broke through Hammy. He knew himself walking in the tunnel with Tam Docherty behind him. He knew a man diving into his own death to push Hammy out of his. He saw the stunning speed with which Tam must have moved. He felt those last handprints burned into his back . . . He stood accepting the magnitude of an unasked for gift. The generosity of it made it hard to breathe. There passed through him like a lightning-bolt love for someone who had always been for him just a hard wee man.

Conn gasped and recoiled. They saw a hand projecting from the
rubbish, fixed in its final reflex, Tam Docherty's hand. It was pulped by
the weight of the fall. The hand was clenched.[336]

The symbol is bathetically obvious; the clenched fist is both defiant and
prophetic of a world that must be made fit for the likes of Tam
Docherty. McIlvanney's proletarian romanticism is flawed with the
faults of the genre and his sentimentality frequently seeps between
the lines of his tough prosaic stance.

37. GEORGE MACKAY BROWN: ELEMENTAL RHYTHMS

Scottish realism (with its tendency to mix naturalism and proletarian romanticism) had developed simultantously with Scottish symbolism (with its corresponding tendency to mix Platonism and mysticism). Some writers see this as an either/or choice between the
manner of George Douglas Brown and the mood of Neil Gunn;
other writers make the best of both worlds. Neil Paterson – in his
nautical *The China Run* (1948) and his *Behold Thy Daughter* (1950)
with its communal dependence on fishing focused on the memorable
heroine Thirza Gair – showed himself to be influenced by Neil
Gunn but also capable of an individual verbal economy. Iain Crichton Smith (whose poetry is discussed elsewhere in this book) might
have been tempted to overuse symbols. Instead he has concentrated
modestly on the evocation of the vulnerability of a central character,
most successfully in his portrayal of Mrs Scott in his *Consider the
Lilies* (1968), a novel of the Clearances. Smith's other novels, including *The Last Summer* (1969) and *My Last Duchess* (1971), are
rather stiff, indeed stuffily schoolmasterly in tone and topic. Smith's
talents are better suited to the short story and he ranks with Fred
Urquhart and George Mackay Brown as Scotland's finest writers of
short stories. George Mackay Brown, in fact, is arguably the most
subtle writer of short stories Scotland has produced. In his stories –
collected in *A Calendar of Love* (1976), *A Time to Keep* (1969),
Hawkfall (1974), *The Sun's Net* (1976) – he creates a timeless mood
as he mixes observations of modern Orkney with historical incidents
derived from the *Orkneyinga Saga* and images suggested by the
archaeological evidence of prehistoric life in Orkney. Orkney is
Brown's world. He was born in Stromness in 1921 and has lived
there ever since, apart from periods of illness (at Aberdeen where
he recuperated from an attack of TB) and formal study (at Newbattle Abbey and Edinburgh University where he read English and did

postgraduate work on Gerard Manley Hopkins). Although virtually all his work is set in the parish of Stromness and could be classified as parochial in the literal meaning of the word, his universal insights have shown the strength of a writing that is entirely rooted in a particular place possessed by a community that changes only superficially with the passing of chronological time. Brown has published two novels, one a triumph and the other an exercise in fictional hagiography.

Greenvoe was published in May 1972 when George Mackay Brown was fifty, a late start for a first novel. The author was not, of course, a novice but a man with five collections of poetry and two collections of stories behind him. Moreover he was a man who had already mapped out the artistic territory he was interested in exploring. What was novel about *Greenvoe* was the way in which Brown showed how magnificently he could sustain his thematic material over such an extended structure. For *Greenvoe* is not a conventional novel in the sense of the steady unfolding of a gripping narrative – in fact all the really dramatic action is compressed into the last chapter. It is rather the imaginative investigation of a way of life as it is revealed through various people who together make up a community. The village of Greenvoe (meaning green-bay) on the imaginary island of Hellya is well on the way to self-destruction; outside events simply make the death more dramatic.

Ostensibly the novel describes the five typical days that precede the official demise of Greenvoe. The year is 1968 and Greenvoe survives on fishing, farming, and gossip. The men of Greenvoe gravitate to Bill Scorrodale's Greenvoe Hotel while the women congregate around the village shop run by the scheming Joseph Evie and his bitter wife, Olive. The whole set-up looks like the parochial fag-end of an insular existence where, as one of the locals puts it, 'Here we are much as usual. Not a thing happens in this place'.[337] Always a writer who sees several sides of a situation, Brown presents the story of the fall of Greenvoe on three distinct levels.

The first level is the immediate present and the technique employed is fictional realism. What happens on this everyday level revolves around three fishermen: Bert Kerston, whose habitual drunkenness corresponds to his wife's endless nagging; Samuel Whaness, an industrious fisherman who awaits the coming Knoxian heaven in the company of his barren wife, Rachel; and The Skarf, a devout Marxist, who has forsaken fishing to write up the history of the island. During the days that follow Bert Kerston gets beaten up by his son for neglecting his pregnant wife; Samuel Whaness almost drowns when he gets out of his depth, both literally and theologically; and The Skarf imposes his history of Hellya, an 'arrogant slanted rigmarole'[338], on anyone who will listen. These three men are clearly differentiated but they all have the fisherman's love-hate relationship with the sea that sustains them and torments them; gives them a livelihood and threatens their lives.

Still on the level of fictional realism, Brown contrasts the lives of this trinity of fishermen with the lesser characters in the book. Ivan Westray, ferryman and modern Viking, makes erotic overtures – urgently in the case of Miss Margaret Inverary, the sexually frustrated schoolteacher; contemptuously in the case of Inga Fortin-Bell, the laird's grand-daughter. Alice Voar, twenty-nine-year-old spinster, has seven children by different fathers and her uninhibited sensuality is counterpointed against the near-mindless cogitations of Timmy Folster, a meth-drinking beachcomber. Timmy is not the only one who drinks, however; we learn that the parish minister Simon McKee is an alcoholic with quite a few skeletons in his drink-cupboard. His mother, old Mrs McKee, is haunted by the ghosts of her presbyterian conscience. Calvinism has taught her to be plagued by guilt, so she is sure she must be to blame for the moral weakness of her son.

Such is the state of affairs in Greenvoe, but the island has a rich Orkney history and the historical narrative – the second level of significance – is presented through The Skarf. What he writes in 'an old cash-book that Joseph Evie the merchant had thrown out'[339] comprises the heritage of the island. In four stretches of historical narrative The Skarf tells the story of Hellya. After the first shadowy settlers had come to the caves of Keelyfa, an adventurous Mediterranean people had come with their sacred jar of seedcorn and their architectural ability to build the Broch of Ingarth at Keelyfa so they could keep out invaders. The Viking invaders, though, swept all before them and one of them, Thorvald Harvest-Happy, brought agricultural expertise to the island. In this way the great circle of life could flourish: the sun could bring corn out of the earth. After the Vikings came feudalism, then capitalism, and The Skarf awaits the coming of the Marxist Millennium. His ears are constantly attuned for the coming 'music of the Children of the Sun'.[340]

The Skarf's dream is not central to the book: his presentation of the past is. For his words show the Broch of Ingarth is the seminal point of the island. Near this Broch, in the year in which the novel takes place, a timeless ritual is being observed at the Bu farm. This is the third level of significance, ritual symbolism; and it is enacted in dramatic form. We are introduced to the members of the Ancient Mystery of the Horsemen, a secret society who meet in the stable of the Bu, three miles from Greenvoe. According to the rites of this society old Mansie Anderson of the Bu is Lord of the Harvest. During the novel he takes his son Hector through the six initiation rites of the Ancient Mystery of the Horsemen. The six rites embody, in symbolic form, the crucifixion and resurrection of corn. A stone symbolises death; the lifting of the stone allows life to break through again just as corn shoots through a field cleared of stones or as Christ rose again when the stone was removed.

Greenvoe is divided into six chapter and – given the importance Brown attaches to numbers – there is nothing arbitrary about this. The six chapters correspond to the six stations in the initiation rites of the Ancient Mystery of the Horsemen. Each chapter ends with a station and a dusk so that the next chapter can open with the dawn of a new day full of the possibility of renewal. Chapter one contains the Station of the Plough; chapter two the Station of the Seed; chapter three the Station of the Green Corn; chapter four the Station of the Yellow Corn; and chapter five the Station of the Dead. It is at this point – the opening of the sixth and final chapter – that the measured pace of the novel changes abruptly so that instead of another day a catastrophe dawns on Greenvoe, the technological catastrophe embodied in Operation Black Star.

For into the everyday life of Greenvoe has come a mysterious guest to stay at Bill Scorrodale's hotel. He is isolated in his room, deliberately cut off from the people. He sits alone all day and rumours buzz like bees around his person. Some of the locals surmise that he might be a writer but Ivan Westray asks rhetorically: 'How the hell can a man write a book about a place if all he does is sit on his arse at typewriter?'[341] Eventually the guest is seen for what he is through the eyes of an Indian packman Johnny Singh (who narrates chapter Three in the form of a letter to his uncle). The man is yet another personification of Progress:

> He is a bureaucrat. He is Western Man arrived at a foreseen inevitable end. I see it now. He rules the world with a card index file.[342]

He has come on behalf of Operation Black Star, a military-technological project that requires the island of Hellya – but not its people. So the village is to be flattened, the community aborted, the past obliterated. The mechanical present is to be imposed on the island regardless of the needs or wishes of the people.

Inevitably Operation Black Star brings wealth to some – to the Evies, to Bill Scorrodale, to Ivan Westray. Timmy Folster it brings to an institute in Kirkwall, while old Mrs McKee fades away into a second childhood. Bert Kerston gets a job as a ghillie on Hrossey (the Norse word, meaning 'island of horses', for the Orkney mainland); the Whanesses go to Hrossey to stay with Rachel's brother; Miss Inverary goes back to Edinburgh. The Skarf is briefly employed as a clerk with Operation Black Star then, when it is discovered he is a Marxist, he is sacked. He gives himself to the sea, drowning in a dream of the Song of the Children of the Sun. Most dramatic of all, though, is the recalcitrance of Mansie Anderson of the Bu, the symbolic Lord of the Harvest. He is politely indifferent when he is told the authorities want to sink a gateway to Black Star through the cornfield of the Bu. His resistance is short and bitter; he is forcibly evicted from his land. After all this destruction the authorities abandon Operation Black Star fifteen months after its inception. They leave and they seal off the island so that it cannot be contaminated by humanity.

Ten years later on midsummer eve Mansie Anderson returns with seven men to Greenvoe. Like the men who brought the sacred jar of seed-corn to Hellya they land at the cliffs of Keelyfa; then they make for the Broch of Ingarth:

> Round here they had sown Hellya's first grain and reaped its first harvests; this was where they had made their music and laws and myths. This navel had attached many generations of Hellyamen to the nourishing earth.[343]

They have come to complete the last station in the initiation rites, to invoke the spirit of resurrection. By this symbolic act they hope to restore agricultural life to the island; in its wake this will bring back people. So the future of Hellya depends on their response to the midsummer sun. The book ends as the seven men stand in the sun suffused with the promise of resurrection:

> The Lord of the Harvest raised his hand. 'We have brought light and blessing to the kingdom of winter', he said, 'however long it endures, that kingdom, a night or a season or a thousand ages. The word has been found. Now we will eat the drink together and be glad'.
> The sun rose. The stones were warm. They broke the bread.[344]

Rather than present a continuous narrative, Brown has divided his text into episodic fragments that have a contrapuntal interdependence. Several things happen simultaneously. We are aware of the past (Skarf's narratives) and the timeless symbols (the drama of the Mystery of the Ancient Order of Horsemen). The montage has to be rearranged in the mind of the reader. The Tolstoyan method of the multiple viewpoint enables Brown to present a solitary event as if it were seen through the various facets of a prism. For example, it is incidental to Inga Fortin-Bell's erotic daydream that, lying and thinking of D. H. Lawrence's story 'Sun', she is startled by the 'chug-chug of a motor-boat'; that she then 'squinnied at the name on the bow, shading her eyes: *Siloam*.'[345] However, pages later, while the reader is still in some suspense as to what will happen in the coming confrontation between Inga and Ivan Westray, we get the viewpoint of the presbyterian Whaness on the *Siloam*: 'That shameless hussy was still lying on the table-rock. Samuel Whaness turned his eyes away sternly. She was even more naked than before'.[346] This expert manipulation of the multiple viewpoint gives depth and conviction to the writing.

The only time the episodic technique is suspended is when Mrs McKee's imaginary prosecutor presents to the court the evidence of the old woman's responsibility for Simon's alcoholism. This lasts for twenty-six pages and really constitutes a marvellous short story in itself, the tale of a hypersensitive man seeking spiritual solace in drink. Throughout that sequence, throughout the book, the texture of the prose is appropriately rich. Like Dylan Thomas in *Under Milk Wood*, Brown delights in the familiar poetry offered by a catalogue of everyday objects:

> Mrs McKee gathered the cups and plates, the marmalade pot, Simon's quarter-eaten egg, the toast-rack, the butter-dish, the cream-jug, the sugar-bowl, the salt-and-pepper, the teapot, the crusts, on to a tray, and carried it through to the kitchen.[347]

A mundane, yet lively, list of that sort brings the prose down to earth so that the provocative symbols relate to a real world. At the end of the book, as the village of Greenvoe collapses around her, the old infirm Mrs McKee is used as a vehicle to convey, symbolically, the image of time collapsing, going into reverse back to the birth and beginning of her wayward alcoholic son:

> she was young again . . . She remembered . . . Simon awash with lupins and dew; Simon's head in lamplight, bent over his theology books; Simon constellated with measles . . . Simon quiet as apples in his cradle; the slow throb and curve and quest of the foetus in her womb.

Such technical virtuosity is never an end in itself for Brown is principally concerned with the spiritual quality of life (especially since he was converted to Catholicism in 1961). He has said that 'In a wholesome society the different estates are stitched together in a single garment'[348]; in Greenvoe the land was neglected, the fishermen divided. Brown seeks to preserve the ancient elemental rhythms that motivate an ideal community. These rhythms (he believes) can be supplied by folk art, or by the waves of passion that follow martyrdom.

Without art and, in Brown's book, without religion any community will wither. The idea of redeeming society by weaving the Seamless Garment pervades his second novel *Magnus* (1973). The image is a biblical one (*John* 19:22): 'Then the soldiers, when they had crucified Jesus, took his garments . . . and also his coat: now the coat was without seam, woven from the top throughout.' This Seamless Garment of Christianity can be rewoven by a saint, we are asked to believe: particularly the Orkney saint, Magnus, who was martyred on Egilsay in the twelfth century. Some twenty years after Magnus's brutal death his life was recorded, in Latin, by an Orcadian priest Master Robert; the events of Magnus's life are also contained in the *Orkneyinga Saga*. These accounts, and the scholarly biography of *St Magnus – Earl of Orkney* (1935) by the Kirkwall businessman John Mooney, are the sources of Brown's novel. He has, naturally, translated the recorded events into his own artistic terms. Basically, though, the story is briefly retold. When Earl Thorfinn, Orkney's mightiest ruler, died, his earldom passed into the joint care of his sons Paul and Erlend. This divided rule was inherited by Paul's son Hakon and Erlend's son Magnus. For seven years the two contended for sole control of the islands before agreeing to a peace conference on Egilsay at Easter 1117 (the exact date varies between 1115 and 1117). As the cousins had agreed, Magnus arrived with two ships; Hakon, on the other hand, came with eight. When the landowners of Orkney insisted on an immediate solution, the politic Hakon put himself forward as the most suitable ruler. Magnus, realising the danger he was in, tried to save his life by suggesting that he be banished or imprisoned. The Orkney landowners would have none of this: death was to be the final solution. Magnus then accepted the inevitability of death: he was executed by Hakon's cook Lifolf who, at Magnus's request, hammered the axe into his forehead. In 1919 the shattered skull of Magnus was found in a secret tomb in St Magnus Cathedral. The story is immensely dramatic but it is difficult for a non-Catholic to see what was particularly saintly in Magnus's murder: he tried to avoid death then humbly accepted it. What else could he do?

Still, the opening of *Magnus* directs the reader to the very earthiest level of existence. Mans, the peasant representative of common humanity in the novel, has to plough Revay hill facing the tidal island, the Brough of Birsay. His ox is lame so Hild, his woman, has to pull the wooden plough so they can make seven furrows on the hill. Counterpointed against this are events that Mans can only see at a distance on the Brough of Birsay. A wedding is taking place between Erlend and Thora. The title of this first chapter, 'The Plough', underlines the symbolic nature of impregnation. The peasants thrust their seed into the furrowed earth; Erlend sows his human seed in Thora. the mother of Magnus. As the peasants finish their work Erlend and Thora embrace in bed and the seed of Magnus is planted:

> a great sacrificial host surged between the loins of bridegroom and bride, and among them a particular chosen seed, a summoned one, the sole ultimate destined survivor of all that joyous holocaust.[349]

In this astonishingly intimate way Magnus is deliberately set apart from the other characters in the novel. He is 'chosen', he is 'summoned'. He has been put on earth for a divine purpose. His otherworldliness is contrasted with the earthiness of Mans who speaks with the voice of the oppressed through the ages. There is no attempt to portray Mans as simply a man of his time, a twelfth-century peasant. Mans is timeless, he is downtrodden man, and his indignant complaint against the world could well issue from the voice of a modern radical:

> The honest labourers, they're kept under by a few parasites, Yes,
> parasites ... A parasite is a person who does no work, no, but he lives
> in luxury all the same. And who provides the parasite with his silks, and
> his silver and his flagons? *I* do.[350]

Anachronism is, in fact, one of the main stylistic features of *Magnus*. Magnus and Mans: twin aspects of mankind, the saint and the sower of seed. In his reluctant way Mans works his own agricultural miracles by lifting stones so that corn can rise in an image of resurrection; Magnus is not to be so lucky. Although a radical, Mans is glad there are folk for him to look down on, the tinkers John and Mary who stroll through poverty and miracle and time in *Magnus*. The likes of Magnus, the ruling classes, are held in contempt by Mans.

Magnus is, technically, an immensely ambitious novel. The counterpoint between Mans and Magnus, the use of Brechtian alienation effects, the exhilarating mixture of heroic and contemplative prose, the frequent time-shifts: these testify to a rare literary gift. Where the novel does suffer is when the author succumbs to the danger of reification – the taking of symbols for material objects. The whole novel hangs on the image of the Seamless Garment of sanctity. If we remain unmoved by this image we must inevitably find flaws in the novel. An image illuminates a text but cannot entirely comprise it. In *Greenvoe* the symbolic material was successfully integrated with reality because we were impressed by the brilliantly close observation of a whole community of characters. In *Magnus* only the peasant Mans and the tinkers Jock and Mary are given a solid fictional identity. Magnus is conspicuous by his corporeal absence. No doubt this was the intention of the author but he owed it to non-Catholic readers to explore the man Magnus instead of dogmatically accepting his sanctity.

38. HONOURABLE EXCEPTIONS: RAE, NYE, GORDON

Brown's fiction covers an imaginative area the reader can readily identify. His writing works in terms of artistic wholeness as all of it is informed by a vision. Few other modern Scottish writers have achieved such an impact being content, instead, to offer fragments and (less frequently) experiments that do not cohere. There are honourable exceptions. Hugh C. Rae, who was born in Glasgow in 1935, is an astoundingly prolific author, equally productive under his own name and assorted pseudonyms (R. B. Houston, Robert Crawford, Stuart Stern, Jessica Stirling). He has functioned as a highly skilled craftsman, deploying various modes in the interests of a rather calculated Scottishness:

> Very early in my career as a novelist (bearing in mind that it was vocation as well as profession) I realised that I had to find a framework for what I had to express about the Scottish scene and, at the same time, provide the general reading public with footholds. I elected to write the *criminal roman*, using an act of violence as the tin-opener with which to open up areas of the Scottish character that, to my mind, hadn't been too fully treated in fiction. I went in off the deep end, stuffed to the gills with Sartre and with the concept of R. D. Laing as an arch priest of that odd schism in character which is so manifest in the hide-bound Scots.[351]

The result was *Skinner* (1965), a persuasive examination of the psychopathic personality of a killer. In subsequent novels Rae has dissected violence in other, less obvious, forms yet he never seems entirely sure which direction his writing is taking him in.

Rae's respect for traditional forms (to the extent that he has gone in enthusiastically for parody and pastiche) recalls the generally conservative Scottish attitude to literary technique. The Scottish fictional mind is not, by nature, experimental. Ironically enough, two novels classed as experimental – Sydney Goodsir Smith's *Carotid Cornucopius* (1964) and Robert Nye's *Falstaff* (1976) – are both based on a seventeenth century Scottish model, namely Sir Thomas Urquhart's vigorous translation of the first three books of Rabelais's *Gargantua and Pantagruel*. Smith phantasmagoric account of his hero's epic drinking bouts in Edinburgh is full of childish puns and cliquish allusions to boozy capital characters; Nye's dramatic monologue resurrects Shakespeare's hero to tell his outrageously arrogant side of his story. Neither Smith nor Nye was born in Scotland: Smith (whose poetry is discussed on pp. 47–51 and whose play *The Wallace* on pp. 296–8) revelled in his acquired Scottishness; Nye became an honorary Scot during the years he spent in Edinburgh where he wrote *Falstaff*. Giles Gordon, who was born in Edinburgh in 1940, has shown an experimental approach in several novels – notably the abruptly episodic *100 Scenes from Married Life* (1976) – which deal comically with the delights and poignantly with the disappointments of marriage.

39. KENNAWAY AND CHARACTER

It is rare, for various reasons to come across a Scottish writer responsible for an entirely satisfactory oeuvre. Probably the geatest loss to Scottish letters in recent years has been James Kennaway, whose published work nevertheless adds up to a total experience. Kennaway's prose style was modelled on American originals: he used both the fluent beautifully-phrased, knowingly world-weary affectations of F. Scott Fitzgerald and the taut, syntactically-tight mannerisms of Hemingway. This artistic commitment rubbed off in real life for an Oxford friend, Godfrey Smith, remembered James and Susan Kennaway as 'a charismatic couple: Scott and Zelda with manners'[352], while Kennaway's widow claimed that he 'lived his life at an orgiastic pace'.[353] He was never entirely happy about his flashy lifestyle (made possible from an income augmented by scripts for films as commercially successful as *The Battle of Britain*). According to Susan, James was plagued by moralistic doubts:

> I suspect that the Calvinistic shades of his Scottish upbringing were actually responsible for these doubts. He believed in certain areas of self-restraint, or self-inflicted punishment; long gruelling runs that took the wind from him and that did nothing to reduce his weight; immensely long working hours even when the inspiration was not at hand. In his list of enjoyable things to be denied he did not, however, include his absorbing interest in sex and women[354]

Kennaway was born in Perthshire in 1928; his father was a lawyer-cum-businessman and his mother a doctor. His circumstances were comfortable, even affluent. In 1941, though, his father died and Kennaway went to Glenalmond School, near Perth. By nature he was competitive and possibly his competitive nature was nurtured in his public school. Anyway, his schooldays are recreated with considerable comic effect in two stories concerning the boy visionary Taylor Two. 'The Dollar Bottom' represented his breakthrough as a writer when he sold it to *Lilliput* in 1953; a sequel, 'Taylor's Finest Hour', was written in 1958 as a get-well-gift from Kennaway to his father-in-law. In both these tales Taylor Two concocts money-making schemes: first, he creates an insurance scheme to provide financial cover for beatings; then he turns his adolescent talents to providing sexual advice.

From the beginning Kennaway showed that his special art lay in creating memorable characters and the proof of this is the way his best creations can be lifted from the printed page to live again in another dimension: his first two novels became splendid films (one after being a stage play) and 'The Dollar Bottom' story, as directed by Roger Christian, won an Oscar for the Best Short Feature Film of 1981. Kennaway himself was a bit of a character who constantly examined his own personality in journals and various drafts for novels. By training he was an establishment man; in his novels he shows individuals reacting against established traditions. Kennaway had first-hand knowledge of academic, military and professional institutions. He was educated at Oxford, served as an officer in the Cameron

Highlanders. From 1951 to 1957 he worked as a commissioning editor for Longmans Green.

An immense amount of hard work went into the making of a Kennaway novel, as Susan Kennaway remembered:

> James used to say that for every slim novel that he published he would write an average of a million and a half words, which was not an exaggeration. The differently coloured drafts of each novel, which led from one to another, piled up in crumpled heaps under the windows and on every shelf in his study . . . The trouble was that the character in the first book would become the character in the second book and the happening in the third book would reappear in the fourth or fifth, so it was extremely difficult to sort out one group of papers from another, one set of characters from another.[355]

That sheer literary slog may have assuaged the Calvinistic conscience that was seemingly so strong in Kennaway. It also worked. His prose was polished until it gave off a glow. His first novel, *Tunes of Glory* (1956), represented a brilliant debut. The talent was prodigious, the assurance astonishing, the skill with dialogue remarkable. The book spelled out the theme of rivalry that runs right through Kennaway's work: in *Tunes* it is Jock versus Barrow for the soul of the battalion; in *Household Ghosts* (1961) it is Pink and Stephen versus David for the love of Mary; in *Some Gorgeous Accident* (1967) it is Link versus Fiddes for the attention of Susan. Generally the format is triangular with two males competing for prestige and psychological and/or sexual reward.

Tunes opens atmospherically, with the snow making Campbell Barracks a world within a world, a law unto itself. In command of the battalion is Jock Sinclair (DSO and bar), a larger-than-life figure who glories in being the centre of attention. Jock has presence as Kennaway conveys with his incisively exact descriptive prose: 'Jock tipped forward in his seat and put his clenched fists on the table. The flat eye grew narrow; the meat on his face quivered, and along the table conversation died on the lips. He made a suppressed sound which was still something of a shout . . .'[356] Jock has been a superb wartime commander but in peacetime he is a bit of a misfit, an anachronism with more muscles than manners and no sense of decorum. At home he is the domestic tyrant forbidding his daughter Morag the freedom he himself seeks with the actress Mary Titterington. All the social graces Jock so conspicuously lacks are possessed by the new Colonel – Basil Barrow, of Eton, Oxford and Sandhurst. Jock, with his habit of self-dramatisation, resents the Colonel's intrusion in the affairs of the battalion. He is, by Jock's reckoning, an effete outsider. Whereas Colonel Barrow came up (so Jock believes) the easy way, Jock came up 'by way of Sauchiehall Street, Barlinne gaol, and the band. I was a boy piper'.[357]

Appearances deceive, however, and it will be Kennaway's characteristically creative delight to turn expectations upside down. He knows his characters so intimately he can afford to let them give themselves away by physical and verbal gestures. There is a linguistic norm the protagonists observe; in *Tunes* both Jock and Barrow are as eloquent as the military presence allows. They are both institutional men. As the reader soon realises Jock and Barrow are not exact opposites. It is Jock who is the sentimentalist and Barrow who is so brittle he eventually breaks down. Jock Sinclair, in fact, is a totally convincing version of a type familiar in Scottish fiction. He is the urban hardman with the heart of gold (which is generally the same as the bellyful of whisky Jock takes). When the showdown comes it is traumatic: Jock strikes a corporal he finds (innocently enough) with his daughter. The Colonel · cannot act decisively enough to resolve the situation and begins to dance to Jock's tune which is glorious for Jock and humiliating for the Colonel who takes his own life. The book ends with a mad dash of tradition as Jock regresses to the emotional origins of his self-destructive Scottishness.

Household Ghosts, Kennaway's second novel, considers the persistence of the past in an incestuously close family situation. Charles Henry Arbuthnot Ferguson – Pink to his chums – and his sister Mary have grown up under the influence of parental decadence. Daddy, Colonel Sir Henry Ferguson, has been held responsible for a (probably apocryphal) family scandal (involving card-cheating and resignation from London clubs) and Mummy has died an alcoholic. Pink and Mary have the financial security of Daddy's Perthshire farm to protect them from the outside world, and they tighten their togetherness by a secret language of their own devising and shared memories of their life together. Mary, uneasily married to Stephen Cameron, manager of Daddy's farm, is intent on an affair with David Dow, a Calvinistically grim physiologist whose letters to her provide an alternative angle to the formal third-personal account of the events.

The story gets under way at a Young Conservative country dance in Dow's Academy (so called after the first headmaster, David Dow's father). In the gymnasium the festivities proceed with a tatty flourish while in Classroom IV Pink and Mary go through their paces, raking over the past and shutting out the present. Mary, however, is confessional by nature and tells David about her life with brother Pink and Mummy:

> You've been home, you know where – just by the top of the stairs by the nursery gate, there's a linen cupboard there, We'd hide in it . . . [Mummy] came in once and found us in the same bed and I thought there would be an awful rumpus. Macdonald [the Nanny] never used to allow us in the same bed. She said that's how keely children slept. But Mummy wasn't really angry at all. She put on all the lights, she blinked,

then she moved across to us. I remember it like yesterday. Then she sat down at the end of the bed pitched forward and her hair was all undone. She kind of pushed us through the bedclothes as if we were the dogs under the blankets. I kept my eyes tight shut until I heard her. I thought she was laughing, but she wasn't. Tears were pouring down her cheeks.[358]

David, with his grimly literal outlook, wants to have Mary on his own terms. This means persuading her to do without Stephen and Pink. The tactic of relentless pressure works; Stephen tries to kill himself and Pink goes off to a 'baronial nut-house'.[359] David comes to despise himself for his negative influence, his destructive presence:

I went to great lengths to break her faith in the two people who loved her . . . I was doing everything in my power to suppress the one contemporary sign of that splendid vitality which I had ever come across. They christened her Mary. I cast myself, perversely, as Knox . . . That we are the perverts and the peeping-toms, the sex maniacs and even the murderers, we, the sons of the righteous, everybody knows. But we are something else, whose childhood was stolen from us, who never, without correction (not necessarily punishment) told Mary's splendid stories; who never went with Alice through the looking-glass. It is the curbing of our imaginations, the firm guidance back to the grammar and the prose, that make us so hungry now for experience. But for a special sort of experience; a kind of imagination of the flesh. We are the tinkers, who move on; who invite experience but flee from consequence. At the last moment our eyes turn furtively away. This is to say that we are the most dangerous of all: the permanently immature. And for that I blame the angels.[360]

That grim joylessness makes David Dow the epitome of Scottish sins of omission. Pink and Mary, with their compulsive myth-making, stand at the opposite extreme for the euphoric irresponsibility of the art of fiction. It is appropriate that Kennaway said, in a diary entry of 1961, '*Tunes of Glory* (novel) proved only, to me, that I could characterize, i.e. write. *Household Ghosts*, that I could feel'.[361] It was Pink, the fictionalist, who survived the book to be brought back as the central figure of a play and a film (both called *Country Dance*); David Dow was reduced in importance, conflated with Stephen to form Douglas Dow, Mary's tediously literal husband.

Kennaway's next two novels – excluding, that is, *The Mind Benders* (1963), which is the book-of-the-film – show him concentrating his mind wonderfully on the theme of rivalry. *The Bells of Shoreditch* (1963) conforms to the traditional triangular pattern as Stella Vass has to choose between two men: Andrew, her weak but likeable husband; and J. T. Sarson, Andrew's boss and the ruthless chairman of a merchant bank. Stella is the creative centre of the book. There have been many novels showing the Scottish hardman with a heart of gold. Stella is the first genuine hardwoman. Actually the hardwoman projection turns out to be a pose so that Stella becomes more than a stereotype and displays all the vulnerability of Kennaway's apparently invincible protagonists. She is a political animal, proud that her socialism was made in Glasgow. She has 'real Glasgow hostility'[362] as well as a profoundly sexual presence. When she discovers that Sarson has sacked Andrew she calls up her sexual allure to seduce Sarson (or so she thinks) and drops her Clydeside morals. In betraying her socialist past and helping the cause of capitalism she feels she is kicking 'Jimmy Maxton in the teeth'.[363] This leads her to believe that 'All socialists like us are insecure and to cure that there's nothing like a real dose of insecurity'.[364] *Some Gorgeous Accident* (1967) is another exploration of the male-male-female triangle. It is, for the usually sharply cinematic Kennaway, a curiously unresolved novel. According to Susan Kennaway it is confessional. Kennaway developed a passionate regard for the spy novelist John Le Carré (David John Cornwall); he regarded him as a rival writer, a competitive friend, and a man capable of loving his wife, Susan. He was right. In the book Susan, an American writer, is loved by both James Link, an Irish photographer, and Dr Richard Fiddes, who runs a surgical clinic in London. Link is Kennaway, Susan is Susan Kennaway, Fiddes is Le Carré. For once the vitality of the real-life characters saves, rather than spoils, a work of fiction.

The Cost of Living Like This, which appeared after Kennaway's death, shows a stylistic novelty as the book – with its frequently shifting narrative viewpoint and blending of appearance and reality – has a surrealistic Sparkian tone. Julian, an economist, is dying of cancer. He attempts to salvage what is left of his life by renewing his sexual awareness in an affair with Sally, the office junior who (at seventeen) is twenty years younger than him. This complicates his relationship with his wife, Christabel. Sally is a swimmer (a competitor) and has to go to Glasgow to swim in a race. Fortuitously Julian and Christabel also gravitate towards Glasgow which turns out to be a suitable place for disease and despair. The doings of the three are observed by Mozart Anderson, a philosophical referee whose interpretative words cut across the action like a chorus working up to a catastrophe. Julian gets injured in a student demonstration and is taken to hospital – conveniently, since he is dying anyway. Christabel attempts suicide; Sally, the competitor, succeeds where Christabel failed. The book displays a devastatingly detached style of writing which shows Kennaway dealing with tragedy in a clinical manner utterly devoid of rhetoric. His final book went a bit further along the same road.

Kennaway's final work also shows his mind taking an increasingly allegorical turn. At the time of his death he was working on the

fourth draft of a new novel; it was subsequently edited and arranged
by his friend Lynn Hughes and published as *Silence* (1972). It is a
new departure for Kennaway, a religious allegory composed in the
terse telegraphic prose of Hemingway. It is also, though brief, an
attempt to come to creative terms with a massive contemporary
problem. Kennaway's last book is controlled in spite of the subject
matter for it deals with the violence associated with the civil war of
American racism. It is set in an unidentified American city, probably Chicago. The hero (and the word is apposite here) is a middle-
aged doctor, Larry Ewing, astonished by the extent of his involvement in the race war.

Ewing's daughter Lilian is, we immediately learn, lying in a state
of shock in a city hospital. She has been assaulted. Ewing discusses
the situation with his son-in-law Mike Angel, a merchant banker;
and with his son Lawrence Junior, one of Angel's employees. Lilian
is the archetypal innocent, at least in the version authorised by
Angel: 'He hitched a lift with her from the club after their Saturday
dance. He failed to seduce her. He hit her. He failed to rape her ...
He literally pissed on her. Shoved her out of the car. Dumped her.
And blew. It was about ten below zero last night, but she got to a
phone. I picked her up'.[365] Reluctantly the doctor joins the posse
out for revenge as they cruise into the black ghetto in search of the
villain. A race riot erupts in which the doctor, symbolically wounded in the side like a latter-day Christ, is lucky to escape with his life.
He blunders into an abandoned room and is roughly treated then
rescued by a black girl called (he later discovers) Silence. She is
athletic – Amazonian almost – in appearance and says nothing. She
just smokes pot and hums Sinatra numbers. Silence has been ghetto-
trained to dislike privileged whites like Ewing but helps him in spite
of herself. She takes him to a dentist's apartment where Ewing
reads a newspaper account of the riot. Silence, he now learns, is
wanted by the police for participating in the lynching of Lawrence
Junior.

Nevertheless the doctor is attracted to Silence and indebted to
her for an escape from the black ghetto. Realising the risks she has
taken on his behalf he comes back to find her martyred, crucified
by outraged black extremists, nailed to the door:

> She was naked. They may have gang-banged her first, but probably not.
> Nobody will ever know. She was standing, or almost standing, stark
> naked. Her back was like an uncooked steak that had been thrashed by a
> tennis racket strung with wire.
>
> And the doctor thought, Maybe it *is* Sunday, but there is no longer
> any belief. So help me, they didn't do as much to Christ.[366]

Ewing realises that he and Silence are representative of 'the power
and the glory of God and the indelible cruelty of man'.[367] He has

become her partner in suffering as ancient as humanity: 'Look what's become of Adam and Eve; that's what the doctor thought'.[368] Eventually the couple seek shelter in a slaughterhouse where they are discovered. Nothing can break the bond forged by shared suffering. The doctor recovers sufficiently to dread the injuries the police will inflict on Silence in their clumsy attempts to make her speak. In a final existential act the doctor kills Silence rather than let her be broken. So ends a savage allegory, a view of the world as an arena bleak and emptied of love.[369]

40. GORDON WILLIAMS: THE SCOT AS VICTIM

Kennaway's characters are unpredictable; in the work of Gordon Williams the Scotsman is presented as an assertive loner ashamed of revealing any sensitivity and anxious to compensate for inadequacies by inflicting pain on a supposedly hostile world. It is a view of the Scot as victim who is out to get his own back on the society that warped him. William's novels are fast and physical and he is especially adept at dramatising the problems of being Scottish and ashamed of it.

Williams was born in 1934 and educated at the John Neilson Institution in Paisley where he had 'an averagely happy childhood in the Ferguslie Park scheme, known locally as The Jungle, where my father was *the* police constable'.[370] Both parents encouraged him to read and the fact that a great-uncle had published a book about his missionary experiences in Venezuela 'made authorship seem a not unattainable possibility right from the start'.[371] From the age of twelve he spent all his school holidays doing farm work; seeing little future in agriculture, he got a reporter's job on the *Johnstone Advertiser* then did his RAF National Service in Germany before going to London to continue his journalistic career. Exposure to the might-have-been complaints of Fleet Street journalists gave him 'the idea that one would either write a book by thirty or drift on in a sea of gregarious booziness and jolly cynicism'.[372] For more than ten years he toiled on his RAF novel *The Camp* (1966) but achieved his first literary success with 'a fast little bit of nonsense' called *The Last Day of Lincoln Charles* (1965).

He began with very definite views on the novel, feeling that too much contemporary fiction had too little factual backbone. Accordingly he wrote a cycle of semi-autobiographical novels and served a self-designed apprenticeship of seven novels, each concentrating on a different technical aspect of fiction. He still feels that fiction is limited by its practitioners:

Current British fiction is a specialist minority activity hermetically sealed from society at large, a therapeutic exercise for the writers and a snobbish or elitist consumer status symbol for the book-buyer. I cannot imagine any authoritarian regime having to ban many British novels even if the regime had heard of them.[374]

Just how strongly that mental pugnacity activates his own creative work is shown in three novels, in particular: *The Camp, From Scenes like These* and *Walk Don't Walk.*

Williams's angry attitude to Scotland is evident throughout these novels. He seems to regard his native land as a detestable breeding-ground for failure, a good place to get the hell out of. In *The Camp* Ritchie Brown from Coatbridge adapts himself easily enough to the mindless conformity of RAF life. He becomes a fairly typical Scot as studiously inelegant as this exchange with Senior Aircraftsman Harvey Sampson shows:

'Aye, that's richt, ma wee English laddie,' said Ritchie, shaking his head Harry Lauder style. 'Ye're a gey clever laddie, but ye'd be nane the worse o' a guid kicking.' 'I think I almost understood some of that,' said Harvey. 'The bit about kicking. Don't you agree, Taff, the Scots mentality places undue emphasis on brutality as an expressive medium?'[375]

In some respects the eponymous camp could stand as a symbol for the thugly Scotland Williams so tellingly reduces to the proportions of its prejudices: 'Of course, the food's abominable and there's nothing to do but get sloshed and every bod on the section hates everybody else, but apart from that it's dead easy.'[376] In showing how the Scottish myth of virility imposes itself on Ritchie – 'He needed to do something manly'[377] – Williams also shows something sick in the Scottish psychological conditioning.

From Scenes Like These (1968) amplifies the analysis of Scotland already apparent in *The Camp.* It is a novel about a potentially outstanding youth, Dunky Logan, who succumbs to the deadening impact of his environment and ends up well on the way to being a model of the drunken foul-mouthed Scot that civilised people keep away from. As we learn, from a meeting with his ex-teacher Ian Nicol, Dunky is imaginative but not strong enough to break away from the archetypal pattern for he longs to be a real man and, in the circumstances, that means being a hard-drinking pain-in-the-neck: he 'wanted to get a job, be a hard case, a real working man, not a silly schoolboy whose brain was affected by too many pictures'.[378] Dunky is a promising footballer and this familiar passion allows Williams to introduce a finely turned piece of irony, reinforcing the ironical use of the novel's Burnsian title: 'That was the greatest thing he could imagine in the whole world, being picked against England – he'd *die* for Scotland'[379] Indeed, the novel suggests, Dunky will die for Scotland and all it stands for.

In its use of colloquial modes and rhythmic prose *From Scenes Like These* is influenced by Gibbon's *A Scots Quair* – which is cited by the teacher Nicol in the novel. The recurring images of defeat are sustained in a total portrayal of failure: Dunky's father is paralysed, his mother is downtrodden, the Ayrshire farm Dunky works on is a grind, the East Ayrshire Cup Final is a personal disaster, and the only hope is the age-old Scottish dream of emigrating to Canada. Some of the set-pieces in the novel are brilliantly handled: for example, the two football matches and the description of the horse in the knacker's yard which should be compared to the slaughterhouse scenes in Archie Hind's *The Dear Green Place*.

In the first chapter of *From Scenes Like These*, Williams expatiates on the linguistic division in Scottish life: 'Was it being a guttersnipe to talk your own country's language? It would be a lot healthier if folk spoke one way . . . Why teach kids that Burns was the great national poet and then tell you his old Scots words were dead common?'[380] This dilemma seems to have discouraged Williams from going as far as Gibbon did in resuscitating Scots prose. Williams probably felt a need to distance himself from Scotland so that with the chronological progress of his fiction he becomes less and less attached to his origins. *Walk Don't Walk* (1972), which is set in the USA, begins with a metrical prologue describing 'A Scots Burgh Boy's Dream of America' and here we see the reasons for Williams's Scotophobia. MacDiarmid posed the rhetorical question 'Scotland small? Our multiform, our infinite Scotland *small*?'[381] Williams regretfully answers in the affirmative by recalling a childhood that depended more on cinematic dreams than the prevailing Scottish nightmare:

> Oh aye, America was our bigtime dream place
> in the years of gas masks and shrapnel.

At the end of the prologue Williams puts, as clearly as anywhere in his prose, his insight into Scotland the Pathetic:

> We knew our country was smalltime dump
> where nothing ever happened and
> there was nothing to do.
> And nobody had a name like Jelly Roll Morton.

Walk Don't Walk is a picaresque novel with indigenous antecedents for, as the American scholar Francis Russell Hart rightly pointed out, it 'echoes and often equals, in a later milieu and idiom, Linklater's *Juan in America*.' [382] The hero, boozy Scottish Graham Cameron, flies to the USA to promote his trendily permissive novel *The New Ladies' Man*. The narrative, which constantly shifts between first and third person, takes Cameron all over America until he acquires the tastes of the seasoned transatlantic commuter. All he actually does is quest guest on TV chat-shows, get drunk, and fail to seduce Sally Weber who handles author promotion but not authors as excruciatingly Scottish as Cameron.

Like many Scots reared on the movies as surrogates for home-grown glamour, Cameron's vision is in Technicolor: 'it was hard to remember he was not taking part in a film. A short, wide man in white sports coat and brown slacks showing two inches of white sock had the same smooth, blond quiff and sweep as Alan Ladd. A big-gutted man walked exactly like Robert Mitchum, shoulders back, belly out. The women, too, suggested some film star or another.'[383] Cameron is star-struck and his only answer to the energy of America is the inertia of his Scottish background. The joke of contrasting a Scottish sensibility with American sophistication is what makes Cameron such a ridiculous figure in the New World. He has just not got the cultural credentials to make it in the land of his dreams. Still, his 'smalltime' background provides some memorably funny moments. On a radio show Cameron is asked about Swinging London and replies 'Mind you, I was brought up in Scotland, which is pretty old-fashioned. We're still shocked by sex after marriage.'[384] The sayings of this stage-Scotsman go down well, we learn, for a studio assistant tells Cameron 'That was a top interview'.[385]

Williams impresses most as a fictional performer with an unusually extensive stylistic repertoire. *The Camp* shows his ability to create a claustrophobically atmospheric novel; *From Scenes Like These* reveals tragic aspects of Scottish life; *Walk Don't Walk* contains a wealth of comic episodes; *The Upper Pleasure Garden* (1970) gives the lowdown on journalists; and *Big Morning Blues* (1974) portrays a Scotsman on the make in a shady part of London. In some ways I regard *The Siege of Trencher's Farm* (1969) – sensationally filmed, by Sam Peckinpah, as *Straw Dogs*–as Williams's most accessible novel since it is a thriller that penetrates to the very essence of male aggression. Williams still regards himself as a developing writer: 'by and large I regard everything up till now as apprentice work'.[386] For a self-styled apprentice he has done uncommonly well and his versatility assures continuing vitality.

41. FULL CIRCLE: HERDMAN, MASSIE, SMITH, GRAY

Fortunately for Scottish fiction new talents continue to emerge and their development will help determine the direction of the Scottish novel of the future. John Herdman's *A Truth Lover* (1973) showed imaginative ability; *Pagan's Pilgrimage* (1978) poked fun at Scottish archetypes from Hogg's justified sinner onwards. Herdman, who was born in Edinburgh in 1941 and educated at Cambridge, chose to confront the reader with deliberate caricatures rather than characters: the dour presbyterian father, 'a Scotch preacher of the old school, and a man of infinite hypocrises'[387]; the unthinking salt-of-the-earth socialist Wee Tam; and Lord Gadarene, the absentee landlord who only visits his 50,000-acre Highland estate during the grouse-shooting season. I suppose the massed Scottish consciousness is full of such figures.

In the events that unfold in the novel this unholy trinity of stereotypes give some external reality to the tale; they are like well-used stage-props for the reader to shove around in the theatre of his mind. However, the real tension in the book arises from the internal conflict between the narrator, Horatio Pagan, and his *alter ego* who appears in various disguises – as childhood bogeyman, mysterious visitant and Satanic tempter. The substance of Horatio Pagan's pilgrimage is his hilarious struggle with himself.

Horatio is apparently destined for failure from his early days in Edinburgh. He fails to get on with his father, fails in his musical ambitions, fails to take a degree at Cambridge, fails to settle down in his uncle's second-hand bookshop, fails hopelessly with the two women who pass through his life. Yet like many Scottish failures Horatio is solipsistically sure he has the seeds of greatness within him, just waiting for a monstrous birth. He confidently asserts that he is a 'superior being'[388]; all he needs is, like Dostoevsky's Raskolnikov, to commit one decisive act to shatter the complacency of the world. His world, that is. With the help of his *alter ego*, Horatio decides he is the ultimate Superman: 'I was set apart to improve the lot of mankind by acts of public and private assassination'.[389] He sets out for the Highlands with the murder of Lord Gadarene on his mind and brings matters to a comic conclusion.

A more delicate talent (which reveals itself in Firbankian hints and Sparkian gestures) is deployed by Allan Massie in three novels: *Change and Decay in All Around I See* (1978), *The Last Peacock* (1980) and *The Death of Men* (1980). Massie was born in Singapore in 1938 and was educated at Glenalmond (where Kennaway had been before him) and Cambridge. His Scottishness is a matter of ethical attitude for he worries about moral issues which transcend the sense of place: 'Outside my imagination, I was, and long remained, quite ignorant of Scotland; in important respects of course I still am'.[390] Massie is a fastidious stylist. In his *The Death of Men* he uses the first-person approach as a genuine artistic device for the events that occur in the novel are only meaningful as a matter of interpretation. There are many ways of looking at facts so the novel suggests two in particular. Christopher Burke is an English journalist whose matter-of-factually opportunistic responses are uncomfortably familiar to the average reader who can absorb headline-hitting tragedy as regularly as he can digest a hot breakfast.

Another way of looking at the same story is presented by Raimundo Dusa whose diary makes up the bulk of the book. Raimundo is an elderly gent, a bit of a dilettante who spends his time hanging round cafés and bars, pondering the book (on the Emperor Augustus) he is supposedly writing, and looking back to his time in the Washington Embassy. He is a decadent, fidgeting – if not fiddling – while Rome burns with political passion. Raimundo's main claim to fame is the fact that he is the brother of Corrado, the leading Christian Democrat politician. As journalists (like Christopher Burke) and forever making his brother the metaphorical key to the Italian crisis, Raimundo reflects that there 'are those who consider Corrado the most powerful man in Italy; but keys of course have no autonomous power'.[391]

While Raimundo deals languidly with his everyday life he is aware that his celebrated brother is in an increasingly bizarre political position. The Christian Democrats are widely regarded as unreliable and are opposed by an astonishing variety of Leftist groups ranging from the Communist Party to the Partisans of the Proletariat (PDP). Anxious to avert political violence, Corrado advocates the Historic Compromise which, as his wayward son Bernardo explains, will accommodate the politically timid Communist Party and thereby 'create conditions in which counter-revolutionary ameliorating reforms are possible'.[392] In the schematic world of extremist politics it is possible, therefore, to see the liberal Corrado as the most subtle and treacherous enemy of revolution. He is inevitably the politician the PDP decides to kidnap in a gesture calculated to traumatise the Italian government.

Massie has used the Aldo Moro kidnapping of 1978 as the suggestive basis for his book, though he emphasises in a prefatory note that 'I have used only such aspects of the case as are public property. This is a work of fiction, with all the aspirations of a novel'.[393] He is right to draw the distinction between fact and fiction for a considerable amount of creative effort has gone into the making of this novel. The characterisation is admirably sharp so there is a convincing interplay between American innocents and Italian intriguers and the various members of the Dusa family. Massie has thought through the implications of his story in order to develop his theme on an allegorical level. The Italian family is a microcosmic version of the Italian state: Raimundo reflects, 'I'm left with just my books and my cat and, of course, what no Italian can entirely escape, the Family'[394] and subsequently holds on to 'that eternal Italian reality, the only thing we are prepared to trust, the Family'.[395] Massie is an intelligent writer with an interest in human frailty. He has a nice turn of phrase and a fine line in images, as witness the vivid simile whereby 'Fear enters the room like a blind man tapping his white stick round the skirting-board.'[396]

There seems to be no shortage of new talent in Scottish fiction. Massie's third novel, for example, was published in the year that saw the appearance of two other notable novels. Anne Smith's *The Magic Glass* (1981) gives a feminist variant on the idiom of proletarian romanticism. The author, a miner's daughter from Leven, has no illusion about the class she describes and there is no great distance between her and her material. The narrative style is integrated into the abrasive texture of the novel which is about the attempts of a working-class girl to keep her hopes intact in a culturally deprived world. It gives an authentic inside account of what a female feels about an aggressively male environment. Stella, the heroine, is able to cope with the physical toughness of her environment but she is sexually insecure. Having fallen for another girl, Morag, she asks her father if there are 'women poofs'.[397] He answers in the affirmative:

> Not being able to deny her crush on Morag, feeling it to be a fine thing, she hated him, momentarily, and got up abruptly and went and was sick in the toilet, raging 'God you *bastard*, you *bastard*. how *could* you? Is this your idea of a joke or what?' Her father, with his excessive admiration for the manly virtues, had made her believe that the highest thing a woman could achieve was to be like a man. She had done her best to live up to it—even then she carried two little india-rubber balls, one in each coat-pocket, for he'd told her that if she squeezed them as hard as she could all day, she would develop 'a grip like a man'. She was sick with betrayal: it was unbearable, as if he had fed her fat just to throw her to the wolves. She had thought he loved her and was bringing her up to succeed, but the truth was, he had been rearing her like any bit cattle, and teaching her tricks to amuse himself, to make up to himself, she thought, 'for the shitty son he never had'. And then she relented to God—it wasn't God's fault, 'But where the hell *are* you, God?' she begged.[398]

Alisdair Gray's *Lanark* (1981) is an epic experiment, a linguistically rich exploration of city life as experienced by an artist. Basically it is a phantasmagoric Glasgow novel with roots in the Scottish tradition that has endured since the publication of George Douglas Brown's *The House With the Green Shutters* in 1901. It is a tradition that recognises the persistence of the past. Scottish novels are still haunted by history; Scottish authors are still pressurised by the past. Styles do not disguise the national cultural inheritance. The coarse texture of Anne Smith's prose and the careful polish of Alasdair Gray's have in common a consciousness of Scotland as a national issue still to be settled. In *Lanark* Gray has an Index of Plagiarisms which includes an entry on Brown, George Douglas: 'Books 1 and 2 owe much to the novel *The House with the Green Shutters* in which heavy paternalism forces a weak-minded youth into dread of existence, hallucination, and crime'.[399] That brings the story of the twentieth century Scottish novel right back to the beginning; it is a long line that describes a vicious circle.

REFERENCES

1   G. K. Chesterton, *Robert Louis Stevenson*, Hodder and Stoughton: London, 1927, pp. 68–70

2   Muriel Spark, *The Prime of Miss Jean Brodie*, Macmillan: London, 1961 (Penguin edn, p. 88)

3   George Blake, *Barrie and the Kailyard School*, Arthur Barker: London, 1951, p. 42

4   Ibid. p. 17

5   Ibid. p. 18

6   J. M. Barrie, *Sentimental Tommy*, Cassell: London, 1896, p. 234

7   J. M. Barrie, *Plays and Stories*, J. M. Dent: London, 1962, p. 244

8   James Bridie, *Tedious and Brief*, Constable: London, 1944, p. 98

9   James Veitch, *George Douglas Brown*, Herbert Jenkins: London, 1952, p. 22

10   Ian Maclaren, *Beside the Bonnie Brier Bush*, Hodder and Stoughton: London, 1898, pp. 29–32

11   George Douglas Brown, *The House with the Green Shutters*, Cassell: London, 1901 (First Novel Library edn, pp. 137–9)

12   James Veitch, op. cit., p. 153

13   George Douglas Brown, op. cit., p. 1

14   T. S. Eliot (ed.), *Literary Essays of Ezra Pound*, Faber: London, 1954, p. 23

15   George Douglas Brown, op. cit. p. 242

16   Ibid. p. 189

17   James Veitch, op. cit. p. 167

18   George Douglas Brown, op. cit. p. 4

19   Ibid. p. 2

20   Ibid. pp. 88–89

21   Ibid. p. 24

22   Mark 3 : 25

23   George Douglas Brown, op. cit. p. 13

24   Ibid. p. 31

25   Ibid. p. 75

26   Ibid. pp. 191–2

27   Ibid. p. 200

28   Ibid. pp. 216–17

29   *The Scotsman*, 2 Octo. 1972

30   J. MacDougall Hay, *Gillespie*, Constable: London, 1914; Canongate reprint (1979), p. xvi

31   Ibid. p. 39

32   Francis Russell Hart, *The Scottish Novel*, John Murray: London, 1978, p. 13

33   J. MacDougall Hay, op. cit. p. 1
34   Ibid. pp. 8–9
35   Ibid. pp. 440–1
36   Ibid. p. 446
37   Ibid. p. 383
38   Ibid. p. 232
39   Ibid. pp. 196–8
40   Ibid. p. 73
41   Ibid. pp. 424–5
42   Ibid. p. 273
43   Lewis Grassic Gibbon, *A Scots Hairst*, Hutchinson: London, 1969, p. 175
44   Ibid. p. 82
45   Ibid. pp. 144–5
46   James Leslie Mitchell, *Spartacus*, Jarrolds: London, 1933. (Hutchinson reprint 1970, p. 55)
47   Ibid. p. 64
48   Ibid. p. 97
49   Ibid. p. 284
50   Ibid. pp. 286–7
51   Lewis Grassic Gibbon, *A Scots Hairst*, p. 124
52   Ibid. p. 125
53   Ibid. p. 125
54   Ibid. p. 127
55   Ibid. p. 136
56   Ibid. p. 141
57   Lewis Grassic Gibbon, *A Scots Quair*, Jarrolds: London, 1946 (new edn, 1950, p. 130)
58   Ibid. p. 31
59   Ibid. p. 36
60   Ibid. p. 44
61   Lewis Grassic Gibbon, *A Scots Hairst*, p. 154
62   Lewis Grassic Gibbon, *A Scots Quair*, p. 54
63   Ibid. p. 43
64   Ibid. p. 19
65   Ibid. p. 27
66   Ibid. p. 74
67   Ibid. p. 37
68   Ibid. p. 97
69   Ibid. p. 138
70   Ibid. p. 19
71   Ibid. p. 5
72   Ibid. p. 30
73   Ibid. p. 49
74   Ibid. p. 64
75   Ibid. p. 58
76   Ibid. p. 31
77   Ibid. p. 146
78   Ibid. p. 131
79   Ibid. p. 28

80   Ibid. p. 89
81   Ibid. p. 104
82   Ibid. p. 22
83   Ibid. p. 112
84   Ibid. p. 112
85   Ibid. p. 112
86   Ibid. pp. 99–100
87   Lewis Grassic Gibbon, *A Scots Hairst*, pp. 248–9
88   Neil M. Gunn, *Whisky and Scotland*, Routledge: London, 1935 (Souvenir Press reprint, 1977 pp. 49–55)
89   Neil M. Gunn, *The Atom of Delight*, Faber: London, 1956, p. 32
90   Ibid. p. 24
91   Ibid. pp. 24–5
92   Ibid. pp. 29 and 271
93   Neil M. Gunn. *Bloodhunt*, Faber: London, 1952, p. 233
94   Neil M. Gunn, *Morning Tide*, Propoise Press: Edinburgh, 1931, p. 14
95   Francis Russell Hart, op. cit. p. 351
96   Neil M. Gunn, *The Lost Glen*, Porpoise Press: Edinburgh, 1932, p. 9
97   Ibid. p. 340
98   Ibid. p. 204
99   Ibid. p. 35
100   Ibid. p. 100
101   Ibid. p. 23
102   Ibid. p. 240
103   Ibid. p. 118
104   Ibid. p. 132
105   Ibid. pp. 249–50
106   Neil M. Gunn, *Sun Circle*, Porpoise Press: Edinburgh, 1934, p. 9
107   Ibid p. 338
108   Neil M. Gunn, *Butcher's Broom*, Porpoise Press: Edinburgh, 1934, p. 21
109   Ibid. p. 72
110   Ibid. p. 9
111   Ibid. p. 14
112   Ibid. p. 21
113   Ibid. pp. 426–8
114   Neil M. Gunn, *Highland River*, Porpoise Press: Edinburgh, 1937 (Arrow edn, pp. 41 and 50)
115   Ibid. p. 113
116   Ibid. pp. 122–3
117   Neil M. Gunn, *The Silver Darlings*, Faber: London, 1941, p. 26
118   Ibid. p. 43
119   Ibid. p. 100
120   Ibid. p. 133
121   Ibid. p. 563
122   Ibid. p. 229
123   Ibid. pp. 567–8
124   Ibid. p. 145
125   Ibid. p. 324
126   Ibid. pp. 583–4

127 Neil M. Gunn, *The Serpent*, Faber: London, 1943, p. 67
128 Ibid. pp. 166–7
129 Ibid. pp. 234 and 249
130 Neil M. Gunn, *The Green Isle of the Great Deep*, Faber: London, 1944, p. 10
131 Ibid. p. 41
132 Ibid. p. 98
133 Ibid. p. 119
134 Ibid. p. 228
135 Neil M. Gunn, *The Drinking Well*, Faber London, 1946, p. 116
136 Ibid. pp. 461–2
137 Neil M. Gunn, *The Well at the World's End*, Faber: London, 1951, p. 17
138 Ibid. p. 20
139 Ibid. pp. 18–19
140 Ibid. p. 291
141 Neil M. Gunn, *Bloodhunt*, p. 233
142 Neil M. Gunn, *The Other Landscape*, Faber: London, 1954, p. 40
143 Ibid. pp. 65–8
144 Ibid. p. 307
145 A. J. Cronin, *The Citadel*, Victor Gollancz: London, 1937, p. 200
146 Norris McWhirter (ed.), *Guinness Book of Records*, Guinness Superlatives: Enfield, 1981, p. 97
147 Anna Buchan (O. Douglas) and others, *Farewell to Priorsford*, Hodder and Stoughton: London, 1950, p. 13
148 John Buchan, *John Burnet of Barns*, Lane: London, 1898, p. 20
149 John Buchan, *The Thirty-Nine Steps and The Power-House*, Blackwood: Edinburgh, 1966, p. 4
150 John Buchan, *John Burnet of Barns*, p. 316
151 John Buchan, *Memory Hold-The-Door*, Hodder and Stoughton: London, 1941, pp. 193–4
152 John Buchan, *Prester John*, Nelson: London, 1910, p. 209
153 Anna Buchan (O. Douglas), *Unforgettable, Unforgotten*, Hodder and Stoughton: London, 1945, p. 143
154 John Buchan, *Sick Heart River*, Hodder and Stoughton: London, 1941; (Macdonald reprint 1981, pp. 221–1)
155 Cited in typescript biography of Neil Munro by the author's granddaughter Mrs Lesley Bratton
156 Neil Munro, *The Daft Days*, Blackwood: Edinburgh, 1907, Inverary edn, p. 1
157 Neil Munro, *Para Handy Tales*, Blackwood: Edinburgh, 1955 (Pan edn, pp. 14–15)
158 Neil Munro, *John Splendid*, Blackwood Edinburgh, 1898 (Inverary edn, pp. 32–3)
159 Neil Munro, *The New Road*, Blackwood: Edinburgh, 1914 (Inverary edn, p. 33)
160 Compton Mackenzie, *Sinister Street*, Martin Secker: London, 1913 (Penguin edn, pp. 492–3)
161 Ibid. p. 11
162 Ibid. p. 12

163 Compton Mackenzie, *The Adventures of Sylvia Scarlett*, Macdonald: London, 1950, p. 686
164 Compton Mackenzie, *My Life and Times: Octave Seven 1931–1938*, Chatto and Windus: London, 1968, p. 301
165 Ibid. p. 60
166 Compton Mackenzie, *The East Wind of Love, Book One*, Chatto and Windus: London, 1973, p. 10
167 Ibid. p. 177
168 Ibid. p. 263
169 Ibid. p. 93
170 Compton Mackenzie, *The North Wind of Love, Book Two*, Chatto and Windus: London, 1973, pp. 12–13
171 Hugh MacDiarmid, *Lucky Poet*, Methuen: London, 1943, p. 26
172 Compton Mackenzie, *The Monarch of the Glen*, Chatto and Windus: London, 1941 (Penguin edn, p. 11)
173 Tom Driberg, *Ruling Passions*, Cape: London, 1977 (Quartet edn, p. 146)
174 Compton Mackenzie, *The East Wind of Love, Book One*, dedication p. 3
175 Eric Linklater, *Fanfare for a Tin Hat*, Macmillan: London, 1970, p. 324
176 Ibid. p. 40
177 Eric Linklater *The Man on My Back*, Macmillan: London, 1950, pp. 198–9
178 Eric Linklater, *Juan in America*, Cape: London, 1931, p. 65
179 Eric Linklater, *Fanfare for a Tin Hat*, p. 11
180 Eric Linklater, *Juan in America*, pp. 105–6
181 Eric Linklater, *The Man on My Back*, pp. 230
182 Ibid. p. 224
183 Eric Linklater, *Magnus Merriman*, Cape: London, 1934, p. 54
184 Eric Linklater, *Laxdale Hall*, Cape: London, 1951 (Macdonald reprint, 1981 p. 67)
185 Ibid. p. 50
186 Ibid. p. 148
187 Eric Linklater, *Roll of Honour*, Rupert Hart-Davis: London, 1961, p. 9
188 Ibid. p. 217
189 Ibid. p. 213
190 Hugh MacDiarmid, *Selected Essays*, Cape: London, 1969, p. 157
191 Norman Douglas, *Late Harvest*, Lindsay Drummond: London, 1946, p. vii
192 Norman Douglas, *South Wind*, Secker and Warburg: London, 1917 (Penguin edn, p. 6)
193 Norman Douglas, *Late Harvest*, p. 58
194 Norman Douglas, *South Wind*, pp. 226–7
195 Ibid. p. 178
196 Ibid. p. 179
197 Ibid. p. 80
198 Bernard Sellin, *The Life and Works of David Lindsay*, Cambridge University Press: Cambridge, 1981, p. 12

199 David Lindsay, *A Voyage to Arcturus*, Methuen: London, 1920 (Gollancz reprint, 1963, 1968), p. 35
200 Bernard Sellin, op. cit., p. xi
201 Ibid. p. 31
202 Ibid. p. 55
203 Ibid. p. 174
204 Ibid. p. 166
205 Ibid. p. 168
206 David Lindsay, *A Voyage to Arcturus*, p. 145
207 Bernard Sellin, op. cit. p. 198
208 David Lindsay, *A Voyage to Arcturus*, p. 42
209 Ibid. p. 118
210 Ibid. p. 16
211 Ibid. p. 24
212 Ibid. p. 25
213 Ibid. p. 51
214 Ibid. p. 71
215 Ibid. p. 82
216 Ibid. p. 135
217 Ibid. pp. 247–8
218 Ibid. p. 248
219 Ian Macpherson, *Wild Harbour*, Methuen: London, 1936 (Paul Harris reprint, 1981, p. xi)
220 I. F. Clarke, *Voices Prophesying War 1763–1984*, Oxford University Press: Oxford, 1966 (Panther edn, p. 170).
221 Ian Macpherson, *Wild Harbour*, p. 14
222 Ibid. pp. 36–7
223 Ibid. p. 20
224 Ibid. pp. 251–2
225 Ibid. p. 41
226 Cover of *Scotia Review 10*, Wick, August 1975
227 Fionn Mac Colla, *At the Sign of the Clenched Fist*, Macdonald: Edinburgh,1967, p. 204
228 Ibid. p. 204
229 Fionn Mac Colla, *And the Cock Crew*, Maclellan: Glasgow, 1945 (Souvenir Press reprint, 1977, p. 20)
230 Ibid. p. 21
231 Ibid. p. 26
232 Ibid. p. 35
233 Ibid. p. 35
234 Ibid. pp. 45–6
235 Chapter 1 of *At the Sign of the Clenched Fist* for Mac Colla's views on the notion of the winning side in history
236 Fionn Mac Colla, *At the Sign of the Clenched Fist*, p. 42
237 Fionn Mac Colla, *And the Cock Crew*, p. 100
238 Fionn Mac Colla, *The Ministers*, Souvenir Press: London, 1979, p. 254
239 Ibid. p. 15
240 Robin Jenkins, *A Far Cry from Bowmore*, Gollancz: London, 1973, p. 64

241 Robin Jenkins, *A Toast to the Lord*, Gollancz: London, 1972, p. 12
242 Ibid. p. 9
243 Ibid. p. 54
244 Ibid. p. 153
245 Ibid. p. 212
246 cf. Mac Colla's *The Ministers*
247 Robin Jenkins, *A Would-Be Saint*, Gollancz: London, 1978, p. 60
248 Ibid. p. 63
249 Ibid p. 66
250 Fred Urquhart, *Palace of Green Days*, Quartet: London, 1979, p. 163
251 *Books in Scotland 2*, Edinburgh, Autumn 1978, p. 5
252 Maurice Lindsay (ed.), *As I Remember*, Hale: London, 1979, p. 174
253 Letter, 6 August 1979
254 Fred Urquhart, *Time Will Knit*, Methuen: London, 1938, (Ace edn, p. 32)
255 Fred Urquhart, *Jezebel's Dust*, Methuen: London, 1951, p. 15
256 Ibid. p. 21
257 Fred Urquhart, *The Dying Stallion*, Rupert Hart-Davis: London, 1967, p. 118
258 Ibid. p. 116
259 Robert Millar and J. T. Low (eds.), *Ten Modern Scottish Short Stories*, Heinemann: London, 1973, p. 8
260 Ibid. p. 14
261 Letter, 6 August 1979
262 David Toulmin, *Blown Seed*, Paul Harris: Edinburgh, 1976 (Pan edn, p. 20)
263 Letter, 11 June 1981
264 Jessie Kesson, *The White Bird Passes*, Chatto and Windus: London, 1958 (Paul Harris reprint, 1980, p. 109)
265 Ibid. p. 38
266 Ibid. p. 40
267 Ibid. pp. 8–9
268 Ibid. p. 43
269 Ibid. p. 28
270 Ibid. pp. 124–5
271 Anthony Burgess, *The Novel Now*, Faber: London, 1967, p. 134
272 Nigel Tranter, *Robert the Bruce: The Path of the Hero King*, Hodder and Stoughton: London, 1970, p. 335
273 Naomi Mitchison, *You May Well Ask*, Gollanz: London, 1979, p. 164
274 Naomi Mitchison, *Cloud Cuckoo Land*, Cape: London, 1925 (Great Historical Novels edn, 1967, pp. 128–9)
275 Naomi Mitchison, *You May Well Ask*, p. 164
276 Dorothy Dunnett, *The Ringed Castle*, Cassell: London, 1971, p. 10
277 Ibid. p. 17
278 Ibid. p. 23
279 Jane Duncan, *My Friends the Miss Boyds*, Macmillan: London, 1959, p. 260
280 Jane Duncan, *My Friend Sashie*, Macmillan: London, 1972, p. 42
281 Ibid. p. 12
282 Ibid. pp. 14–15

283 Ibid. p. 22
284 Ibid. pp. 98–9
285 Ibid. p. 99
286 Francis Russell Hart, *The Scottish Novel*, p. 296
287 Letter, 22 April 1979
288 Muriel Spark, *The Prime of Miss Jean Brodie*, Macmillan: London, 1961 (Penguin edn, pp. 108–9)
289 Ibid. p. 26
290 Ibid. p. 8
291 Ibid. p. 9
292 Ibid. p. 31
393 Ibid. p. 85
294 Ibid. p. 120
295 Ibid. p. 125
296 Ibid. p. 125
297 Ibid. p. 39
298 Muriel Spark, *The Driver's Seat*, Macmillan: London, 1970 (Penguin edn, p. 50)
299 Ibid. p. 25
300 Ibid. pp. 106–7
301 Muriel Spark, *Not To Disturb*, Macmillan: London, 1974 (Penguin edn, p. 58)
302 Ibid. p. 12
303 Ibid. pp. 74–5
304 Muriel Spark, *The Hothouse by the East River*, Macmillan: London, 1973 (Penguin edn, p. 119)
305 Ibid. p. 127
306 Ibid. p. 45
307 Ibid. p. 71
308 Ibid. p. 63
309 Ibid. p. 135
310 Ibid. p. 139
311 Joan Lingard, *The Prevailing Wind*, Hodder and Soughton: London, 1964 pp. 82–3
312 George Blake, *The Paying Guest*, Collins: London, 1949, p. 22
313 Ibid. pp. 54–5
314 George Blake, *The Shipbuilders*, Collins: London, 1935 (new edn, 1944, p. 5)
315 Ibid. p. 12
316 Ibid. pp. 13–14
317 Ibid. p. 329
318 Ibid. p. 242
319 *The Scotsman*, 28 July 1979
320 Ibid.
321 Alan Sharp, *A Green Tree in Gedde*, Michael Joseph: London, 1965, p. 162
322 Ibid. pp. 35–6
323 Ibid. p. 270
324 Ibid. pp. 256–7
325 Ibid. pp. 337–8

326   Archie Hind, *The Dear Green Place*, Hutchinson: London, 1966, p. 33
327   Ibid. pp. 12–13
328   Ibid. p. 53
329   Ibid. pp. 34–5
330   Ibid. pp. 63–5
331   Ibid. pp. 106–7
332   William McIlvanney, *Docherty*, Allen and Unwin: London, 1975, p. 25
333   Ibid. p. 181
334   Ibid. p. 192
335   Ibid. p. 210
336   Ibid. p. 301
337   George Mackay Brown, *Greenvoe*, Hogarth Press: London, 1972 (Penguin edn, p. 19)
338   Ibid. p. 110
339   Ibid. p. 10
340   Ibid. p. 259
341   Ibid. p. 158
342   Ibid. p. 99
343   Ibid. p. 277
344   Ibid. p. 279
345   Ibid. p. 125
346   Ibid. pp. 129–30
347   Ibid. p. 122
348   George Mackay Brown, *An Orkney Tapestry*, Gollancz: London, 1969 (Quartet edn, p. 76)
349   George Mackay Brown, *Magnus*, Hogarth Press: London, 1973, p. 26
350   Ibid. p. 20
351   Letter, 12 June 1979
352   James Kennaway, *Tunes of Glory*, Longman: Harlow, 1956 (Mainstream reprint, 1980, introduction)
353   James and Susan Kennaway, *The Kennaway Papers*, Cape: London, 1981, p. 7
354   Ibid. pp. 8–9
355   Ibid. pp. 12–13
356   James Kennaway, *Tunes of Glory*, p. 11
357   Ibid. p. 23
358   James Kennaway, *Household Ghosts*, Longman: Harlow, 1961 (Mainstream reprint 1981, p. 30)
359   Ibid. p. 185
360   Ibid. pp. 173–5
361   James and Susan Kennaway, *The Kennaway Papers*, p. 70
362   James Kennaway, *The Bells of Shoreditch*, Longman: Harlow, 1963 (Mainstream reprint, 1981, p. 151)
363   Ibid. p. 197
364   Ibid. p. 200
365   James Kennaway, *Silence*, Cape: London, 1972, p. 19
366   Ibid. p. 87
367   Ibid. p. 89

368 Ibid. p. 92
369 cf. the tone of *Silence* with Susan Kennaway's account of her husband's final days in *The Kennaway Papers*
370 Letter, 17 March 1979
371 Ibid.
372 Ibid.
373 Ibid.
374 Ibid.
375 Gordon Williams, *The Camp*, Secker and Warburg: London, 1960 (rev edn, Allison and Busby: London, 1980, p. 45)
376 Ibid. p. 17
377 Ibid. p. 63
378 Gordon Williams, *From Scenes Like These*, Secker and Warburg: London, 1968 (Mayflower edn, p. 12)
379 Ibid. p. 35
380 Ibid. p. 23
381 Hugh MacDiarmid, *Complete Poems*, Martin Brian and O'Keeffe: London, 1978, p. 1170
382 Francis Russell Hart, op. cit. p. 316
383 Gordon Williams, *Walk Don't Walk*, Hodder and Stoughton: London, 1972 (Quartet edn, p. 383)
384 Ibid. p. 109
385 Ibid. p. 109
386 Letter, 17 March 1979
387 John Herdman, *Pagan's Pilgrimage*, Akros: Preston, 1978, p. 5
388 Ibid. p. 18
389 Ibid. p. 27
390 Trevor Royle (ed.), *Jock Tamson's Bairns*, Hamish Hamilton: London, 1977, p. 68
391 Allan Massie, *The Death of Men*, Bodley Head: London, 1981, p. 33
392 Ibid. p. 101
393 Ibid. p. 6
394 Ibid. p. 7
395 Ibid. p. 163
396 Ibid. p. 94
397 Anne Smith, *The Magic Glass*, Michael Joseph: London, 1981, p. 168
398 Ibid. p. 169
399 Alasdair Gray, *Lanark*, Canongate: Edinburgh, 1981, p. 486

Part Three

DRAMA

42.   IN SEARCH OF A TRADITION

A cursory look through a catalogue of twentieth century Scottish play-titles would convince the casual observer that we are dealing with a drama that dwells exclusively on the past. Scottish history has exerted such a dramatic, indeed melodramatic, influence on Scottish playwrights that a play on a contemporary subject is the exception rather than the rule. There are plays about Bruce and Wallace, about James VI and Bothwell, about the Highland Clearances and the Wars of Independence but there are comparatively few plays that indicate what it is like to live in modern Scotland. As Scottish drama is largely a twentieth-century phenomenon this habit of looking back in anguish might seem puzzling; however, if we remember that the Scot typically bears a grudge about the real and imagined wrongs of yesteryear we can understand this need to dramatise historical incidents that shaped modern Scotland. There is, too, the need for contemporary dramatists to manufacture an instant tradition; they are, in a sense, writing the plays that might have existed if the country had enjoyed a strong, unbroken tradition of indigenous drama. There are, after all, many who would agree with Maurice Lindsay: 'The Scot, however, has yet to prove himself a master of the theatre. Sir David Lyndsay's *Ane Satire of the Thrie Estatis* remains our solitary major masterpiece; and it was written more than four hundred years ago.'[1] As Scotland is so vocal about its political status its artists can easily imagine themselves to be the acknowledged legislators of their world; they can feel an urgent obligation to compensate for cultural deprivation. Throughout the unfolding of Scottish drama there has been a desire to establish the tradition that never was and, collectively, the dramatists have been in hot pursuit of a national character. Although some dramatists have performed heroically at times a distinctively national theatrical idiom has not, so far, emerged. Instead we have evolution, through a process of argument and achievement, of a Platonic ideal of Scottish drama against which real productions are tested. If we think of a tradition as a set of formal challenges to which succeeding practitioners can respond, then we have to lament the lack of continuity in the Scottish theatre. A national tradition issues a more specific challenge to the writer: in trilingual Scotland he has to decide whether to write in English or Scots (or even in Gaelic, though that choice is open to very few). To write in Scots usually implies a political commitment to autonomy; to write in English is to compete with writers who are blessed with a real tradition. What is the Scottish dramatist to do? Alexander Reid had no doubts about the matter:

> If we are to fulfil our hope that Scotland may some day make a
> contribution to World Drama as individual and valuable as that made by

Norway in the nineteenth and by Ireland in the present century, we can only do so by cherishing, not repressing our national peculiarities (including our language), though whether a Scottish National Drama, if it comes to birth, will be written in Braid Scots or the speech, redeemed for literary purposes, of Argyle Street, Glasgow, or the Kirkgate, Leith, is anyone's guess. That it will be written in some sort of Scots however is quite certain.[2]

Reid's contention that the ideal Scottish National Drama will utilise 'some sort of Scots' does, of course, put additional pressure on the Scottish dramatist. J. M. Barrie's plays were aimed at a London target and found their mark so accurately that he has been unfairly set aside as a 'Scotsman on the make', indifferent to the theatrical requirements of his native land. James Bridie, who did just occasionally use 'some sort of Scots', has been accepted as a national dramatist. However, there is little doubt that Bridie, like Barrie, craved international appreciation. In his pronouncements on the theatre he avoided narrowly nationalist squabbles and presented himself as a craftsman doing his job: 'The Theatre itself is a place for viewing or seeing things. The thing it presents to our vision is the drama. Drama consists of people doing things. It takes the form of a play, which is a method of passing time when there is nothing better to do.'[3] That abecederian statement of 1937 must have infuriated those who sought to capitalise on the ideal of the Scottish National Drama. Bridie wanted a drama that did more than adhere to a few theoretical principles.

In the 1970s there was something of an explosive revival of dramatic activity in Scotland and most of the plays were written in 'some sort of Scots'. Still the revivalists were aware of working in a vacuum because few twentieth century Scottish plays survived their first productions and even fewer texts are available. Donald Campbell, one of the leading dramatists of the 1970s, made this point forcefully:

> Scottish drama, it often seems to me, is stuck in a rut, doing the same thing over and over again, simply because neither dramatist, director, actor or audience realise that the ground has been covered already. What is the difference, I wonder, between the 'social documentary' drama of the Unity Theatre in the 'forties and the more recent successes in this genre by such as Bill Bryden, John Byrne and Tom McGrath? . . . I can't escape the feeling that plays like *Willie Rough*, *The Slab Boys* and *The Hard Man* might have been even stronger and more powerful if their authors had had the chance to at least read these earlier plays.[4]

Those who dread the allegedly omnipresent Scottish disease of parochialism would welcome a situation that forced dramatists to seek inspirational models outside their own country. If Scottish dramatists had to learn their craft from touring plays, from classics staged in the Edinburgh International Festival, from work transmitted on the mass media they may have been helped rather than hindered.

43.   A SCOTTISH NATIONAL THEATRE

Scotland is of course, a small country with poorly cultivated theatre-going habits. A purely Scottish play is, therefore addressed to a tiny minority who cannot finance a national theatrical effort. Admittedly the ideal of a Scottish National Drama assumes that a great Scottish play will earn the respect of the world but first it must make a splash in the Scottish pond. To do so it invariably requires a subsidy. A move to set up a Scottish Theatre Trust as a company of national stature took the form of a submission to the Scottish Arts Council who had financed the preliminary investigations. According to a newspaper report the Scottish Theatre Trust would be both national and international:

> Outlining the company's policy, Mr [Ewan] Hooper said that its repertoire should consist of the best existing Scottish plays, translations by Scottish writers of European and other classics, and new plays by Scottish writers. He said they were setting out to achieve international standards of production. 'I only hope that this company may go back to the original ideas of the Abbey Theatre of Dublin and present drama of international significance by concentrating on what is around us.'[5]

Again there is compulsion to step back in time: to 1904 when the Abbey Theatre opened and, more pertinently, to 1924 when the Abbey was officially recognised as the Irish National Theatre.

The Scottish theatre has lived in the shadow of the Abbey; the great plays produced there astonished Scotland and it is worth noting that Glasgow Unity Theatre commenced its professional life in 1946 with a production of Sean O'Casey's *Purple Dust*. The Dublin commodity has seemed ready made for import to Scotland though Scots have to learn that the fact it has not arrived does not necessarily mean they have missed the boat. They have (changing the metaphor) to remember the vagaries of a chicken-and-egg quandary: Scottish plays cannot wait for a Scottish National Theatre and may well help to bring one into being. Kenneth Tynan, who did so much to establish a National Theatre in London, warned Scots against putting too much faith in duplicating the Abbey pattern: 'I think that, as what you might call the Celtic twilight school has produced what has turned out to be the least durable of Irish plays, the 'chip on the shoulder' Scottish play is probably a forlorn hope in the theatre.'[6]

44. THE PULPIT VERSUS THE STAGE

During the Edinburgh International Festival of 1977 the Scottish Society of Playwrights held a conference to discuss, among related matters, the possibility of a Scottish National Theatre. In his contribution to the discussion Hector MacMillan observed:

> The history of Scottish theatre takes the form of a series of almost totally isolated bursts of creative energy – a series of quanta between which there is no immediately accessible link – quanta spaced so far apart in time that no overall pattern is immediately obvious to the newcomer at any particular moment.[7]

This disjointed development of Scottish drama obtained until the twentieth century when Scottish writers began increasingly to apply their talents to the stage. It is a remarkable fact that a country without a definite theatrical traditional has been able to simulate one in recent years. For the early history of Scottish drama is, fundamentally, a tale of three plays (though scholars have conjectured a lost world of forsaken plays). Sir David Lynsday's *Ane Pleasant Satyre of the Thrie Estatis* had a royal premiere before the Court at Linlithgow in 1540 and a revised version (performed at Cupar in the presence of James V) was published in 1602. It was a massive spectacle that was spectacularly revived – in Robert Kemp's modernised text – by Tyrone Guthrie at the second Edinburgh International Festival of 1948. Ironically enough, considering the Kirk's part in suppressing Scottish drama, it was produced by the Scottish Theatre in the Church of Scotland Assembly Hall (initially on 24 August).

Guthrie had been asked, by the Festival Committee, to direct Scottish actors in a classic Scottish play. It was an ambitious request:

> Barrie, it was agreed, was not, at all events in the present epoch, whatever his future reputation may be, of classical status. Bridie was a member of the committee and did not wish his work considered. I was asked to read Home's *Douglas*, Ramsay's *Gentle Shepherd*, and *The Three Estates*.[8]

The two plays Guthrie rejected are of some relevance. Allan Ramsay founded Scotland's first organised theatre (in Edinburgh's Carrubber's Close) in 1736 in the hope of building a new tradition on the basis of his ballad opera *The Gentle Shepherd* (first performed in 1729 as Scotland's answer to Gay's *The Beggar's Opera* of 1728). Although the Licensing Act closed Ramsay's theatre in 1737 the seeds had been sown and drama might have developed had it not been for the opposition of the Kirk.

'What Knox really did was to rob Scotland of all the benefits of the Renassiance', wrote Edwin Muir[9] in a misguided moment. It is too easy to blame Knox for everything that has gone wrong with Scotland and he will not do as the stage villain of a propagandist piece. Knox was not averse to entertainment:

> Knox went to plays, if he could approve their content: we know he saw one that graced a St Andrews wedding, in which Kirkcaldy of Grange, then holding Edinburgh Castle for Queen Mary, and still very much alive, was taken and hanged.[10]

As the principal force behind the Scottish Reformation, which triumphed in 1561, Knox bequeathed to the Scots a cause which some of them turned into a creed. In 1574 the General Assembly turned its wrath against plays drawn from Scripture and the following year censured entertainments associated with saints' days; the ecclesiastical condemnation was endorsed by the Scottish parliament in 1581. With this precedent in mind, the Scottish clergy took it upon themselves to transform a dislike of drama into a theological principle:

> The Kirk nurtured the concept that the playhouse was the domain of Beelzebub . . . Of the various elements which explain the poverty of the Scottish stage, religious censure is paramount.[11]

It was against this background that John Home's *Douglas* was premiered at the Canongate Theatre, Edinburgh, on 14 December 1756. Home was minister of Athelstaneford so the Kirk had special reasons for railing at a play that inspired a member of the first-night audience to call out 'Whaur's yer Wully Shakespeare noo?' It was the popularity of this pseudo-Shakespearian tragedy that alarmed the Kirk, who were fearful that worshippers might transfer their allegiance from the pulpit to the stage.

On 5 January 1757 the Edinburgh Presbytery issued an Admonition and Exhortation against Home's play. The opening of this invective deserves to be cited here as demonstrating, more eloquently than anything else, the sort of influential opposition potential Scottish dramatists were up against:

> The Presbytery taking into serious consideration the declining state of religion, the open profanation of the Lord's Day, the contempt of public worship, the growing luxury and levity of the present age – in which so many seem lovers of pleasure more than lovers of God – and being particularly affected with the unprecedented countenance given of late to the Playhouse in this place, when the state of the nation and the circumstances of the poor, make such hurtful entertainments still more pernicious, judged it their indispensable duty to express in the most open and solemn manner, the deep concern they feel on this occasion. The opinion which the Christian Church has always entertained of stage plays and players as prejudicial to the interest of religion and morality is well known, and the fatal influence which they commonly have on the far greater part of mankind particularly the younger sort, is too obvious to be called into question.[12]

The matter did not end there, for Home was persuaded to resign from his ministry on 7 June 1757. The Kirk had spoken: it considered the theatre to be a diabolic rival and was determined to fight it. It was an unequal battle, for in a Scotland that had lost its court and its parliament the rule of law was excessively clerical. Scottish writers virtually abandoned the theatre until the dawn of the twentieth century by which time the opinions of presbyterian ministers no longer mattered to them. The long theatrical silence remained a matter of concern, though. In 1790, thirty-three years after the *Douglas* affair, Robert Burns posed a question that was to wait many years for an adequate answer. In his 'Prologue for Mr Sutherland's Benefit-Night, Dumfries' he wrote:

> Is there nae poet, burning keen for fame,
> Will try to gie us sangs and plays at hame? . . .
> There's themes enow in Caledonian story,
> Would show the tragic muse in a' her glory.
>   Is there no daring Bard will rise, and tell
> How glorious Wallace stood, how hapless fell?
> Where are the Muses fled that could produce
> A drama worthy o' the name o' Bruce?

Where are the Muses fled? The Muses, Thalia and Melpomene, had fled from the Kirk. When they returned, more than a century later, they were cautious in their visits to Scottish writers.

If we think of some of the finest theatrical moments in the twentieth century – for example, J. M. Synge's *The Playboy of the Western World* (1907), Eugene O'Neill's *Anna Christie* (1921), O'Casey's *The Shadow of a Gunman* (1923), Arthur Miller's *Death of a Salesman* (1947), Tennessee Williams's *A Streetcar Named Desire* (1948), Samuel Beckett's *Waiting for Godot* (1954), John Osborne's *Look Back in Anger* (1956), Harold Pinter's *The Caretaker* (1960) – the Scottish contribution is conspicuous by its absence. That should be remembered in any discussion of modern Scottish drama lest we get carried away by rhetoric and propaganda. No Scottish play has yet made the rest of the world sit up and take notice. Moreover there are no theatrical innovations that have been born and bred in Scotland – another Scottish cultural paradox. Though there has been no long tradition of Scottish drama, modern Scottish drama is tradition-bound, reluctant to take chances. Within the limits of its safety-first inhibitions twentieth century Scottish drama has been attended to by several dramatists even if few of them have had more than one play in them.

45. BARRIE: SCOTSMAN ON THE MAKE

The most commercially successful twentieth century Scottish dramatist, J. M. Barrie (1860–1937), has paid for his success in terms
of critical neglect. It has become the custom to treat Barrie's life as
more inherently dramatic than his plays and to regard him as an
English rather than a Scottish dramatist. In the Edinburgh Festival
Fringe of 1974 Jon Plowman's short piece *The Peter Pan Man* portrayed Barrie as an unstable person schizophrenically divided between his public persona and the inner man he described, in his
speech *Courage*, as M'Connachie. Here is the relevant passage from
Barrie's Rectorial Address (delivered at St Andrews University on 3
May 1922):

> My puppets seem more real to me than myself, and I could get on much
> more swingingly if I made one of them deliver this address. It is
> M'Connachie who has brought me to this pass . . . I am the half that is
> dour and practical and canny, he is the fanciful half; my desire is to be
> the family solicitor, standing firm on my hearthrug among the harsh
> realities of the office furniture; while he prefers to fly around on one
> wing.[13]

Barrie was being characteristically contrary as a prelude to his serious treatise on courage. Yet his exegetists have made the mistake
of treating his work as an escapist flight from his psychological problems. Andrew Birkin's study *Barrie and the Lost Boys* (1979) – and
the same author's television series that preceded its appearance –
exposed the most intimate details of Barrie's life so relentlessly that
the public are apt to forget he was a creative writer and not simply a
sentimentalist who suffered from emotional immaturity.

It is true that Barrie's life was punctuated by tragedy; that he felt
intensely his mother's grief on losing her favourite son; that he was
appalled at the deaths of Arthur and Sylvia Llewlyn-Davies; that he
was prostrate when, in the *in loco parentis* role he so magnani-
mously adopted, he had to live with the death of George Llewlyn-
Davies in the First World War and the drowning of Michael Llewlyn-Davies in 1921. In some ways his life was played out on a vicarious level for he was a substitute David to his mother Margaret
Ogilvy and a substitute father to the Llewlyn-Davies boys. To Mary
Ansell he was a sham husband for 'Barrie was impotent and the
marriage had never been consummated'.[14] With so much playacting
and roleplaying in his career it is exquisitely apt that his creative
work managed to combine fantasy and wish-fulfilment in such a rewarding fashion. We must remember, though, that it was creative
and not confessional work.

Barrie was a writer with an instinctive appreciation of public taste and had an early success with a dramatisation of his novel *The Little Minister* (1897). His theatrical flair was confirmed by the charming period comedy *Quality Street* (1902) and *The Admirable Crichton* (1902) in which his eponymous butler represented a competent variant of the Figaro theme. *Peter Pan* (1904) cleverly exploited the Celtic myth of Tir nan Og. The play itself quickly assumed legendary proportions though its perennial appeal has eclipsed Barrie's more thoughtful plays. The notion that he deserted his Scottish origins is refuted by *What Every Woman Knows* (1908) in which Barrie put a convincingly calculating Scotsman, John Shand, on the London stage. Barrie may have valued success but he was able to appreciate the inhumanity that goes with the pursuit of success for its own sake. In John Shand he created a character who is familiar enough to his fellow countryman: the arrogant boor whose antics may be comic but whose nature is far from funny. In fact this emerges in an early exchange between Shand and David:

DAVID: You have a name here for high moral character.

JOHN: And justly.

DAVID: Are you serious-minded?

JOHN: I never laughed in my life.[15]

What London audiences found so amusing in Shand – his total humourlessness – is not guaranteed to raise a laugh in Scotland. Barrie's wit must have made him a misfit in Scotland and he took a humorous revenge by casting the stage Scot as John Shand with all his inconsistencies. Shand proclaims his pride but is not too proud to strike the celebrated bargain with the Wylies: £300 a year in exchange for a promise to wed Maggie. As we watch Shand's inexorable progress David makes his finely turned speech about the Scotsman on the make. The paradoxical conclusion to the play (in which it emerges that the ostensibly domestic Maggie is the power behind the throne) is an unflattering comment on the Scottish male, who depends on women while professing to be superior to them. For all the fun and games Barrie has with his characters he is astute enough to incorporate in the play his own cure for Scottish negativity, namely laughter. Shand condemns himself (and many of his countrymen) by failing to see the joke he represents:

JOHN: I never was one for fun. I cannot call to mind, Maggie, ever having laughed in my life.

MAGGIE: You have no sense of humour.

JOHN: Not a spark . . . I remember reading of some one that said it needed a surgical operation to get a joke into a Scotsman's head.

MAGGIE: Yes, that's been said.

JOHN: What beats me, Maggie, is how you could insert a joke with an operation.[16]

Barrie was equally effective on a smaller scale and his habit of poking fun at the success he was supposed to take so seriously is perfectly illustrated in his one-act play *The Twelve Pound Look* (1910). The central character, Sir Harry Sims, evaluates the world in terms of its commercial status; he possesses the cash-register mentality. Throughout the play Sir Harry's inflated ego seems to float over him like a bloated travesty of the conventional halo, then Barrie sharpens the drama to a point that pricks this bubble of pomposity. When Sir Harry's former wife, Kate, returns like a ghost to rattle the bones of his past before him he turns a blind eye to this apparition of the new woman. It is comic, of course, but not without an incisive cutting edge.

Barrie was not limited to plays about material success. In *Mary Rose* (1920) he drew on a more subtle side of his nature; the play is more like a dramatic expansion of a folk ballad than the usual drawing-room comedy associated with the London stage. The plot of *Mary Rose* is so simple – a young girl is enchanted on an island, and makes two disappearing acts into Tir nan Og – that there is a temptation to dismiss the play as a further instance of Barrie's temperamental infantilism for, like Peter Pan, Mary can never grow old. This temptation should be resisted in deference to the quality of Barrie's imagination. The second act of the play, set on the magical Outer Hebridean island, is beautifully controlled. Mary, married to Simon Blake, has come to the island in the company of the young Highlander Cameron who is the proverbial product of the Reformation: the Scotsman with a volume of Euripides in his pocket. The dialogue between Cameron and the young married couple shows how Barrie could mimic a Gaelic speaker's English speech-rhythms with more manners than mockery:

> CAMERON: It iss not Mr Blake's learning; he has not much learning, but I haf always undertood that the English manage without it. What I admire in you iss your ferry nice manners and your general deportment, in all of which I haf a great deal to learn yet, and I watch these things in Mr Blake and take memoranda of them in a little note-book.
>
> MARY ROSE: Mr Cameron, do tell me that I also am in the little note-book?
>
> CAMERON: You are not, ma'am, it would not be seemly in me. But it iss written in my heart, and also I haf said it to my father, that I will remain a bachelor unless I can marry some lady who iss ferry like Mistress Blake.[17]

46.   THE SCOTTISH NATIONAL PLAYERS

Had Barrie chosen to apply all his talent for speech to the Scottish theatre, using the sort of linguistic dexterity that distinguishes his story 'Farewell, Miss Julie Logan', modern Scotland might have had a great national dramatist to be proud of. However, he did not and it is idle to speculate on what might have been the case. In the event it was a much lesser talent, Dr John McIntyre (1869–1947), who tried to build a recognisably Scottish drama. McIntyre adopted the pseudonym John Brandane and acted on his belief that the first step to a national drama was a permanent theatre devoted to Scottish plays. In 1921 his *Glenforsa* (co-written with A. W. Yuill) helped launch the Scottish National Players who formed, the following year, the Scottish National Theatre Society with the avowed aim of establishing a Scottish National Theatre. Brandane's most substantial play, *The Glen is Mine*, was first performed at the Athenaeum, Glasgow, on 25 January 1923. Like *Glenforsa* it is set on the imaginary Hebridean island of Eilean Aros (actually Mull where Brandane had practised as a doctor). It uses the tension of a father-versus-son conflict (to avoid death duties Colonel Murray has made over his property to his son Charlie who intends to exploit it commercially) and sets Gaelic romanticism against Lowland realism. Appropriately enough the dialogue is given the benefit of pseudo-Gaelic speech-rhythms and it has been argued that Brandane's work consequently marks 'the point when Scottish drama was leaving the initial stages of imitation'.[18] It is doubtful if Brandane had any permanent influence on the direction of Scottish drama though his work with the Scottish National Players deserves to be remembered.

The Scottish National Players (who remained in existence until 1947) presented much work that has since been forgotten but the implicit notion they paraded of a Scottish National Theatre was so promising that each production was treated as a possible step in the creation of the ideal Scottish National Drama. Gordon Bottomley's *Gruach*, presented by the Scottish National Players at the Athenaeum on 20 March 1923, had an enormous impact; as astute an observer as George Blake wrote: 'I myself would select the first performance of Gordon Bottomley's *Gruach* ... as revealing to the young Scots playwright the larger possibilities of the native theme.'[19] Bottomley (1874–1948), the son of a Yorkshire businessman, was introduced to Scottish themes by his mother, Ann Maria Gordon. He was an enigmatic and backward-looking figure, well described as 'a Victorian whose roots were in the 'nineties'.[20] In 1913 he wrote *King Lear's Wife* as a retrospective prelude to *King Lear* and in 1918 *Gruach* as a retrospective prelude to *MacBeth*; The idea of inviting comparison with Shakespeare suggests vaulting ambition. Gruach, the future Lady MacBeth, is about to marry her cousin Conan, Thane of Fortingall, when she meets MacBeth. The two are instantly attracted and leave Fortingall Castle for the events that will form the basis of the Shakespearean drama. Conan is left with his own thoughts:

> If I touch Gruach
> I feel her body go hard beneath my hand,
> And danger crouching there: if she does nothing,
> She makes me feel outside her.
> I would not wed her if she had no land:
> The inconvenient wisdom of my mother
> Is not to be avoided; land is land.
> The knightly stranger shall not imperil it.[21]

Bottomley apparently believed that this sort of stilted verse would have a ready audience in Scotland; his hopes were never realised. Bottomley's work represented another false dawn. In contrast to the bookish mode of writing favoured by Bottomley there was a corresponding move to naturalism that at least located the roots of a native tradition in the making. Joe Corrie (1894–1968) provided a vigorously contemporary idiom that now seems fresher than the work of Brandane or Bottomley. Corrie was a miner and his proletarian pieces – *The Poacher* (1926) and *The Shillin' A Week Man* (1927) – were performed by the Scottish National Players, and are, whatever their structural faults, authentically of the people Corrie knew so well. Corrie was an accomplished poet and his verbal vivacity was engagingly exploited in his many one-act plays. One of them, *The Dreamer*, is set in the depressed 1930s and reveals the difficulties of escaping from an inhuman environment. Though the requirements of middle-class audiences would have inhibited a lesser man than Corrie he was able to compose poignant speeches demonstrating the eloquence of a stylised Scottish working-class speech. Mary remonstrates with her father about his defeatism:

> MARY: I left school to go and work on the pitheid. And noo ye want me to drift into the life that has made my mither an auld woman at forty-five . . . The same auld thing day after day. Never a blink o' sun gettin' into oor lives ava'. Ragged men standin' at street corners, weary weemin wi' hungry weans clingin' to their skirts. Chimneys pointin' to the sky and no' a wisp o' smoke comin' oot o' them; wheels rustin' in the air; and the hale toon becomin' yin great big slum. It's hell, Faither . . . hell!
>
> JOCK: Ach! it's no as bad as that, Mary.[22]

47.   JAMES BRIDIE: THE DOCTOR'S DILEMMA

In 1937 James Bridie gave the Galt Lecture to the Greenock Philosophical Society and included Brandane and Corrie in his list of Scottish dramatists. The catalogue is introduced with Bridie's usual levity:

Perhaps you have never heard of the Scottish theatre. If you have not, I
think it probable that you will before very long. In the meantime, it is
possible to see, in many towns and villages in Scotland, what Scottish
dramatists have found in the vein that seemed to be exhausted. Mr Joe
Corrie is bringing life out in the miner's row. Mr T. M. Watson has
found it in the mean streets. Mr Donald MacLaren has found West of
Scotland villages full of it. Mr John Brandane has filled the stage with
the smell of heather and peopled it with odd, delightful, distinctive
creatures. Mr Roxburgh and Miss Christine Orr in the East, Mr
Rowntree Harvey in the North-East, Mr Neil Gunn himself in the
North-West have discovered that the moon is not yet cold.

The Scottish theatre is still young and immature and its playwrights
have to pull hard against the collar. Its history is short and it is too soon
to expect greatness from it.[23]

Bridie did not include himself in that list yet his plays survive while
the other authors he mentions have been largely forgotten. Bridie,
unlike them, was the genuine article: an intuitive man of the
theatre.

In a Scottish theatrical context Bridie is a major figure: a man
whose plays were performed with success in Glasgow, London and
New York with no loss of Scottishness; a man who produced a complete oeuvre; a man who had the organisational drive to create institutions that would guarantee the future of drama in Scotland. In
an international context he is less significant, often reduced to the
level of Shaw's disciple. In a study of radicalism in modern drama,
for example, he merits only passing consideration:

This piquant Shavian combination – small electric shocks and 'massive
conversation pieces', to use Bridie's phrase – has proved a very
attractive, though terribly dangerous model for later playwrights.
Bridie's own comedy followed a similar pattern: he loved to open with
an outrageously improbable event, like the calling up of the devil in a
Scottish manse on a wet Sunday (*Mr Bolfry*) and move into a debate on
manners and morals, with the devil or equivalent character (an archangel
in *Tobias and the Angel*) leading the discussion. There are strong echoes
in that situation of the hell scene in Man and Superman. And there are
many other Shavian echoes in Bridie's comedy.[24]

There is no doubt that Bridie took from Shaw the notion of the
theatre as an arena for argument. At the same time he was the first
genuine dramatist to explore the Scottish psychology; he was in a
uniquely privileged position to do so.

James Bridie was born Osborne Henry Mavor in Glasgow on 3
January 1888, studied medicine at Glasgow University, and qualified
as a doctor in 1913. His profession was of great importance to his
theatrical outlook, for the doctor is circumvented by a strict ethical
code and is able to see human beings at their most vulnerable. Moral posturing and human fragility are the twin supports of Bridie's
stage. He invariably presents a moral dilemma in his plays and it is

usually a doctor's dilemma as in *The Switchback, A Sleeping Clergyman, The Anatomist, Dr Angelus*. Bridie took from Shaw the dramatically fascinating figure of the Superman then brought the Superman down to earth by confronting him with a conscience-stricken Everyman (or Everywoman). The Shavian Superman is a character we are asked to admire; Bridie's Supermen invoke more pity than admiration.

Bridie's first play, *The Switchback*, was written in 1922 (the year of *Ulysses* and *The Waste Land* and the debut of Hugh MacDiarmid) but rejected by Glasgow Repertory Theatre. The following year Bridie joined the board of the Scottish National Theatre Society and began an administrative interest in the theatre that would eventually lead to the founding of the Glasgow Citizens' Theatre in 1943 and the Glasgow College of Drama in 1950. In 1928 Tyrone Guthrie produced *The Sunlight Sonata* at Glasgow's Lyric Theatre and it was in the wake of this that *The Switchback* was first performed, on 9 March 1929, by the Birmingham Repertory Theatre.

The Switchback deals with the fall of a country doctor, Mallaby, who is corrupted by two visitors, Pascal and Burmeister, who offer him – respectively – fame and money. Mallaby has discovered a cure for tuberculosis but the premature announcement of this breakthrough brings down the wrath of the Royal Academy of Medicine. Mallaby is struck off the medical register, Mallaby's wife takes up with the wealthy Burmeister and Mallaby himself takes to drink before going off to Palmyra and the promise of a new beginning in archaeology. It is an interesting plot, handled with great stagecraft; Bridie's skill was apparent throughout and there is no hint of the apprentice in the making of the play. Mallaby is a megalomaniac who wants only the kingdom of heaven regardless of the consequences for others. This was a theme Bridie was to make his own.

Bridie's most successful early play, *The Anatomist*, was first performed on 6 July 1930 at the Lyceum Theatre, Edinburgh; a year later Tyrone Guthrie staged it at the Westminster Theatre, thus ensuring that Bridie's first London production would be a memorable one. The play is arguably the finest piece of drama conceived in Scotland since Lyndsay's *Thrie Estatis*. In his Author's Note to *The Anatomist* Bridie is typically self-effacing about his creation of the hero, as if it were a simple matter of editing:

> The principal figure is Robert Knox, the anatomist, who was so
> theatrical in his life and habit that it is possible to transfer him almost
> bodily to the stage. A few heightened effects have been added, and his
> rhetorical style has been adapted slightly to fit modern standards, but I
> believe the character as it stands in the play is a fair deduction from what
> we know of the man.[25]

In fact the character of Knox is a masterly piece of invention; he is recast as the archetypal Bridie Superman, a person so enraptured by his intellectual superiority that he is convinced he is beyond good and evil.

The play opens in 1828 in a withdrawing room in Edinburgh; Dr Knox comes to the home of the Dishart sisters, Mary and Amelia, to obtain some light relief in flute-playing. Before Knox makes his entrance it is obvious that he inspires both devotion and dread: his disciple, Walter Anderson, adores him whereas Walter's fiancee, Mary, finds him repulsive. Like other Bridie heroes, Knox has an affectation of omniscience and is given to massive generalisations:

> KNOX: The vulgarian , the quack and the theologian are confronted with the Universe. They at once begin to talk and talk and talk. They have no curiosity. They know all about it. They build a mean structure of foolish words and phrases, and say to us, 'This is the World.' The comparative anatomist *has* curiosity. He institutes a divine search for facts. He is unconcerned with explanations and theories. In time, when you and I are dead, his facts will be collected and their sum will be the Truth. Truth that will show the noblest thing in creation, how to live. Truth that will shatter the idol Mumbo Jumbo, before which man daily debases his magnificence.[26]

Some critics – like Helen L. Luyben in her book *James Bridie: Clown and Philosopher* (1965) – have puzzled over the author's ambiguous attitude to such figures as Knox. Bridie's fondness for the megalomaniac surely lies in the impressive verbal flourish of megalomaniac outpourings. After all, his was a drama of discussion. Dr Knox condemns those who 'talk and talk and talk'; McCrimmon, in *Mr Bolfry*, condemns 'Rhetoric! Rhetoric! Rhetoric!'[27] Mary Queen of Scots, in *John Knox*, condemns 'sermons, sermons, sermons'.[28] Yet Bridie's plays are precisely made of words, rhetoric and sermons. Structurally they comprise a series of incidents leading up to a vocal clash between Superman and his accuser. In Bridie's Scottish drama opposites attract, often fatally.

To illustrate this we need only look at the way the domestic affairs of Act I give way to the realistic conflict of Act II in *The Anatomist*. Walter has been rejected by Mary and seeks solace in a low drinking dive in the Canongate. He is approached by two Edinburgh girls out for a good time. In his drunkenness Walter substitutes this Mary for his own Mary before falling into a fitful sleep. At this point the bodysnatchers, Burke and Hare, enter and Bridie handles their Irish speech with humour and accuracy:

> BURKE: It's a fine night, Mister Nebby, glory be to God, an' I'm that dry that me throat feels the like of the insides of a lime-kiln. Will you give us a couple gills of malt? An' be quick about it.
>
> NEBBY: Hae you the siller to pay for it?
>
> BURKE: Silver is it? Holy St Joseph, will you listen to him, Bill! Silver is it? There's what's better than silver, a note. And you can take an' nail it

to the counter, if you've a mind to, so long as we have drink for the worth of it.[29]

Burke and Hare subsequently make off with Mary and when Walter is sober enough to show up at Dr Knox's rooms he recognises the corpse and realises that his idol is the patron of the bodysnatchers.

The final act of *The Anatomist* mixes farce and melodrama. Bridie could assume that audiences were already familiar with the facts of the Burke and Hare case: how Hare gave evidence against his accomplice who was hanged. Given this inevitable outcome Bridie counterpoints it against a little romance: the reconciliation of Walter and Mary and Knox's attempt to woo Amelia. Knox is sufficiently shaken by scandal to admit his responsibility for the deaths of those he regarded as insignificant means to a glorious end. He also admits to Amelia that he feels overwhelmed by her femininity:

KNOX: You understand me so well. You see the little pink shivering boy crouching within this grotesque, this grisly shell of a body. You are sunshine to me, Amelia. You are safe harbourage in storms. I love you. You are everything to me. I love you.[30]

It is an incongruous moment, the sort of situation Bridie relishes: the Superman reduced to his innate insecurity.

One of the triumphs of *The Anatomist* is the way Bridie manages several layers of linguistic activity. Knox is astonishingly eloquent, often carried away by his verbose logic; Walter attempts to duplicate Knox's speech but, when drunk, lapses into genteel Scots; Burke and Hare talk in broad Irish accents; and the Dishart maid uses Scots. It is characteristic of Bridie's sense of humour that Amelia should learn the details of Burke's execution through an outrageous pun. The Disharts have been on holiday and have to be informed about the reason for the civic unrest.

MAID: But is was the croods, Mem. A' the gangrel buddies in the toun raging roun' the streets, crying, 'Gie us Hare! Gie us Hare!'

AMELIA: Give us whose hair? Do compose yourself, Jessie Ann.[31]

As Amelia is slow to grasp the horror of the situation the maid has to spell it out to her and when she does so Bridie shows how expertly he could use Scots in a theatrical situation:

MAID: The riots, Mem. Ower the heid o' the hanging. Burke, Mem. I saw them hang him wi' my own eyes, Mem. Fornenst my Auntie's hoose in the High Street. Faces on a' the causies and faces at a' the windies. And oh, ye should ha' seen him, Mem. He'd a naipkin ower his heid. And a big fellow in a black surtout took awa' what he was staunin' on, Mem. And he played paw paw for it wi' his feet and syne birled roond three times. And syne he gied a kin' o' a hunch wi' his shouthers and syne he hung still. And oh! I was feart, Mem![32]

Patriotic purists might be disappointed that Bridie reserved his Scots for tertiary characters; he wanted his captive audience to understand every syllable.

In the 1930s Bridie consolidated his reputation with *Tobias and the Angel* (1930) and *A Sleeping Clergyman* (1933). The biblical drama uses the reductive technique of bringing exalted characters down to earth; Tobias is lifted from the Book of Tobit and transformed into a picaresque hero who can take care of himself. *A Sleeping Clergyman*, which Bridie considered his masterpiece, is a polemical work which takes an argumentative stand against genetic determinism. For Bridie, God is not dead but simply nodding: he is the titular sleeping clergyman and is described, in the stage directions, as a huge white-bearded figure. The human drama that unfolds does not rouse God from his slumber, the inference being that modern life is not divinely ordained but simply what the participants make of it.

Charlie Cameron, a medical Superman in search of a cure for the ills of humanity, is dying of tuberculosis in his squalid rooms. He is visited by Dr William Marshall, then by Marshall's sister Harriet who tells Cameron she is carrying his child. Cameron, above such things as cosy domesticity, asserts his egoism immediately:

CAMERON: If I was sure I was going to die, I believe I'd marry you all right. But I'm not going to die. I'm going to fight and work and live, and I'm going to fight without any long-haired, soft-skinned, piping-voiced bag of whims and vapours hanging round my neck. And you can make up your mind to that – you 'recreation of the warrior.'[33]

When Cameron dies, in spite of his own prediction to the contrary, his landlady, Mrs Hannah, enunciates the theme of the play:

MRS HANNAH: It's a bad end you'll come to, aye, and your children and your grandchildren if you have any. Bad all through. Bad to the bone.[34]

Cameron's bastard, Wilhelmina, is raised by Dr Marshall and the gossips confidently expect her to turn out to be a carbon copy of her father:

OLD LADY: This man Cameron was almost a maniac. He was bad through and through, body and soul. He had consumption. He drank. He stole money from Will. He had all sorts of unmentionable associates. The kindest thing to think was that he was insane. And there you are. You see what I mean.

YOUNG LADY: I see. Heredity . . . I mean, I've read a lot about it, and it's awful. You have it running through generation after generation. A lot of us think something ought to be done – oh, well – to prevent people like that getting married at all. But, then, they didn't get married.[35]

This folklore about the sins of the father being visited on the child seems to be apt enough with regard to Wilhelmina who poisons the father of her illegitimate twins, an act witnessed by Dr Marshall. However, Cameron's grandchildren, Charles and Hope, are living contradictions of the perniciously ignorant talk of heredity. Charles discovers a wonder cure for the world's ills while Hope works her own wonders on the League of Nations. *A Sleeping Clergyman* is a play that transcends its own didactic programme. The action is more dramatic than is usually conceded in a Bridie play and the dialogue sustains a sense of urgency.

In a long productive career Bridie added several plays to the British repertoire and showed that Scotsmen need not be stagey caricatures. He was quintessentially Scottish in his choice of thematic material which illustrated the coexistence of divinity and banality in individuals. Bridie had a wide range, being able to produce serious plays, diabolic diversions like *Mr Bolfry* (1943), biblical dramas, and farces like *What Say They?* (1939) and *It Depends on What You Mean* (1944). Always he was alert to the Scottish character. In later years he began to retrace some of his own steps. *John Knox* (1947) is little more than a theatrical redaction of documentary sources; *Dr Angelus* (1947) is a variant on *The Anatomist*. Cyril Angelus, a hero modelled on the Glasgow murderer Dr Pritchard, poisons his mother-in-law and his wife but feels spiritually justified in doing so as it enables him to survive with his irresponsibility intact. It is not a conventional thriller – there is never any doubt as to Angelus's guilt – but a pathological presentation of megalomania. To achieve the necessary depth Bridie introduces two secondary characters who represent innocence and experience: Johnson, Angelus's naive assistant; and Sir Gregory Butt, a cynical old man. When these two first meet Bridie presents them as complementary forces whose alliance will destroy Angelus (whose name suggests the fallen angel rather than a melodramatic figure of pure evil). The extremes suggested by Johnson and Butt give rise to some fine comic touches: Bridie's vision of the world is basically a recreation of a Scottish divine comedy. Hugh MacDiarmid, who was not given to showering easy praise on anyone, said of Bridie: 'It is far from absurd to call him the Scottish George Bernard Shaw. He was unquestionably the greatest playwright – the only really great one even – Scotland has yet had.'[36]

48. SPEAKING SCOTS: ROBERT McLELLAN

In Bridie's work the dream of Scottish drama was a reality, even if his critics found him altogether too flippant and too wasteful of what was a large talent. Bridie had shown that to be born in Scotland was

not an impossible burden for a dramatist. A less commercial playwright who was never to achieve the output (nor the recognition) of
Bridie did address himself directly to the creation of a Scottish
National Drama. As Alexander Reid put it: 'Bridie had put a thinking head on the shoulders of the new theatre. It was McLellan's
great service to put a Scots tongue in the Scots head.'[37] Robert
McLellan (b. 1907) had been influenced by MacDiarmid's resuscita-
tion of Scots and felt he could avail himself of this in his attempt to
build completely Scottish plays. He delved into Scottish folklore for
Jeddart Justice (1934) and *Toom Byres* (1936); produced a satirical
comedy on clerical standards in *The Hypocrite* (1967); and revitalised Scottish history in his finest play, *Jamie the Saxt*, which was first
performed in Glasgow's Lyric Theatre, by the Curtain Theatre
Company, in 1937.

The problem for the dramatist was how to combine the rhythm of
oral Scots with the artificiality of dictionary Scots. A synthetic language can work perfectly for poetry which is a literary law unto itself; in the theatre the speech must sound dramatic, must communicate instantly. McLellan not only managed a fluent Scots but could
take liberties with the language in the interests of character dif-
ferentiation. A good example of this is the treatment of Queen
Anne who uses, in *Jamie the Saxt*, what MacDiarmid (in *A Drunk
Man Looks at the Thistle*) called 'wild fowl Scots' – an equivalent of
pigeon English. On her first appearance, in Act I, she is trapped in
her Danish accent as she bandies words with Ballie Morrison and
Laird Logie:

THE QUEEN: See, the last time I see ye I couldna speak. I speak nou.
Logie he say I hae a guid Scots tongue in my heid afore lang.

LOGIE: Yer Grace, ye talk like a native already.

THE QUEEN: Ah Logie, ye flaitter me. But Bailie. My Leddy Vinstar.
Ye haena met her. She is my freind frae Denmark. Margaret, this is the
Bailie Morison. He is a magistrate of the Toun. He is gey, what ye say,
kenspeckle. And he is gey weill-aff. He has mony ships that sail to
Flanders. Eh, Bailie?

BAILLIE M: Weill, ane or twa.

THE QUEEN: Ane or twa. He disnae ken. But ke kens fine. He daesna
like to, what ye say, blaw his ain horn, eh?[38]

Jamie the Saxt deals with the relationship between James VI and
Francis Stewart, 5th Earl of Bothwell, whose maniacal plots
threatened the stability of Scotland. Bothwell (whose father was a
bastard son of James V and whose mother was the sister of Mary
Queen of Scots' Bothwell) was, historically, an audacious man
while James VI's caution bordered on cowardice. In McLellan's play
the king appears as a typically Scottish henpecked husband who has
enough to contend with without the intervention of his illegitimate

kinsman. Jamie is full of sound and fury and signifies, thanks to his royal position, something significant for Scotland. He was, after all, the king whose Anglophilia deprived Scotland of its crown in 1603. McLellan does not treat the king as a complete fool but gives the man a certain shrewdness.

The play opens in 1591 when Jamie is under pressure and reacting with panic. He is worried about Bothwell's diabolism and the hostility of the Kirk. He is, comically, a man *in extremis* who tells his court so:

THE KING: Ye're traitors, ilka ane o ye! Ye wad hae yer King gang ilka day in terror o his life! What kind o country's this, that Bothwell's alloued to leive? Has he no made sic a wrack o the Palace that I canna bide in it? Has he no haen aa the witches in Lothian raisin storms on the watter whan I was crossin ower wi Annie there frae Denmark? Has he no haen dizzens o them stickin preens in my cley corp, and brewin pousins for me oot o puddock's bluid? And ye mak a steer, certies, because we hae sent oot a warrant against ane o his closest freinds![39]

Jamie is, in other words, that egregious Scottish figure – the blamer. Everyone is out of step bar himself; though titular head of Scotland he cannot control the country and has to content himself seeking out scapegoats.

In Act II Jamie is face to face with Bothwell whose strength of character emphasises the weakness of the king. Here the reductive manner is used to bring out the humour of the situation. The spectacle of a king caught with his trousers down is too good a comic situation for McLellan to miss and he understandably makes a set-piece of the scene:

BOTHWELL: Gin ye dinnae gie in I'll cairry ye owe to the winnock juist as ye are!

THE KING: (*Almost in tears*) Aa richt. I'll gie in the nou. But by God wait!

BOTHWELL: (To ATHOLI) Whaur are his breeks?

THE KING: They're in the closet.

BOTHWELL: Fetch his breeks, Lennox.

LENNON: (*indignantly*) My Lord, ye forget yersell'.

OCHILTREE: I'll fetch them . . . (*coming in from the closet*) This is the only pair I can fin.

BOTHWELL: They'll dae. Help him into them.[40]

In that exchange the great men of history are cut down to the size of childish participants in a drama whose importance escapes them.

In the fourth and final act of the play the extent of Bothwell's perfidy is revealed as he is discovered to be in league with the Papists. Jamie now has Bothwell in a trap and is ready to assert himself. At last the king has come of age and chooses his moment of triumph to indulge in a spot of *schadenfreude*; he gloats on the fall of his foes and anticipates, with pleasure, his English coronation. The king's feelings are conveyed in Scots that is both sensuous and dramatically apposite:

> THE KING: Aa that I hae wished for is promised at last! Bothwell on the
> scaffold, the Papists houndit doun, the Kirk in my pouer, England ahint
> me, and then, in the end, the dream o my life come true! It gars my
> pulse quicken! It gars my hairt loup! It gars my een fill wi tears! To think
> hou the twa pair countries hae focht and struggled. To think o the bluid
> they hae shed atween them, the touns they hae blackent wi fire, the
> bonnie green howes they hae laid waste. And then to think, as ae day it
> sall come to pass, that I, Jamie Stewart, will ride to London, and the twa
> countries sall become ane.[41]

Jamie the Saxt was an experiment that modestly succeeded; Scots could work on the stage and be the stuff of entertaining comedy without forcing audiences to rush to the etymological dictionary. However, there was a limitation implicit in the experiment, for the Scots-writing dramatist ran the risk of appealing only to the minority of Scots who were willing to pay for the Scottish National Drama – and there were few of them. English audiences were suspicious of the Scots tongue and, in Scotland itself, the notion persisted that the stage was a hallowed temple where actors spoke in the tongues of Angles. McLellan's language did not travel the way O'Casey's did and depended on the participation of accomplished Scots speakers: Duncan MacRae, for example, gave the first performance of *Jamie the Saxt* a virtuoso presentation, as did Ron Bain, as Jamie, in the 1982 revival of the play by the Scottish Theatre Company.

49.   UNITY AND DISUNITY

While the New Scottish Drama had a voice it had no permanent venue. The Scottish National Theatre Society was wound up in 1934 though the Scottish National Players remained in existence until 1947. Bridie, with the backing of the Council for the Encouragement of Music and the Arts, founded the Glasgow Citizens' Theatre in 1943 (and built on this by founding the first school of drama in Scotland, the College of Drama of the Royal Scottish Academy of Music, in 1950). Some Scots felt Bridie was too much a pillar of the establishment to operate as unopposed leader of Scottish drama and, impressed by the activities of London's Unity Theatre Club (founded 1936), set up a Glasgow branch of Unity. Glasgow Unity Theatre began as an amateur organisation and made its professional start in 1946. The company had some notable successes – with

Robert McLeish's *The Gorbals Story*, James Barke's *Major Operation* and, perhaps their most powerful production, George Munro's *Gold in His Boots* (1947) which dealt with football as Scotland's main religion – but found it ultimately impossible to continue without Arts Council money. Bridie, incidentally, is said to have had a hand in removing Glasgow Unity's subsidy.[42] Though Glasgow Unity failed to create mass support for its politically committed productions it did encourage some outstanding actors who cherished the vigour of the proletarian theatre. One of them, Roddy McMillan, was to become closely involved with the director Bill Bryden whose own proletarian dramas recalled the aspirations of Glasgow Unity.

50. HISTRIONIC HISTORY: REID TO KEMP

In 1948 the Guthrie production of *The Three Estates* represented a summit in twentieth century Scottish drama (though the play itself was from another era). Here, vividly enacted before packed audiences, was the vitality the Scottish drama had once possessed. Robert Kemp's version, which stripped an epic down to manageable proportions, seemed not only magnificent but, in its satirical verve, supremely relevant to Scotland. McLellan, it seemed, had been right: Scots was fit for the stage. The challenge was there for modern Scottish dramatists to respond to. Two of them did, though in vastly different ways, Alexander Reid's *The Lass Wi' the Muckle Mou'* – first performed by the East Lothian Repertory Company at Dunbar on 24 October 1950 and later by Glasgow Citizens at Ayr – gave Scotland a modern comedy that is constantly revived.

When Reid published *Two Scots Plays* in 1958 (the other play being *The World's Wonder*, about Michael Scott, the original Wizard of the North) he felt it necessary to preface the book with a polemical declaration of intent:

> The Scottish dramatist, so far as his intentions are serious, is not, as so many people still seem to think, trying to write an English kind of play about Scotland or elsewhere in Scots. He is trying to make an original Scottish contribution to world drama which will be as distinct from the English contribution as the English contribution is from the French, American or Russian . . . Scottish literature and the Scottish use of language can be separated in theory and not in practice. For two hundred years we have been trying to write like Englishmen and at the end of it we can only say with enormous labour what a native English writer, otherwise of equal power, says spontaneously out of nature.[43]

Reid's play is an extension of the old ballad of Thomas the Rymer. True Thomas, after an agreeable sojourn with the Queen of Elfland, has come back to the real world to find material for a ballad. As the essence of balladry relies on narrative immediacy Thomas is looking for a ready-made tale (which turns out to be the plot of the play):

THOMAS: I've got it aa charted oot in my heid. I want a story – a true yin, mind you! – that begins wi some sort of a struggle – a fecht, if possible. Then, it's got to hae a dollop of sentiment in it, for the weemen ye ken. Eftir that I want a grand climax in which the key character has to make a desperate choice atwixt true glory and mere warldly considerations. Hinnermaist I need a pathetic ending – for that's my speciality.[44]

When Thomas arrives at the home of Sir Gideon Murray he finds the real world is artistically unpromising. Instead of the anticipated feud between the Murrays and the Scotts, Sir Gideon is languishing in hypochondriacal inactivity. Sir Gideon explains the tribulations of the peaceful life:

SIR GIDEON: Things are very different on the border syne you were here last. The days o the pike are done, man. They're done. D'ye ken this? . . . Things are that centralised wi the king in Embro noo that a man canna hing yin o his ain tenants on his ain gallows wi'oot some birkie fae Holyrood pokin' his neb in and spierin awkward questions.

THOMAS: Man, ye'll be tellin' me there's nae mair fechtin in a meenit!'

SIR GIDEON: There isna, Thomas. There hasna been a fray here for twa years . . .

THOMAS: It soonds awfa dreich.[45]

Thomas is, of course, appalled at this state of affairs for he is already under a severe artistic handicap: the Queen of Elfland had denied him poetic licence, forced him to tell only the truth in the making of his ballad. Fortunately for Thomas a Border skirmish develops between the old enemies; the Murrays capture Willie Scott and offer to spare his life only if he will marry Meg Murray whose massive mouth is a figment of the folk imagination (thanks to a vindictive rhyme of Thomas's). Thomas does his best to persuade Willie to choose the gallows rather than matrimony but love – or the love of survival – conquers all at the close of the play. Thomas is left with no alternative but to return to Elfland and his queenly muse.

Reid, in this play, has used the past in a theatrically impressive way: rather than pedantically choosing a celebrated historical event he has chosen to draw on the timeless dimension of the traditional ballads. There is nothing quaint or antiquarian about *The Lass Wi' the Muckle Mou'*; it is a fine atmospheric comedy that carries its Scots learning lightly. Whereas some Scots plays are thinly disguised political statements about the condition of Scotland, Reid's comedy owes its durability to its dramatic objectivity.

In 1948 Sydney Goodsir Smith was one of those enthralled by

Guthrie's production of *The Three Estates*; consequently he decided to produce his own play for the open stage. Smith, a fervent Scottish Nationalist, wanted a patriotic hero who could rouse Scotland from its apathy, for the intention of his play is to provoke the moral indignation of a Scottish audience. Smith's *The Wallace* was first staged in the Assembly Hall at the 1960 Edinburgh International Festival and proved a popular focus of political discussion. *The Wallace* lacks dramatic subtlety for the hero has no tragic flaw; even his inordinate pride is justified by Smith. The tragedy of *The Wallace* (which is revealingly subtitled 'A Triumph in Five Acts') is that the hero is forsaken by his peers. If there had been more Wallaces, so the logic of the play runs, Scotland would have won a substantial victory sooner than Bannockburn. Moroever, as Wallace is presented as Bruce's moral superior in the play, that freedom would have been that more permanent.

As a romantic poet first and foremost Smith could no more avoid rhetoric than he could avoid baring his nationalistic convictions in public. In Act I, Wallace arrives as a very parfit knight. He has married Mirren Bradefute and come to her Lanark home for the bridal. On learning that the Sheriff of Lanark has made amorous advances to Mirren, he rushes out for revenge; while he is away the Sheriff comes and kills Mirren. Wallace is horrified at the spectacle but his grief turns to heroic determination and he vents his feelings in a lyrical speech:

> We'll greit
> Nae mair, but cry up daith and fire,
> Destruction! Ah, Mirren! Here was
> The Maist beauteous flouer o' the flock,
> Here was my luve, here Scotland
> Incarnate, the White Rose breathin
> In a lassie's form . . . [46]

Act II is set in Wallace's headquarters in the Tor Wood near Falkirk. Wallace has a great victory (Stirling) behind him and is ready to drive Edward I out of Scotland. Despite his triumph he is unable to get the Scottish nobility to rally round him in sufficient numbers. Here the internal divisiveness of Scotland is well expressed. Wallace's creed is simple and straightforward:

> Monie a man has deed, my lord,
> And monie mair will dee or Scotland
> Breathes free air again. [47]

The Scottish nobles cannot, however, bring themselves to serve under Wallace because he is their social inferior. As Bruce puts it:

> We canna serve under ye, Wallace,
> Nae mair nor could ye under a tapster.
> Ye hae nae rank. [48]

With friends as opportunistic as Bruce and Comyn, Wallace's efforts are vitiated. His magnanimity is played out against the petty squabbling of the nobles; thus Smith's hero is not only a leader of men but a man of the people who puts his faith in the folk:

> In the end, my friends,
> We've nane but the folk; they've nocht
> To loss but life and libertie
> But gin we've them, we've aa. They're Scotland,
> Nane ither.[49]

Wallace then goes his way to certain defeat and as Act III opens at the court of Edward I in Stirling in 1304 we learn – from the counterpointed chroniclers who introduce each act – that Wallace now lives the life of an outlaw. In a rather gratuitous moment Edward I has some recalcitrant Scots humiliated for the entertainment of his guests and he is clearly cast in the role of stage villain.

After Edward I has arranged the capture of Wallace (which takes place in Act IV) the finale of the play, set in the Great Hall of Westminster, consists of a debate between Edward I and Wallace. Wallace, of course, wins hands down. His execution is a matter of routine and here Smith bends history by having Edward I offer a dukedom to Wallace who naturally treats the offer with contempt. When Wallace's brutal sentence is read out Bruce springs to his feet and declares undying opposition to England, a gesture that ensures Wallace has the last laugh and, indeed, the stage directions have Wallace laughing as he is taken away to be butchered.

Though *The Wallace* can be treated as a piece of special pleading rather than a play it is a brave venture. Few Scottish dramatists have attempted to write on such a grand scale; it is a mighty conception marred by inexpert execution. Still, it would be wrong to convey the impression that Scottish drama progressed solely on the basis of single memorable plays for any movement needs its day-to-day momentum. This was provided in the 1940s and 1950s by several writers, two of whom should be cited with honour. Alexander Scott (see p. 53) did much to give Scots prominence in the 1950s. He wrote three verse plays in Scots – *The Jerusalem Farers* (1951), *The Last Time I Saw Paris* (1951) and *Untrue Thomas* (1952) – and had three full-length satirical comedies produced by Glasgow Citizens. One of these, *Right Royal* (1954), has been successfully revived on radio and television and at Perth under the direction of Ian Cuthbertson. More pertinently, Robert Kemp, the son of a minister, used much of his energy to enrich the theatrical life of Scotland. As chairman of the Gateway Company in Edinburgh from 1953 to 1960 he helped instil theatre-going habits in Edinburgh; and as the man responsible for the modern version of Lyndsay's *The Three Estates* he had a shaping hand in one of the supreme moments of twentieth century Scottish drama.

Kemp was a clever craftsman who brought a real polish to the genre of the Scottish historical play. *A Trump for Jericho* (originally *Walls of Jericho*) – performed by the Scottish National Players in 1947 – is set in an Edinburgh rocked by the theological Disruption of 1843 and Kemp continued to evoke Scotland's past: *The Saxon Saint* (1949) presents the ostensibly pious Saint Margaret as a formidable figure instrumental in transforming Celtic Scotland into a feudal state on the English model. In 1951 *The King of Scots* was performed in the nave of Dunfermline Abbey (where Robert the Bruce is buried) and *The Other Dear Charmer* was performed by Glasgow Citizens at Ayr. The second of these plays, revolving around the epistolary courtship between Robert Burns and Mrs Agnes McLehose, is perhaps the most sensitive thing Kemp composed. The poet appears as a sexual opportunist rather than an incurable romantic; his final decision to choose Jean Armour in preference to the Edinburgh grass widow reflects a pragmatic wish to shelter behind the tolerance of his ain folk. It was predicable, given Kemp's background, that he would eventually essay a play on the great Reformer; *Master John Knox* (1960) was commissioned by a special committee appointed by the Church of Scotland to mark the fourth centenary of the Reformation. As in Bridie's play on the same subject, Kemp is often content to reproduce the recorded words of the principals. When the common folk have their say the play is lifted on to a more imaginative level:

SERGEANT: Aye, Jock, guid morrow to you! And my auld friend Cuddie! How's times?

CUDDIE: Gey thin!

SERGEANT: Then you'll be ready for my news! There's wark for us, fellows!

CUDDIE: I'll believe that when I see my first week's pay!
Och, there's plenty wark o' a kind, I'll no deny,
But what true soldier would tak service
Wi' our Scots lords, aye adding to their tails,
But never wi' siller for their wages?
I'd rather beg my bread![50]

The practitioners of the Scottish National Drama produced good plays without ever producing an undeniably great one. Probably this was due to a failure of nerve, a compulsion to forever play for safety. Donald Campbell sees it differently and his attitude is worth recording:

So what went wrong? Why did Robert Kemp die without writing the masterpiece of which he was so obviously capable . . . ? Why has Alexander Reid fallen silent and why has Alexander Scott steadfastly and determinedly refused . . . even to consider writing another play? Most important of all, why did Robert McLellan (arguably the finest playwright that Scotland has produced in recent times) turn his back on theatre writing twenty years ago? . . . To my mind, the real explanation of the demise of that particular school of Scottish dramatists lies in a . . . sinister direction. The theatre in Scotland at that time was the most anglicised area of Scottish life, with the great majority of its denizens having a vested interest in a career structure whose pinnacle lay in London. Since most of these people had nothing to gain (and a great deal to fear) from a theatre in Scotland that was anything more than an off-shoot of provincial English theatre, they regarded the New Scottish Drama as a threat to their livelihoods – and correspondingly killed it.[51]

That conclusion is worthy of inclusion in a whodunnit and omits to acknowledge that the Scottish National Drama did not die away; it faded away in the 1960s and returned in the 1970s with younger writers like Campbell himself replacing Kemp, Scott, Reid, Smith and McLellan.

51.   A SMALL STAGE: SCOTTISH DRAMA IN THE 1960s

In the 1960s a more subdued style of drama was favoured in Scotland and tended to emanate from the Traverse Theatre Club which was founded, in Edinburgh in 1963, by the young American impresario Jim Haynes. The Traverse increased its grip on the Scottish theatrical conciousness when Giles Havergal took over the artistic direction of the Glasgow Citizens' Theatre in 1969 and studiously avoided native Scottish plays. Stanley Eveling, who was born in Newcastle upon Tyne in 1925, came to Edinburgh in 1960 to teach philosophy at Edinburgh University:

> What drew me to the Scottish theatre was being in Edinburgh at the time of the opening of the Traverse and it being the sort of place that would want to put on the sort of plays I then wanted to write. Since I am a Geordie I can't either claim or perceive any Scottishness in my plays although I suppose there is a sort of rough northern character to them.[52]

Eveling began by refining Absurdist conventions then developed a more robust style in which his love of paradox and irony could be related to realistic, and disturbing, situations. *Come and Be Killed* (1967), in which a superficial young man is made to face the reality of the abortion he has so kindly arranged for a girlfriend, is a theatrically strong idea in action. Eveling has still to improve on it.

Cecil Taylor, another leading light of the Traverse during the 1960s, began with very definite notions on the nature of the theatre but later settled into community drama work in Northumberland. He was born in Glasgow in 1929, grew up in its Jewish community

and died in his native city in 1981. Like Arnold Wesker, he found
the Jewish working-class ambiance propelled him into political activism. For him the theatre was the stage on which would be enacted
the contours of the coming revolution. He was forced to rethink his
position and came to favour a less strident programme:

> A gradual scaling down is the best description of my development as a
> playwright. Starting with the aim of the theatre as a potent instrument of
> the revolution, I have been beaten down to theatre as another of the
> communication arts. I used to write plays . . . genuinely convinced they
> would move the workers, by the insights they gave into great political
> truths, to the revolution. I now write plays . . . to communicate my
> narrow, odd vision of the world as I see it at the time of writing.[53]

Taylor's play *Allergy*, produced at the Traverse in 1966, was
calculated to alienate earnest left-wing politicos as it took their most
sacred beliefs as the stuff of comedy. It is, fundamentally, a triangular sex situation with political overtones. Jim, editor of a socialist
journal regularly preaches to the converted (all 200 of them) in his
sectarian editorials. He has come to a cottage in Ross to write a
treatise on Marxism; into his fantasy life comes a determinedly un-
conventional couple. Christopher works as a journalist but keeps his
conscience clean by writing for Jim's journal. Barbara is convinced
that she and Christopher will become financially independent from
the proceeds of her typing and his creative writing. Christopher's
confidence about rearranging the world is undermined by his terror
of disturbing his personal serenity. He, a married man with children, comes, out in a rash at the thought of having an affair with
Barbara. While she is out of the room he shows Jim the red marks
of his sexual martyrdom:

> CHRISTOPHER: I've had slight attacks when I even started getting
> ideas . . . One of the girls in the office . . . Long, red hair . . . combed
> straight down . . . You know what it is. It's an allergy.
>
> JIM: To women?
>
> CHRISTOPHER: To adultery.
>
> JIM: Impossible.
>
> CHRISTOPHER: I'm telling you[54]

This preposterous situation is developed by Taylor to illustrate
the timorous nature of the kitchen revolutionaries. When Barbara
sees the rash she cannot countenance an affair with Christopher who
angrily leaves her to Jim's tender mercies. *Allergy* is anecdotal and
as slight as the easy targets involved; *Bread and Butter* (1967) is a
bigger play on a bigger theme. It spans thirty-four years in the lives
of two Glasgow Jews, Alec and Morris, and depicts the erosion of
their political aspirations as they abandon their youthful idealism
and sink into middle-aged apathy.

Although there are comically ridiculous assertions in the play, as when Morris acknowledges that, while no Marx or Lenin, he has 'something to contribute to Socialist thought – a few original ideas'[55], the play amounts to a poignant study of self-deception. Alec and Morris proclaim their belief in dynamic change and human dignity but constantly resort to self-pity:

MIRIAM: We can be sure whatever happens, we'll never starve, or freeze. And we'll always have a roof over our heads.

ALEC: And bread and butter. I can make a meal out of bread and butter. Good, tasty white bread with thick yellow butter, with salt. I'm telling you. We should never have anything worse to eat in our lives than good wholesome bread and butter![56]

As the full horror of the twentieth century unfolds, vicariously, for Alec and Morris their response never rises above self-interest. Everything is grist for their mill of conversation; they chatter while the world burns. It is a finely written play and Morris's despairing speech at the end is a well-drawn character's final articulation of his predicament:

MORRIS: You're right, Alec. Who am I to criticize anybody? Over half a century, and what have I achieved? . . . What have I done? What have I achieved? So I stopped buying South African fruit. They're still persecuting niggers there. So I marched against the bomb. They're building bigger and better ones. So I protested against Hitler's anti-Jew laws. He killed off six million of us! I went round and collected money for the Spanish Republic. Franco's still killing off Communists there. What was it all for? Where did it get us, Alec? What's the meaning of it all, Alec? My head's swimming, Alec. I just keep turning it this way and that way. I'm at the end of the road.[57]

Taylor's images of self-induced hopelessness are integrated into the verbal fabric of a thoughtful play.

Asked about his reaction to the much-vaunted Scottish Dramatic Revival of the 1970s Cecil Taylor replied: 'I'm not sure when people talk about a revival in Scottish drama, if they aren't really ignorant of the fact that Stewart Conn, Stanley Eveling and myself had already revived it many years before.'[58] Conn, born in Glasgow in 1936, has been not only a dramatist but, in his role as radio producer with the BBC, a patron of Scottish drama. His *I Didn't Always Live Here*, produced at the Glasgow Citizens' in 1967, is set in contemporary Glasgow and uses flashbacks to the 1930s (Act I), the Second World War (Act II) and the postwar period (Act III) to disrupt the unity of time. The two main characters, Martha and Amie, live opposite each other and dwell on memories of defeat and humiliation. Martha remembers her husband, whose vitality was crushed by the pressure of Glaswegian life; and she talks to her budgie who turns out to be a symbol for her dead son (who died in a cage). If the symbolism is forced, Conn's sturdy use of language is the main strength of the play. Martha's big speech in the final act is not only revealing but announces the hardman theme that proved irresistible to the dramatists of the 1970s:

MARTHA: Mind I told you I didn't always live here, I started off in the south side, in Govan? Well, I lived with my brothers Tommy and wee Alex – he was the youngest. And three closes up was big Francis Duggan . . . Well, one night wee Alex's in himself, and there comes a banging at the door . . . So Alex opened the door, and there was Tommy, with his face slashed to bits and the blood running down his jacket. And wee Alex says 'Who done that to you Tommy? Tell me who done it and I'll get him. I'll kill him,' and Tommy . . . leans forward, with what's left of his face, the blood streaming off him, and he says 'If you must know, it was Big Francis Duggan.' And wee Alex stands stock still. And he says in a kind of whisper. 'Aw Tommy, you must've said something for to offend him.' There you are, that was Big Francis Duggan . . . Well, it's cheered me up a bit telling you that.[59]

Conn's *The Burning*, which Bill Bryden directed at the Royal Lyceum in 1971, reworked the material first presented in McLellan's *Jamie the Saxt*. Conn is a derivative dramatist who possesses more finesse than originality. In his historical play James VI is an evil idiot, a man without dignity but prey to his own irrationality. By contrast Bothwell's schemes seem positively wholesome. Conn's talent shows itself in single speeches rather than in the overall texture of the play. He has a flair for semi-autonomous scenes rather than long stretches of action. When young Effie (whose affair with Bothwell leads up to her burning) is interrogated by the king, James VI acts like a man disfigured by perversion:

JAMES: Think of it! Your flesh, one with his. As he prises your body, and takes his fill . . . Bothwell on top, yourself working below . . . panting and huffing, his body making its mark . . . breath fiery, as he splits you . . . your breasts like petals, beneath his thrust . . . opening to him . . . love swelling and rising . . . limbs entwinit and threshing . . . his seed spilling, your juices commingling . . . soft flesh worked to a frenzy as he rides you and rides you . . . festooned in your lust![60]

Conn could also write plays like *The Aquarium* (1973), which utilises the Oedipus complex, and his constant shifting from idiom to idiom makes him a typically restless figure in Scottish drama. His stylistic diversity shows the range of genres at the disposal of the Scottish dramatist: the historical drama, the psychological study, the working-class conflict. All these possibilities had been tested on Scottish audiences and the native stage was set, as it were, for a play that summed up the strengths of Scottish drama to date. This Bill Bryden provided in *Willie Rough* which opened, under Bryden's own direction, at the Royal Lyceum Theatre on 10 February 1972.

With its high level of ensemble playing the play initiated a new wave of naturalism that swept over Scottish drama.

52.   REVIVAL: BILL BRYDEN AT THE LYCEUM

Bryden, born in Greenock in 1942, had made an early reputation as a director: first, in London, at the Royal Court from 1966 to 1971; then, in Edinburgh, at the Royal Lyceum from 1971 until 1975 when he returned to London as an Associate Director of the National Theatre. *Willie Rough* was something of a sensation in Scotland though opinion on its merit was divided: some saw the play as the salvation of Scottish drama; others felt that Bryden had taken over the Lyceum in pursuit of his own personal ambitions. The critical praise showered on *Willie Rough* was tempered by a negative chorus of resentment. Russell Hunter, a fine actor who has appeared in one-man shows written by W. Gordon Smith, epitomised the antagonism directed at Bryden's play:

> I can't say I was a fan of *Willie Rough* . . . these plays are largely a sort of twentieth-century Celtic twilight . . . I am, you know, all in favour of a bit of theatrical graffiti: BILL BRYDEN IS NOT RABBIE BURNS! – or better – IBSEN O.K. BILL BRYDEN YA BASS.[61]

That kind of reaction could only have been aimed at a play that forced Scotsmen to think about the nature of Scottish drama. *Willie Rough*, in its capacity as a topic of heated conversation, made Scotsmen intensely theatre-conscious for the first time in many years.

Bryden was in an enviable position as a man who could commission and cast plays at the Lyceum. As a director he could make sure that his own plays received the best possible treatment. Accordingly he gathered around him, in his period at the Lyceum, some of the finest actors in Scotland; they gave *Willie Rough* the kind of performance that most new dramatists could only dream about. The play is set in Greenock between February 1914 and June 1916. In order to obtain a job at the shipyard Willie has to pay his way past the foreman. Unlike certain of his fellow-workers, Willie is no timorous workhorse whose principles can be exchange for the promise of employment. He sees himself as a man of integrity dedicated to political agitation in the interests of socialism. His hero is the Scottish Republican, John MacLean:

> WILLIE: He's a great man. I really believe that. His meetins are the only thing I've got tae look forward tae 'cept gaun hame tae the wife and weans at night. An' just look at me nou. I'm sore ashamed o myself, sae I am! Willie Rough sittin here waitin tae see if he's bought 'imsel' a job.[62]

Willie is elected shop steward at the shipyard and, disgusted at the war fever infecting the shipworkers, has MacLean and Willie Gallacher speak to the workers. While the war in Europe obsesses the men Willie is increasingly involved with the class war on the home front and organises a strike for a tiny wage increase. When the strike-breakers are called in the workers are brutally suppressed and one-legged Hughie, a solid secondary character, is shot. Willie comes to Greenock Royal Infirmary to comfort Hughie on his deathbed:

WILLIE: But it wisnae your fight, Hughie. I tellt ye to stay out o it.

HUGHIE: I wis tryin tae help ye, Willie. When I saw our boys gettin stuck intae thae dirty bastards, I just had tae try an blooter wan or two wi the auld crutch. I couldnae help mysel'. I'm leanin against this waa layin about me, when this big red-heidit fella starts runnin for the gates. He had somethin' in his haun, ye see? I shouted: 'Where the fuck did that come frae?' It looked lik a gun, but I thought it was a wee toy. It didnae look lik a real wan. I didnae think it was gonna blow ma fuckin leg aff.[63]

Bryden's technique is to employ realistic dialogue in an emotionally charged theatrical atmosphere and the result has been construed as sentimental by critics who know less than Bryden does about the realities of working-class life. Bryden is not guilty of letting heroically noble and unbelievable workers strut about the stage (though he does just that in a later play, *Civilians*); he prefers to enlist vernacular speech-rhythms to suggest the sensitivity that is often buried beneath a selfconsciously rough proletarian exterior. If *Willie Rough* is an embarrassing experience for some that is perhaps a comment on the theatrical assumptions of a public conditioned to éxpect the soft option of fantasy – not a condemnation of Bryden's use of realism. Bryden ends his play by having Willie agitate himself out of a job; after writing a seditious article he serves a jail sentence. He has, ironically, paid for his integrity by inflicting hardship on his family. This pessimistic finale is firmly in the antiheroic tradition associated with Sean O'Casey. The Abbey had, to some extent, finally come home to Scotland. Bryden was fully aware of the Irish precedent and, for a while, it seemed as if he could create the requirements of a Scottish National Theatre from the company he had assembled at the Lyceum.

Bryden's next play, *Benny Lynch*, which he directed at the Lyceum in 1974, is subtitled 'Scenes from a Short Life'. By winning the World Flyweight Championship in 1935, Benny Lynch became a folk hero whose memory is treasured by the Scottish working class. In his heyday Benny Lynch seemed the living image of the pugnacious Scot: the wee fellow who could battle his way through life whatever the problems. Tragically, he died a broken – and broken-hearted – man. While acknowledging the immense athletic skill of

Benny, Bryden plays on weaknesses that make the character representative of Scotland. For all his gifts Benny is a born loser. He has courage and talent but remains the victim of his limited outlook; outside the ring he cannot rise above the mediocrity of his greatest ambition which is that Glasgow should belong to him. Boxing ability is meaningless to Benny except as a passport to instant recognition in Glasgow. When Glasgow turns its back on him he squanders his life in alcoholic abuse and displays appalling temperamental insecurity. If Arthur Miller's *Death of a Salesman* can be seen as a comment on the American Dream, *Benny Lynch* can be taken as a cautionary tale about the Scottish Nightmare.

Benny is haunted by the poverty that humiliated him as a child. He never grows out of its shadow. When Wilma Lafferty taunts him about his early life he becomes first violent, then philosophical:

BENNY: *You* were a'right. You had a mother an' a father. 'Where's ma mammy?' I used tae say tae the old man, 'Where is she?' 'Oot.' 'Oot where?' 'Och, she's wi' that big waistcoat-tearer frae the Garngad!' That was ma mother. When the boys said she was a cow, I didnae know what they were talkin aboot. No at first. Gie'd them a doin for it when I found out, but. My old man's suffered, so he has. I'll see'im all right. I'd like tae buy'im a car, ye know? He's got a steel plate in his heid. Imagine that. Frae the War. We don't know we're livin, Wilma.[64]

Benny Lynch evolves in episodes and some of these amount to scenes of tremendous power. In the fourth scene, set in the office of Benny's manager, George Dingley, Mrs Lafferty has come for a showdown. Wilma, we learn, is pregnant by Benny, a married man; the honour of Glasgow is at stake. Dingley, preoccupied with the imminent world championship bout, realises that Wilma's condition could cause a scandal so he reluctantly sees Mrs Lafferty and Wilma. His money does most of the talking and Mrs Lafferty is reduced to a pathetic figure who proclaims her pride but is too poor to afford it:

MRS LAFFERTY: You must have a lot tae dae. I'm that sorry for takin up yur time. She's ma ain daughter, but I don't know what she'd dae once she saw the wean. Ye know how it is? Naebody would go through a' that for nothin'. My last . . . a wee brother for her . . . was still-born . . . I don't want her tae go through that, an' if she kept it she'd be wantin Lynch tae support it an' the wife would find oot, an' his troubles would never be over.[65]

When Dingley hands over some money for an abortion Mrs Lafferty takes it with the comment 'I feel dead cheap, so I dae'.[66]

Towards the end of the play – when Benny has lost his title, his friends, and his self-respect – there is another scene of great pathos. It is now 1943 and a Salvation Army girl, Alison, stops in the street as Benny is thrown bodily from a pub. He is now a typical Glasgow down-and-out of the period; he wears an old cap, a raincoat tied with string, and working boots. Alison has no idea of his vanished glory and when he reveals his identity she is baffled. Stripped off his last illusions Benny gives Alison his remaining possessions – the world championship trophy and his dressing-gown – and dismisses her. He then turns to face the bombers that buzz over Glasgow:

> BENNY: I want to die. I don't want to be an old man . . . Come on ya Hun-faced whures! There's no wan Gerry can beat me. I'm Benny Lynch! That's me. I'm Benny Lynch! Can ye hear me up there? I'm Benny Lynch . . . Don't burn the docks! Aim for me! Give us a drink. Somebody. Anybody. I'm Benny Lynch! I take on all comers. Pound a round . . . They've missed me again. Look at the flames. How could you no have drapped wan right here! Feart, is that it? Ha! Nothin' tae be feart o noo. Nae speed. Nae punch an' nothin' left tae pawn.[67]

Since he moved to the National Theatre Bryden has written a play, *Old Movies* (1977), about the writing of a filmscript. Although one of the characters, Ford, speaks in a Glasgow accent there is little of the vitality of Bryden's first two plays. It is not even a complete change of direction, for Ford introduces material already incorporated in Bryden's other plays:

> FORD: I saw Benny Lynch beat Small Montana at Wembley. Great night. Great experience. Like seeing the Mantegna Christ in Milan for the first time or Bogart.[68]

Bryden is actively involved in projects in the cinema and in television; whatever future he makes for himself he will be remembered as the man who brought urgency and expertise to the Scottish dramatic scene is the 1970s. For that reason his play *Civilians* (1981) was a disappointment, as if the former enthusiasm had faded.

53. THE IMPACT OF 7 : 84

The year after *Willie Rough*'s first appearance at the Lyceum in 1972, there was another dramatic development in Scotland: the advent of the 7 : 84 Company (Scotland). Although drawn to political dogma the Company preserved a stylistic flexibility and arrived at a style of delivery that owed as much to popular entertainment as it did to theatrical conventions. We have stressed the paucity of tradition in Scottish drama but we should not forget the importance of the music hall in keeping theatres open. Harry Lauder and Will Fyffe were, after all, superlative performers who captivated audiences in Scotland; Lauder even became an international celebrity. This popular tradition has never entirely vanished: the comedian Billy

Connolly, who has also written stage plays, is virtually a bawdy rein-carnation of Lauder. For all its Brechtian effects, the 7 : 84 Company could not have functioned as it did without recourse to Scottish music hall patter.

The 7 : 84 Theatre Company was first formed in London in 1971 and took its name as the result of a statistic asserting that 7 per cent of the population owned 84 per cent of the capital wealth. John McGrath, a founder-member of the London-based company, then moved to Scotland to develop 7 : 84 as a touring group of players. He has stressed the kind of theatre he wants:

> The kind of theatre which 7 : 84 has done a great deal to establish in Scotland is there to present the realities of working class life and history directly to working class audiences, without translating it into the language of the middle class 'theatre' that has dominated our stages since the 1890s. It has its roots in the popular tradition of entertainment, and it takes the values of the working class very seriously . . . Any theatre that concentrates on 'emotional' plots and does not question the structures that underlie its characters' lives is being political by default. We choose to examine political issues openly because they shape the reality we all live in.[69]

Clearly, then, those who take their seats for a McGrath play are not meant to be passive spectators but potential participants in the political action dramatised before their eyes. McGrath had an un-likely background for a Scottish theatrical revolutionary: he was born in Birkenhead in 1935 and had first attained prominence as the co-founder and original director of the television series *Z-Cars*. His concept of the theatre as a place of class conflict had its genesis in the Epic Theatre developed by Brecht and Piscator in the 1920s. Here is Brecht's concise definition of Epic Theatre:

> The essential point of the epic theatre is perhaps that it appeals less to the feelings than to the spectator's reason. Instead of sharing an experience the spectator must come to grips with things. At the same time it would be quite wrong to try and deny emotions to this kind of theatre.[70]

McGrath does not seduce his audience; he confronts them with a political proposition. He is enough of a showman, though, to under-stand the public need for entertainment and the vivacity of his work made him and his Company something of a cult in Scotland. Just as committed young Scotsmen of the 1960s had worn badges proclaim-ing their allegiance to the Campaign for Nuclear Disarmament, so in the 1970s the red badges of the 7 : 84 Company were conspicuous by their presence on Scottish lapels.

In 1973 McGrath toured Scotland with his *The Cheviot, The Stag and the Black, Black Oil* and dazzled the country with his recreation of the tragi-comedy of Scottish history. Apparently the actors were encouraged to contribute to the making of the play and McGrath described the finished product as the work of the Company as a whole. *The Cheviot* used songs, jokes, music hall sketches, parodies, anecdotes, documents and plain propagandist statements to remind Scotland of the iniquities of the Highland Clearances. The play was suitable for performance on the stage, in small halls, in any *ad hoc* setting and the actors assumed several roles as if to remove all vestiges of illusionism. Serious political issues alternated with knockabout farce. For example, a passage lamenting the depopulation of the Highlands was immediately followed by a farcical speech by a property-shark:

ANDY: The motel – as I see it – is the thing of the future. That's how we see it, myself and the Board of Directors, and one or two of your local Councillors – come on now, these are the best men money can buy. So – picture it, if you will, right there at the top of the glen, beautiful vista – The Crammem Inn, High Rise Motorcroft – all finished in natural, washable plastic granitette. Right next door, the 'Frying Scotsman' All Night Chipperama – with a wee ethnic bit, Fingal's Cafe – serving seaweed suppers in the basket and draught Drambuie. And to cater for the younger set, yous've got your Grouse-a-go-go.[71]

One of the reasons for the success of 7 : 84 was the way the cast drew the audience into the action as if all present at a given performance were involved in an open conspiracy against authority. The actors did not seem to be simply parroting lines they had been paid to learn but rather expounding an argument they all believed in. The sheer camaraderie of the Company helped them through subsequent productions which did not live up to the promise of *The Cheviot*. *Little Red Hen* (1975) is based round a choice bit of Scottish folkwisdom ('Ye cannae teach yer granny tae suck eggs') and the play brings together a wide-eyed Scottish Nationalist girl and her granny who remembers how in the 1930s (when MacLean, Maxton and Gallacher were active) the workers were bought off with parliamentary democracy. *The Game's a Bogey* (1975) counterpoints the tragedy of the martyred John MacLean with the life of a married couple, Geordie and Ina. McGrath hammers home the propagandist point that the workingman is always open to exploitation by ruthless employers. By this time the Company had become predictable and repetitive and needed to return to basic principles of showmanship. This they did with *Joe's Drum* (1979).

Joe's Drum is an attempt to present the voice of the people or, in Scottish parlance, Ra Voice Orra Peepul. 'General' Joe Smith was an eighteenth century Cowgate cobbler, a proletarian demagogue who stirred the Edinburgh mob to acts of rebellion like the Porteous Riot of 1736 when, as Joe says in McGrath's play, 'If Black Jock Porteous was tae hang oor hero fur the crime o' no payin' Excise duties; then we wad hang Black Jock fur murderin' six innocent people o' Edinburgh . . . And we took Jock Porteous tae the Grassmarket and hang'd him oorsels – very quiet and orderly.'[72] At the beginning of the play Joe rises from the grave, after two centuries, in response to 'the thunderous apathy of the devolution vote'.[73] Thumping out his message on his drum he accuses the audience of treachery for not ensuring a Scottish Assembly at the very least:

> JOE: Ye had yer chance to beat yer ain drum – And what did you dae? Oh, I'll tell you what you did – Oh I've been watchin ye – 'What me?' ye'll be saying, 'Ah've done naethin', Wisnae me.' Aye right, that'll be correct. *Naethin'* ye've done *naethin'*.[74]

What follows is an illustrated lecture by Joe on the virtues of mob rule, a polemical discourse enlivened by songs and a parade of revolutionary heroes like Thomas Muir of Huntershill, Robert Hamilton and James Connolly. Those who come to see 7 : 84 know what to expect so McGrath is really preaching to the converted, entertaining a captive audience with his own vision of Scottish Republicanism. In relying on topical material he runs the risk of his plays becoming dated by the passage of time but it is a risk he is prepared to take. He has personally helped to undermine the idea of the theatre as a means of escape from the real world and the general impact of 7 : 84 has encouraged at least two men associated with it to write their own plays: John Byrne and John Bett. Byrne was born in Paisley in 1940, the son of a labourer in the Clyde shipyards, and began his creative life as a painter. He designed the sets for *The Cheviot* and other 7 : 84 productions and in 1977 used his own money to stage *Writer's Cramp* at the Edinburgh Festival Fringe. The play (in which John Bett played the part of the narrator, thus retaining the 7 : 84 link) delighted audiences with its satirical ingenuity and mock-heroic mood and won a Fringe First Award from *The Scotsman*. It is a portrayal of a Scottish self-styled man of genius, Francis Seneca McDade, who never rises above the level of his innate idiocy. His epistolary confessions are punctuated by extracts from his written works and it is in these that Byrne's addiction to parody is deployed. Here is an extract from McDade's novel *Pass the Buns, Dolly*:

> Flicking idly at the large boil on his cheek, Peter saw at once that all was not well with Mandy. As she stood by the fire and allowed the flames to lick at her jodhpurs he could tell by the set of her narrow shoulders that Rupert had been up to his old tricks. 'Rough day, old girl?' He put the query as nonchalantly as he was able with the paris bun lodged under his dentures. Peter dropped his gaze to the floor and in an effort to cover the terrible awkwardness he felt prised off one of his boots. 'Not especially,' said Mandy icily. 'Why do you ask?' Peter felt the words sting the back of his neck and looked up sharply.[75]

McDade, who turns out to be of German parentage (for which

blunder he is imprisoned during the Second World War), expires at the end of *Writer's Cramp*. His amorous exploits were referred to in Byrne's play *Cara Coco* (1981) in which McDade's wife, Pamela Crichton-Capers, turns out to be yet another graphomaniac. In 1978 Byrne's *The Slab Boys* was presented at the Traverse before going to London to receive the *Evening Standard* Award for Most Promising Playwright; the play has also been seen in the USA which suggests that modern Scottish drama can travel. Byrne had worked as a slab boy (paint mixer) in a Paisley carpet factory in the 1950s and his re-creation of the shop floor was both amusing and nostalgic. An unholy trinity of slab boys act up outrageously when they are introduced to a stranger from another world: a university student who does not speak their language. The narrative drift of the play is slight, the banter between the main characters is often uproarious, and the evocation of the 1950s is exact; a sequel, *The Loveliest Night of the Year* (1979), takes two of the principals, Spanky and Phil, to the staff dance and reveals still more of their compulsive posturing. Byrne's determination to draw on his own background guarantees the period charm of his comedies but his characters tend to be caricatures. *Normal Service*, which was commissioned by Hampstead Theatre Club and produced in 1979, is basically a duplication of the main features of *The Slab Boys*. This time the place of work is a television studio (and Byrne worked as a graphic artist with Scottish Television in the 1960s); once again the workers have to cope with a hopelessly disorganised corner of the world. As usual the patter is fast and funny but the play is little more than a series of jokes strung together by interchangeable characters.

John Bett (b. 1949) was one of 7 : 84's star actors. His professional experience is reflected in his comedy *Street Fighting Man* (1978) which is an insider's exposure of the infighting that goes into the preparation of a play; or so Bett would have us believe. Here the actors are high on bitchiness; they mutter their token protests but can never actually stand up to the pretentious director who lords it over them. The play-within-a-play format is a well-worn ploy and the camp mannerisms of actors have always been fair game for the satirist. Still, Bett manages to invest his theatrical travesty with genuine comic effects and he has a sharply vindictive turn of phrase. His skill at dramatising the behind-the-scenes banality of the theatre is impressive as witness the following exchange:

DOSSER: All this 'dear heart' bullshit – that's not real. That's drama school '30s theatre. (*Extravagant*) Deep scarlet drapes. Footlights. The magic of the theatre. Bouquets. Walk down curtain calls. Have you seen the notices, darling?

TONY: No, I haven't dear. Did they mention my exit to the shrubbery or my red dress in the last act?

DOSSER: These are the bastards that nearly killed the theatre. Christ, to hear them talk you'd think they'd invented it.[76]

54. TOM GALLACHER: THE ARTIST AS HERO

The verbally snappy comedy of Byrne and Bett is a contrast to the characteristically earnest plays that came out of Scotland in the 1970s when social realism was the order of the day. There was, though, an individual voice who resisted most of the developments that had been made in Scotland. Tom Gallacher, born in Dunbartonshire in 1934, has been drawn to a somewhat ponderously cerebral drama that deals with a critical stage in the life of an intellectual Superman. Gallacher's own intellectual heroes are Ibsen and Kierkegaard and he is attracted to metaphysical problems:

> My initial motive for writing drama was philosophical rather than theatrical. I have since evolved a synthesis which is just, both to philosophy and to drama . . . I'm delighted at the revival of Scottish drama. My main concern is that most of the new work is small-scale, 'Fringe' orientated and there is very little sign of development from 'Fringe' theatres to 'Mainstream' proscenium theatres – where it must go if it is to last . . . My own (serious) work is built to last and therefore is always being revived either in original or in translation. In 1978 there were seven separate productions of my plays in Scotland alone.[77]

In 1972, the year of the revival associated with Bill Bryden's *Willie Rough*, Tom Gallacher's own *Revival*! was presented at the Eblana Theatre, Dublin; it subsequently played in London and was first presented in Scotland at Pitlochry Theatre on 14 July 1975. Gallacher's play is not much more than a pleasant theatrical cocktail comprising a measure of Ibsen with a strong dash of Stoppard (whose work has also influenced Byrne and Bett). Bernard Kevin, an arrogant retired actor-manager, has become a recluse and discovers, from one of three doctors, he has only a month to live. When he is offered a come-back part in a revival of Ibsen's *The Master Builder* he decides to end it all histrionically by staging his own death in the final fall. Kevin is playing a role: inside this role he is an actor playing the role of meditative thinker inspired by Kierkegaard's philosophy. When his theatrical suicide is botched he resorts to instinct and decides to soldier on with his career.

Schellenbrack (1973) deals with another Great Man. The eponymous hero is visited by an English critic, Ivor Cope, who wants to make him the subject of a book dealing with his contribution to European thought. Cope comes with news that the Nobel Prize has been awarded to Schellenbrack but discovers an Ibsenist skeleton in the cupboard: Schellenbrack is subject to bouts of insanity and has to be kept under lock and key. Furthermore he has a mother-fixation, keeps a black book of his enemies, and indulges in insane scribblings. Schellenbrack, like other Gallacher characters, is apt to blame the world for his anguish when in fact his is not the real world but a solipsistic invention:

SCHELLENBRACK: It's the same everywhere. I wrote as though I might
be able to cast potent spells which would change the room and the street
and the night. And when it was written I wanted everyone to see – not
that I could write, but, that it was me . . . That is what a writer is *for*.
Any artist! He is the man given the power to reach deep into himself and
pluck out some vital part. To tear it out, joyfully, like a gift – and give it
to whoever will listen, and say: 'I have done this for you.'[78]

Gallacher is one of the most selfconsciously literary men operating
in modern Scottish drama; he is also capable of fine vernacular writing as his radio play *Perfect Pitch* (1979) proved.

55.   PROLETARIAN DRAMA: McMILLAN AND MacMILLAN

A real feeling for the theatre informs Roddy McMillan's *The Bevellers* which Bill Bryden directed at the Lyceum in 1973. McMillan
was born in Glasgow in 1923 and joined the Unity Theatre as a
teenager. His first play, *All in Good Faith*, was performed at Glasgow Citizens' in 1954; *The Bevellers* was his only other play. He
died in 1979. *The Bevellers* is a play about craftsmen (glass-
bevellers) surviving into an age of mass production. Bob, the foreman, has a pride in his craft but the other men simply pass their
time and wait for the day – or the day depicted in the play – to end.
The opening of the second Act is a vividly histrionic set-piece. Norrie, the put-upon new boy, is larking in the rafters when he sees
Dan the Rouger trying his hand with another man's girl friend. As
the Rouger is about to succeed he spots Norrie and lambasts him
with an extraordinary speech that represents what Scots might
sound like if it had a theatrical tradition behind it:

ROUGER: Ya knee-crept, Jesus-crept, swatchin little fucker, ah'll cut the
bliddy scrotum aff ye! Ah'll knacker an' gut ye, ah'll eviscerate ye! Ya
hure-spun, bastrified, conscrapulated young prick, ah'll do twenty year
fur mincin you. Ye hear me? Ah'll rip ye fae the gullet tae the groin,
ah'll incinerate ye! . . . Ye see this culet? Ah'll make a bayonet o this an'
come up therr an' get ye. Ah'll stow ye in the rubbish, an' the rats'll
guzzle whit's left o ye. Ah'me comin up![79]

McMillan is one of the few dramatists who has elevated Scots above
a cosy conversational level.

Only a few months after Roddy McMillan's play was first performed at the Lyceum, Hector MacMillan's *The Sash* was premiered
(on 13 August) at the Edinburgh Festival Fringe. The proximity of
these productions contributed to the impression that the Scottish

theatre was alive as never before, with one fine play following another. Hector MacMillan was born in the east end of Glasgow in 1929, left school at fourteen, and lived abroad before returning to Scotland to run his own electronics business. After selling a play, *To Stand Alone* (1966), to Scottish Television he decided to concentrate on drama. *The Rising* (1970) dealt with the abortive insurrection of 1820 and the historical theme was carried over into *Royal Visit* (1971) which satirised George IV's trip to Edinburgh in 1822. Although *Royal Visit* predictably sets the nobility of the workers above the decadence of the king the most telling feature of the play is its characterisation, not its political content; Sir Walter Scott, who stagemanaged the royal visit, is deglamourised and interpreted as a sycophant who hogs the stage.

Neither of these plays carried the impact of *The Sash* which, when it transferred to the Pavilion Theatre in May 1974, became the talk of Glasgow. The theme of religious bigotry reflected a way of life that Glaswegians had learned to live with; MacMillan helped them to laugh at their prejudices. Andrew Keir's performance as Big Bill MacWilliam certainly helped to give the play a mass appeal but *The Sash* mainly proclaimed its own merits as a theatrically valid exercise in iconoclasm. As the play opens Bill is preparing for the Orange March of 12 July and his hungover son Cameron is sickened by his fanaticism. A young girl, Georgina, comes to Bill's flat and flirtatiously encourages his obstreperous behaviour. Bill's noise alarms his neighbour, Bridget, a Catholic spinster from Ulster. When she brings Una, her pregnant niece, up to Bill's flat to shame him into silence a furious argument erupts. Una has experienced the full horror of the Ulster situation but her nervous and physical fragility do nothing to assuage Bill's crudity:

> BRIDGET: She's got to suffer this, after them firin a big rubber bulit at her! In her condition! (*lifts Una's smock, draws down the waistband of her jeans.*) Show them where it hit you, darlin. (*Una, struggling to hold her emotions in control, thrusts her aunt away.*)
>
> BILL: (*cold, hard*) Oh, Ah think we can aw see where she got the, eh (*very suggestively, miming Bridget's accent*) big rubber bulit![80]

After further commotion with Bridget and Una, Bill is accidentally pushed out of the window – a physical defenestration alluded to in Act II when Cameron says 'We should fling the hale fukn religious thing oot the fukn windae!'[81] The explosive first act is followed by a didactic second act. Here MacMillan consciously collects the inherently dramatic pieces into a neat political package and the second half of the play is an anticlimax. Cameron and Una find common ground in socialism and the injured Bill has to swallow his Protestant pride and let Bridget nurse him. Unable to go on the march Bill eventually retires to hospital resplendent in his sash; the play ends with the cast singing a song of proletarian unity. MacMillan, on the evidence of the first Act of *The Sash*, has many of the attributes of the accomplished dramatist (a good ear for dialogue, an insight into his characters, a passion for the subject under scrutiny). He also has the energy to deal impatiently with contemporary life in Scotland.

56.   ARGUMENT AND AGGRESSION: CAMPBELL AND McGRATH

Theatrical conditions in Scotland have, to some extent, dictated the shape of the new plays; it is difficult for emerging writers to secure a production at a large theatre and the Traverse has long been the natural home of experiment. As we have seen, the Traverse actively encouraged the work of writers like Cecil Taylor and Stanley Eveling in the 1960s and in the 1970s it offered similar facilities to a new generation of writers. Due to the spatial restrictions of the Traverse – which in 1969 moved from the Lawnmarket to the Grassmarket – a type of chamber play evolved. It had a small cast, a minimum of scenery, and episodic action. Two plays premiered at the Traverse in the 1970s showed how effective this format could be: Donald Campbell's *The Jesuit* and Tom McGrath's *The Hard Man*. There are striking similarities between the two pieces: claustrophobic atmosphere, a concern with the nature of crime and punishment, the vulnerability of an individual at the hands of his captors, the uninhibited use of dialect, the influence of American movies. At the end of *The Jesuit*, Father John Ogilvie is approached by Archbishop Spottiswoode who advises him to escape and avoid bloodshed in Scotland; we are later told he acted with uncharacteristic cowardice on the scaffold (though, as a Catholic, he could hardly have assisted at his own execution). Now the source of that is the 1939 film *Angels With Dirty Faces* in which James Cagney, at the prompting of a priest, feigns fear of the electric chair to disenchant the slumkids who worship him. Another Cagney film, *Each Dawn I Die* (1939), provides a horrific account of the abuse of authority in prison – which is exactly what Tom McGrath shows in *The Hard Man*.

Donald Campbell (b. 1940) wrote *The Jesuit* in 1973 – at which time he had no idea of John Ogilvie's imminent canonisation. It took him some time to find a theatre willing to stage the play but it was eventually performed at the Traverse on 4 May 1976. The play is set in 1614–15, in the reign of James VI and I, and recreates the struggle between Father John Ogilvie and John Spottiswoode, Archbishop of Glasgow. Ogilvie has been apprehended but the authorities are not quite sure what to charge him with as the mere fact of being a Catholic is not a capital offence in Scotland. It is Spottiswoode's task to disover whether Ogilvie is guilty of treason.

Ogilvie, we learn, is an archetypal outsider. He has spent almost all his life outside Scotland; he is a member of the nobility and so isolated from popular feeling in Scotland; he is a priest unable to sympathise with the tenets of the Reformed religion; and he is linguistically out of step with his fellow countrymen. Ogilvie is the only person in *The Jesuit* who speaks English, and his affected speech irritates Spottiswoode and infuriates the soldiers who have to guard him.

Ogilvie's apparent determination to become a martyr appals Spottiswoode, who has little time for gestures. Although convinced of Ogilvie's involvement in a Papish plot to murder the king he tries to persuade Ogilvie to change his deposition:

OGILVIE: Why are you doing this? Why are you trying to persuade me to change my deposition? . . . . In your eyes, I am a potential assassin. Why should you seek to allow me to escape with my life?

SPOTTISWOODE: There are larger issues at stake.

OGILVIE: Larger than the King's safety?

SPOTTISWOODE: Larger than the life of one extremely ineffectual conspirator! Look, Ogilvie. If you are banished, I will be quit of ye – alive or dead, it's aa the same to me!

OGILVIE: (*with a deep breath*) Then I am afraid that it will have to be dead. For I cannot and will not change my deposition.

SPOTTISWOODE: Certes man, are ye wyce?[82]

There is the contrast between the realist and the idealist that is sustained through Campbell's play. An additional element of realism is worked into the script in the treatment of the four soldiers who have to deal with Ogilvie and his divine ambitions. They are remarkably contemporary figures who could have been lifted out of a backstreet in Glasgow almost any time in the twentieth century. They provide a chorus of common humanity and offend even each other. After an argument, between Wat and Andrew, Sandy has his say:

SANDY: I'll no argy wi ye, Wattie. But ye're a lucky bugger tae be sittin there the nou. Andro's a haurd man, Wat. He's no lived as lang as he has for naethin. His sword'd have been through your guts afore ye'd got yer ain clear o the scabbard! Jist dinnae try that again, son. I'm warnin ye!

WAT: Aye? Weill maybe . . . (*look towards the door*) but I still say ye cannae trust thae papish bastards![83]

The theme of proletarian violence is the subject of McGrath's *The Hard Man* which was first staged at the Traverse on 19 May 1977. In the published version the play is jointly credited to

McGrath and Jimmy Boyle, the convicted murderer whose artistic activities have made him something of a cultural celebrity in Scotland. His participation in the play adds credibility to the scenes of brutality though it also means that the central figure, Johnnie Byrne, is depicted as a martyr rather than a murderer. Society, according to this play, is the real villain. The play occasionally takes the form of a confrontation between Byrne and the audience who, as members of a society that inflicts institutional violence on prisoners, are meant to feel guilty.

The drama of Bryne's violent progress from petty-thief to gangster is played out against a bleak background of social deprivation; a chorus of Windae-hingers supplies the framework within which Byrne operates. He is always anxious to relate his antisocial behaviour to his background and always articulate:

> BYRNE. Blades. Hammers. A splinter of glass. Anything did –
> just so long as it made a mark. A new dimension had entered my life. A
> new reality had opened up for me. Violence . . . in the world I come
> from, violence is its own reason. Violence is an art form practised in and
> for itself. And you soon get to know your audience and what it is
> impresses them. You cut a man's face and somebody asks you, 'How
> many stitches?' 'Twenty' you say, and they look at you – 'Twenty? Only
> twenty? Christ, you hardly marked him.' The next time you cut a face
> you make a bit more certain it will be news.[84]

When Byrne is imprisoned he is treated with the same inhumanity he once showed to his fellow citizens. It is a tribute to McGrath's prowess as a dramatist that he manages to make the audience sympathise with Byrne when he is tormented by the jailers.

Since writing these plays both Campbell and McGrath have been productive. Campbell's *Somerville the Soldier* (1978) deals, like *The Jesuit*, with a martyr: Alex Somerville who, for writing a political letter to the press in 1832, was court-martialled and sentenced to two hundred strokes of the cat-o-nine-tails. A more sensitive play, *The Widows of Clyth* (1979), explores the aftermath of a Caithness tragedy of 1876 when a fishing boat went under and five widows were left to cope with twenty-six children. McGrath continued to investigate contemporary subjects; *The Innocent* (1979) looks at drug addiction in the 1960s. Scottish theatre has, thanks to the efforts of twentieth century dramatists, much to be proud of and there is a solid foundation for the work still to come. As Hector MacMillan, speaking for Scottish dramatists in general, said:

> At present, though we have pushed the Scottish theatrical boat out
> further than ever before, we still cannot be sure we have durable and
> seaworthy craft on our hands. Theatres will have to live a little more
> dangerously before we know that. The majority of these will do so only
> in response to somebody else's *fait accompli*. Perhaps dramatists will
> have to make the move by forming and controlling their own company.
> This would imply a maturity big enough to put aside the traditional

bitching of the Scottish cultural scene long enough to mount a sustained attack on the common enemies. I suppose that is asking a lot of the nation that has for so long connived at, when not actively contributing to, its own cultural demoralisation – but there are signs.[85]

As Scottish drama moved into the 1980s there was a period of adjustment after the various excitements of the 1970s. The Scottish Theatre Trust became established as the Scottish Theatre Company; as such it attempted to encourage a national creative effort. The dramatists interpreted this as a commitment to themes that had already achieved some success with the public. Bill Bryden's *Civilians* (1981), set in Second World War-torn Glasgow, brought to the stage the drawn-out proletarian romanticism associated with George Blake's novel *The Shipbuilders* (1935); Donald Campbell wrote plays around the lives of Stevenson and Burns; sentimentalism affected Hector MacMillan whose *Capital Offence* (1981) portrayed whores with hearts of gold surviving in the hypocritical Edinburgh so conveniently close to the theatrical imagination. The public did not seem too impressed and yet the dramatists demand a symbiotic relationship with the public. John McGrath, speaking at a conference in Edinburgh on 'Scottish Theatre in the Eighties' summed up the feeling: 'It all depends on the audience, and here Scottish theatre has its greatest untapped resources. Given their respect for the theatre and their intelligence, Scottish theatre could take off in many directions all at once'.[86] So the Scottish dramatist remains in a state of uncertainty: waiting, not for something to turn up but for someone to turn to.

REFERENCES

1   Maurice Lindsay, *History of Scottish Literature*, Robert Hale: London 1977, p. 439

2   Alexander Reid, *Two Scots Plays*, Collins: London 1958, p. xiii

3   James Bridie, *Tedious and Brief*, Constable: London 1944, p. 14

4   *Chapman 23–24*, Spring 1979, p. 33

5   *The Scotsman*, 29 January 1980

6   *Scottish Theatre 2*, April 1969, p. 6

7   SSP Conference Report, Glasgow 1977, pp. 11–12

8   Sir David Lyndsay adapted by Robert Kemp, *The Satire of the Three Estates*, Heinemann: London 1951, p. vii

9   Edwin Muir, *John Knox*, Cape: London 1929, p. 309

10   Agnes Mure Mackenzie, intro. to James Kinsley (ed.) *Sir David Lindsay: Ane Satyre of the Thrie Estaits*, Cassell: London 1954, p. 13

11   Terence Tobin, *Plays by Scots 1660–1800*, University of Iowa Press: Iowa 1974, p. 9

12 *Edinburgh Courant*, 7 Jan. 1757
13 J.M. Barrie, *Plays and Stories*, Dent: London 1962, p. 202
14 Janet Dunbar, *J.M. Barrie: The Man Behind the Image*, Collins: London 1970, p. 184
15 J.M. Barrie, *The Plays*, Hodder and Stoughton: London 1928, p. 332
16 Ibid. pp. 344–5
17 Ibid. p. 563
18 Kurt Wittig, *The Scottish Tradition in Literature*, Oliver and Boyd: Edinburgh 1958, p. 315
19 George Blake, intro. to J.M. Reid (ed.), *Scottish One-Act Plays*, The Porpoise Press: Edinburgh 1935, p. 9
20 Claude Colleer Abbot, intro. to Gordon Bottomley, *Poems and Plays*, The Bodley Head: London 1953, p. 16
21 Ibid. p. 210
22 J.M. Reid (ed.), op. cit, p. 112
23 James Bridie, *Tedious and Brief*, Constable: London 1944, pp. 105–6
24 Katherine J. Worth, *Revolutions in Modern English Drama*, G.Bell: London 1972, p. 103
25 James Bridie, *A Sleeping Clergyman and Other Plays*, Constable: London 1934, p. xi
26 Ibid. p. 22
27 James Bridie, *Plays for Plain People*, Constable: London 1944, p. 206
28 James Bridie, *John Knox and Other Plays*, Constable: London 1949, p. 80
29 James Bridie, *A Sleeping Clergyman and Other Plays*, Constable: London 1934, p. 31
30 Ibid. pp. 62–3
31 Ibid. p. 50
32 Ibid. p. 51
33 Ibid. p. 19
34 Ibid. p. 22
35 Ibid. p. 26
36 Hugh MacDiarmid, *The Company I've Kept*, Hutchinson: London 1966, p. 237
37 *Jabberwock 6/1*, 1959, p. 5
38 Robert McLellan, *Jamie the Saxt*, Calder and Boyars: London 1970, pp. 26–7
39 Ibid. p. 40
40 Ibid. p. 55
41 Ibid. p. 129
42 David Hutchison, *The Modern Scottish Theatre*, Molendinar: Glasgow 1977, p. 104
43 Alexander Reid, *Two Scots Plays*, Collins: London 1958, pp. xi–xii
44 Ibid. p. 11. (In quoting from Reid's play I have restored the original Scots.)
45 Ibid. pp. 31–2
46 Sydney Goodsir Smith, *The Wallace*, Oliver and Boyd: Edinburgh 1960, p. 43
47 Ibid. p. 56
48 Ibid. p. 58
49 Ibid. p. 61

50   Robert Kemp, *Master John Knox*, The St Andrews Press: Edinburgh 1960, pp. 103–4
51   *SSP Newsletter 2/11*, June 1979, pp. 16–17
52   Letter, 10 June 1979
53   James Vinson (ed.), *Contemporary Dramatists*, St James Press: London 1973, p. 751
54   Jim Haynes (ed.), *Traverse Plays*, Penguin: Harmondsworth 1966, p. 114
55   *New English Dramatists 10*, Penguin: Harmondsworth 1967, p. 199
56   Ibid. p. 165
57   Ibid. pp. 219–20
58   Letter, 7 June 1979
59   Stewart Conn, *The Aquarium, The Man in the Green Muffler & I Didn't Always Live Here*, John Calder: London 1976, p. 156
60   Stewart Conn, *The Burning*, Calder and Boyars: London 1973, p. 90
61   *Chapman 111/1*, 1974, p. 3
62   Bill Bryden, *Willie Rough*, Southside: Edinburgh 1972, pp. 24–5
63   Ibid. p. 70
64   Bill Bryden, *Benny Lynch*, Southside: Edinburgh 1975, p. 34
65   Ibid. p. 41
66   Ibid. p. 42
67   Ibid. p. 92
68   Bill Bryden, *Old Movies*, Heinemann: London 1977, p. 15
69   Programme note for *Joe's Drum*
70   John Willett (ed.), Brecht on Theatre, Eyre Methuen: London 1973, p. 23
71   John McGrath, *The Cheviot, The Stag and the Black, Black Oil*, West Highland Publishing: Breakish 1974 (rev. 1975), p. 23
72   John McGrath, *Joe's Drum*, People's Press: Aberdeen 1979, p. 23
73   Ibid. p. 8
74   Ibid. p. 8
75   John Byrne, *Writer's Cramp* typescript, p. 15
76   John Bett, *Street Fighting Man* typescript, p. 19
77   Letter, 30 May 1979
78   Tom Gallacher, *Revival! and Schellenbrack*, Molendinar: Glasgow 1978, p. 97
79   Roddy McMillan, *The Bevellers*, Southside: Edinburgh 1974, pp. 50–1
80   Hector MacMillan, *The Sash*, Molendinar: Glasgow 1974, p. 39
81   Ibid. p. 65
82   Donald Campbell, *The Jesuit*, Paul Harris: Edinburgh 1976, p. 33
83   Ibid. p. 79
84   Tom McGrath and Jimmy Boyle, *The Hard Man*, Canongate: Edinburgh 1977, p. 16
85   Letter, 17 June 1979
86   *The Scotsman*, 2 Nov. 1981

BIBLIOGRAPHICAL NOTE

Individual works and studies of individual writers are cited in the text and described in the endnotes. The literary and linguistic background to Scottish literature is discussed in the following books:

Aitken, A.J. and McArthur, Tom (ed.), *Languages of Scotland*, Chambers: Edinburgh 1979

Craig, David, *Scottish Literature and the Scottish People 1680–1830*, Chatto and Windus: London 1961

Hart, Francis Russell, *The Scottish Novel*, John Murray: London 1978

Hutchison, David, *The Modern Scottish Theatre*, Molendinar Press: Glasgow 1977

Lindsay, Maurice, *History of Scottish Literature*, Robert Hale: London 1977

Muir, Edwin, *Scott and Scotland*, Routledge: London 1936

Murison, David, *The Guid Scots Tongue*, Blackwood: Edinburgh 1977 (rev. 1978)

Power, William, *Literature and Oatmeal*, Routledge: London 1935

Smith, G. Gregory, *Scottish Literature*, MacMillan: London 1919

Thomson, Derick, *An Introduction to Gaelic Poetry*, Gollancz: London 1974

Wilson, Norman (ed.), *Scottish Writing and Writers*, Ramsay Head: Edinburgh 1977

Wittig, Kurt, *The Scottish Tradition in Literature*, Olivera and Boyd: Edinburgh 1958

Individual collections of Scottish poetry are likewise identified in text and endnotes. The following anthologies will be found useful:

Lindsay, Maurice, *Modern Scottish Poetry*, Carcanet: Manchester 1976

MacQueen, John and Scott, Tom, *The Oxford Book of Scottish Verse*, Clarendon Press: Oxford 1966

Scott, Alexander, *Modern Scots Verse 1922–1977*, Akros: Preston 1978

Scott, Tom, *The Penguin Book of Scottish Verse*, Penguin: Harmondsworth 1970

There are several anthologies of Scottish short stories, notably:

Gordon, Giles and Urquhart, Fred, *Modern Scottish Short Stories*, Hamish Hamilton: London, 1978

Hendry, J.F. *The Penguin Book of Scottish Short Stories*, Penguin: Harmondsworth, 1970

Since 1973 the Scottish Arts Council and Collins have published an annual anthology of *Scottish Short Stories*.

INDEX